SOCIAL MARKETING

Principles and Practice

Happy reading — and I hope it
helps in your work.

SOCIAL MARKETING

Principles and practice

Robert J Donovan

Nadine Henley

IP Communications
Melbourne
2003

IP Communications Pty Ltd
Level 1
123 Camberwell Road
East Hawthorn Victoria 3123
Australia
Phone   +61 3 9811 6818
Fax   +61 3 9813 3979
E-mail   ipcomm@bigpond.com
www.ipcommunications.com.au

ISBN 0 9578617 5 3

National Library of Australia Cataloguing-in-publication data
Donovan, Robert J., 1944- .
Social marketing : principles and practice.
1. Social marketing. 2. Marketing. I. Henley, Nadine,
1952- . II. Title.
658.8
Bibliography.
Includes index.

Edited by Sandra Goldbloom Zurbo, Melbourne
Production management and design by Club Tractor Production Services, Melbourne
Typeset by Desktop Concepts, Melbourne
Cover photograph © Fairfax Photos
Indexed by Judy Clayden
Printed by BPA Print Group, Melbourne

Table of contents

Preface

Social marketing was originally defined as simply the application of marketing principles and tools to the achievement of socially desirable ends. However, with the increasing adoption of marketing techniques by public health and other social change agents there has been a trend toward defining social marketing as the application of marketing concepts, tools, and techniques to any social issue. In this sense some people talk about applying social marketing as though social marketing was an entity distinct from marketing. In our view, while there clearly are differences between commercial marketing and social marketing (as there are between marketing fast-moving consumer goods to domestic consumers and marketing industrial products to manufacturers), social marketing is simply an area of application for marketing techniques. Hence, this book is firmly based on the basic principles of marketing. It reminds public health and other social change agents who have enthusiastically adopted commercial marketing techniques that marketing—when applied correctly—is more than just a bag of advertising and promotional tools; it is both a philosophy and a set of principles about how to achieve mutually satisfying exchanges between marketers and consumers. Marketing, and therefore social marketing, relies on a comprehensive and fully integrated approach to achieving campaign objectives.

At the same time, this book broadens the definition and domain of social marketing. First, to preempt debate about who decides what is socially desirable, this book proposes the United Nations Charter on Human Rights as the authoritative source for defining what constitutes a socially desirable goal. Second, and following the United Nations Charter, the 'social' in our social marketing emphasises the social determinants of individual and population health and wellbeing. Social marketing not only targets individual behaviour change, but also attempts to bring about changes in the social and structural factors that impinge on an individual's opportunities, capacities, and right to have a healthy and fulfilling life. Social marketing targets individuals and groups in legislative bodies, government departments, corporations, and non-profit organisations, who have the power to make policy, regulatory and legislative changes that protect and enhance people's health, wellbeing, and quality of life.

This book is a blend of the authors' practical commercial marketing know-how, hands-on experience in developing and implementing social marketing campaigns, and extensive involvement in formative and evaluative research across a broad variety of health and social policy areas. The principles of social marketing are illustrated with numerous examples of practical application from the field. The book synthesises and offers a new perspective on a large body of research previously published in both Australian and international publications, providing a broad-based context, particularly for the Australian contribution to the field, which has been considerable over the years. The book also reports on several previously unpublished, ongoing research projects and postgraduate studies. Our intention is that a number of groups find this book useful: social marketing and health promotion researchers, practitioners, lecturers, and students.

Acknowledgements

Geoffrey Jalleh, Associate Director of the Centre for Behavioural Research at Curtin University contributed significantly to chapters 6 (Research) and 12 (Sponsorship) as well as assisting considerably in other ways for which we are very grateful. Dr Tom Carroll and Ms Laurie Van Veen contributed the immunisation case and Mr Bruce James contributed the TravelSmart case in chapter 14. Chapter 12 drew on the work of Professor Billie Giles-Corti and other colleagues in the Health Promotion Unit at the University of Western Australia and chapter 15 drew on the work of colleagues at NFO Donovan Research and the Family and Domestic Violence Prevention Unit (Leonie Gibbons warrants a special thank you). Mr Richard McKenna's comments on chapter 7 were most helpful. The authors would like to thank the anonymous reviewers of the proposal and completed text for their insightful comments. The first author acknowledges the support of the Cancer Foundation of Western Australia and acknowledges Healthway as a major provider of grant support for much of the research reported herein. We would also like to acknowledge various colleagues who, by their collaboration on the research reported here or on other research projects and interventions, have contributed to the foundations of this book: Garry Egger, Ross Spark, D'Arcy Holman, John Rossiter, Jo Clarkson, Mark Francas, Donna Paterson, and Susan Leivers.

Finally, a personal thank you to Cobie and Peter for all their patience and support throughout this process and to our publisher, Alan Fettling, for his ongoing encouragement.

The authors would also like to thank the following institutions and individuals for permission to reproduce copyright material:

Academy for Educational Development (ch. 13, fig. 13.2); *Accident Analysis and Prevention* (ch. 6, fig. 6.1); Dr Claudia Amonini (ch. 5, figs 5.7, 5.8, 5.9 and 5.10); Adbusters (ch. 8, fig. 8.7); Annual Reviews (ch. 13, fig. 13.1); *Australia and New Zealand Journal of Public Health* (ch. 6, box, 'Measuring impact evaluation via odds ratios'); Australian Associated Press P/L (ch. 12, fig. 12.3); Australian Association of National Advertisers (ch. 8, table 8.2); Australian

Marketing Institute (ch. 7, AMI code of professional conduct); American Marketing Association (ch. 9, table 9.2); Australian National Tobacco Campaign (ch. 4, fig. 4.2, 'Cigarettes cause strokes' image, 'Cigarettes cause lung cancer' image; and ch. 11, fig. 11.1); Blackwell Science Ltd (ch. 9, skin cancer advertisement); Cancer Foundation of Western Australia (ch. 4, fig. 4.1, and ch. 10, fig. 10.4); Commonwealth of Australia, Communicable Diseases Branch (ch. 11, fig. 11.6); Department for Community Development, Western Australia (ch. 10, FaCS logo and ch. 15, fig. 15.5); Distilled Spirits Industry Council of Australia (ch. 8, Voluntary Alcohol Beverages Advertising Code); Health Canada (ch. 4, fig. 4.2, first 'Cigarettes cause lung cancer' image, and 'Cigarettes cause mouth diseases' image); *Health Affairs* (ch. 13, table 13.1); Healthway (ch. 12, figs 12.4 and 12.8); Human Kinetics Press (ch. 9, table 9.5); *Journal of Research for Consumers* (ch. 4, fig. 4.7); McGraw-Hill Australia (ch. 11, table 11.1); Market Research Society of Australia (ch. 6, table 6.1); National Heart Foundation of Australia (ch. 8, fig. 8.6); Open University Press (ch. 5, fig. 5.1); Peters & Brownes (ch. 8, fig. 8.5); Dr A. Peterson (ch. 10, table 10.1, which was produced for a project unrelated to her current role as Assistant Administrator, Bureau of Global Health, USAID); Queensland Health, ch 10, figs 10.2, 10.3 and 10.6); Dr John Rossiter (ch. 5, table 5.1); Dr Ross Spark (ch. 6, figs 6.5, 6.6a and 6.6b); Sage Publications (ch. 9, fig. 9.3); Soul City (ch. 11, fig. 11.4); The McGraw-Hill Companies (ch. 5, table 5.2 and ch. 13, fig. 13.3); Transperth (ch. 13, fig. 13.4); University of Chicago Press (ch. 5, fig. 5.4, and ch. 9, box, 'Targeting opinion leaders'); United Nations Office of the High Commissioner for Human Rights (ch. 7, excerpts from UN Universal Declaration of Human Rights); West Australian Newspapers Ltd (ch. 11, fig. 11.3); and Western Australian Office of Road Safety (ch. 4, fig. 4.5 and ch. 6, figs 6.3a, 6.3b, and 6.3c).

Chapter 1

Social Marketing and Social Change

Introduction

Social marketing is concerned with helping to achieve and maintain desirable social change. Social marketers are among a number of professionals working to achieve social change. Sometimes social change occurs unplanned and with generally benign or even positive effects such as in the introduction of the printing press or the telephone. In other cases, change can be violent as it was in the French and Russian revolutions. Change can have devastating health effects as it did in the industrial revolution with the introduction of underground mining and factories that were unhealthy and unsafe.

While ideological and religious causes are still catalysts for social change in many parts of the world, most social change is occurring as a result of rapidly changing technology, with implications not only for the developed countries where these changes originated, but also for developing countries where they are often applied.

Changes in communication technology led to cultural intrusions, usually American-based, and to company and personal names, such as McDonald's, Michael Jordan, and Nike, being known even in the remotest and poorest parts of the world, particularly among the young. Changes in industrial technology have led to unemployment or redeployment, with subsequent social upheaval.

All these events, including the marked decline in physical inactivity as a result of labour-saving devices in the home and workplace and the advent of computer-driven home entertainment systems, have consequences for health. As our colleague Garry Egger has said, 'It's not Ronald McDonald who's causing the current obesity epidemic in developed countries, it's Bill Gates.'

In countries that once constituted the Soviet Union, social and economic changes have led to a marked increase in heart disease, especially among the unemployed and underemployed. Social marketers (and other social change practitioners) are called on to use their skills not only to achieve socially desirable change, but also to counter undesirable social change.

Social change practitioners are involved in a wide variety of areas, from changing practices and cultures within industrial organisations, government bureaucracies and institutions, to achieving change within local communities, state and national groupings. For example, environmentalists such as Greenpeace are seeking to change the way people treat the environment, public health professionals are attempting to change the way politicians view preventive health versus medical 'cures', progressive educationalists are attempting to change the way teachers view learning and conduct their classes, and organisational psychologists are attempting to change the way workers react to changing technology and work practices. In this book we will argue that social marketing has much to contribute to all of these areas, but that social change practitioners in these other areas can also assist social marketers develop comprehensive social marketing campaigns.

We would argue that the value of social marketing is that it is the one discipline to embody, within the one framework, most of the principles, concepts and tools necessary for the development and implementation of effective social change campaigns.

According to Ross and Mico (1980), social change can be brought about through any or all of several different methods. These range from passive to active acceptance by the community, for example:

- the diffusion of ideas, products, and services throughout society, often led by opinion leaders and the mass media
- consensus organising by interested parties
- planned or political action such as lobbying, legislation, and election campaigns
- confrontational methods via threats of reactive action if agreement is not met
- non-violent disruptive protests (for example, boycotts, strikes)
- violent disruption through riots and revolution.

Social marketing makes its major contribution in understanding and facilitating social change in all of the non-confrontational methods noted above, but particularly in facilitating diffusion and adoption.

Key point: Social marketing is best viewed within a broad context of social change.

Marketing and business

Just as business in general relies on marketing tools to attract (and satisfy) customers, so too does the business of social change. While no business relies solely on marketing (that is, finance, production, transport, and warehousing, etc, are all essential), without marketing of some sort, the company could not survive. No matter how good a product is, if consumers are not made aware of how it could meet their needs, and if it is not readily available and affordable, the company will fail. In short, marketing is a necessary but not sufficient factor for success.

All other things being equal (for example, costs of production, and distribution, etc.), the most successful businesses are those with the best marketing. By 'best marketing' we do not just mean the best ads or high-incentive promotions, but the best techniques to reach and attract the attention of the target audience in a way that involves them, products and services that better deliver benefits that satisfy their needs, and at a price customers consider equitable.

Like any other business the business of social change relies on the use of marketing tools to achieve its goals of attracting and satisfying its target groups. No matter how intrinsically good our product, say, energy conservation, if we do not

- inform people as to why energy conservation is necessary
- show them how they can buy products or adopt behaviours that conserve energy without undue cost or effort
- demonstrate how energy conserving behaviours meet individual and community needs and
- in a way that attracts and holds their interest,

then we cannot expect people to buy and act on our message. Similarly, if we do not do the same for legislators and corporations we cannot expect to achieve regulatory and policy changes to provide support for individual behaviour change.

What is marketing?

Marketing has been variously defined. The American Marketing Association's (AMA) current definition (which, incidentally, is under review) is: 'Marketing is the process of planning and executing the conception, pricing, promotion, and distribution of ideas, goods and services to create exchanges that satisfy individual and organisational goals.' (It is noteworthy that 'ideas' was included only in 1985.) For many people it is simply the tactics used by companies to sell their products and services, that is, the first half of the AMA's current definition above.

The second half of this definition is the basis for what has been called the 'marketing concept' (or 'philosophy') as a way of doing business: '... to create exchanges that satisfy individual and organisational goals.' The key words here refer to 'satisfying exchanges'—for both the buyer (the benefits derived from the product or service meet the customer's needs) and the seller (at a price that meets costs and returns a profit).

The marketing concept proposes that company profits are gained via the identification and satisfaction of consumer needs. This emphasis, known as a 'consumer orientation', is on maximising consumer satisfaction with resultant repeat purchasing and favourable word of mouth. The orientation is long-term and aims to establish an ongoing relationship with the customer. In this sense marketing is distinguished from the 'selling orientation', in which the emphasis is on the short-term goal of making the sale, regardless of whether the item is best suited to meet the customer's needs.

The quote attributed to Henry Ford when referring to his T Model Ford—'They can have any colour they want so long as it's black'—is often cited as demonstrating the selling orientation, as are the tactics of timeshare and door-to-door encyclopaedia salespeople. Other orientations contrasted with marketing's customer orientation are the 'product' and 'production' orientations. The former focuses on developing the best possible product—with little attention paid to whether customers want or can afford such a product; the latter focuses on obtaining the most cost-efficient production, packaging, and distribution processes with scant regard for how this might affect the consumer. Needless to say, excluding monopoly or cartel situations, commercial organisations that do not place sufficient emphasis on the consumer orientation will fail in the long run. We will have more to say on the consumer orientation in chapter 2.

Defining social marketing

Social marketing was originally named—as were other subbranches of marketing such as business-to-business or industrial marketing—to refer to a specific subarea of marketing. In actual practice what occurred was that the modern marketing techniques developed for consumer products began to be applied by other areas of business as they saw the apparent success of these techniques. These subdisciplines became demarcated as it was realised that, although the principles and tools of marketing could be applied in the different areas, the marketplaces were very different for each. Marketers in each of these areas required an understanding of these marketplaces in addition to their understanding of marketing per se. Hence, we now have texts and courses entitled Industrial or Business-to-Business Marketing, Services Marketing, Financial Services Marketing, Government or Public Sector Marketing, Events Marketing, Sports Marketing, and even Religious Marketing. So too social marketing came about as marketers and social change practitioners began to apply marketing techniques to social campaigns.

What distinguished early social marketing efforts from other areas was that social marketing was not for commercial profit; nor was it promoting a particular organisation (that is, the domain of not-for-profit marketing). Rather, social marketing campaigns appeared to be conducted for the common good.

Incidentally, just as many original applications of consumer goods marketing to other business areas failed (see Baker 1996, p. 25), so too have many attempts to apply marketing to social causes. However, this is generally not because marketing is inappropriate in these areas, but because marketing concepts and techniques have been misinterpreted and poorly applied. Too many early (and recent) social marketing campaigns were conducted by health and social policy professionals who lacked marketing expertise or were led by marketing or advertising professionals who lacked an understanding of the health or

The social marketing listserver has a burst of activity every so often with respect to 'defining social marketing'. Much of this is semantic with various contributors taking perhaps perverse intellectual delight trying to think of exceptions to whatever definition is proposed by someone else. We think that the vast majority of social marketing practitioners have been doing quite well without a precise definition, and pedantic semantic posturing serves little useful purpose.

social policy area in question. Given that the most visible aspect of consumer goods marketing was advertising, many uses of marketing simply involved the addition of advertising to the organisation's promotional strategy. A classic example was that of the early adoption of 'marketing' by Australian universities to compete for students. This generally involved the appointment of a marketing manager, the creation of a slogan, and the advertising of their various courses, with too little regard for factors such as teacher quality, timetabling, job opportunities, etc.

Social marketing, as it was first defined by Kotler and Zaltman (1971), simply referred to the application of the principles and tools of marketing to achieve socially desirable goals, that is, benefits for society as a whole rather than for profit or other organisational goals: '... the design, implementation and control of programs calculated to influence the acceptability of social ideas and involving considerations of product planning, pricing, communications and market research' (p. 5).

An often cited definition in the past 5 years has been Andreasen's (1995, p. 7) definition: 'Social marketing is the application of commercial marketing technologies to the analysis, planning, execution, and evaluation of programs designed to influence the voluntary behaviour of target audiences in order to improve their personal welfare and that of their society.' We have previously preferred Kotler and Zaltman's definition because of its simplicity, wide generalisability, and because it avoids unnecessary and generally unhelpful definitional debates. In this view, a health promoter's use of sponsorship (a marketing tool)—to ensure that entertainment venues are smoke-free or that healthy food choices are available—is an example of social marketing.

We consider Andreasen's definition too constrictive in its emphasis on *voluntary* behaviours. For example, a social marketing campaign for the National Heart Foundation, with an end goal of individuals consuming less saturated fats, might also target biscuit manufacturers to persuade them to substitute saturated fats in their products with polyunsaturated fats. While this requires a voluntary behaviour change among the food company executives, the end-consumers' change in saturated fats intake is involuntary. Furthermore, from our point of view, if the social marketers lobbied legislators to enforce such substitutions (that is, individual voluntary behaviour by legislators, involuntary by food manufacturers and their consumers), this would still be social marketing.

This voluntary restriction is somewhat inconsistent with the practice of marketing anyway. For example, commercial sponsors of events often negotiate exclusive merchandising arrangements, such that the customer has little or no choice but to consume the sponsor's product. For the 2000 Olympics, the only credit card accepted by the ticketing agency was Visa (an Olympic sponsor). Similarly, commercial sponsors in American schools have exclusive merchandising contracts for a wide range of products, and health promoters use sponsorship to ensure that healthy food choices are available at entertainment venues, that the venues are smoke-free, and that access is available to people with disabilities (Corti, Holman, Donovan, Frizzel & Carroll 1995a). Hence, we would modify Andreasen's definition to 'Social marketing is the application of commercial marketing technologies to the analysis, planning, execution, and evaluation of programs designed to influence the voluntary *or involuntary* behaviour of target audiences in order to improve the welfare of individuals and society.' We further extend this definition to accommodate two key points underlying this book's approach to social marketing, especially as we wish the field to develop.

- First, much of the debate about defining social marketing and the common good centres on how to establish this so-called common good in pluralistic societies (that is, who decides what is good?). While we believe that this is rarely an issue in practice we propose the United Nations Universal Declaration of Human Rights as our baseline with respect to the common good (<see http://www.unhchr.ch>).

- Second, most social marketing to date, particularly in the public health and injury prevention areas, has focused on achieving individual behaviour change, largely independent of the individual's social and economic circumstances. There is now overwhelming evidence that various social determinants influence health over and above individual behavioural risk factors and physical environment risk factors (Wilkinson & Marmot 1998). These social determinants result from the social structure of society in (interrelated) areas such as the workplace, education, literacy and community cohesion. Hence, we see a primary future goal of social marketing as achieving changes in these social determinants of health and wellbeing (Donovan 2000b; Mechanic 1999).

Our view is that the domain of social marketing is not just the targeting of individual voluntary behaviour change and changes to the environment that facilitate such changes, but the targeting of changes in social structures that will facilitate individuals reaching their potential. This means ensuring individuals' access to health services, housing, education, transport, and other basic human rights that clearly impact on health status (Gruskin, Plafker & Smith-Estelle 2001). This will require the targeting of individuals in communities who have the power to make institutional policy and legislative change (Andreasen 1997; Hastings, MacFadyen & Anderson 2000). There are a number of examples of this in developing countries; there is also an urgent need for a social marketing approach to empower indigenous communities in Australia.

A brief history of social marketing

Social marketing has its roots in public education campaigns aimed at social change. Kotler and Roberto (1989) report campaigns to free the slaves in ancient Greece and Rome and history records many attempts by governments in particular to mobilise public opinion or educate the public with respect to health or edicts of the government of the day. These efforts perhaps reached a peak of sinister sophistication with the expertise of Joseph Goebbels in Nazi Germany in the 1930s and similar attempts by the Allies to rally their own populations to the war efforts in the 1940s (see chapter 11, 'Media'). The propaganda expertise developed in the 1940s was then applied, initially mainly in the USA, to a series of topic areas such as forest fire safety, crime prevention, cardiovascular disease, and so on. It is perhaps most evident recently in the anti-smoking and HIV/AIDS campaigns of the 1990s.

Although some would argue that these early public education campaigns were primarily media-based campaigns rather than comprehensive social marketing campaigns (Fox & Kotler 1980), nevertheless, socially desirable products (for example, war bonds) and attitudes (for example, towards women working) were promoted heavily in ways indistinguishable from commercial marketing. In any case, in the 1970s social marketing was being applied far more extensively in developing countries than in developed countries (Manoff 1985) in areas such as family planning, rat control and other hygiene and sanitation areas, agriculture, and attitudes towards women (Rice & Atkin 1989).

The 1980s saw rapid growth, both in Australia and overseas, in the application of marketing concepts to public education campaigns across a broad range of activities, including injury prevention, drinking and driving, seat belt usage, illicit drugs, smoking, exercise, immunisation, nutrition, and heart disease prevention (Egger, Donovan & Spark 1993; Fine 1990; Kotler & Roberto 1989; Manoff 1985; Walsh, Rudd, Moeykens et al. 1993). Egger, Donovan & Spark (1993) point to a number of factors influencing this.

- The realisation by behavioural scientists and health professionals that, while they were expert in assessing what people should do, they were not necessarily expert in communicating these messages, nor in motivating or facilitating behavioural change
- The apparent success of marketing techniques in the commercial area and the observation that the discipline of marketing provided a systematic, research-based approach for the planning and implementation of mass intervention programs
- Epidemiological research findings about the relationships between habitual behaviours and long-term health outcomes. Within public health this led to campaigns aimed at prevention of the so-called lifestyle diseases such as heart disease and cancer.
- A focus on lifestyle diseases initially led to an emphasis on individual responsibility and individual behaviour change (Egger et al. imply that this

was an undue emphasis), a view consistent with the capitalist philosophy of individualism and rational free choice, which many saw as synonymous with commercial marketing.

Some critics of social marketing (and health promotion) have claimed that this individual focus philosophy largely ignores the social, economic, and environmental factors that influence individual health behaviours. While some social marketing campaigns deserve this criticism this is not an inherent characteristic of social marketing. One of the fundamental aspects of marketing—and hence, of social marketing—is an awareness of the total environment in which the organisation operates and how this environment influences, or can itself be influenced to enhance, the marketing activities of the company or health agency (see Hastings & Haywood 1991; Buchanan, Reddy & Hossain 1994; Hastings & Haywood 1994). Our definition of social marketing explicitly acknowledges the influence of the social and physical environment on individual behaviour.

Social marketing: what it is—and what it is not

The latest outbreak of defining social marketing on the Social Marketing listserver occurred in December 2000, with various contributors anguishing over such things as how one defines the common good and who in the community decides what is good, what the word 'social' means, whether the term should be restricted to individual voluntary behaviour, and so on. We take an eclectic and pragmatic view, but our underlying premise is that what distinguishes social marketing from other areas of marketing is the primary end goal of the campaigners. If the National Heart Foundation (NHF) were to undertake a campaign to reduce the amount of cholesterol in people's diets using advertising and promotions aimed at increasing fruit and vegetables consumption and via lobbying manufacturers and fast food outlets to reduce their use of saturated fats, this would be social marketing. If the NHF formed a partnership with various fruit and vegetable marketers in such a campaign these commercial partners would not be engaging in social marketing. While the impact of increased fruit and vegetable consumption would have a desirable social health outcome, this is not their goal: their goal is an increased profit.

Not-for-profit marketing

Not-for-profit marketing refers to not-for-profit organisations using marketing to achieve organisational goals. If the NHF were to undertake a fundraising drive using direct mail and mass media advertising, this would be not-for-profit marketing. While the NHF's aims overall are for the common good, raising funds in competition with other charitable organisations is an organisational goal rather than a common-good aim. Similarly, if a library used marketing techniques to build its customer base and attract funds to achieve its goals of growth and its positioning of having an up-to-date library of music videos and CDs, this would be not-for-profit marketing. However, if the library undertook to increase the literacy of people in the community it served and this was the primary aim of the program the library would be engaging in social marketing. Such a program might, of course, result in increased use of the library, but this would be a means to the primary goal.

Cause-related marketing

Cause-related marketing refers to a commercial entity forming a partnership with a prosocial organisation or cause, such that sales of the commercial organisation's products benefit the prosocial cause (Webb & Mohr 1998). In some ways this is similar to sponsorship (or prosocial marketing; see below), where the prosocial organisation allows the commercial entity to promote its association with the prosocial organisation in order to improve people's attitudes towards the company and its products. The difference is that, in cause-related marketing, the return to the prosocial organisation is directly related to product sales. Again this is not social marketing as the commercial organisation's main aim is to achieve increased sales or some other marketing objective; it is simply using the social goal as a means to this end. Cause-related marketing has become relatively popular in the USA ever since, in 1983, American Express offered to donate 1 cent to the restoration of the Statue of Liberty for every use of its card. In Australia there has been less direct linking to sales. Perhaps the best known was Coles's 1991–3 linking of purchases from Coles outlets to the provision of Apple computing equipment to participating schools (Kotler, Armstrong, Brown & Adam et al. 1998).

Prosocial marketing

Prosocial marketing refers to a commercial organisation promoting a prosocial cause related in some way to its target audience. For example, in Australia Kellogg's features on its cereal products messages targeting young children about bullying; on its Guardian pack it promotes a message about folate from the Northcott Society for Crippled Children. Kellogg's is also a major sponsor of the Surf Life Saving Association (Kellogg's 'Surf Safe Summer'). Prosocial marketing is similar to sponsorship in that the commercial organisation hopes to achieve an increase in positive attitudes to itself and its products through an association with the prosocial organisation or issue.

In many cases an apparent concern for a social issue is directly related to the commercial organisation's interests, for example, a condom manufacturer providing information on HIV transmission, insurance companies promoting screening, and cereal manufacturers providing information on fibre and colorectal cancer. A variation on this is where the commercial organisation joins with its critics to minimise the harm done by its products, for example, alcohol marketers mounting or supporting responsible drinking campaigns, packaging companies supporting and promoting recycling and clean-up campaigns, and cigarette manufacturer Phillip Morris funding domestic violence shelters. In many cases the commercial organisation's primary motive is to avert criticism or regulation rather than achieving a socially desirable goal.

Societal marketing

Societal marketing is sometimes confused with social marketing. Kotler et al. (1998) use this term to refer to companies that act in socially responsible ways in the achievement of their profit goals (for example, companies that voluntarily use biodegradable products and recyclable packaging in production processes, etc.). This was considered an extension of the original marketing concept from profit through identification and satisfaction of consumer needs to profit through identification and satisfaction of consumer needs 'in a way that preserves or improves the consumer's and the society's well-being' (Kotler et al. 1998, p. 20).

Corporate philanthropy

Societal marketing is often linked with social responsibility and corporate philanthropy. Corporate philanthropy, such as The Body Shop's secondment of staff to Romanian orphanages and McDonald's Ronald McDonald houses, is viewed as altruistic, with no direct link to increased sales or other commercial goals. However, corporate philanthropy has direct and indirect benefits to the company's profitability via positive effects on employees and external stakeholders and the community (Collins 1993); along with social responsibility and an interest in social causes, corporate philanthropy appears to be on the increase (Osterhus 1997; Drumwright 1996). Since 1991 Qantas has raised almost $5 million for UNICEF: its staff are raising money for aid projects in Zimbabwe and Thailand; in 1998, the company raised $410 000 for the Starlight Children's Foundation through sales of a Christmas carols CD (McCoy 2000). This new era of social responsibility augurs well for social marketers looking for resources and partnerships.

There clearly are elements of overlap between these various areas that utilise marketing concepts and tools. Figure 1.1 attempts to show the relationship between them. For example, prosocial marketing appears to be the intersection of social marketing and profit marketing, while cause-related marketing combines elements of profit marketing and non-profit marketing.

Social marketing and social change tools

Social marketing as proposed by many social marketers (mainly by academics, less so by practitioners) has been restricted to the classical marketing techniques and has excluded areas such as lobbying, legislative and policy action, and structural change (for example, Andreasen's (1995) emphasis on individual, voluntary behaviour change). However, marketers use a number of tools to achieve sales and profit goals. Business lobbies government for policies and legislation that facilitate business operations such as restricting competition—

Figure 1.1 Variants of marketing applied to socially desirable causes

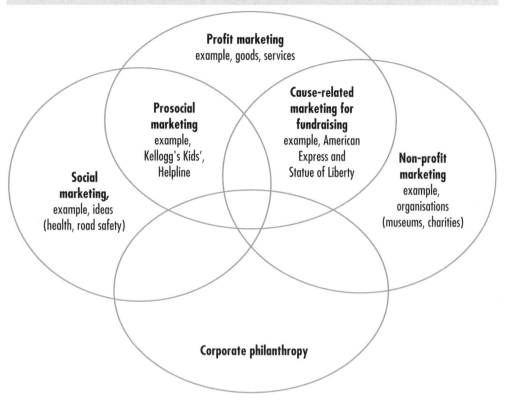

especially from imports, tax breaks for research and development of new products, plant and retail location incentives, fuel subsidies, and so on, all of which have a bearing on the company's marketing efforts. For example, Australian margarine manufacturers lobbied long and hard for legislation to allow margarine to be coloured like butter to increase its acceptance to consumers, a move vigorously opposed by the dairy industry. Similarly, antitobacco campaigners have lobbied government to ban tobacco advertising, to increase tax on tobacco, and to restrict smoking in public places.

Is lobbying for the social good social marketing? From our point of view, if the lobbyist considers the interaction an exchange and is concerned with the needs of the lobbied (that is, the politician or legislator), it is social marketing.

Such lobbying is, of course, consistent with commercial marketing anyway— as noted above—since actions such as lobbying are included in the promotion element of the marketing mix in terms of influencing the environment in which exchanges take place (Kotler et al. 1998, p. 519). Furthermore, if the key core concept of marketing is the exchange process, whereby one party exchanges something of value with another party to the perceived benefit of each, then much of human activity—not just that of commercial organisations—could be termed 'marketing'. In this sense we agree with Piercy (1991) and Baker (1996) that virtually all organisations engage in some form of marketing (that is, attempting to achieve satisfying exchanges with stakeholders), although many would not label it as such and some would make more efforts with some stakeholders than others. For example, many government department CEOs extend far more effort keeping their minister happy than they do keeping their clients satisfied.

Education, motivation and regulation

Elsewhere (Egger et al. 1993; Donovan 2001; see also chapter 11) we describe the three major methods of achieving campaign objectives as

- to educate (information)
- to motivate (persuasion)
- to advocate (sociopolitical action).

Education and persuasion are aimed at individual behaviour change and advocacy is aimed at achieving structural change at the social, physical, and legislative level. We distinguish education/information and motivation/persuasion in much the same way that health education is distinguished from health promotion. Health education involves the provision of information in a more or less dispassionate, objective scientific manner, where the target audience is left to make an informed choice. Education can be effective in achieving behaviour change when ignorance is the major barrier.

However, information per se is often insufficient to bring about behaviour change. Persuasion—and health promotion—involves the provision of information, products, and services so as to directly influence the target audience to adopt the source's recommendations. In health education we would dispassionately inform the target audience of the constituents of inhaled tobacco smoke, how the lung cells metabolise this smoke, and how tobacco is related to a number of illnesses. In health promotion, we would dramatise the ill-health effects and attempt to increase the target audience's perception of the severity of the illness and the likelihood of personally being afflicted, stress that quitting smoking would vastly reduce, if not eliminate, the possibility of suffering a smoking-related illness, and offer nicotine-replacement therapy products. We could also lobby to restrict tobacco advertising and institute non-smoking areas in public places. That is, following the World Health Organization's Alma Ata declaration, health promotion is also concerned with the influence of social and physical environment factors.

Rothschild (2001) proposed that there are three overall methods for achieving desirable social change: education, motivation, and legislation. Rothschild's framework appears similar to ours, although he views motivation as the domain of social marketing and differentiates it from education and legislation. He sees all three as complementary and, where relevant, cooperating means of achieving desirable social change. However, in our view, education/information is part of marketing, as are attempts to achieve a legislative context that facilitates the marketing effort. Hence, while different professionals might be necessary to implement these three methods, they are all part of what we would call a comprehensive social marketing campaign. In the case of tobacco, legislative restrictions on advertising and promotion, packaging requirements, and no-smoking areas would constitute the legislative component of a comprehensive approach.

This more comprehensive view of social marketing reflects our background in the public health area, where advocacy for legislative and policy change has played a major role in areas such as tobacco and gun control. The environmental protection area has also used advocacy as its major method for achieving social change. The law has long been used to assist in public health areas, from mandatory notification of various infectious diseases and indicators of child abuse to restrictions on the sexual behaviour of HIV positive people, requirements for food handling and food processing, and so on. Similarly, racial vilification and antidiscriminatory laws are used to influence social norms in tolerance campaigns although some commentators, such as Hugh Mackay, question the use of so-called educative laws to achieve changes in cultural mores or morality. In our opinion, such laws can be a positive force for change, especially if accompanied by education as to why the laws are there.

Legislation and unintended effects

It is claimed that mandatory bicycle helmet use has resulted in increased injury and death rates in the UK as a result of cyclists taking less care through a false sense of security; and many people giving up cycling and returning to the use of their car, hence decreasing their physical activity (Wardlaw 2000).

Social marketing campaigns in many areas exploit existing laws or are used to create favourable public opinion to support further enforcement strategies (for example, road safety, illicit drug use, underage alcohol and cigarette use, etc.). In Australia this is particularly so in the road safety area in which graphic advertising and accompanying publicity have been used to create public support—or at least neutralise opposition—to regulatory measures such as increased fines, hidden cameras, and compulsory random breath testing. Today, social marketing techniques are being used to achieve policy and legislative change at local, state, national, and international levels. In 2000 the European Union parliament adopted policies on tobacco packaging that were to apply to all member countries (Smith 2000). Public health lobbyists are attempting to achieve international agreements on a broad range of issues that impact social welfare and public health.

Social marketing and health promotion

As noted above attempts to achieve social change have been around for a long time. While these may not have been called social marketing, they share many of the same techniques and principles. Consider the case of health promotion. Health promotion has been defined as a more proactive stance than health education, in that whereas health education attempted to inform people—and then left them to make a so-called informed choice—health promotion attempts to not only inform but also to persuade people to cease unhealthy behaviours and to adopt healthy behaviours. Health education focused on bio-medical information, risk factors, and diseases in a fairly dispassionate format. Health promotion, on the other hand, uses highly graphic, emotion-arousing appeals to dissuade people from unhealthy habits, such as smoking. It also uses positive appeals to wellness, self-esteem, and mental alertness to persuade people to adopt healthy behaviours. Health promotion also places considerable emphasis on environments in which health promotion takes place (for exam-ple, health-promoting schools, health-promoting workplaces, health-promot-ing cities, etc.).

A perusal of health-promotion campaigns and health-promotion texts might give a marketing savvy reader the sense that only the name has been changed. Interestingly, some of these texts include a section or chapter on social marketing as just one way of approaching a health-promotion campaign (including ones co-authored by Robert J. Donovan, co-author of this book; see also, Egger et al. 1993; Egger, Spark, Lawson & Donovan 1999).

In short, there are a number of principles, concepts, and tools that are or should be used to develop and implement effective social change campaigns. These are drawn from disciplines such as psychology, sociology, social research, and communication. We would argue that the value of social marketing is that it is the one discipline to embody most of these principles, concepts, and tools within the one framework.

Social marketing and social mobilisation

Based on social change programs in developing countries, McKee (1992, p. 107) defines social mobilisation as

> the process of bringing together all feasible and practical inter-sectoral social allies to raise people's awareness of and demand for a particular development program, to assist in the delivery of resources and services and to strengthen community participa-tion for sustainability and self-reliance.

He lists legislators, community leaders (religious, social, and political), corpora-tions, and the target audience themselves (the 'beneficiaries') as targets via lob-bying, mass media, training, participation in planning, sponsorship, study tours, and so on, to bring about the 'mobilisation' of all these groups to ensure a pro-gram's success. In this sense McKee sees social mobilisation as incorporating and supporting a social marketing campaign with specific objectives. In our view, we see the terms as synonymous, with his list of mobilisation targets simply being the list of necessary stakeholders to engage for maximal impact.

McKee's framework is particularly relevant in developing countries where intersectoral alliances and government support for programs is relatively weak, or where there may even be hostility towards the program. In developed countries, government departments, NGOs, corporations, and community organisations are more likely to be positive towards the program—although moving these positive attitudes into cooperative action still requires considerable effort.

McKee's framework is useful because it highlights all the target groups for any campaign, although their relevance will vary by issue, resources, and campaign objectives.

Major target groups for social marketing/social mobilisation

- National and state policy makers, legislators: political mobilisation
- Service providers, funders: government mobilisation
- Opinion leaders, NGOs, local government, unions: community mobilisation
- Businesses, business organisations: corporate mobilisation
- Individuals and group beneficiaries of the program: beneficiary mobilisation

For example, a campaign against bullying we are implementing in a Western Australian town was initiated by the then member of the state legislative assembly. The campaign has a board consisting of representatives of several state government departments and the commonwealth government (including education, family and children's services), and community organisations. Major companies in the area have been approached for financial support, schools are incorporated in the program, and individual parents, children, and members of the community have been consulted and will participate in the campaign.

Another example of a social marketing approach that embodies the principles of social mobilisation is the American Centers for Disease Control and Prevention's (CDC) (1996) Prevention Marketing Initiative (yet another term). This HIV prevention program targeting adolescents in five locations used media, skills workshops, contests, condom distribution, promotional merchandise, public events, and influential opinion leaders to reach its goals.

Concluding comments

There are three main ways of looking at or defining social marketing.

- Social marketing is simply a bag of tools or technologies adapted mainly from commercial marketing and applied to issues of social importance.
- Social marketing, via the marketing concept (or philosophy), is a way of approaching an issue that emphasises the perspective of the target audience.
- The end goal of any social marketing campaign is to contribute to achieving a socially just society.

In this book social marketing occurs when all three of the above are present. Furthermore, this book retains the definition of social marketing as derived from the key concepts of commercial marketing, but broadens the domain of social marketing from the application of commercial marketing techniques to the achievement of socially desirable goals to the application of the marketing concept, commercial marketing techniques and other social change techniques to achieving individual behaviour changes and societal structural changes that are consistent with the UN Universal Declaration of Human Rights.

Social marketing seeks to inform and persuade and, where deemed necessary, to legislate to achieve its goals. The relative emphasis on each of these will depend on formative research, resources, the nature of the issue, and the prevailing sociocultural norms and values. For example, mandatory seat belt usage was introduced in Australia with minimal public resistance. However, similar attempts in the USA were met with considerable resistance because they were viewed as an infringement of citizens' rights. In some cases, therefore, social marketing campaigns are undertaken to bring about positive community attitudes to facilitate legislative change. For example, road safety advertising and publicity campaigns serve to convince the public that increased fines and surveillance and detection methods are necessary.

Virchow stated 150 years ago that 'medicine is a social science, and politics nothing more than medicine on a grand scale'. That is, a society's health is very much dependent on the way that society structures itself. Factors affecting the health of populations may be different to those affecting the health of individuals. While the health care system deals with the proximate 'causes' of illness, broader social change is necessary to deal with population causes.

The broader approach we advocate is consistent with the National Academy of Sciences' Institute of Medicine 2000 report into social and behavioural intervention strategies for health. They conclude (p. 6) that interventions need to

- 'focus on generic social and behavioural determinants of disease, injury and disability' (societal level phenomena)
- 'use multiple approaches (for example, education, social support, laws, incentives, behavior change programs) and address multiple levels of influence simultaneously (individuals, families, communities, nations)'
- involve sectors 'that have not traditionally been associated with public health promotion efforts, including law, business, education, social services, and the media'.

The report concluded that although environment-based strategies have the greatest population effect, far more progress had been made in developing individual-oriented health interventions than environmental-oriented interventions (Orleans, Gruman, Ulmer, Emont & Hollendonner et al. 1999). We feel there is a clear need for social marketing to help redress this situation; other social marketers (Goldberg 1995; Hastings et al. 2000) have also pointed this out.

Influences on health and well-being*

Interaction between…	Context shaped by …
Biology—genetics	Age and gender
and	
Behaviour—lifestyle, risk factors	Race and ethnicity
and	
Environment—physical, social	Socioeconomic status

* National Academy of Sciences 2000

Chapter 2

Principles of Marketing

Introduction

Chapter 1 emphasised the 'social' in social marketing. This chapter defines the 'marketing' in social marketing by briefly reviewing the major principles of marketing. It is these principles that form the core of a social marketing approach. Unfortunately, many campaigns that have been labelled 'social marketing' have not been based on an adequate understanding of these principles, leading to unjustified criticisms of social marketing and unjustified claims of its ineffectiveness.

For many health and social change professionals, social marketing is seen as synonymous with the use of media advertising and publicity to promote socially desirable causes. Given that the basic product or primary resource of many social marketing campaigns is information (Young 1989), this view is not unexpected. However, the use of the media is only one component of a total marketing process: the product or service must be designed to meet the customer's needs—it must be packaged and priced appropriately, it must be easily accessible, it should be trialable (if a large commitment is required), intermediaries such as wholesalers and retailers must be established, and, where relevant, sales staff must be informed and trained.

In the same way, a campaign that aims to promote improved parenting behaviour must be based on more than just advertising. Programs and strategies are required at community level, parenting courses must be developed and offered, self-instruction materials made available, the activities promoted must be doable (that is, within the target group's capacities) or learnable (that is, skills must be defined and training must be available for specific activities), and the courses and materials must be easily accessible and affordable.

Marketing is all about satisfying one's customers. Marketing therefore permeates (or should) all areas of an organisation:

- it affects the finance department with respect to prices customers are prepared to pay, how they would like to pay (cheque, credit card, or cash), and what sort of credit terms are desired

- it affects the production department in terms of desired product varieties and packaging
- it affects transport and distribution in terms of where customers prefer to buy the product, and the attitudes of retailers to stocking arrangements and instore promotions
- it affects staff training in terms of what factors enhance or detract from customer satisfaction, for example, how the receptionist treats a customer, how staff are dressed, and how clean the premises are can all have as much to do with customer satisfaction as the actual service the organisation provides. And it is customer satisfaction that will ensure the success and profitability or otherwise of an organisation.

Given that marketing is often defined in terms of delivering products and services that meet customers' needs and that profitability results from customer satisfaction, British author Nigel Piercy (1991) considers that any organisation with customers (or clients) relies on a marketing process, whether they call it that or not.

Nigel Piercy's marketing view

- Every organisation has customers.
- For all organisations, at the end of the day, the only thing that really matters is the long-term satisfaction of customers.
- Therefore every organisation relies on a marketing process.

Marketing basics

There is much jargon and perhaps some mystique attached to the term 'marketing'. Some social change practitioners are very cynical about its philosophical appropriateness and its potential effectiveness while others have a blind, optimistic faith in its ability to achieve all sorts of objectives. Each of these views stems from an objectification of marketing as either an individual-based, capitalistic approach or a bag of highly successful manipulative techniques—or both. Piercy (1991, pp. 7–8) takes a very pragmatic view on what is really marketing. This is his view, with which we concur.

Every organisation has customers—even if it is difficult sometimes to decide just who they are. For a public housing department, identifying its customers (or clients) appears relatively easy: all existing and potential tenants and purchasers who qualify for public housing assistance. However, taxpayers and society in general are also interested in the type and location of public housing. Many public housing projects of the 1960s and 1970s, especially highrise blocks, ended up becoming ghettos of crime and social disorder that pleased neither the primary customers, their neighbours, or the taxpayers who paid not only for the bricks and mortar, but also for the social ills exacerbated by these developments.

The police service also has quite diverse customers: criminals in their care, the general public, shop and other property owners, and so on. The Department of (Road) Transport has a broad variety of customers: road users—bicyclists, motorcyclists, car, truck, and bus users, as well as road transport firms, organisations and communities that rely on road transport, pedestrians, and so on. All these different groups have needs—some of which are conflicting—and demand products and services to meet these needs. Determining priorities of needs is one of the major issues facing government departments and one of the major ethical dilemmas for social marketers (see chapter 7).

For all organisations, at the end of the day, the only thing that really matters is the long-term satisfaction of customers

This is the only reason for the existence of an organisation, whether it be commercial, non-profit, or government, and the only way it can survive. Take customers away and organisations cease to exist. Customers' long-term satisfaction is often more difficult to define and achieve in the public and NGO sectors than in the private sector. Nevertheless, the point is that if public sector and non-profit organisations really wish to achieve their vision and mission statements they must first identify and then satisfy their customers' needs.

In past experience with the public sector it was evident that many such organisations put organisational goals ahead of client satisfaction goals. For example, public housing was designed, located, and built primarily to achieve financial and productivity indicators, not the long-term satisfaction of users— and often with disastrous effects, as noted above. Similarly, road transport departments would focus on miles of road built and maintained rather than on road safety indicators, traffic noise, and road users' satisfaction with traffic flow, convenience, and so on. Fortunately, with the rise of customer charters, many government departments in Australia are at least aware of customer needs, even if they currently only pay lip service to satisfying those needs.

Therefore, every organisation relies on a marketing process.

The most important marketing tasks are not necessarily carried out by a specialist marketing department or person, but by front-counter staff, telephone-answering staff, or delivery staff.

A customer's impression of an organisation is based on their experiences with the people who represent that organisation, whether they are an accounts person responding to a customer querying their account, the person who delivers the product to the customer's home or factory, or the staff member answering the phone. Good marketing means that each of these organisation staff recognise the need to treat the customer with dignity and respect. Too many organisations fail to appreciate that all their staff influence customer satisfaction. Public sector organisations in particular need to implement a marketing orientation before they can properly adopt social marketing to meet their campaign objectives. Thus, a family and children's services department should first understand the need to treat its captive clients as customers before it can maximise the effectiveness of adopting a social marketing approach to, say, attracting parents to enrol in parenting courses.

Piercy further states that marketing is very simple in concept (that is, common sense), but very difficult to implement in practice. Even for those with a will it's not that easy. A survey of the faithful at the American Marketing Association's Customer Satisfaction Congress in 1994 found that only 16 per cent said their company had a very successful customer satisfaction strategy (*Services Marketing Today*, July/August 1994). Similarly, although many public sector (and commercial) organisations now have customer charters many have failed to fully—or even partially—implement these charters. Piercy claims— and we agree—that the reason why is a lack of real commitment by senior management. How many public sector heads actually spend time at the front counter? How many take the time to attend community meetings? How many read whatever customer research their department does undertake? In the authors' experience, very few.

Principles and practices of marketing

A number of aspects of product and service marketing such as market segmentation, market research, competitive assessment, the use of product, price, promotion and distribution tactics, pretesting and ongoing evaluation of campaign strategies, and models of consumer behaviour adapted from the psychological and communications literature have been discussed in the context of social marketing (for example, Hastings & Haywood 1991; Kotler & Roberto 1989; Lancaster, McIlwain & Lancaster 1983; Lefebvre & Flora 1988; Manoff 1985; Novelli 1990; Solomon 1989).

Those we consider most relevant are those discussed by Donovan and Owen (1994); they are outlined below (figure 2.1).

- **Two fundamental concepts**   *Consumer orientation*
                                                        Exchange concept
- **Three overarching principles**   *Customer value*
                                                        Selectivity and concentration
                                                        Differential advantage
- **Three defining features**   *Use of market research*
                                                        Integrated approach to implementation
                                                        Monitoring and influencing environmental forces

We will present and illustrate each of these in turn.

The marketing concept: a consumer orientation

Piercy's major point is that marketing is about focusing an organisation on identifying its customers and its customers' needs and then directing resources to

Figure 2.1 Basic principles of marketing

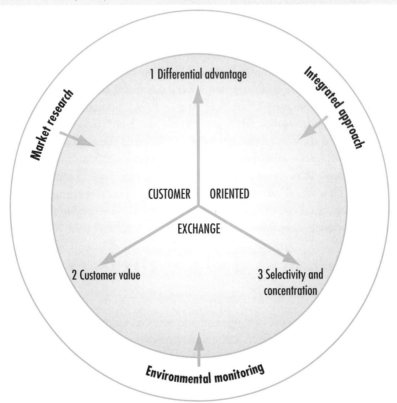

meeting those needs. It is this customer orientation view of marketing that we most endorse and that permeates all of the other principles and concepts dealt with below. Beverley Schwartz, of Fleishmann-Hillard in Washington DC, expresses the consumer orientation in social marketing in her statement that 'the problem is not what to *tell* people, but what to *offer* them to make them want to change'.

This customer orientation is also known as 'the marketing concept'. Organisations with a consumer orientation are contrasted with organisations that have production, product, or sales orientations. These orientations focus on the needs of the seller rather than the buyer (Kotler 1989). In contrast, a customer focus seeks profits through the identification of customer needs, the development of products and services to meet these needs, and the pricing, packaging, promotion, and distribution of these products in accordance with consumer habits, aspirations, and expectations.

The first author (RJD) was once employed by the Swan Brewery which, at that time (the 1970s), enjoyed a near monopoly in Western Australia. In 1971 the Swan Brewery employed its first marketing manager, and in 1972 Donovan was employed as the company's first market research officer (MRO). However, while the company had employed a marketing manager, they had not embraced the marketing concept. They saw the marketing function as that of just a more sophisticated sales department that would design more stylish can and bottle labels, develop professional-looking (expensive) television ads, and sell more beer in overseas markets by lavishly entertaining import agents in various countries. The company was still largely in the hands of the brewers, the finance people, and the production– packaging managers. The brewers' dominance meant that the consumer got what the brewers considered beer should look and taste like, regardless of consumer research indicating different preferences. The dominance of the production–packaging manager meant that packaging was dictated by what was easiest and least costly rather than what consumers preferred (for example, an initial reluctance to introduce six-packs), the dominance of the finance people meant that credit terms were inflexible to hoteliers and liquor store owners, and that all areas of the brewery first considered cost implications rather than customer satisfaction implications. The MRO's research, for example, revealed retailers and customers complaining about cartons coming apart. Nevertheless, it took considerable effort to convince the production people to apply two applications of glue rather than one, which they were reluctant to do because of the increased cost.

Even the marketing manager had not fully adopted a consumer orientation. While he was concerned about customer satisfaction in some areas he was motivated more by a desire to reach quarterly and annual sales goals (against which his performance was assessed) than to achieve long-term customer satisfaction. When customer research revealed that many (older) beer drinkers wanted only one or two glasses of a 750 mL bottle per night, and hence looked for all sorts of ways to stop the remainder going flat, the MRO suggested a screwtop for 750 mL bottles. The marketing manager dismissed this outright and delivered his mantra: 'Mr Heinz made his fortune not from the mustard people ate, but from the mustard they left on their plate.'

Can social marketing be based on customers' needs?

A basic distinction between social and commercial marketing is that social marketing campaigns are often not based on needs experienced by consumers, but on needs identified by experts. This is true. Communities might prefer their resources to be spent on hospitals rather than on disease prevention, and on tougher prisons rather than rehabilitation. On the other hand, whereas epidemiological evidence indicates smoking and physical inactivity are greater causes of morbidity and mortality, a government might allocate far more resources to antidrug campaigns because a majority of voters considers drugtaking a more important issue. So government resource allocation is not only informed by experts, but also by party philosophy, lobbying from various specific interest groups, and voter opinion polling. At the same time, there is at least the

Good service people make their customers feel important

From a social marketing view a consumer orientation means viewing individuals, regardless of their position or circumstances, as equal human beings, with a right to dignity and respect. This requires an empathy with their needs and a caring, compassionate approach to their immediate situational as well as long-term needs. This is particularly important when dealing with disadvantaged people.

appearance of increasing community consultation on priorities for health and social policies.

In 2001 in Western Australia, the Medical Council, an advisory group to the Health Department, conducted what it called 'citizen juries' to obtain community input to decisions about health care resource allocation. These juries consist of small convenience samples of citizens who are presented with information by health experts, then asked to consider the information and make recommendations on priorities for resource allocation. The usefulness of these juries beyond traditional qualitative research methods with health consumers has yet to be demonstrated.

Regardless of who decides the priorities, a marketing approach emphasises that the development, delivery, and promotion of the message and products or services must be carried out in accordance with consumer needs. For example, messages about immunisation must be in a language consumers understand, the promised benefits must be relevant, and the messages must be placed in media that consumers attend to. A number of studies have shown that, while things are improving, much health education and other literature emanating from government departments is written at a readability level far higher than the average reader level and contains jargon understandable only to other professionals in the area (Rudd, Moeykens & Colton 1999). It appears that many authors of such material are attempting to meet their peers' approval rather than attempting to make the literature easily comprehensible to end consumers.

In the 1970s the first author's research company was commissioned by the then West Australian State Housing Commission (SHC) to assist them implement an urban renewal program (Donovan, Close, Woodhouse, Hogben 1979). We suggested the then radical step of having the Commission's architects actually meet with the people for whom they were designing homes and units and recommended that the Commission open information centres in areas to be renewed. We also suggested that the CEO and other senior executives appear at an open meeting in the renewal area to answer residents' questions. To ensure that the SHC executives could answer these questions we recommended a small survey of residents to determine what questions residents would be likely to ask. Hence, the SHC could prepare appropriate answers. The SHC accepted all of these suggestions, but initially as a means of mollifying the residents rather than out of a genuine concern for the residents' needs.

However, as a result of participating in these activities and seeing the benefits first hand (for example, reduced resident anger and complaints, feelings of goodwill arising from listening and cooperating, etc.), a profound cultural shift occurred within the Commission staff involved. The renewal program then proceeded with a distinct and genuine consumer orientation to the extent that Commission staff took over the social marketing role that the research company had previously performed.

Perhaps the most important outcome of this project was that it at least temporarily removed the confrontational them-versus-us attitude that still pervades many public sector organisations, where staff view the customer or client as the enemy. Perhaps the reason why universities are still struggling with their marketing programs is that many staff still believe that teaching would be so much better if it were not for the students.

The concept of exchange

The concept of exchange has long been described as the core concept of marketing: 'Marketing is the exchange which takes place between consuming groups and supplying groups' (Alderson 1957, p. 15). An essential factor differentiating exchanges from other forms of need satisfaction is that each party to the exchange gains and receives value and, at the same time, each party perceives the offerings to involve costs. Hence, it is the ratio of the perceived benefits to the costs that determines choice between alternatives (Kotler & Andreasen 1987). Kotler (1988) lists the following as necessary conditions for potential exchange:

- there are at least two parties
- each party offers something that might be of value to the other party
- each party is capable of communication and delivery
- each party is free to accept or reject the offer
- each party believes it is appropriate or desirable to deal with the other party.

There is some debate as to whether the exchange concept is truly present in many social marketing areas. If it is not, is it really social marketing?. Elliott (1995) takes the view that a voluntary exchange as it occurs in commercial marketing differs from the exchange that takes place in social marketing and that it is an 'intellectual contortion' to consider that 'exchange' means the same as when a consumer exchanges dollars for a refrigerator and when a smoker gives up smoking for a longer, healthier life (Elliott 1995).

Elliott has a point. In the commercial world the exchange is always between two parties; in social marketing, depending on the issue, the exchange of something of value may appear to take place within rather than between the parties. For behaviours such as immunisation, time and effort on the part of the consumer is exchanged for a healthy life through prevention of diseases; for the health organisation, resources are exchanged for lower morbidity and mortality, and lower health costs. Consistent with Maibach (1993), we take the view that some sort of exchange is usually always present, even if primarily intra-individual, somewhat complex or ill-defined. Nevertheless, neither our definition in chapter 1, nor those of Andreasen (1995) and Kotler and Zaltman (1971) relies on the inclusion of exchange in the definition of social marketing.

More pragmatically, the lessons for social marketers from the exchange concept are that we must

- offer something perceived to be of value to our target audiences
- recognise that consumers must outlay resources such as time, money, physical comfort, lifestyle change, or psychological effort in exchange for the promised benefits
- acknowledge that all intermediaries enlisted to support a campaign also require something of value in return for their efforts (De Musis & Miaoulis 1988).

In short, 'the social marketer's task is to maximise the perceived benefits and minimise the perceived costs associated with the advocated change' (Goldberg 1995, p. 350).

In Piercy's terms the customers for a physical activity campaign would include GPs, commercial health club operators, local government recreational officers, community health instructors, health promotion and fitness professionals' associations, volunteer workers, sponsors, and so on. For example, health promoters have too often assumed that the medical and paramedical professions' shared common goal of public health enhancement would be sufficient to ensure their support. But each intermediary should be considered a distinct target market with their own needs and values that must be included in an exchange process. Hence, promotions to GPs asking them to recommend exercise to their patients must be designed with the GPs' needs in mind; that is, materials distributed to GPs should be easy to use, easy to distribute, and should improve their understanding of the relationship between physical activity and physical and mental health.

Customer value: the concept of the marketing mix

The principle of customer value emphasises that products and services are purchased not so much for themselves, but for the benefits they provide to the buyer (Lancaster 1966). This point was reportedly well made by Revlon's Charles Revson in his statement that, 'In the factory we make cosmetics; in the store we sell hope.' Levitt's more mundane example was that although people may buy a quarter-inch drill what they want is a quarter-inch hole (Kotler 1988, p. 243).

Customer value is provided not just by the tangible product or the service per se, but by all the so-called four Ps that constitute what is known as the marketing mix. The four Ps are:

- *Product* (brand name and reputation, packaging, etc.)
- *Price* (monetary cost, credit terms, etc.)
- *Promotion* (advertising, sales promotion, publicity and public relations, personal selling)

- *Place* or distribution (physical distribution, number and type of outlets, opening hours, atmosphere in outlets, availability of public transport, availability and ease of parking).

The marketing manager's task is to blend these four Ps to provide maximal value to selected market segments. For example, customer value can be increased by reducing time and effort costs in obtaining the product (for example, wide distribution, vending machines in appropriate locations, internet ordering), making the product trialable before commitment (for example, sample packs, inoffice/inhome demonstrations, seven days free trial), easy to pay for (for example, credit card acceptance, layby, hire purchase), and easy to use (for example, user friendly packaging, instructions on use, free training courses). The total value of a particular perfume is determined not only by its fragrance, but—and arguably more so—by its packaging, brand name, brand positioning (brand image), price, and outlet reputation.

A fifth P—*People*—is often added for services marketing (Baker 1996), given the frequent inseparability of the service provider and the actual service. In social marketing, of counselling services for example, people aspects are crucial. The lesson from commercial services marketing is that staff training, especially in interpersonal skills, is essential for successful completion of the exchange transaction. Unless domestic violence counsellors, say, have empathy with their clients and have the ability to maintain rapport, perpetrators will discontinue counselling.

A concept that ties the two aspects of customer benefits and the four Ps together is Kotler's (1988) concept of the *core* product, the *augmented* product and the *tangible* product. For example, the tangible product might be a computer. The augmented product involves after-sales service, training, warranties, associated software, a widespread consumer-user network, and so on. The core product is better management decision making. In fact, many companies compete more on augmented product features than on tangible product features (Levitt 1969).

In the promotion of physical activity the core product might be a longer, healthier life through cardiovascular disease-risk reduction, the actual product might be an aerobics class, and the augmented product might include a creche, off-peak discount rates, clean hygienic change rooms, and a complimentary towel.

The notion of augmented product emanates directly from a consumer orientation, an approach that continually seeks to identify customers' needs and attempts to meet them. Public sector welfare organisations often have large numbers of waiting clients, many of whom are women with young children who have probably arrived somewhat tired and frazzled—especially in the summer—after some time on public transport. A social marketing consumer orientation would result in the waiting areas having an area for children to play, the provision of toys and games, refrigerated water fountains, adequate and comfortable seating, and easily accessible toilets and washrooms.

Market (customer) segmentation: the principle of selectivity and concentration

Market segmentation is probably the most important and most established concept in marketing. At a fundamental level it is obvious that the young differ from the old in product requirements and tastes, as do the sexes. But there are far more and sometimes better ways than demographics to segment markets to maximise campaign resources. For example, some people rarely read newspapers, others are avid television watchers, different people respond to different types of appeals. Some people respond only to self-interest appeals, others to civic duty appeals, some to fear, others to guilt; some are already positive toward the use of water conservation devices, others see them to be too costly and ineffectual, and so on.

Market segmentation involves dividing the total market into groups of individuals that are more like each other than they are like individuals in other groups. The fundamental issue is to identify groups that will respond to different products or marketing strategies, and, for commercial organisations, to select and concentrate on those segments where the organisation can be most competitive. We have suggested elsewhere the term 'customer' rather than 'market' segmentation, as 'customer' is more personal and prevents distancing ourselves psychologically from our customers.

The segmentation process involves three phases:

1   dividing the total market into segments and developing profiles of these segments
2   evaluating each segment and selecting one or more segments as target markets
3   developing a detailed marketing mix (that is, the four Ps) for each of the selected segments.

The concept of market segmentation again derives directly from a consumer orientation. To segment adequately clearly requires a comprehensive understanding of customers and is therefore heavily dependent on appropriate market research. Segmentation is fundamental to developing social marketing campaigns and is dealt with in chapter 9.

Competition and the principle of differential advantage

In marketing the principle of differential advantage refers to an analysis of the marketer's resources versus those of the competition with the aim of determining where the company enjoys a differential advantage over the competition. Companies are most likely to be successful in areas where they enjoy a differential advantage. Commercial organisations regularly carry out SWOT analyses on themselves and their competitors—audits of the organisation's strengths and weaknesses, and identification of current and future opportunities and threats in the environment. Social marketers should do likewise, remembering that

Monitoring the competition: messages in alcohol advertising

Jones and Donovan (2001) analysed the messages young people perceived in ads for UDL's vodka-based drink. They showed that these ads promoted the drink as a facilitator of social relationships by removing inhibitions, especially those with the opposite sex, and that the drink had direct mood effects such as inducing relaxation, removing worries, and making the drinker feel good. These messages are consistent with the reasons for young people's consumption of alcohol in general. Jones and Donovan point out that these messages are in fact against the alcohol industry's self-regulatory code and that public health professionals need to be vigilant with respect to the alcohol industry's activities.

strengths and weaknesses cover financial, human, and technological resources. Many social marketing campaigns directed at youth fail because the people involved have little understanding of youth culture.

This principle is useful at even the most basic stage of identifying just who or what is the competition in a particular instance. Interestingly, and particularly with (global) moves towards privatisation and outsourcing, many public sector organisations are now realising that competitors are being forced upon them or that they face growing competition from the private sector expanding into traditionally public areas For example, while private detective agencies have been around for many years, recent years have seen a dramatic increase in private security organisations such that police services are expressing concern about 'protecting their turf' (Harvey 2001).

What is the competition to increasing physical activity? The answer is any other leisure time activity such as watching television, movies, hobbies, etc. The strategy of attempting to increase physical activity levels via day-to-day activities recognises that allocating a set period of time for exercise faces far more formal competition than does an attempt to increase incidental physical activity.

In a wider sense the principle of differential advantage relates to monitoring and understanding competitive activity, sometimes to emulate or follow such activity, or, in other cases, to preempt or counter competitors' activities. A study of alcohol advertising and promotion, for example, can assist in understanding appeals to young people. Similarly, advocacy groups need to monitor industries such as the tobacco industry and attempt to preempt anticipated industry moves.

The use of market research

It should be apparent that effective marketing is a research-based process with ongoing research in various areas: testing new products, surveys to identify consumer dissatisfaction with current offerings and opportunities for improvement, pretesting advertising and promotions, surveys of attitudes to competitors' offerings, pricing, and packaging research, and so on.

The major use of research in social marketing campaigns to date has been in understanding target audiences' beliefs, attitudes, and behaviours, the development and pretesting of communication materials (advertising, posters, brochures, PSAs), measures of exposure to campaign materials, and pre–post surveys or periodic surveys to assess changes in attitudes, beliefs, and behaviour over the duration of campaigns. Examples of some research questions we have looked at in various social marketing campaigns include the following.

- What do people understand by the term 'bullying'?
- What would motivate domestic violence perpetrators to seek help?
- What are food vendors' attitudes to including health food alternatives on their menus?
- What healthy lifestyle issues (for example, exercise, dietary fat reduction, smoking cessation, etc.) do the community perceive as priorities for action?
- What tangible products can be developed to facilitate the adoption of health-promoting behaviours or to reduce risk (for example, no-tar cigarettes, low-fat foods, quit smoking kits, exercise videos, etc.)?
- What social and structural facilitators and inhibitors need to be taken into account when promoting increased physical activity?
- Who are the relevant influencers of youth fashion and music preferences?
- What motivates young people's alcohol, tobacco, and illicit drug use?
- What messages about indigenous people are most likely to neutralise negative stereotypes?
- What factors influence GPs' use of health-promoting brief interventions?
- What would increase residents' participation in urban renewal decisions?
- What would increase residents' involvement in a recycling program?

Our framework for research is based on that of Coyle, Boruch and Turner (1987) who delineated four types of evaluation designed to answer four questions:

- Formative research   What message strategies and materials would work best?
- Efficacy research   Could the campaign actually make a difference if implemented under ideal conditions?
- Process evaluation   Was the campaign implemented as planned?
- Outcome evaluation   What impact, if any, did the campaign have?

Research in social marketing not only requires an understanding of consumer research methods, but, increasingly, an understanding of epidemiological research methods, as many campaigns are based on such data. Also, given the greater complexity of social marketing areas, research designs can often be more complex or require more indepth analysis and a broader variety of approaches than research into commercial products. Furthermore, we believe that the researchers themselves should have some background in the social sciences, not just in marketing or economics.

Research and evaluation methods are covered in chapter 6.

An integrated planning process

The marketing process is an integrated process, such that elements of the marketing mix—the organisation's resources, the use of market research, and the selection and concentration on specific market segments—are all combined to maximise the value of the organisation's offerings to the consumer and profit to the company.

In simple terms a perfume's packaging must be consistent with its price, its brand image, and its retail distribution. An expensive perfume clearly must be accompanied by expensive- looking packaging and an elegant, stylish image rather than, say, an outdoors or disco fun image, and it must be available only from upmarket outlets. Market research is needed to ensure a viable target segment exists for the perfume, outlets and shelf space must be negotiated for distribution of the product, and advertising and publicity timed to take advantage of gift buying seasons—and certainly not until distribution has been completed. Such a simple adage as 'No advertising until the product is on the shelf' is often forgotten by both commercial and social marketers. Many campaigns in the social welfare area (for example, domestic violence, child abuse) often lead to services being overloaded, because demand was underestimated, was not adequately planned for, or because there was insufficient time to put them in place because the minister or CEO wanted to do something in a hurry simply to be seen to be doing something.

An integrated approach implies the need for a systematic strategic planning process: the setting of clearly defined overall goals, the setting of measurable objectives to meet the overall goals, the delineation of strategies and tactics to achieve these objectives, management and feedback systems established to ensure that the plan is implemented as desired, and to avert or deal with problems as they arise. Egger, Donovan, and Spark (1993) have presented what they called the SOPIE approach to campaign planning: situational analysis, objective setting, planning, implementation, and evaluation. This will be covered, along with other planning methods, in chapter 13.

The environment

Commercial marketers are keenly aware that the marketing process takes place in a changing environment and that this environment must be monitored continually to identify potential opportunities and to avoid potential and actual threats to the company and its products or services. Aspects of the environment that influence both commercial and social marketing include:

- *political–legal* (for example, exhaust emission requirements, antimonopoly laws, food labelling regulations, and rulings on the use of words such as 'natural', 'fresh', etc.)
- *economic* (for example, the introduction of low-priced alternatives during recession periods, changes in spending patterns such as reduced petrol consumption, and hence, reduction in miles driven and number of accidents

---

Who killed Princess Diana?

Would Princess Diana be alive today …
if her driver hadn't been affected by alcohol?
if the vehicle hadn't been speeding?
if she'd been wearing her seatbelt?
An *individual, voluntary behaviour* focus would emphasise the above questions.
An *environmental* perspective would add …
if French authorities had followed standard practice and installed guardrails between
the concrete pillars in the tunnel?

- *technological* (for example, changes in packaging and production methods, whole product categories such as typewriters becoming virtually obsolete)
- *social and cultural* (for example, the demand for environmentally friendly packaging and products, the consumer movement, yearnings for traditional values)
- *demographic trends* (for example, increase in single person and single parent households, growing Asian-born population, the ageing of the population).

However, social marketing takes a broader view in that it recognises that the environment plays a role in bringing about or exacerbating poor health and antisocial behaviours and that individual change is often limited, if not impossible, to achieve or sustain without concurrent or preceding environmental change. For example, people's levels of physical activity are related to opportunities in their immediate physical environment. This is not just in terms of access to facilities such as squash and tennis courts, swimming pools, and commercial health centres (gyms), but also in terms of whether attractive parks are nearby, whether the neighbourhood is safe to go walking, jogging, or cycling (in terms of traffic and likelihood of assault or harassment), whether the footpaths are maintained, and so on (Corti 1998; Stokols 1992; Sallis, Hovell, Hofstetter et al. 1990).

Similarly, a community's or individual's response to a delinquency program or a positive parenting practices program will be very much dependent on factors such as the level of unemployment in the community, the level of income and home ownership, educational opportunities (Hawkins & Catalano 1992), and other measures commonly known as 'social capital' (Putnam 2000). An ecological perspective also considers the role the environment can play regardless of individual risky behaviours. We will cover these wider environmental implications in chapter 3.

Differences between commercial and social marketing

Can we sell brotherhood (and healthy lifestyles and human rights) the way we sell soap?

Many years ago Wiebe (1952), in his article 'Can we sell brotherhood like we sell soap?', questioned whether marketing principles and practices could be applied to non-commercial areas. Clearly, the answer has been 'yes', although there are perhaps obvious differences between selling soap and selling, say, alcohol moderation, just as there are obvious differences between high-involvement products such as fashion clothing, life insurance, and earth-moving equipment versus low-involvement products such as laundry detergent, insecticides, and icecream. Consumers' buying decisions (sources of influence, amount of effort involved, and so on)—and hence marketing approaches—are clearly quite different across these product categories. Nevertheless, while specific tools and tactics may differ the overall principles of commercial marketing are more or less applicable to selling socially desirable products.

The major differences between social and commercial marketing, as noted by various social marketers and commentators (Rothschild 1979; Bloom & Novelli 1981; McKee 1992; Egger, Donovan & Spark 1993; Rangan, Karim & Sandberg 1996) and from our own experiences, can be summarised as follows.

- Defining and communicating the product is far more difficult in social marketing, especially when different experts may have different views on the subject. Developing the National Physical Activity Guidelines for Australians went through ten drafts following development by two key stakeholder workshops and then being mailed three times to a large sample of health and physical fitness professionals, as well as undergoing scrutiny by a twelve-member scientific advisory committee (Egger, Donovan & Giles-Corti 1998; Egger, Donovan, Giles-Corti, Bull & Swinburn 2001).

- In social marketing the product is often information designed to bring about attitudinal and behavioural change; less frequently do social marketers have tangible products to sell and, even where they do, the primary task is to sell the idea (or core product). For example, people must first be convinced that water conservation (the idea) is desirable (and that their contribution would be meaningful) before they can be convinced to purchase water-limiting attachments for their plumbing.

- Commercial products tend to offer instant gratification whereas the promised benefits of many social marketing campaigns are often delayed. This especially applies to many health behaviours.

- The exchange process is far easier to define in commercial marketing than in social marketing.

- Social marketing attempts to replace undesirable behaviours with behaviours that are often more costly in time or effort and, at least in the short term, less pleasurable or even unpleasant. Changes in parenting practices require considerable patience and persistence, withdrawal from addictive substances can be physiologically very traumatic, breaking long-established social and subcultural influences can be difficult.

- Behaviours targeted in social marketing campaigns are often extremely complex, at both a personal and social level, and far more so than are the behaviours involved in purchasing most commercial products. Racist beliefs, attitudes and behaviours are far more complex than any purchasing behaviour.

- Many targeted behaviours, especially health behaviours, are inconsistent with social pressures. Consuming alcohol is a normative behaviour in Australia, with excess consumption not only condoned but encouraged among young males (Pettigrew 2000; Donovan 1997). One of the aims of social marketing is to shift behaviours such as recycling and condom use from unusual to normative behaviours while maintaining others such as children's immunisation as normative behaviours.

- Social marketing often asks the target group to accept a reduction in personal benefits or increase in personal costs to achieve a societal benefit which they may or may not directly benefit from. This applies particularly to corporations in areas such as packaging, land clearing, and toxic waste disposal.

- Commercial marketing mostly aims at groups already positive towards the product and its benefits, whereas social marketing is often directed towards hard-to-reach, at-risk groups who are often most antagonistic to change.

- Intermediaries and stakeholders in commercial marketing are far fewer in type and generally far easier to deal with (although perhaps more costly) than those in social marketing. Antidrug campaigns targeting youth involve a broad variety of intermediaries: health department staff, youth drug workers, drug clinics, school authorities, local government authorities, the police, sport coaches, and youth entertainment operators. Commercial retailers can be influenced by monetary and promotional incentives in a straightforward negotiating process. Influencing GPs to cooperate in a health promotion campaign is far more complex, and gaining cooperation from different government departments or NGOs requires substantial skills.

- Political considerations are far more frequent in social marketing. This applies not only to more obviously sensitive areas such as HIV/AIDS, but to all areas that are vulnerable to party philosophy and government policy.

- Commercial marketing mainly operates within social systems that are conducive to the marketers' goals and that facilitate the marketing and purchasing processes. Commercialisation, privatisation, sponsorship, and the dominance of brand names in sport and entertainment all support a consuming culture. On the other hand, social marketing is operating in many areas where social systems not only inhibit success, but actually exacerbate the targeted problem and possibly contributed to the problem in the first place. Hence, social marketing is often—and should be more often—directed not just towards changes in individual behaviour, but also towards changes in systems and social structures that operate to the detriment of the wellbeing of populations. For example, is there any point in running no smoking campaigns or positive parenting campaigns in communities of high unemployment, extensive drug use, high rates of domestic and street violence, and poor and overcrowded housing? (On the other hand, is it ethical *not* to run antismoking campaigns in these areas if other communities are getting the campaign?)

■ Ethical questions and issues of equity are far more complex and important in social marketing (for example, victim blaming). Commercial marketing practices suggest that non-smokers be offered a discount on their life insurance policies. Given that a high proportion of smokers are lower-income people likely to suffer from greater morbidity than upper-income people anyway, is it ethical for health professionals to encourage private health insurers to offer this incentive?

■ Social marketing programs are often limited in comprehensiveness, duration, and evaluation by available funds.

■ Successful commercial marketers have a genuine concern for their customers' needs—not just their money. Social marketers share this concern, but at a deeper level. Social marketers' transactions with their clients have the underlying goals of enhanced self-esteem, empowerment, and enhanced wellbeing.

Concluding comments

While the techniques and principles of marketing are applicable to any consumer decision their effective application to health and social policy areas requires an understanding of both marketing and the content areas in which they are to be applied. In practical terms this requires close cooperation between marketing experts and staff within the content areas, as well as behavioural scientists with expertise in program design and implementation, research and evaluation, communication theory, and attitude and behaviour change.

With respect to the above principles of marketing it is the consumer orientation that most defines a marketing approach. It is a consumer orientation that forms the basis for many of the other marketing concepts and that distinguishes social marketing from other frameworks for achieving social change. What the discipline and philosophy of marketing also provide is a comprehensive planning framework for the development, implementation, and evaluation of campaigns. It brings together concepts that are not necessarily new to those working for social change and demands that they be considered.

Chapter 3

Social Marketing and the Environment

Introduction

In this chapter we look at aspects of the environment that are relevant to social marketers. First, we briefly discuss the legal, technological, political, and socio-cultural aspects of the environment within which social marketers operate. Then we look in more depth at the ways the environment impacts on people's health, called the environmental determinants of health. There is a strong focus in social marketing and in our society generally on the individual's responsibility for adopting healthy lifestyle behaviours, a 'downstream' approach. However, in this chapter, we outline the evidence that social and economic factors beyond the individual's control have a powerful effect on overall health. Social marketers can increase the effectiveness of their campaign strategies by being aware of these determinants and considering an 'upstream' approach that creates changes in the environment itself.

The 'upstream'–'downstream' metaphor comes from a frequently cited fable in public health involving people, a river, and a cliff. Clinical medicine is seen as rescuing people who have fallen off the cliff into the river and been swept downstream. Preventative medicine is seen as going upstream to erect fences on the edge of the cliff so that people will not fall in. As Chapman and Lupton (1994) explain the downstream approach involves heroic rescues, racing ambulances, new technologies, and grateful patients. There are many opportunities for dramatic news stories and political capital. Upstream approaches have much less news value. Prevention is far less newsworthy than rescue since, as they point out, successful prevention strategies result in nothing happening.

A variation on this analogy is to see the downstream approach as addressing the individual person with recommended behaviours that will help them to negotiate the river safely, that is, skills to stay afloat or swim, hence, a focus on quitting smoking, eating right, exercise, etc. The upstream approach addresses preventative measures that can be put in place by agencies and organisations that will bring about desired individual behaviour, sometimes without the individual's conscious volition, for example, a reduction of smoking can be achieved by banning cigarette advertising and taxing cigarettes. Upstream approaches targeting legislators can be much more cost-effective than downstream approaches targeting individuals. In South Africa, for example, the decision was taken in 1995 to legislate that all salt should be iodised in order to ensure universal access to iodised salt (Marks 1997). At the time only 30 per cent of households used iodised salt, which was slightly more expensive than ordinary salt. Rural and low-income people were less likely to have access to the iodised version or to purchase it. The alternative downstream approach of a lifestyle modification program to educate the whole population to choose iodised salt would have been much more costly and inevitably fallen short of the 100 per cent compliance obtained by the upstream approach.

One criticism of the downstream focus on individual behaviour is that it encourages victim-blaming, holding people entirely responsible for behaviours that are not entirely within their control (Hastings, MacFayden & Anderson 2000). However, disadvantageous social factors outside the individual's control can foster unhealthy behaviours such as substance abuse and addictions. The individual should not be left with the whole responsibility of their behaviour (Wilkinson & Marmot 1998).

Smith (1998) argued that social marketers should consider environmental change first. Only when all possible structural changes have been adopted to make it easier for people to change should we resort to trying to persuade individuals to change their behaviour. Stokols (1996) has argued that there will inevitably be blind spots when focusing on either the individual or the environment. He advocates social ecological analyses that complement current approaches in health promotion by focusing on the interplay between the environment and the individual. Stokols's approach will be discussed later in the chapter.

Upstream strategy in the UK : using legislation to restrict pack sizes of OTC drugs to reduce self-poisoning

Parallelling increases in sales, the misuse of paracetamol has been a major cause of liver poisoning and a number of deaths in the UK . In September 1998 legislation was introduced that limited packet sizes of paracetamol, salicylates and their compounds in pharmacies to thirty-two tablets (previously no limit) and elsewhere to sixteen (previously twenty-four). Specific warnings were added to the packs and to a leaflet inside the pack. The rationale for this legislation was that analgesic self-poisoning is often impulsive, associated with low suicidal intent, and with little knowledge of the possible severe consequences. Hence, limiting availability was expected to lead to less misuse.

In the year following introduction of the legislation deaths from paracetamol and salicylates poisoning decreased by 21 per cent and 48 per cent respectively; liver transplant rates after paracetamol poisoning declined by 66 per cent. Furthermore, the number of tablets taken in overdoses decreased by 7 per cent and the proportion involving thirty-two or more tablets decreased by 17 per cent and 34 per cent for paracetamol and salicylates respectively (Hawton, Townsend, Deeks et al. 2001).

Environmental analysis

As with marketing in general the success of a social marketing campaign depends in part on the marketer's accurate analysis of the complex environment in which the campaign appears. The purpose of the environmental analysis is to understand and monitor the environmental factors, predict the impact of these factors on the organisation's performance, and make strategic decisions that will enhance competitiveness. Environmental factors include political–legal, demographic–economic, social–cultural, and technological–physical environment factors (Kotler 2001). These factors are described separately but must be analysed in terms of their interactions. For example, a demographic change such as population growth will have impacts on the physical environment by depleting resources and increasing pollution (Kotler 2001). All these factors are subject to change and, in our contemporary world, are changing at an ever increasing rate. Environmental analysis takes account of the current environment, but also tries to anticipate future trends and developments (Kotler 2001).

Like any other marketers social marketers must continually monitor the environment so as to be aware of competitive activities, opportunities for exploitation, factors requiring preemption, and changes in attitudes, values, and practices. Similarly, but more importantly than for commercial marketers, social marketers must focus on ways of changing the environment. Factors such as price, promotion, product, and place are generally seen as within the control of the organisation while environmental factors are generally seen as uncontrollable, or largely uncontrollable constraints on marketing activity (Zeithaml & Zeithaml 1984; Kotler 2001). Zeithaml and Zeithaml (1984) argued that marketers typically neglect opportunities to bring about desired environmental changes. This may not be surprising in commercial marketing where the physical, social, legal, technological, and political environments are generally conducive to achieving sales and profit goals.

On the other hand, the physical, social, legal, technological, and political environments either passively or actively often operate to inhibit desirable social change. It is in these areas that social marketers must begin to direct greater efforts. For example, social marketers can identify opportunities to modify the regulatory environment by lobbying government or industry organisations, or to change the technological environment by developing an innovation. Similarly, a good understanding of current sociocultural trends can result in more effective communications with target audiences.

Political–legal

Monitoring the political–legal environment means being alert to possible changes in legislation, government priorities, and the influence of numerous pressure groups that lobby government (Kotler 2001). An upstream approach open to social marketers is to increase the level of political will to make policy changes. This can be achieved by changing social norms and by increasing salience and concern over social issues in the general population (Henry 2001).

Changes in government may have an effect on social marketing priorities. This has been seen recently in the Bush administration in the United States where there have been changes in policy relating to the physical environment (greenhouse gas emissions) and abortion, as well as a change in the inclusion and exclusion of organisations in the process of making health policy decisions (DeYoung 2001). Social marketing is often used to complement changes in legislation as well as to reinforce existing legislation. For example, the introduction of compulsory random breath testing (RBT) state laws in Australia were supplemented with campaigns to inform people about the new law. Similarly, a campaign advocating the benefits of wearing a bicycle helmet preceded the introduction of a law making it compulsory.

Demographic–economic

The demographic environment is analysed by noting trends in population growth, distribution (for example, urban–rural) and movement, as well as demographics of age, gender, education, household characteristics, and ethnicity. Marketers need to understand the characteristics of the ageing baby boomers (people born between 1941 and 1960) as well as those of Generation X (born between about 1961 and 1981), Generation Y (born between about 1982 and 2002), and even the future Generation Z (to be born between about 2003 and 2023). These generations differ on many dimensions, such as in their preference for green products and packaging, interest in recycling, and their attitudes towards convenience foods.

Economic trends associated with demographics include income, disposable income, and patterns in savings, debt, and credit (Kotler 2001). As unemployment increases the economy slows down and companies may respond by abandoning the development of luxury products in favour of low-cost, generic alternatives. If the price of petrol increases people may drive less. A reduction in road fatalities might have more to do with the price of petrol than with a road safety campaign. Failure to analyse the environment might lead to an inflated assessment of the value of a campaign. Among the many profound effects of the terrorist attacks on 11 September 2001 was the negative economic effect of people staying home and spending less money. President Bush urged the American public to return to the shopping mall. In what we might view as a rather tasteless display of the primary role of consumption in American society, 15 000 posters were distributed in San Francisco depicting the American flag with shopping-bag handles ('Fighting the good fight' 2001).

Social–cultural

The social–cultural environment includes the broad beliefs, values, and social norms that people hold, how persistent the core values are over time, how norms shift over time, and the existence of subcultures (Kotler 2001). Core values are reinforced by the family and all the major social institutions, including schools and churches. It is unlikely that social marketers would be able to change core values through a marketing campaign. In the USA attempts to ban the sale of alcohol during the prohibition era were unsuccessful, indicating that a core value was being targeted. On the other hand, social norms, or secondary values, may be more accessible to change such as changing perceptions about drink driving. People have been amenable to accepting a new social norm in Australia—that drink driving is not acceptable.

One of the sociological problems that social marketers have to consider is the difficulty of targeting hard-to-reach audiences. These audiences may be hard to reach because they have little access to mass media, for example, the homeless. Or they may be hard to reach because they belong to subcultures that are more resistant to social marketing messages, for example, addicted drug users and prisoners. Sometimes social marketers have to accept that it is not cost-effective to expend limited resources on reaching intractable groups (Andreasen 1995). On the other hand, it has been said that there are no hard-to-reach audiences only hard-for-us-to-reach programs and that an innovative social marketer may set out to discover the unique networks of communication inherent within such groups (Cooke 2001).

An example of a social marketing campaign sensitive to sociocultural factors is an American campaign to prevent illness in young children associated with the preparation of a holiday dish, chitterlings (Peterson & Koehler 1997). It was found that it was safer to cook chitterlings by first preboiling them for 5 minutes and that this simple change in cooking method was effective in preventing a severe form of diarrhoea that was killing African-American children. However, it was recognised that this method of cooking chitterlings would be non-traditional for many families. The problem was overcome by enlisting the support of African-American grandmothers who were able to recommend the new method as being safer for children with no difference in taste (confirmed by a taste test by the researchers), and that it also made the job of cleaning easier and faster. The success of this campaign was measured in the fewer deaths of young children and the number admitted to hospital after the bacterium incubation period following Thanksgiving and Christmas festivities. (This campaign is discussed more fully in chapter 10.)

Social marketers can adapt communication objectives to the different needs of target groups in different social classes. Social class is a useful market segmentation variable. It meets all of Rossiter's (1987) four main criteria for segmentation, that is, the resultant segments are substantial enough to be worth developing marketing strategies for, relatively easy to measure, relatively easy to access, and sufficiently different in potential responsiveness to make segmentation worthwhile.

Durgee (1986) discussed a number of research studies on class differences in the UK and the USA and found some distinctions between social class that would be useful for marketing strategy. (It would be important to check that differences found at one time in one culture are still current and relevant to the target market today. In other words, what was true of English lower classes in 1970 may not be true of English lower classes today.) An interesting difference found between classes is in the way they perceive time. Lower classes were found to have a stronger orientation to the present so messages that focus on the immediate benefits of changing behaviour would be more suitable for this target market. More future-oriented higher classes may respond more to messages describing long-term health benefits. Similarly, differences have been found between classes in the use of language. Lower classes were more likely to use concrete, literal language so messages targeting them should focus on specific and individual benefits. Global benefits could be described in messages targeting higher social classes who were attracted to more symbolic, abstract language (Durgee 1986).

Technological-physical

Technological trends also need to be considered, including the rate of technological change, the budgets available for technological innovations, and the commercial opportunities for new technologies (Kotler 2001). From the social marketer's viewpoint campaigns will only be effective if we have appropriate technology: to iodise salt, manufacture safe helmets, measure consumption of alcohol in a breath test, and so on. Equally, it is important for the social marketer to know when the technology does not yet exist to support legislation on a social marketing issue, for example, 'Don't Drive Tired'. These campaign messages must relate to the intrinsic value of not driving when fatigued (reducing the risk of an accident) rather than relying on an extrinsic punishment (getting caught). Recent technological advancements mean that we now have fast response ambulances equipped with life-saving machines, which has resulted in a decline in deaths from cardiovascular disease and road accidents. On the other hand, high production-value advertisements for fast cars equipped with safety items such as air bags evoke a sense of thrill and invulnerability that has to be counteracted with effective road safety messages, often at a fraction of the car manufacturer's advertising budget.

The physical environment is affected by technological change, usually in a negative way. Raw materials, often finite, non-renewable resources such as oil, are being used up. Finite renewable resources such as forests may be depleted and even resources that are seen as infinite, such as air and water, may be at risk from pollution in the long term (Kotler 2001). The physical environment includes the climate, which can have a major effect on people's behaviour as well as their risks. For example, people might feel less like being physically active in the winter and might eat foods higher in fat. People in tropical climates need to be protected against malaria while people in northern Canada would need to know how to protect against frostbite. The physical environment exerts a powerful influence on what people do. Making a simple change to the environment is sometimes more effective than running an expensive campaign. For example, if pedestrian injuries at a junction can be traced to inebriated people stumbling out of a tavern on the corner it will be more efficient to put up a barrier than to run a campaign to moderate their drinking or their behaviour as pedestrians.

Food for thought

The influence of each of these aspects of the environment and the interaction between them can be illustrated by looking briefly at some of the many issues relating to food in contemporary times: fast or convenience food, functional or designer food, genetically modified (GM) foods (also emotively called 'Frankenstein foods' [Schmidt 2000]), and green or clean food.

Fast or convenience food includes takeaways, drivethroughs, casual dining, delis, and preprepared supermarket meals (Hollingsworth 2001c). Functional or designer foods are foods supplemented with vitamins, herbs, minerals, amino acids, or manipulated in some way, such as altering animal feeding practices to produce leaner products ('Functional food' 1999; Van Elswyk 1993). These include energy bars, probiotic yoghurts and other dairy foods, calcium-fortified dairy products, cholesterol-lowering margarines, cereals and meat products, anti-oxidant fortified fruit juices, soups containing echinacea, caffeine, and guarana-enriched beverages, and functional confectionary such as diabetic sweets and dental gum (Hollinsworth 1997, 1999, 2001a, 2001b; Sloan 2000a). Probiotics have become big business. For example, in Japan in 2001, every day 24 million people drank Yakult, a probiotic drink, and Nestle has developed infant formula with cultures to prevent diarrhoea (Hollingsworth 2001b). Green or clean foods are organic, preservative-free, all-natural, and free of genetic modification.

The political–legal environment around food has included major issues in Europe relating to mad cow disease and foot and mouth disease, and subsequent European import restrictions, with considerable impact on the economic environment as well. Genetic modification has been a major issue with regulations imposed on GM crops and a move in Australia to label clearly whether products contain GM ingredients. Safety concerns are another issue with calls for some products, such as caffeine drinks, to be restricted, especially for children and young people. There are serious health concerns as many of the ingredients, for example, of functional beverages, have not been tested in combination and may have adverse effects, particularly on young people, who are the primary target market (Hollingsworth 1997). A single beverage product, Brainwash, contains at least the following ingredients: 'ginseng, buchu, jalapeno, capsicum, caffeine, ginger, citric acid, ginkgo leaf, skull cap (a herbal sedative), ma huang (ephedrine), mad dog weed' (Hollingsworth 1997, p. 45).

McDonald's is now the most recognised brand in the world (Schlosser 2001). However, there are political implications in the globalisation of major fast food producers and other corporations, as seen in the protest demonstrations by S11 against the World Economic Forum meetings in London (1999), Seattle (1999), Davos (2000), Washington DC (2000), and Melbourne (2000). These protests brought together an unusual combination of diverse groups unified in their objection to corporate globalisation, including anarchists, environmentalists, socialists, unionists, union leaders, students, and farmers (Henderson 2000). Farmers may have particular reason to be concerned about the effect of globalisation on the domestic environment. Schlosser (2001, p. 8) argued that fast food producers have gained control over American agribusiness, changing the rural social environment, with independent family farmers now operating as hired hands of large corporate farm businesses. There are legal issues about what health claims can be made for functional foods on the nutrition labels (Sloan 2000a) and whether such products should come under the definition of food or drugs. The regulations relating to drugs are much more stringent (Functional food 1999). The term 'nutraceutical' has been coined for the new classification (Hollingsworth 1997). Recently the UK government included nutrition in the remit of the Food Standards Agency, acknowledging that food is a public health issue and that nutrition is an important aspect of any strategy on health (White 1998). This might appear self-evident but the lobbying power of the food industry has consistently blocked public health attempts to address dietary issues. For example, in 2000, the US Department of Agriculture attempted to include in official dietary guidelines a recommendation to limit consumption of sugar. The sugar industry lobbied on the basis that such a guideline would hurt their business and that there was no proof of a link between sugar and obesity. The word 'limit' was not included in the guidelines (Brownlee 2001).

In the demographic–economic environment it would seem that consumers generally prefer clean foods, foods that do not contain preservatives or GM ingredients (Hollingsworth 2000; Sloan 2000b, 2001). With so much research and development into genetic modification it will be necessary to consider the public concerns and whether these concerns can be overcome if a market is to be successfully constructed for the product (Bender & Westgren 2001). At present, consumers are afraid of the risks involved in GM foods and unwilling to accept claims of benefits (Wansink & Kim 2001). Consumers are concerned that non-genetically modified crops cannot be protected from 'genetic trespass' from GM crops (Lehrman 1999), which concern has reduced public confidence in basic food products.

Younger and ethnic groups are more likely to buy organic foods (Hollingsworth 2000; Sloan 2001), while the designer–functional foods appeal to baby boomers as they move into their fifties and become concerned with ageing (Wrick, Friedman, Bewda & Carroll 1993; Hollingsworth 1999). Value is now being added to ordinary grocery foods by cutting the planning and preparation time off cooking (Sloan 2000b; Hollinsworth 2001c). This is already seen in the variety of prepared salads and vegetables in supermarkets today. The American market for fast food grew from about US$6 billion in 1970 to US$100 billion in 2000 (Schlosser 2001).

In the social–cultural environment there are trends to fast foods, convenience foods, vegetarianism, organic, and clean foods. The first generation to grow up entirely in the fast food era is now reaching adulthood (Sloan 1998). Fast food, with its high fat content, is blamed in part for the epidemic of obesity in developing countries (Schlosser 2001). Yet fast food franchises have moved into some American hospitals (as well as many American schools) so that it is now possible to enjoy a Big Mac and fries before checking out after a triple bypass operation (Brownlee 2001).

There has also been an increase in the consumption of preprepared foods. The main reason given for serving preprepared foods at home is lack of time, with only 25 per cent of people planning meals before 9 o'clock in the morning and 50 per cent waiting until after 4 o'clock in the afternoon (Sloan 2000b). This is in keeping with the change in work patterns and household characteristics, with more women in the workforce, and smaller family units.

The proliferation of functional foods has been attributed to the interest in alternative medicine and self-care. The American Dietetic Association has taken the position that 'the availability of health-promoting functional foods in the US diet has the potential to help ensure a healthier population' (American Dietetic Association 1999, p. 1278). It also stated its intention to work with the government, food industry, scientists, and the media to inform the public of potential benefits.

In the technological–physical environment there have been major developments in food science. Fourteen classes of phytochemicals that may inhibit the growth of cancer tumours have been identified in common foods including garlic, liquorice, cruciferous vegetables (cabbage, broccoli, and cauliflower) and soybeans (Caragay 1992). There may be many more sources; for example, a research team discovered that thirty-nine commonly used dietary plants in Thailand prevented the growth of tumours (Ohigashi, Murakami & Koshimizu 1996). Some caution has been advised and there has been a call for human feeding studies to investigate the physiological effects of these substances. Adding some phytochemicals to food might reduce the risk of one disease but increase the risk of another (Kurzer 1993). Experiments have been conducted on animal feeding practices, for example, feeding omega-3 fats to chickens. The eggs are higher in omega-3 (good) fats and lower in saturated fat, with an acceptable flavour that can be used in processed products such as mayonnaise, although the poultry meat is generally not acceptable to consumers (Van Elswyk 1993).

The advances in the genetic modification of foods, such as built-in pesticides, may please farmers and produce healthy yields, but generally have not been accepted by consumers (Lehrman 1999). There may be no discernible difference in taste but consumers object on a cognitive level. Another interesting development is the genetic modification of pigs crossed with spinach genes, turning 20 per cent of the saturated fatty acids into healthy linoleic acids (BBC News 2002). Whether the consumer can be persuaded that the meat will be healthier to eat has yet to be seen.

Environmental determinants of health and wellbeing

We now address the influence of environmental determinants on health and well-being. It has long been known that the poor and disadvantaged have poorer health than their richer counterparts. The differences have largely been attributed to

- *differences in risk behaviours*, such as poor diet, smoking, alcohol and drug abuse and poor personal hygiene, or
- *differences in the physical environment*, such as poor sanitation, overcrowded housing, lack of adequate heating, exposure to pollution, or
- *both* individual and environmental factors.

Other factors that affect health include lower rates of literacy and reduced access to medical services, both linked to lower socioeconomic status (Wilkinson & Marmot 1998).

Improved housing reduced illness in children in Malawi

The importance of housing standards for health is well accepted, but few studies have provided rigorous data on this effect. A well-designed study of a Habitat for Humanity Housing project in Malawi showed that improvements in housing were accompanied by a significant reduction in respiratory, gastrointestinal or malarial illnesses among children under 5 years compared to children in traditional homes (Wolff, Schroeder & Young 2001).

However, differences in lifestyle, deprivation, and the physical environment only partially account for differences in health status. Poverty clearly contributes to poor health at the bottom of the scale, but in developed countries most people have access to adequate food, clothing, shelter, and medical care. Comparisons between countries suggest that it is not the average level of income that determines health status, but the size of the gap between rich and poor within a country (Wilkinson & Marmot 1998; Donovan 2000b). As social marketers we usually focus on advocating individual behaviour change. In fact we have been accused of being 'hopelessly biased in favor of messages and individual change' (Smith 1998, p. 15). However, it is part of the social marketer's task to look at the need for structural change. To do this we must not underestimate the powerful effect of the social milieu on people's health (Lomas 1998).

Obesogenic environments

Swinburn, Egger, and Raza (1999) have proposed a framework to identify obesogenic environments, environments that promote or facilitate obesity in the population. The basic framework analyses physical factors (what foods and physical opportunities are available), economic factors (the costs), political factors (the rules), and sociocultural factors (the attitudes and beliefs).

Physical environment determinants

Other than physical environments most associated with 'absolute poverty' (Marmot 2000) (that is, poor and overcrowded housing, inadequate sanitation and rubbish removal, lack of plumbing and clean water supplies, insufficient protection against temperature extremes, and exposure to toxic fumes), physical environments act in a number of ways. For example, certain geographical regions are more prone to various diseases than others, so that mosquito control is far more important in tropical regions than in temperate zones. Similarly, vaccination with HIB to protect against meningococcal meningitis is far more important in some parts of Africa than in Australia. Given the poor physical conditions in which many indigenous people live in remote communities environmental health workers (EHWs) play a crucial and different role in these communities than they do in the suburbs.

In health promotion physical activity is one area that is receiving increasing attention from an ecological perspective. It is now widely accepted that participation in physical activity is likely to be influenced by the quality and design of the physical environment (Dishman 1990; Sallis et al. 1990; King, Jeffery, Fridinger et al. 1995; Hansen 1959). The physical environment affects participation in two ways:

- *incidental* physical activity is encouraged or discouraged through energy-inducing or energy-reducing design of the urban environment, buildings, and household appliances
- *planned* physical activity is encouraged (or discouraged) by providing (or not providing) accessible, convenient, safe, affordable, and appealing recreational opportunities (Sallis et al. 1990; Hahn & Craythorn 1994; King et al. 1995).

Automatic opening gates, escalators and elevators, push-button appliance controls (including windows in cars), the expansion of electronic entertainment devices, and the provision of parking close to worksites and entertainment venues all serve to decrease incidental physical activity. Attractive parks and walkways, safe cycleways separated from vehicular traffic, and beach access serve to increase planned physical activity.

A striking feature of an environmental approach to increasing physical activity is the need for active involvement of disciplines and sectors outside of health, including local government, urban planning, architectural design, transport, and property developers (Corti 1998; Harris, Wise, Hawe et al. 1995; Giles-Corti & Donovan 2002)

Social determinants

Health indicators that have been found to correlate with social class include mortality rates, birth weights, incidence of obesity, heart disease, lung disease, asthma, cancer, diabetes, lower back pain, sick days, smoking, alcoholism, teeth

The physical and social environment influences physical activity

Billie Corti (1998; Giles-Corti & Donovan 2002) showed that, in addition to people's beliefs and attitudes with respect to physical activity, physical and social environment factors were important predictors of people's levels of physical activity. The physical environment appeared to influence walking at recommended levels. Compared with those in the bottom quartile of access to public open space the odds of walking as recommended were 47 per cent higher in those in the top quartile of access. Compared with those who had major traffic and no trees in their street the odds of achieving recommended levels of walking were nearly 50 per cent higher in those who had one or other of these or some trees and minor traffic. Similarly, compared with those who had no footpath and no shop in their street, those who had access to either one or both of these attributes were about 25 per cent more likely to achieve recommended levels of walking. In terms of the social environment the odds of achieving recommended levels of walking increased with the numbers of significant others who exercised weekly with the respondent over the past 3 months—58 per cent higher in dog owners and nearly 3.5 times higher in those who knew of four or more significant others who exercised with the respondent over the past 3 months.

brushing, seat-belt use, physical activity, television watching, diet, accident rates, suicide, depression, and mental health (Henry 2001; Wilkinson & Marmot 1998; Yen & Syme 1999).

Despite the popular notion that chief executives suffer more stress and are more likely to die of a heart attack, evidence clearly indicates that people in higher positions are less likely to suffer from disease. People on the lower rungs of the social ladder have generally twice the risk of serious illness and premature death than those near the top (Wilkinson & Marmot 1998). Interestingly, a continuous gradient has been found between each level so that health declines progressively the further down the ladder you go (Wilkinson & Marmot 1998; Henry 2001). Data from the British civil service in the 1960s showed that there were significant differences in health across the five classes of public servants, all of which were relatively affluent (Marmot, Rose, Shipley & Hamilton 1978). In a follow-up study in the 1980s Marmot and colleagues found the same differences in morbidity still existed 20 years later among the classes of British civil servants (Marmot, Smith, Stansfield, Patel et al. 1991; Marmot 2000).

The work environment can have a major impact on health. Health improves as people have greater control over their work environment, more opportunity to use their skills, and greater rewards (including money, status and self-esteem) (Wilkinson & Marmot 1998). The negative effects of a poor work environment can be mitigated somewhat in a workplace where there is strong social support (Wilkinson & Marmot 1998). Interestingly, studies of both primates and humans show greater risk of cardiovascular disease in those in subordinate positions (Wilkinson & Marmot 1998; Henry 2001).

The Whitehall studies (Marmot, Rose, Shipley & Hamilton, 1978; Marmot, Smith, Stansfield, Patel et al. 1991) followed 10 000 British civil servants with a 25 year mortality follow-up. These showed a social gradient related to all-causes morbidity and mortality: there was a fourfold difference in mortality between men in the bottom grade of the civil service compared with men in the top grade and each higher level in the employment hierarchy was associated with less morbidity and mortality even when holding all other factors constant. A large number of European and American studies show relationships between a number of social factors and health. For example, in one study, the best predictors of coronary heart disease were social isolation, depression, anxiety, and low control at work; others have shown HDL cholesterol levels to be related to employment grade—independently of other risk factors.

Link and Phelan (1995; 1996) in the USA suggest that the differences are due to differences in resources such as knowledge, money, and social connections that allow people to avoid risks and minimise disease consequences. However, this only explains the lower risk factor rates among higher social classes. Other researchers (for example, McEwen in the USA, Marmot in the UK) have begun to look at the body's physiological response to stress (that is, immune and hormonal responses) in terms of the relationship between these responses and causes of morbidity and mortality.

People with low control of their work, those living in poverty, those experiencing racism, and those with little social support generally experience far greater sustained or chronic stress than those higher up the social scale. Marmot and others postulate that it is the additional and sustained stress experienced by those lower down the social scale that not only increases an individual's vulnerability to lifestyle risk factors, but, through effects on the hormonal and immune system, also independently contributes to morbidity and mortality. A number of studies—with humans and animals—support the notion that higher-status individuals not only experience less stress (in terms of physiological responses), but recover more quickly than do those of lower status.

Whatever the cause might be it is clear that some fundamental factors are operating to sustain the social gradient of disease.

*Wilkinson & Marmot 1998

Social class and self-efficacy

Self-efficacy is the individual's sense that they can exert control over their environment and the sense that they are able to perform deliberate and conscious behaviours, such as quitting smoking, if this is what they want to do. The concept of self-efficacy has received much attention in the threat appeals literature, where it is theorised to be a critical factor in determining whether a threat appeal will motivate the recipient to take appropriate action (when self-efficacy is high) or to adopt a maladaptive response (when self-efficacy is low) (Witte 1993; 1998; Snipes, LaTour & Bliss 1999; Witte & Allen 2000). Perhaps not unexpectedly, given less access to power and resources, self-efficacy has been found to be associated with social class. Lower-class respondents have been found to have a limited sense of mastery, a greater sense of perceived constraints (Lachman & Weaver 1998, cited in Henry 2001), and a more fatalistic attitude towards their health (Chamberland & O'Neill 1998, cited in Henry 2001). This fatalistic, pessimistic view of the future leads to limited planning for the long term and reduced persistence with long-term healthy behavioural patterns (Henry 2001).

Economic determinants

It is tempting to think that all that is needed to reduce the effect of social determinants is a more equal distribution of wealth. Mayer (1997) studied the true effect of income on children whose basic material needs were already being met through income-support programs. She concluded that doubling the income of low-income families would improve some outcomes (such as raising children's test scores by a couple of points and the years of education by a couple of months), but it would not have a significant effect on health outcomes unless accompanied by changes in the non-economic domain such as the years of parents' education, the age of young mothers, the experience of racism and single parenthood (Mayer 1997).

It has been suggested that the effect of relative deprivation and income inequality may be a reflection of low social capital and that it is the effect of low social capital that causes negative health effects (Kawachi, Kennedy, Lochner & Prothrow-Smith 1997). This idea is receiving growing attention among social marketers (Hastings, MacFayden & Anderson 2000; Donovan 2000b); it is discussed more fully below.

Non-economic factors

Substance abuse can confound economic determinants. Mayer (1997, p. 151) reports this story told by an assistant principal of an American primary school.

> Drugs are a really big problem here. I had a little girl, a tough little girl, who always had her guard up. One day she just let it all down and began to cry. When I asked her why she was crying she said she just wanted everything to be like it had been in the third grade. I asked what it had been like in the third grade. She said she had gotten a certificate for good attendance and some other award and her mom had hung them up on the refrigerator. She said her mom had been happy. That was before the crack. 'Since the crack my mommy doesn't care any more,' she cried. This mom was not a bad mom. She cared, and she had been good, but she just got into trouble and there is no help for her—no place for her to turn, and now this little girl is miserable.

Additional income alone will not solve this family's problems.

Importance of early childhood

Hawkins, Catalano and colleagues in the United States have demonstrated the importance of protecting children in early childhood from risk factors that could lead to crime, violence, teenage pregnancy, and substance abuse. They have developed a prevention planning system, Communities That Care (CTC) (CTC website, accessed January 2002; Harachi, Ayers, Hawkins, Catalano & Cushing 1996), to promote the positive development of children based on community involvement. They claim that over 400 communities have used their system over the last 13 years with positive results.

CTC is a comprehensive, community wide prevention strategy that is aimed at the prevention of substance abuse and behaviour problems in adolescents (Harachi et al. 1996). The aim of this prevention strategy is to mobilise and train communities to reduce risk factors and increase protective factors that reduce the incidence of uptake of substances such as tobacco, alcohol, and illicit drugs. The program has three phases.

1   The recruitment and training of key community leaders to drive the process, act to recruit other community members, and to oversee the operation of the other phases such as data collection, analysis and intervention planning, and implementation.

2   A risk and resources assessment in order to complete an inventory of the community's health. This phase allows communities to determine which risk and protective factors are important to target for intervention.

3   Planning and implementation of intervention strategies that meet the needs of the community and that have been shown to impact upon the significant risk and protective factors that are relevant to the community.

The process is a lengthy one and there is limited published data on the outcomes of this process. However, process and formative evaluations indicate that this approach is effective in bringing communities together to assess risk and protective factors for substance abuse and then implement evidenced-based strategies to reduce such problems. For example, Harachi et al. (1996) describe a statewide implementation of this approach in twenty-eight communities in the American state of Washington resulting in reductions in adolescent drug abuse. Harachi et al. (1996) describe a replication of this process in thirty-one communities in Oregon.

Factors that protect children from risk are a strong bonding to school, family and friends, healthy beliefs and expectations of success, clear standards against criminal behaviour and early sexual activity, as well as individual characteristics such as resilience, intelligence (though intelligence does not protect against substance abuse), and a sociable disposition (Lehman, Hawkins & Catalano 1994). It is estimated that children develop some of these individual characteristics in early childhood, sometimes as early as 2 years of age. Children's 'habitual ways of responding', such as with persistence and enthusiasm, have been developed by age 2. This is also the critical period for learning emotional control, while social competence with peers begins around age 3 and continues to 6 or 7 years (Williams, Zubrick & Silburn 2001, p. 12). Figure 3.1 suggests that disturbed attachments in early childhood are likely to lead to adult ill-health via substance abuse and other risky behaviours and/or through experiencing greater

Figure 3.1   Importance of early life experiences and social support on adult health

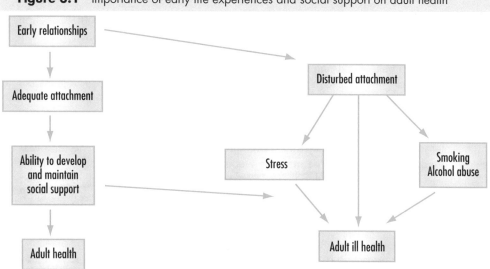

stress in life. Even if a child achieves adequate attachments in early childhood the loss of the ability to maintain social supports can result in adult ill-health.

Poor parenting has been identified as a major risk factor, specifically, failure to supervise children's activity, failure to provide clear expectations for appropriate behaviour, and the use of excessive or inconsistent punishment (Lehman et al. 1994). Other risk factors are availability of drugs and alcohol, high mobility and low attachment to the community, poverty, conflict between family members, the experience of academic failure (seemingly independent of ability), lack of attachment to school, and a family history of addiction or criminal activity (Lehman et al. 1994).

The influence of two protective environmental factors—social bonding to family and to school—was investigated in a non-randomised controlled study conducted in a high crime area in Seattle (Hawkins, Catalano, Kosterman, Abbott & Hill 1999). It provided a multicomponent intervention for children in Grades 1–6, with a follow-up 6 years later. The intervention consisted of inservice training for teachers, parenting classes offered to parents, and developmentally appropriate social competence training for children. The aim was to increase the children's sense of bonding with family and school. There was no

Children's Court judge's profile of a repeat offender

He is a boy, possibly Aboriginal, from a broken home with a working parent and has very little contact with his father. He has witnessed domestic violence and was possibly abused himself. His parents have alcohol and/or drug problems, which he has also begun to develop. He does not go to school, is probably illiterate and roams around unsupervised with his mates. He doesn't have anyone at home to fix breakfast, pack lunch and get him to school, let alone help with homework (Judge Valerie French, quoted in Egan 2002).

Positive parenting

In 1996–7, a social marketing campaign was developed by the Western Australian Family and Children's Services to promote positive parenting techniques. The campaign was intended to assist parents in developing an encouraging parenting style. The campaign built on existing skills to help parents manage their children's behaviour effectively at different stages in their development. The campaign, entitled 'Accentuate the Positive', developed a number of printed and video products and services. It was targeted to parents, teenagers, professional carers, and other intermediaries, distributed via public libraries, shopfront parenting information centres in shopping centres, the internet, via direct response and a parenting information telephone line, and was supported by direct mail, mass media advertising, and publicity. The advertisements modelled encouraging parenting behaviour and portrayed positive emotions including love (hugging the child), excitement (playing with the child), assertiveness (turning off television at bedtime) and humour (amused acceptance of a messy kitchen after the children's attempt to cook). The television advertisement achieved 69 per cent awareness in the target group. Forty per cent of parents said they planned to do something to improve their parenting as a result of a seeing this ad, with 25 per cent saying they had already done so, indicating substantial behavioural as well as attitudinal change. In 1996, 54 per cent of parents agreed with the statement that 'Parents who need help in their parenting role are failures'; by 1997 this had dropped to 44 per cent. (Henley, Donovan & Moorhead 1998). (This campaign is discussed more fully in chapter 10.)

attempt to develop competencies relating to health-risk behaviours such as how to say no to drugs. The children were not informed at the time that they were part of a study and at the follow-up 6 years later they would not have known whether they were in the intervention or control group, minimising possible halo effects.

For a cost per child of US$2991, there were significant positive effects relating to school achievement and behaviour. Positive effects had endured at the follow-up at 18 years: significantly fewer in the intervention group had committed violent delinquent acts by age 18, used alcohol heavily, or had multiple sex partners (Hawkins et al. 1999).

The Triple-P (Positive Parenting Program), developed by Sanders and colleagues in Queensland, is a behavioural family intervention that has been shown to be an effective clinical intervention suitable for adaptation as a population-based strategy. The program aims to reduce or prevent emotional and behavioural problems in children by targeting their parents with a multilevel parenting program. The program develops knowledge, skills, confidence, and teamwork in parents (Sanders 2001). A randomised controlled trial was conducted with parents of 3 year olds at high risk for developing behaviour problems, with a follow-up 1 year later. Parents who received training in parenting strategies observed a significant decrease in disruptive behaviour in their children, compared to the control group (Sanders, Markie-Dadds & Tully 2001; Sanders, Markie-Dadds, Tully & Bor 2000). It has been estimated that if such

The building blocks initiative in Western Australia

This is a behavioural family intervention aimed at improving mental health in children and adolescents by investing specifically in programs targeted at parents of infants 0–2 years. The objectives include promoting a healthy physical environment for a child with advice about safety, hygiene, breastfeeding, and immunisation practices. Other aspects are the importance of a stimulating learning environment for the child and nurturing, consistent, and encouraging parenting practices. This early investment prevention strategy also involves antenatal initiatives, including planning for a healthy pregnancy, promoting healthy behaviours during pregnancy, and reducing risk factors for low birth weight such as smoking. It will be interesting to evaluate how effective these very early intervention strategies will be in reducing the rates of mental health morbidity and mortality in later years.

behavioural family interventions were to be adopted as a universal strategy to reach all eligible families it would reduce the number of children with behaviour problems by 37 per cent in 2 years (Zubrick, Northey, Silburn et al., under review).

Parenting strategies are a key factor in protecting young people. The social chain of risk will only be broken if parents can be persuaded to change the environment for their children so that children can grow up with fewer disadvantages (Wilkinson & Marmot 1998). Many of the psychological characteristics that are associated with poorer health in lower social classes are set in childhood and resistant to change (Henry 2001). Social marketing campaigns could mobilise adults to change by stressing the effect of negative environments on children. Public opinion is likely to blame adults for the conditions in which they find themselves (victim blaming), but will see children as blameless and deserving of support and protection (Mayer 1997; Henry 2001).

Social capital

Social capital was defined by Robert Putnam as 'features of social organization such as networks, norms and trust, that facilitate coordination and cooperation for mutual benefit' (1995b, p. 66). It refers to the degree of interaction between people, both formal and informal, and the levels of civic engagement, trust, mutual obligation, and caring in the community. Some people now believe social capital to be the most important determinant of health (Lomas 1998).

Greater health is associated with a sense of belonging and being valued (Wilkinson & Marmot 1998). Indicators of social capital, such as trust, reciprocity, and participation in voluntary organisations, have been associated with reduced mortality rates (Kawachi et al. 1997). Kawachi et al. (1997) attempted to quantify the effect of social capital. They estimated that an increase in overall trust by 10 per cent in the population would lead to a reduction in the age-adjusted mortality rate of about 67 per 100 000 people per year. Improvements in health can be achieved with increases in community involvement and

Social capital projects in Western Australia

The Western Australian Health Promotion Foundation, Healthway, has funded several studies exploring the relationship of social capital and public health. One major project is the Healthy Communities Project in Narrogin and Dongara/Denison, two small regional centres in Western Australia. This project aims to make the communities a better place to live. Emphasis is placed on empowering the community to determine the issues affecting health and wellbeing and to develop their own tailor-made, localised strategies to address the issues (Frizzell 2001). Strategies include promoting sporting and cultural events, youth dances, a skate park, a youth drop-in centre, children's art classes, and providing opportunities for volunteers to become involved in the community (Skoglund 2001; Stuart 2001). One such opportunity has been a walking partner program in Narrogin that sees young people accompanying seniors on morning and evening walks through the parks (Stuart 2001).

Another, more small-scale, Healthway social capital project is a case study focusing on the ways social capital might increase among the members of a walking group. The Lockridge Walking Group, with around forty-five members from nine different language and cultural groups, has operated in a low socioeconomic area for several years. The researchers have attempted to quantify indicators of social capital in the group by observing norms, networks, skills, and habits in the group members (Bayly & Bull 2001). Another useful project is Janice Dillon's PhD study at Curtin University that has addressed a significant deficiency in the literature on social capital—the difficulty of measuring the construct. Dillon has developed a Social Capital Index using structural equation modelling to determine the multidimensional construct of social capital.

supportive networks that reduce isolation and foster cohesion. Perhaps social capital improves health by increasing people's sense of self-worth (Berkman 1995, cited in Henry 2001). Wilkinson and Marmot (1998, p. 21) concluded that 'in all areas of personal and institutional life, practices should be avoided that cast others as socially inferior or less valuable'.

Social cohesion is in part the product of the physical structure, such as the design of housing estates, and social structure, which includes community centres and opportunities for meeting and interaction (Lomas 1998). Small changes at a local level could make a substantial difference to social capital, for example, by increasing number and size of public spaces, or encouraging architects to design homes with verandahs on the front of houses rather than the back, or by subsidising local clubs (Lomas 1998).

Bearing in mind the current thinking about social capital, social marketers can build in to their communication strategies messages that reinforce social bonds. For example, the director of a drink-driving rehabilitation centre in Queensland reported that high-risk offenders reacted with hostility to the drink-driving campaign slogan, 'If you drink and drive, you're a bloody idiot', feeling personally insulted. However, they seemed to respond more favourably to messages such as 'Mates don't let their mates drink and drive'. The director said,

Offenders ask to be shown gory videos thinking that will help, but most of them have been in multiple crashes already, may even have been responsible for fatalities; they've lived through worse than we could ever show them and that hasn't worked. What works is being drawn into the community, being included.

Donovan, Henley, Jalleh & Slater 1995, p. 141

Social capital protects against binge drinking

Weitzman and Kawachi (2000) found a 26 per cent lower risk for binge drinking (three or more drinks in quick succession) for individuals on campuses with higher than average levels of social capital, where social capital was measured by the average time committed to volunteering aggregated to the whole campus. That is, on campuses where there was generally more volunteering, the incidence of individual binge drinking was lower. Interestingly, as might be expected, the incidence of social drinking (one or two drinks at a time) was higher on campuses with higher social capital.

Although this association is correlational, not causal, a college administration concerned about the level of students' binge drinking may wish to consider implementing initiatives that are intended to increase the level of voluntarism on campus. This strategy may be at least as effective—and may be more effective—than trying to change individual drinking behaviour.

Social ecology

The theory of social ecology in health promotion is another example of the shift from the downstream, individual-focused, lifestyle modification approach to a broader understanding of health protective factors. Stokols (1996) advocated the theory of social ecology as one of three complementary perspectives on health promotion:

- targeting the individual with behaviour change recommendations relating to lifestyle issues such as smoking, substance use, diet, exercise, and safety
- changing the environment to maximise health protective factors by creating a safe place, free from contagious disease and unhealthy levels of stress (caused by environmental factors such as pollution or violence), in which healthy behaviours are actively facilitated and where people have access to health care
- social ecological analyses that attempt to understand the interplay between the environment and the individual, emphasising the interdependence of multiple environments and the contributions of many diverse disciplines.

Thus, while the individual behaviour change approach may be concerned with persuasion theories and health communication and the environmental change approach may consider urban planning and injury control, the social ecological approach focuses on aspects such as cultural change models of health, medical sociology, community health, and public policy (Stokols 1996). The

Reduce parents' smoking; increase parents' knowledge of health and understanding of children's emotional needs; introduce preschool programmes not only to improve reading and stimulate cognitive development but also to reduce behaviour problems in childhood and promote educational attainment, occupational chances and healthy behaviour in adulthood; involve parents in preschool programmes to reinforce their educational effects and reduce child abuse; ensure that mothers have adequate social and economic resources; and increase opportunities for educational attainment at all ages, since education is associated with raised health awareness and improved self-care.

Wilkinson & Marmot 1998, p. 13

major contribution of the social ecological approach is that it provides a systems framework within which behavioural and environmental factors can be integrated, thereby eliminating the blind spots inherent in focusing on either the individual or the environmental approach (Stokols 1996). A typical ecological health evaluation involves different levels of analysis and multiple methodologies, from individual medical examinations to environmental assessments to epidemiological analyses (Stokols 1996).

Concluding comments

There is now a growing movement in public health to address environmental determinants of health in the areas of education, employment, and income by influencing government policy on a broad scale. Social marketing practitioners need to recognise this fundamental shift in public health strategy and to become part of it. Just as public health professionals have needed to familiarise themselves with fundamental marketing principles, so social marketers now need to better understand the fundamental principles and philosophies of public health if we are to play a role in changing the social determinants of health.

As Donovan and Hastings have pointed out, both separately and jointly (Hastings & Donovan 2002), the emphasis of social marketing should shift from marketing voluntary healthy behaviours to individuals in the general population to targeting community leaders who have the power and influence to make major institutional policy and legislative changes.

If we are to have an impact on social determinants social marketers will need to think in terms of group and system effects rather than just individual effects. This may require a cultural shift from thinking of health as the individual's responsibility to seeing it as a collective social responsibility. Thus, the slogan of a major American initiative targeting children and educators, 'Healthy children make healthy communities', would be reversed: we need to build healthy communities if we are to have healthy children (Donovan 2000b).

Chapter 4

Principles of Communication and Persuasion

Introduction

Given that much of what social marketing is about involves communication of information rather than promotion of products, the principles of communication and persuasion are arguably more important in social marketing than in commercial marketing.

In this chapter we first present an overall model of the communication process, which will be followed by a discussion of factors relevant to the first two steps of the communication process: exposure and attention. This includes aspects of how to present messages to have most persuasive impact. We then present one of the most commonly used persuasion models, Petty and Cacioppo's Elaboration Likelihood Model (the ELM). Cialdini's six 'weapons' of persuasion are then described. The weapons, based on the psychological literature and techniques that professional persuaders use to sell their products, can be used in interpersonal interactions as well as in the media. Finally, given that they are probably the most commonly used appeal in social marketing—particularly in health, crime, environmental degradation, and road safety—we present an analysis of threat appeals (and their converse, incentive appeals).

We begin with an overall summary of what factors appear to characterise successful communication campaigns.

Communication principles for successful communication campaigns

A number of overall principles are relevant to conducting successful communication campaigns, that is, campaigns that meet their communication and behavioural objectives (Egger, Donovan & Spark 1993; ONDCP 1997).

1 The receiver is an active processor of incoming information

Paraphrasing Hugh Mackay, 'the receiver acts far more on the message than the message does on the receiver', that is, the impact of a media message is not determined by its content alone. Members of the audience are active partici-pants in the communication process; preexisting beliefs, attitudes, experiences, and knowledge affect attending to, interpretation and acceptance of messages. This is particularly important in sensitive, controversial, or core values areas, where existing attitudes often screen out incoming messages that contradict the individual's existing beliefs and attitudes. Hence, particular care is needed when constructing messages aimed at those antagonistic or sceptical towards the proposed idea or behaviour. These aspects are dealt with in this chapter.

2 Different target audiences may respond to different messages

Target audiences must be segmented by beliefs and attitudes before the devel-opment of targeted messages. This is dealt with in chapter 9.

3 Formative research, including message pretesting, is essential

Given the importance of existing beliefs and attitudes affecting message process-ing, formative research is essential to gain an understanding of each target audi-ence's beliefs and attitudes on the issue to be addressed. Also, following from the above, it is crucial that messages be pretested against target audiences to ensure correct message understanding and that minimal counterarguing occurs. Pretest-ing is also necessary to ensure that messages aimed at primary target audiences do not have unintended negative effects on secondary audiences. Pretesting is cov-ered in chapter 6.

4 Comprehensive, coordinated interventions are most successful

Communication campaigns must be coordinated with other environmental and on-the-ground strategies to ensure attitudinal and behavioural success (see figure 4.1 for the relative impact of communication campaigns vs environmen-tal factors at various stages in the hierarchy of effects).

5 Use multiple delivery channels and multiple sources

Communication campaigns involving a number of message delivery channels and more than one source appear more successful than those that do not.

6 Stimulate interpersonal communications

Mass media-led communication campaigns that stimulate interpersonal com-munications appear more successful than those that do not.

7 Campaigns must be sustained

Communication campaigns must be sustained to achieve and maintain success.

Table 4.1 Relative impact of communication vs environmental factors at various stages in the hierarchy of effects

Effects hierarchy	Communication campaigns	Environmental factors
awareness	very high	low
attitude	high	moderate
intention	moderate	high
behaviour	low	very high

8 Use a theoretical framework

Campaigns that have been guided by theoretical frameworks are more success-ful than those that have not.

The communication process: Rossiter and Percy's six-step model

The Rossiter–Percy model (Rossiter & Percy 1987; 1997) is used to provide the conceptual framework for planning a communication strategy. Following McGuire (1985), Rossiter and colleagues developed a simplified hierarchical six-step model relating advertising exposure to company objectives and profits (see table 4.2). While developed for advertising in a commercial marketing context (Rossiter, Percy & Donovan 1991), the model is applicable to all forms of communication and has been applied in a number of health and social marketing contexts (Donovan & Owen 1994; Egger, Donovan & Spark 1993).

Table 4.2 The Rossiter–Percy six-step communication process

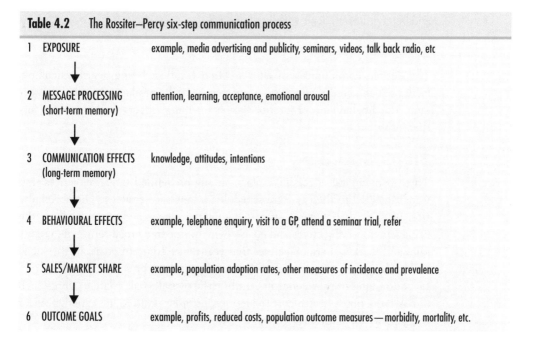

1	EXPOSURE	example, media advertising and publicity, seminars, videos, talk back radio, etc
2	MESSAGE PROCESSING (short-term memory)	attention, learning, acceptance, emotional arousal
3	COMMUNICATION EFFECTS (long-term memory)	knowledge, attitudes, intentions
4	BEHAVIOURAL EFFECTS	example, telephone enquiry, visit to a GP, attend a seminar trial, refer
5	SALES/MARKET SHARE	example, population adoption rates, other measures of incidence and prevalence
6	OUTCOME GOALS	example, profits, reduced costs, population outcome measures — morbidity, mortality, etc.

Step 1

The hierarchy of effects commences with **exposure** of the target audience to the message. Messages may be delivered in a variety of ways (for example, advertising, publicity, edutainment, factual information), and in a variety of media and media vehicles (that is, websites and CD-ROMs, newspaper articles, television ads, billboards, radio talkback, posters, magazine articles, soap operas, hit songs, videos, or face-to-face counselling).

Step 2

Attention to the message, in whatever form it appears, leads to **processing** of the message in short term memory. This involves attention to the message content, emotional arousal, comprehension and learning, and acceptance or rejection of the message. Message execution (the use of colour and graphics), source factors (who delivers the message—whether an individual or organisation), and message content, all influence processing.

Step 3

Processing of the message (and subsequent related messages) results in long-term memory effects called **communication effects**. These are beliefs about, attitudes towards, and intentions with respect to the brand, message topic, or promoted behaviour. The content of the message, the audience's initial attitudes and beliefs, the nature of the message exposure, and the degree of repetition of the message all affect whether, how much, and what components of the message are stored in long-term memory and how easily these can be recalled during decision making. (Issues with respect to attitude formation, intentions, and behaviours are dealt with in chapter 5.)

Step 4

The desired communication effects, when recalled during decision making, facilitate **behavioural effects** such as purchase of the product, or trial of the recommended behaviour, or intermediate behavioural effects such as seeking further information.

Steps 5 and 6

These behavioural effects take place among predefined target audiences that were subjected to the exposure schedule and message strategy. The accumulation of these behavioural effects among the target audiences leads to the achievement of objectives and goals—which, in commercial terms, are usually sales and market share objectives that contribute to profit goals. In the social and health areas, sales or market share objectives may be stated in terms of participation rates or prevalence rates, while the overall goals relate to things such as risk reductions, health cost reductions, or more positive life experiences for the general population (Donovan & Owen 1994).

Taking an example from commercial marketing a teenager (*target audience*) watches a television ad (*exposure*) for a new confectionery bar. The television ad is aired during a show known to be popular with teens. The ad attracts and maintains our teen's attention because it is fast moving, backed by a rap song, and features exciting, colourful graphics. The confectionery bar is shown being shared by several cool-looking teens who exclaim in unison that it 'Tastes great'. A voiceover lists creamy caramel, milk chocolate, and crunchy nuts as the ingredients. Our teen viewer is drawn into the ad, *likes* the music and talent, and *accepts* that the confectionary bar would probably taste good and might be worth trying (*message processing*). The ad appears twice more during the show (*repetition*). Our teen now *knows* the confectionery bar's brand name, what the wrapper looks like, what its major ingredients are, and has formed a tentative positive *attitude* towards trying the confectionery bar (*communication effects*).

A few days later at the local deli, our teen sees a display of the confectionery bars on the counter and *recognises* the wrapping and the brand as those seen on television. Our teen experiences a *positive feeling* toward the confectionery bar and *recalls* the promise of great taste (*communication effects*). The price is slightly cheaper than other popular brands and our teen has sufficient cash, so the decision is made to *buy* and *try* the confectionery bar (*behavioural effects*)— thus, along with thousands of others, contributing to the company's sales and profits.

Another scenario. Our high school athlete has been chosen to try out for the state basketball team (*target audience*). As part of the induction process our athlete attends an orientation evening (*exposure*). One part of the program consists of an International Federation (IF) spokesperson outlining the IF's policy on performance-enhancing drugs (PEDs). A sports doctor then outlines the potential ill-health side effects of drug taking, followed by an inspiring address by a well-known athlete about winning without cheating (*the messages*). A World Anti-Doping Agency (WADA) representative presents the ethical and moral basis for banning PEDs, followed by an outline of the likelihood of being tested in and out of competition and the sanctions for testing positive (*more messages*). Our athlete listens intently (*processing*) and goes away with a manual containing the list of banned substances, test procedures, and a statement on the ethics of doping. Our high school athlete is somewhat confused as to what is banned and why, but feels inspired by the well-known athlete's address and forms an implicit intention not to use PEDs (*processing and communication effects*). The whole evening has left our high school athlete with a greater determination than ever to make the state team.

Our athlete hears little of drugs in sport from official sources over the next few months, but reads the occasional report of positive tests among cyclists and other athletes overseas.

Several months later our athlete appears to have reached a plateau in performance and is competing to make the final team squad with two others, who are currently performing slightly better than our athlete. By now our athlete has become aware that some elite athletes, and not just in basketball, are using performance-enhancing drugs obtained via the health club black market. An assistant coach, who has befriended our athlete and knows our athlete's situation, suggests that he may be able to get some drugs for our athlete and supervise their use (*the decision-making situation*). Our athlete recalls the inspiring induction address and the WADA slogan and feels that to accept the assistant coach's offer would be wrong and inconsistent with the athlete's moral and sporting values (*communication effects*). Our athlete recalls the induction program's tips on how to reject a drug offer and tactfully declines the offer (*communication and behavioural effects*).

These examples also bring to mind that our messages compete with other messages, and that a variety of influences can operate at various points in the exposure–behaviour chain that either facilitate or mitigate against our desired outcome.

Planning a communication strategy

In using the Rossiter–Percy model to plan a communication strategy the chain is in the opposite direction to the exposure process (table 4.3). That is, the campaign planner asks—and then sets out to answer—the following questions.

Step 1   What is our overall goal that the campaign must help achieve?

Step 2   What specific objectives do we want this campaign to achieve?

Step 3   Who do we need to impact to achieve our goal and what do we want them to do?

Step 4   What beliefs and attitudes do we need to create, change, or reinforce to have them behave this way?

Step 5   What sorts of messages do we need to create to have them adopt these beliefs and attitudes?

Step 6   Where, how often, and in what form do we need to expose these messages to reach these people?

It should be noted that this planning process is an iterative, recursive process, in that previous levels in the hierarchy may be modified as a consequence of planning considerations lower down, resulting in even further modifications, and so on.

Principles of exposure and attention

People are faced with hundreds of ads per day through a proliferation of television channels, milk cartons, toilet doors, blimps, bus stops, rented videos, cash register receipts, event entry tickets, school tuckshops, projections on buildings, in the turf of football ovals, players' outfits, yacht sails, and so on, and so on. Advertising is ubiquitous, leading agencies to urge their clients to spend more to

Table 4.3   Campaign planning sequence

The manager defines overall outcome goals and specific measurable objective.

↓

Select specific target audiences among which to achieve these goals.

↓

Specifies behavioural objectives for each target audience.

↓

Delineates the beliefs and attitudes necessary to achieve the behavioural objectives.

↓

Generates the content and type of messages that will be necessary to achieve these beliefs and attitudes.

↓

Determines how, where, how often, and in what form these messages are to be exposed or delivered to the specific target audiences.

be heard amid the din. But it is not just media weight that is needed to attract attention. As one ad executive was quoted as saying, consumers 'are like roaches—you spray them and spray them and they get immune after a while' (Klein 2000, p. 9).

Breaking through the clutter

Australian advertising creative John Bevins uses the following to illustrate the problem of gaining attention in a modern society in which individuals are continually bombarded with messages or information through a variety of channels (referred to as 'clutter') (Donovan 1992b; Egger et al. 1993).

> clutterclutterclutterclutterclutterclutterclutterclutterclutterclutter
> clutterclutterclutterclutterclutterclutterclutterclutterclutterclutter
> clutterclutterclutterclutterclutterclutterclutterclutterclutterclutter
> clutterclutterclutterclutterclutterclutterclutterclutterclutterclutter
> clutterclutterclamourclutterclutterclutterclutterclutterclutterclutt
> clutterclutterclutterclutterclutterclutterclutterclutterclutterclutter
> clutterclutterclutterclutterclutterclutterclutterclutterclutterclutter

Messages that social marketers wish to communicate are hidden in this clutter (like the single word 'clamour' in the left hand side of the third bottom row). The objective is to make our message stand out more, not only through mechanical or stylistic executional processes (for example, 'clamour' would stand out from the clutter if it was in a larger and bolder typeface), but also through a knowledge of psychological factors in human information processing. The most striking such factor is selective attention. This selectivity operates in three ways (Donovan 1992b; Egger et al. 1993):

1 *selective exposure (or attention)*: people expose themselves or pay attention to media and messages that have a personal relevance to them or with which they already agree

2 *selective perception*: when exposed to information that is not in agreement with their attitudes individuals tend to reinterpret this information to be in accord with their existing attitudes and beliefs

3 *selective retention*: when information not in agreement with their attitudes is committed to memory it is often recalled in a way more favourable towards preexisting attitudes and beliefs.

Selective exposure and attention

Selective exposure applies at two levels: the medium or channel and the message. Some people are avid television watchers but rarely read a newspaper; others may read only broadsheet or tabloid newspapers. There are distinct preferences for radio stations or specific announcers. Others will deliberately avoid documentary, fact-based television programs (which is why social marketers have incorporated messages in entertainment vehicles; see chapter 11), and many specialty magazines are read only by small, well-defined audiences. Thus, to even have a chance of reaching some target groups we need to know their media, and leisure, and entertainment habits.

Personalising the message

According to Bevins (1998), much of the fault with public health communication is that its central orientation is:

WE

Health professionals often wrongly start from the assumption that WE know what YOU want to hear. In Bevin's terms, health authorities too often 'go around "weeing" in public' when they should be personalising the message, that is, focusing on the mirror inversion of WE, or

ME

According to Bevins,

Message begins with 'me'. Me singular. Indeed, there is no such thing really as mass communication. It's a contradiction in terms. Communication is an intensely personal, one-to-one process, whether you're doing it over the telephone or over the television network. Uni, Uno, One—is the very heart of communication.

In short, we must recognise that people interpret messages from the perspective of what is in it for me.

At the message level people pay attention to topics in which they are interested, ignoring topics of little interest or of an opposite view. Voters, for example, are more likely to expose themselves to messages of the political parties to which they are already committed (Klapper 1961), and smokers who find it difficult to quit or who want to keep on smoking tend to avoid antismoking messages, but pay attention to news reports that question or contradict the relationship between smoking and ill health.

Selective perception and interpretation

Even if individuals do expose themselves to a message they may not accept that message because of the way they interpret the information. For example, *All in the Family* (an American television version of the British show *Til Death Us Do Part*), which featured a right-wing older-generation couple generally in conflict with a younger generation left-wing couple, turned out attracting far higher ratings than the producers anticipated. Subsequent surveys found that the show appealed to both left-wing and right-wing viewers. Although the show was meant to be satirical of right-wing prejudices, right-wingers saw it as endorsing their views while left-wingers saw it as endorsing their views (Vidmar & Rokeach 1974). Similar effects occur when supporters of opposing football teams view exactly the same incident but disagree vehemently about which way the penalty should have gone.

Inconclusive data are particularly vulnerable to selective interpretation or what is called "biased assimilation'. Lord, Ross, and Lepper (1979) found that when pro and anti advocates of capital punishment were presented with studies showing mixed results on the deterrent effects of capital punishment each group interpreted the results as supportive of their own position. Similar effects are found in racism studies, in which the same data are used by opposing sides to support their positions. Again this reinforces the need for pretesting of messages—among both primary and other target groups to ensure that the desired interpretation is taking place.

Gaining and holding men's attention to messages about health: the 'Healthy Blokes' project*

Given men's general reluctance to visit their doctor unless their health issue is really serious and hence often too late for early intervention one of the main aims of the limited-scope Healthy Blokes project was to stimulate blue-collar men over 40 to have a regular health check. The project also aimed to increase awareness for the main risk factors for heart disease, cancer, and diabetes: poor diet and physical inactivity.

Qualitative research indicated that men would respond to health messages directed specifically to them, that a car maintenance analogy would be well accepted, and that health assessment scores were likely to trigger action (Donovan & Egger 2000).

As part of the project a Cancer Foundation of Western Australia ad (below) was placed in the sporting section of the daily newspaper. The ad was a half page in size and a 'male interest' headline to attract attention. It included a self-assessment questionnaire to attract readership of the ad content and, hopefully, trigger some action if the score indicated action was required. A telephone number was included to provide further information to those who needed it.

Figure 4.1 Is your body due for a checkup and service?

Is your body due for a check up and service?

TAKE FIVE MINUTES TO GIVE YOUR BODY A ROAD TEST.

Circle the number that answers each question best for you. Then add up your score at the end of each column.

NUTRITION

How many days a week do you eat at least 2 pieces of fruit?

Seven	4	One to two	1
Five to six	3	None	0
Three to four	2		

How many days a week do you eat a meal which includes vegetables?

Seven	4	One to two	1
Five to six	3	None	0
Three to four	2		

How do you spread butter or margarine on your bread?

Don't have	2	Thickly	0
Thinly	1		

How often do you eat fatty foods eg pies, pasties, sausage rolls ?

Seldom or never	3
Once or twice a week	2
Three or four times a week	1
Daily or almost daily	0

11-13: You are doing well keep up the healthy diet.
5-10: Umm... you could probably eat a bit better.
0-4: You need help. Definitely call for information.

PHYSICAL ACTIVITY

How many days a week do you participate in physical activity that makes you puff?

Seven	4	One to two	1
Five to six	3	None	0
Three to four	2		

How long do you do physical activity each time?

Thirty minutes or more	3
Fifteen up to thirty minutes	2
Up to fifteen minutes	1
I do not exercise at all	0

How many hours do you sit each day (include home and work)?

Zero to eight hours	2
Eight to twelve hours	1
Twelve or more hours	0

How often do you drive the car when you could walk?

Daily or almost daily	0
Three or four times a week	1
Once or twice a week	2
Seldom or never	3

How often do you walk the dog or the family?

Daily or almost daily	3
Three or four times a week	2
Once or twice a week	1
Seldom or never	0

11-15: Well done – you must be a fit guy.
5-10: There is always room for improvement.
0-4: Leave the remote and go for a walk – NOW!

THE CHECK UP

When was the last time you had a check up with your doctor?

Within the last year	4
One or two years ago	3
Three or four years ago	2
More than four years ago	1
Never	0

Do you know the result of your last cholesterol check?

Yes	1
No/Haven't had one done	0

Do you know the result of your last blood pressure check?

Yes	1
No/Haven't had one done	0

Do you know the result of your last blood glucose check?

Yes	1
No/Haven't had one done	0

Do you know if you are in the healthy weight range?

Yes	1
No	0

7-8: You are the full bottle about you – excellent!
3-6: A check up in the near future is a good idea.
0-2: Definitely make an appointment to see your Doctor.

Disclaimer: The purpose of this quiz is to raise awareness only of your risk factors for cardiovascular disease and type 2 diabetes and certain types of cancer. Evidence proves that early intervention can make a difference.

HEALTHY BLOKES

Your body is like a car, and the older it gets, the more important it is to get it serviced regularly. Start by using this quiz to see if you're in need of an overhaul. If your score is low, see your doctor for some practical advice or call 13 11 20.

* Cancer Foundation of Western Australia

Selective retention

There is some evidence that memory is sometimes reconstructed in line with attitudes and expectations rather than being the retrieval of accurately stored information. In a classic American study, Allport and Postman (cited in Klapper 1961) showed subjects a picture of a confrontation in a subway train between a black man and a white man holding a razor. Subjects were later asked to describe the picture. As the delay from exposure to recall increased, the razor shifted from the white man to the black man's hand, illustrating the influence of prejudice on retention.

Factors influencing the selectivity process

Three major sets of factors influence whether messages are attended to and how they are processed (Donovan 1992b; Egger et al. 1993).

Mechanical executional factors

These factors refer to physical or sensory attributes of the message vehicle such as colour, use of movement, size, and contrast, which attract attention more or

Using mechanical execution characteristics to break through the clutter

clutterclutterclutterclutterclutterclutterclutterclutterclutterclutter
clutterclutterclutterclutterclutterclutterclutterclutterclutterclutter
clutterclutterclutterclutterclutterclutterclutterclutterclutterclutter
clutterclutterclutterclutterclutterclutterclutterclutterclutterclutter
clutterclutterCLAMOURclutterclutterclutterclutterclutterclutter
clutterclutterclutterclutterclutterclutterclutterclutterclutterclutter
clutterclutterclutterclutterclutterclutterclutterclutterclutterclutter

less reflexively. Mechanical factors are particularly important when messages must compete for attention against a large number of other messages or against a strong background. For example:

- eye-catching pictures greatly increase readership of print articles
- colour stands out in largely black-and-white productions
- larger ads attract more attention than smaller ads
- movement gains reflexive attention (for example, flashing lights, moving arrows, etc.)
- isolated stimuli (as in lots of white space around a brief message in a news-paper ad) attract greater attention, as do objects placed in the centre, rather than on the periphery, of the visual field.

Given little attention to the original warning statement on cigarette packets studies in Australia resulted in space, position, and typeface size requirements to enhance the noticeability of cigarette packet health warnings (Donovan & Francas 1985; Centre for Behavioural Research in Cancer 1992).

Novelty is included as a mechanical factor, suggesting that message executions should be continually revised and revived to prevent wearout. It has been suggested that the pool of new pack warnings in Canada—showing graphic, sometimes gruesome, photos of the ill-health effects of smoking—will need to be continually revised to prevent habituation to these warnings (Donovan 2001).

Some factors that appear to attract attention reflexively also have some psychological aspects. For example, sensational headlines ('Headless body in top-less bar'), sex (pictures of scantily clad women), and rare occurrences ('Man bites dog') appear to attract attention and are commonly used by subeditors to attract readership and viewers. These appear to be socially conditioned types of response although there does appear to be a biological basis for a novelty effect (Ornstein 1986).

Psychological factors

Psychological factors refers primarily to factors such as personal interest, prior experiences, and current attitudes and beliefs. People are more willing to respond to messages relating to topics of personal interest or messages that offer a personal benefit ('Good news for frustrated golfers'), and, for high-involvement issues,

Figure 4.2 Health warnings on Canadian cigarette packets*

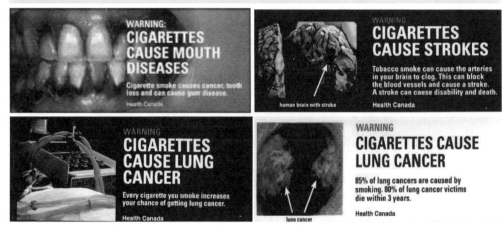

*The image at bottom left is licensed under Health Canada copyright; the two images at right, courtesy of the Australian National Tobacco Campaign.

messages that are consistent with what they already believe ('Boat people are "queue jumpers", says Minister'). Expectations also affect interpretation (that is, people interpret information to be consistent with what they expect) and individuals differ in their ability to attend to and process information.

A *belief* can be defined as a perception that a certain state of affairs exists or is true. An *attitude* can be defined as the extent to which positive or negative feelings are held toward a state of affairs. A *state of affairs* can include objects, people, behaviours, or ideas. The *salience* of a belief refers to the readiness with which that belief comes to mind when the person's attention is drawn to the issue.

Most attitudes are based on a set of beliefs and an evaluation of these beliefs (see chapter 5). Some beliefs may be negative while others are positive. It is important to recognise that many members of a target audience may be ambivalent about an issue. For example, a woman may believe that condoms are a reliable, inexpensive, easy-to-use method for avoiding contracting a sexually transmitted disease. At the same time, she also may believe that condoms reduce pleasurable feelings for her partner, are embarrassing to purchase and present, and are difficult to dispose of afterwards.

For issues where there is a mix of both negative and positive beliefs (as in many health and related policy areas), research suggests that the overall attitude held at a particular point in time depends on the relative salience of the various positive and negative beliefs. Hence, situations that stimulate consciousness of positive beliefs about an issue will increase the likelihood of an individual expressing a positive attitude toward that issue at that time, and vice versa. If the aim is to achieve a change in attitude towards a particular issue the message strategy should first stimulate recall of beliefs favourable to the issue prior to the persuasive component of the message being presented. For example, a target audience may believe that exercise is beneficial to overall health, tones the body, and increases energy, but the audience may lack sufficient motivation to participate. The audience should be reminded of their positive beliefs before— or at the same time as—presenting new reasons why they should increase physical activity. Jalleh (1999) and Donovan, Corti, Holman, West, and Pitter (1993) argue that sponsorships change attitudes in the desired way—at least temporarily—by increasing the salience of beliefs supporting the desired health behaviours (see chapter 12).

Message structure tactics (which may involve both mechanical and psychological factors)

The structure of more complex messages is also important. Message execution tactics, including the language, tone, and style of a message, are important influences on the impact of a communication. Tactics that increase message acceptance in high-involvement controversial areas include the following:

- link the desired belief to an already accepted belief (for example, most smokers accept that tobacco smoke constituents can't be doing them any good; violent men may not accept that their violence harms their partner, but they will accept that witnessing violence affects their children)
- stay within the target audience's 'latitude of acceptance', that is, the claimed threat and/or promised benefit must be credible (Sherif, Sherif & Nebergall 1965)
- use two-sided messages rather than one-sided messages (that is, accept that smoking can be enjoyable, help cope with stress, and act as a social facilitator; accept that some patrons will be upset by smoking bans); this preempts potential counterarguments that might otherwise distract from the message and/or lead to denigration of source credibility and hence rejection of the message
- leave the audience to draw their own conclusions rather than telling them to adopt the promoted stance, that is, 'cool' rather than 'hot' messages (for example, more successful Quit smoking advertisements are those that are seen by smokers—and youth in particular—not to be preaching or dictating to them).

Implications for initiating the communication process (Donovan 1992b; Egger et al. 1993)

When implementing a communication campaign to create awareness of and positive attitudes towards a concept, the first step of the campaign should focus on issues where there is most agreement between the target audience's attitudes and beliefs and those of the campaign source. In many cases these areas

Figure 4.3 Latitude of acceptance

A cartoon shows a fisherman using the distance between his hands to show his friends the size of the one that got away. The man's grandchild notices that the size of the fish varies according to who is being told the story. When the grandchild queries this the fisherman says, 'I never tell a person more than they'll believe.'

of agreement may have low salience (that is, are rarely thought about) or are weakly held. Exposure increases the salience of these attitudes and beliefs and, depending on the persuasive power of the message, can also increase the strength of the attitudes and beliefs.

Approaching the communication process from a point of common agreement also builds source credibility and trust and hence some form of commitment to the source and the message. This approach provides a favourable context within which to neutralise negative attitudes and beliefs and to create positive attitudes and beliefs from a neutral position. Once this platform of credibility is established strategies such as attaching a negative belief to a positive belief to increase the likelihood of acceptance of the negative belief can be implemented.

Cognitive processing models for persuasion: elaboration likelihood model

Cognitive processing models attempt to describe how cognitive processing of messages explains persuasion. The two main models from a psychological perspective are the Elaboration Likelihood Model (ELM) (Petty & Cacioppo 1983; 1986) and Chaiken's (1987) Heuristic Model of Persuasion. From a consumer behaviour/ advertising perspective the two main models are the Rossiter and Percy model (1987; 1997) and the FCB planning model (named after advertising agency Foote, Cone and Belding) (Vaughn 1980; 1986). The ELM model is briefly described here and the Rossiter–Percy model, because it emphasises motivations, in chapter 5.

Petty and Cacioppo (1986) state that there are two routes to persuasion: the *central* route, which involves extensive consideration (or elaboration) of the issue-relevant arguments in the message, and the *peripheral* route, in which the individual does not engage in such elaboration, but rather is persuaded by some factor(s) peripheral to the arguments such as liking (or disliking) the source or the music accompanying the message or some other such cue. Peripheral

Targeting racist stereotype beliefs

Donovan and Leivers (1993) reported a study carried out to determine the feasibility of using paid advertising to modify beliefs underlying employment discrimination against Aborigines in a small country town in Australia.

Qualitative research with opinion leaders, employers, townspeople, and local Indigenous people informed the development of the advertising. Both the research and the content and execution of the print and television advertising were guided by models of attitude change (chapter 5) and various communication principles—primarily, the concept of latitude of acceptance.

The research showed that negative attitudes to employing Indigenous people were based on beliefs that

- very few Aborigines had a job
- very few Aborigines with jobs hold them for a long time
- very few Aborigines have skilled jobs.

These objective beliefs were identified as the basis for subjective stereotypical beliefs that Indigenous people 'are lazy', 'do not want to work', and 'cannot handle responsibility'.

In fact, 60 per cent of local Indigenous people were employed and many had held their jobs for a considerable time. However, given the beliefs of the non-Indigenous population, promoting a 60 per cent employment rate would have met considerable scepticism from a large percentage of the non-Indigenous population. To accommodate people's different starting points, the advertising communication objective was defined as '*increasing* people's beliefs about ...

- the percentage of Indigenous people employed
- the percentage who remain in employment for long periods
- the percentage who are in skilled jobs ...'

regardless of what percentage they currently thought fell into these categories.

Mindful of not telling people more than they would believe, the advertising avoided any statistical information and made no specific claims about Indigenous employment. Instead, each ad—television and press—simply presented the occupational details of four locally employed Indigenous people. The television ad, for example, pictured four people, one at a time, in their workplace. As each person was pictured, their name, occupation, place of work, and length of time employed appeared in print on the screen. Length of employment varied from 2 years to 12 years. In short, this was a cool message that left the audience to draw their own conclusions from the information given.

The research also indicated that any campaign sourced to a government organisation that simply asked people to employ Indigenous people or extolled their virtues and did not indicate that Indigenous people themselves were involved would be greeted with scepticism. That is, the campaign per se also had to be acceptable. To provide a rationale for the campaign to the non-Indigenous population the ad promoted an Aboriginal employment week, was sourced to a local Indigenous group, and ended with the slogan, valued in Australian culture and hence that no one could really argue against—'All anyone wants is a fair go.' A post campaign survey showed that of those aware of the campaign 68 per cent supported it, 28 per cent had no feelings either way, and only 4 per cent opposed it. The effectiveness of the campaign is reported in chapter 11.

processing includes the use of decision heuristics such as accepting 'seals of approval' or following 'expert advice', or such rules as 'if they advertise a lot on television they must be a safe company'. Cialdini's principles of liking, authority, and social proof can all act as heuristics for peripheral route persuasion (O'Keefe 1990).

Petty and Cacioppo claim that central route processing will occur when the individual is motivated and has the capacity to pay close attention to the message content. This is most likely to occur when the issue has high personal relevance and high potential impact on their lives, that is, when an individual is highly involved in the issue. People generally pay far more attention to messages about issues that will affect them directly than to messages about issues of little direct personal relevance. For example, a camera buff will pay far more attention to the technical information in camera ads, seek experts' opinions on the camera, and spend considerable time and effort gathering relevant information before choosing a new camera. An amateur photographer might be more persuaded by the celebrity endorsing the product or the camera's styling. People who are employed directly in the timber industry or whose employment depends on logging will process antilogging arguments very differently from those less affected. The former would require two-sided messages, highly credible statistics, etc., whereas the latter might be persuaded simply by the sincerity of the speaker or the sheer amount of statistics—not what the statistics mean.

Similarly, people with little education in a particular area, and hence little capacity to analyse relevant information, may be persuaded by people in authority in that area or people whom they trust. For example, Indigenous people with little knowledge of Western concepts of disease prevention by vaccination are more likely to be persuaded to vaccinate by the peripheral route than by scientific arguments. Similarly, most people lack the technical background to follow many political and social debates. They tend to be persuaded by source characteristics such as the advocate's physical appearance, apparent sincerity and apparent knowledge ('She sounds as if she knows what she's talking about', 'His deep cultured voice sounds authoritative', 'She's a medical doctor—she should know'). Hence, much advertising for health-related products such as analgesics, cold remedies, and toothpaste rely heavily on peripheral cues such as actors in white coats, graphs, microscopes, and other apparently scientific cues to support their product claims.

The ELM and other cognitive processing models remind us that messages must take into account not just the target audience's initial attitude, but also their involvement or level of interest in the issue and their motivation to process information. Questions in headlines and self-assessment tools (as in the Healthy Blokes ad above) are one way of increasing motivation to attend to a message. Where the level of involvement is high and the target attitude is currently negative close attention must be paid to the actual message content. In fact, attitude change under these circumstances is very difficult. On the other hand, where the attitude is currently negative, but involvement in the issue is low, peripheral cues such as positive imagery can—and should—be used to achieve attitude change.

Hence, a dual strategy is often required, perhaps particularly for teenagers for issues such as binge drinking, sun protection, tobacco and drug use. Many teens view these behaviours as relatively benign in the sense that the ill-health effects are distant or because they intend to modify their behaviour before any permanent damage occurs. Or the behaviours are simply of far less relevance in their lives compared to school work, boy–girl relationships, sport, computer and video games, music, fashion, physical changes in their bodies, parent conflict, and so on. Many young Australian teens, as distinct from their Florida counterparts, and regardless of whether they smoke, simply do not see smoking as a big issue—and certainly not one that non-smokers consider it is worth being activist about (NFO Donovan Research 2000). In this case it is likely that peripheral cues may be more effective in inducing some teen smokers to quit.

The elaboration likelihood model of persuasion suggests that measures of personal relevance, interest in the issue, and knowledge of the area are key measures for use in pretesting messages. The model also supports the use of cognitive response measures in assessing a message's potential effectiveness (see chapter 6).

Cialdini's six principles of persuasion

After reviewing psychological studies of persuasion and spending some time working as a salesperson in a variety of areas, psychologist Robert Cialdini (1984) identified six principles (or sales techniques) related to the psychology of persuasion. All six principles are a result of our social conditioning and hence tend to operate reflexively or unconsciously. In the main these principles are adaptive, but, as Cialdini so entertainingly shows, they can be exploited by unscrupulous salespeople.

Reciprocity

'One should be more willing to comply with a request from someone who has previously provided a favour or concession' (Cialdini 1994, p. 198).

The principle of reciprocity states that we should try to repay, in kind, what another person has provided. We are obligated to the future repayment of favours, gifts, invitations, and so on. This is apparently a universal characteristic of human societies, literally exemplified in the phrase 'You scratch my back, I'll scratch yours'. Similarly, when people say 'much obliged' in response to an act of kindness, they in fact are. This principle is illustrated in the commercial area by the use of free gifts, product samples, and so on, and is clearly evident in political parties in the allocation of the spoils of government.

Given the universal functional utility of this principle it is not surprising that it is very powerful. Politicians often find themselves in compromising situations when they have accepted gifts from certain parties who later on seek political favours. John Wren, the corruptor of policemen, politicians, and others in Frank Hardy's (1950; 1972) novel *Power Without Glory* put it this way: 'Once he'd done a man a favour, he knew he was his.' It is a major reason why direct donations to political figures are (or should be) banned and the identities of donors not revealed to legislators. The invoking of a reflexive obligation to repay is so strong that sometimes people go out of their way to avoid its triggering or feel trapped when it occurs. For example, Cialdini observes that people will cross the street to avoid someone giving out 'free' flowers and then asking for a donation, because they feel unable to accept the flower without making a donation. This illustrates another aspect of this principle, that of an obligation to accept gifts and favours when they occur. Without this the principle simply could not apply.

It is particularly useful to remember this principle in lobbying politicians and forming collaborative networks: provide a useful service to potential partners, funders, and collaborators *before* asking for the favour being sought and show what is in it for them.

Reciprocal concessions

Perhaps the most powerful aspect of the reciprocity principle is this: *an obligation to make a concession to someone who has made a concession to us.* This is particularly important in negotiating agreements—granting a concession triggers an automatic obligation for the other side to make a concession: 'Would you like to buy a $50 raffle ticket? No? Well, how about a $1 donation?' (Gotcha!)

Commitment and consistency

'*After committing oneself to a position, one should be more willing to comply with requests for behaviours that are consistent with that position*' (Cialdini 1994, p. 202). This principle states that making a commitment, particularly a public commitment, to a particular stance leads to greater consistency between beliefs, attitudes, and behaviour. As Cialdini puts it, 'Once a stand is taken, there is an almost compulsive desire to behave in ways consistent with that stand'. Hence signing a pledge to lose weight increases the likelihood of successful weight control, signing a pledge to quit smoking and displaying this on the worksite noticeboard leads to a greater likelihood of attempting to quit. Companies use this principle in many ways, including competitions in which people are asked to 'write in six reasons why brand x is the most wonderful thing in their lives...'

Social marketers can use this principle in a similar way by having people in workshops write out and then publicly state the reasons for adopting the recommended behaviour under discussion, regardless of their initial attitudes. Similarly, the distribution of T-shirts, car stickers, and fridge magnets with energy conservation tips should lead people who accept and display these things to be consistent with their publicly apparent commitment.

This principle can be applied to extend people's commitment to a particular stance ('foot-in-the-door' technique) (Freedman & Fraser 1966). For example, Healthway (the Western Australian Health Promotion Foundation), took a

Promises increase medication compliance

Half of a sample of parents of children with inner-ear infection was asked to promise to administer all the prescribed medication. The other half was simply given the medication and asked to administer all of it (standard procedure). Those asked to promise were more likely to administer all the medication and their children had better recovery than those who made no promise (Kulik & Carlino 1987).

small wins approach in its sponsorship negotiations to getting venues to go smoke-free. Healthway first asked for only areas where food is served to go smoke-free. Adjacent and other enclosed spaces were then negotiated. Finally, Healthway asked for outdoors areas also to be smoke-free. Given the organisations' earlier commitments to smoke-free areas for health reasons the pressure to be consistent with these earlier behaviours was strong when later and greater demands were made.

Fundraising organisations appear to make considerable use of this principle. Potential donors are first asked how good a job they think the specified charitable organisation is doing, whether they support their work, and whether they feel the organisation is an important one in the community. As a variation they might be asked to sign a petition urging politicians to support the organisation. After responding favourably the target is then asked whether they would like to make a donation. How could they refuse?

Social proof

'One should be more willing to comply with a request for behaviour if it is consistent with what similar others are thinking or doing' (Cialdini 1994, p. 201).

'More doctors smoke Camel than any other cigarette' read the ad headline in a 1940s ad. 'Join the club, join the club, join the Escort Club' went a television jingle in the 1960s. Cigarette marketers were at the forefront of advertising claims that 'most' people—or those who mattered—were users of their brands.

The principle of social proof states that people look to the behaviour of others as a guide to what is appropriate or normative behaviour. This applies especially in ambiguous situations and where the others are viewed as similar to themselves. It explains the use of canned laughter in comedy shows and, more seriously, the phenomena of copycat suicides and violence. For example, following a television movie about a single, isolated mother apparently about to smother her child, two women in similar circumstances made similar attempts on their children's lives, with one child actually dying as a result (Wharton & Mandell 1985).

This principle is the basis of current social norms approaches in many alcohol, tobacco, and drug programs aimed at young people. For example, campaigns attempt to inform young people that the vast majority of their number do not binge drink, do not drink and drive, do not do hard drugs, and so on. These sorts of campaigns are important as many pre-university students believe that

Suicides increase following death of Diana

The University of Oxford Centre for Suicide Research found that the rate of suicide among women in general rose 34 per cent and in women aged 25–44 (Diana was 37) rose 45 per cent in the month after her funeral. The researchers suggested that women of Diana's age who experienced the same sort of relationship and psychological problems as she did became more pessimistic and despondent about their capacity to solve these problems (Persaud 2000).

excessive drinking is the norm on university campuses. Hence, they are likely to feel greater pressure to binge drink when they arrive at university than if they believed the norm was moderate or light drinking (Task Force 2002).

It is therefore important to feed back to people the results of successful social marketing campaigns, for example, by highlighting the number of people participating in physical activity events, the number of quitters after a Quit campaign, the number of people complying with water restrictions, and so on.

Liking

'*One should be more willing to comply with the requests of friends or other liked individuals*' (Cialdini 1994, p. 206).

The principle of liking refers to the fact that people tend to comply with the requests of those they know and like. Furthermore, liking is based on perceived and actual similarity: we tend to like people who have similar attitudes, beliefs, and backgrounds to our own. We also tend to like people who are physically attractive with warm, friendly, outgoing personalities. Such models dominate commercial advertising. It was often said that former prime minister Bob Hawke was believed to be so popular with the 'common man and woman' because he not only talked the way they did but he was also felt to understand their everyday problems and aspirations. Selecting role models who have similarities with and empathy for the target audience is crucial in communication campaigns.

Authority

'*One should be more willing to follow the suggestions of someone who is a legitimate authority*' (Cialdini 1994, p. 212).

In our society and many others many people have a deep-seated sense of duty and obedience to those in respected positions. This is no doubt based on the fact, learnt early in life, that people in authority have superior access to information and power. This principle is exemplified in many ways, including automatically following the instructions of someone in uniform or with a title such as 'doctor' (as on the button, 'Trust me. I'm a doctor'). Much advertising contains testimonials from various authoritative sources and is perhaps one of health and social marketing's greatest exploitable assets. 'The Surgeon-General's report on …' has great influence, along with the voices of 'university experts …' on various matters.

Demonstrating empathy increases voluntary disclosure of abuse

Far more women volunteered that they had been sexually or physically abused when the doctor wore a badge reading 'Violence against women is wrong' than when the doctor was not wearing the badge (Murphy 1994).

Unfortunately, health, environmental, social, and other scientists do not always agree on many issues, leading to people being potentially somewhat sceptical or cynical about various warnings and threats issued by government organisations. However, many non-profit organisations and individuals do have high credibility. For example, a recent survey (Jalleh & Donovan 2001) showed that 66 per cent of Western Australians rated the Cancer Foundation of Western Australia as 'very credible' and a further 25 per cent rated it as 'somewhat credible'. Only 3 per cent rated the foundation as 'a little/not at all credible'.

Similarly, individuals such as Fiona Stanley, Rosemary Stanton, Garry Egger, and Norman Swan have high credibility in the health area. William Deane has credibility in the social welfare area. Barry Jones used have it in the science area. However, we lack authoritative leadership in the environmental area.

Scarcity

'*One should try to secure those opportunities that are scarce or dwindling*' (Cialdini 1994, p. 211).

This principle states that things in scarce supply are valued more than if they are plentiful. This principle is exemplified by the 'Only three left!', 'Last chance …' sales tactics and in the country and western song, 'The girls all get prettier at closing time'. The principle of scarcity is exacerbated when there is competition for scarce resources, accounting for the often inflated prices obtained at auctions.

This principle is related to psychological reactance, the tendency to see things as more desirable when they are restricted. Many argue that bans on various behaviours only serve to increase young people's desires for behaviours and substances that they may not otherwise be attracted to. On the other hand, loss of privileges—such as loss of a driving licence—may lead to an increased value placed on the licence and increased compliance in the future.

Tupperware parties illustrate a number of these principles: 'free gifts' are distributed to people when they arrive, members of the audience are asked to stand and say why they have previously bought Tupperware or why they think the products are good. Once one person buys, the social proof principle is activated: people are buying from someone they know and like.

Fear arousal and threat appeals in social marketing communications

A commonly used tactic in health promotion and social marketing campaigns is the 'fear appeal' (Job 1988; France, Donovan, Watson & Leivers 1991; King

& Reid 1990; Donovan, Henley, Jalleh & Slater 1995). Fear (or threat) appeals are based on behavioural learning theory: the threatening message arouses fear (or some other unpleasant emotional state), which is then reduced by the decision to adopt the behaviour that will avert the threat (the fear drive model). Adoption of the recommended behaviour leads to fear reduction, which reinforces repetition of the behaviour (see also the Rossiter–Percy model and Applied Behavioural Analysis, discussed in chapter 5).

Fear appeals are common in a number of health areas (particularly antismoking and road safety) and in areas as diverse as energy conservation, recycling, fire control, and crime control (Rice & Atkin 1989; Salmon 1989). They are also not uncommon in commercial advertising (LaTour, Snipes & Bliss 1996).

However, given conflicting findings in the literature there is some disagreement on their efficacy (Donovan et al. 1995; Backer, Rogers & Sopory 1992). Nevertheless, a number of reviews of the literature have concluded that fear appeals can be effective and that more fear is more effective than less fear— except perhaps for targets with low self-esteem—and provided the recommended behaviour is efficacious and under volitional control (Sutton 1982; 1992; Boster & Mongeau 1984; Job 1988). The question is no longer whether fear appeals *can* be effective, but *when* and for *whom* fear appeals are effective (Donovan 1991).

Fear

Fear is a complex emotion that can be both attracting and repelling. People have been flocking for years to scary roller coaster rides, sideshow tunnels of fear, and horror movies for the experience of fear—albeit safe in the knowledge that the experience—in movies anyway—is only vicarious (Daniels 1977). At the same time, fear can lead to panic when a threat becomes real—such as when a fire breaks out (or is thought to) in the same cinema showing the horror movie or when thousands of radio listeners assumed Orson Welles's radio production of H. G. Wells's *War of the Worlds* was an actual not a fictional broadcast (see chapter 11) (Lowery & DeFleur 1988).

Two types of fear arousal

Some 30 years ago, Leventhal and Trembly (1968) distinguished between two types of fear, which they labelled 'anticipatory' and 'inhibitory' fear. This distinction was highlighted by Higbee (1969) in his seminal review of the literature but has received little attention since. Inhibitory fear, evoking feelings of nausea and horror, results from exposure to graphic, gruesome descriptions and pictures of events such as decapitations in car crashes, bloodied and bruised bodies, and removal of organs in bloody operations. The focus here is on the stimuli evoking automatic or reflexive conditioned responses of fear. Anticipatory fear results from the recipient's cognitive appraisal that the threatened consequences are likely to occur if they ignore the recommended course of action. Similar distinctions can be noted in movies. While movies such as *Chainsaw*

Massacre and *Evil Dead* rely mainly on gruesome scenes of carnage to frighten (or horrify) viewers (that is, reflexive responses) others rely more on arousing the viewers' anticipation of horrific outcomes depending on what actions the actors take (for example, the killer is in the cellar, the lights go off, she grabs a torch and heads down the stairs to the fuse box ...) (anticipatory fear).

While Higbee (1969) drew no conclusions as to the relative appropriateness of these two types of fear, Donovan (1991) has argued elsewhere that it is anticipatory rather than inhibitory fear that health communicators must arouse since it is the link between the threat and the person's continuing unhealthy behaviour that must be established. Results from the current Australian national tobacco campaign with respect to ads depicting the graphic squeezing of fatty deposits from an artery and the cutting in half of a brain suggest that inhibitory fear can enhance anticipatory fear where the threatened consequence is clearly seen to result from the unhealthy behaviour (Hassard 1999).

Observation of a large number of campaigns shows that many health communicators in designing their scare messages have failed to note the distinction between these two types of fear, with many simply using graphic, gruesome scenes without regard to the necessary cognitive link. That is, gruesome and graphic stimuli may have aroused inhibitory fear, but failed to arouse anticipatory fear, leading to a cognitive this-could-happen-to-me response to the threat appeal.

Fear appeals or threat appeals?

The terms 'fear appeal', 'fear arousal', 'threat appeal', and 'threat' are used rather loosely and interchangeably in the persuasion literature (Donovan & Henley 1997; Henley 1999). We have argued elsewhere that the term 'threat appeal' is more appropriate than 'fear appeal' primarily because fear is an emotional response and hence the term 'fear appeal' confounds stimulus (message content) and response (audience reaction) variables (Strong, Anderson & Dubas 1993; O'Keefe 1990).

Focusing on the fear response also tends to distract attention from cognitive responses to threatening messages. The recipient's unprompted cognitive responses during exposure to the message (especially the degree of counterarguing) are a major predictor of overall message effectiveness, as are prompted cognitive measures of threat appraisal such as personal relevance, credibility, and 'likelihood of [it] happening to me' (Rossiter & Percy 1997; Donovan, Jalleh & Henley 1999d).

Fear is only one of a variety of emotions that might be aroused by threat appeals and mediate audience response to the message (Bagozzi & Moore 1994; Stout 1989; Dillard, Plotnick, Godbold, Friemuth & Edgar 1996; Donovan et al. 1995). For example, shame, guilt, sadness, and remorse are emotions widely used in social areas (Bennett 1998), with the Victorian Traffic Accident Commission's ads demonstrating the effective use of guilt and remorse in the area of road safety (Donovan et al. 1999d). Witte (1993) has attempted to define fear

The term 'threat appeal' is preferred to the term 'fear appeal' because
* it encourages a broader study of potentially important mediating emotions and cognitive responses
* it demands a greater focus on stimulus factors (that is, message content and how this is communicated)
* it simultaneously demands a separate and sharper focus on response factors (that is, audience emotional and cognitive reactions to the message.

appeals and threat appeals as two distinct categories. Our framework defines fear appeals as a subset of threat appeals, in which the targeted emotional arousal is fear rather than some other emotion. Use of the term 'threat appeal' rather than the term 'fear appeal' leads to a more precise focus on both the content of threat appeals (stimulus factors, negative outcomes, contingent behaviours) and on response factors (cognitive responses and the generation and role of emotions other than fear).

Defining threat appeals: negative outcomes, threats, and threat appeals

We define a threat appeal as a communication including three major components:

1 a negative outcome
2 a contingent behaviour
3 a source.

The communication might be delivered in any medium and in either advertising or editorial format, that is, a television commercial, radio or press ad, press release, or news announcement, by a brochure or video, or in a face-to-face encounter.

A threat appeal consists of a source stating that some negative outcome will result—or increase in likelihood—as a consequence of non-compliance with the source's recommendation. Source characteristics are particularly important for new issues where the link must be established between the threat and the behaviour in question, and for specific target audiences who might be distrusting of establishment sources (Donovan & Henley 1997; Perman & Henley 2001).

A negative outcome is some event that is perceived by the target audience to be harmful or undesirable (*something bad*) and which, under normal circumstances, would be avoided where possible. The loss of a loved one, blindness, a jail sentence, loss of a limb, and lung cancer are negative outcomes.

Figure 4.4   Threat appeal components (Donovan & Henley 1997)

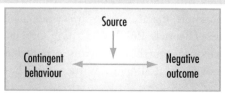

A threat is when some harmful event is perceived by the target audience to be likely to occur to them (*something bad could happen to you*). Stating the lifetime likelihood of blindness for an individual from all causes constitutes a threat.

A threat becomes a threat appeal when a source states that the negative outcome is contingent on the recipient's behaviour and seeks to alter that contingent behaviour (*X says that something bad could or will happen to you **if** you do/do not do …*).

Something bad
(negative outcome)
Something bad could happen to you
(threat)
Something bad will happen to you *if* you do/do not (… some behaviour)
(threat appeal)

The difference between a threat and a threat appeal may be illustrated as follows. The weather bureau announces a high likelihood of a cyclone occurring in far North Queensland. This constitutes a threat. The local State Emergency Service leader recommending that people evacuate the area to avoid injury or loss of life constitutes a threat appeal. Similarly, an ophthalmologist stating the likelihood of blindness occurring because of an existing condition constitutes a threat. Stating the likelihood of blindness occurring if an individual views an eclipse without an appropriate protective device constitutes a threat appeal (Donovan & Henley 1997).

Attributes of negative outcomes

Negative outcomes vary widely and along a number of dimensions (Donovan & Henley 1997; 2000). All of these need to be considered by health promoters when developing a threat appeal in a particular area. What might be an effective negative outcome in some areas for some audiences might not be appropriate in other areas and for other audiences.

Typology of negative outcomes

There are at least four dimensions: physical (for example, disease, disfigurement), social (for example, ostracism, embarrassment), psychological (for example, sense of failure, loss of self-esteem), and financial (for example, property loss or damage, loss of job or income source). It is likely that the relative impact of these will vary by target audience.

Many negative outcomes involve several of these dimensions. For example, a car crash could result in physical injury that results in job loss and subsequent depression. Young, heavy-drinking, blue-collar males who rely on their own motor vehicle for accessing employment sites are concerned about random breath testing (RBT) because losing their driver's licence could mean losing their job (Donovan 1995a).

Degree of perceived control

Natural disasters such as earthquakes, typhoons, and floods occur regardless of the individual's actions. In these cases threat appeals focus on taking action to minimise the consequences of the events. Other negative outcomes, such as the so-called lifestyle diseases and injuries, are at least partly under the individual's control. In these cases threat appeals focus on prevention or minimising the likelihood of their occurrence.

Origins: single or multiple causes

Some negative outcomes have a single cause or a set of clearly related causes (for example, STDs). Others have multiple causes or risk factors (for example, coronary heart disease, diabetes Type II). Messages are easier to generate and comprehend for negative outcomes with clearly defined single causes or few related causes.

Severity

Some negative outcomes have major lifestyle implications (for example, emphysema), whereas others would have little impact on day-to-day functioning (for example, a mild hangover). Different target audiences could have vastly different views with respect to the severity of specific negative outcomes.

Reversibility

Negative outcomes can be described in terms of their permanence or 'reversibility' (Henley 1995). Amputations are non-reversible (although prostheses are available), whereas most STDs are reversible. Given awareness of coronary bypass and organ transplant successes even some major diseases, such as heart disease, might be considered reversible by some people. Ease of reversibility might serve to reduce the perceived severity of a negative event (France et al. 1991). On the other hand, it is desirable that in some cases, such as smoking, the target audience can be assured that any damage they have suffered can be reversed (to ensure response efficacy).

Salience or familiarity

Different diseases and risk factors differ in terms of the ease with which they come to people's minds, which, in turn, is a function of media publicity, previous educational efforts, and individual circumstances. For example, there is generally continuing media publicity about the road toll and heart disease, whereas far less media attention is focused on diabetes.

Lifetime likelihood and imminence

Negative outcomes differ in their estimated lifetime likelihood independently of any contingent behaviour and in their (perceived) imminence (Chu 1966). In general, the more imminent the outcome, the more impact on behaviour change. For example, with respect to smoking, many young people are less deterred by death outcomes in middle age than they are by immediate effects on their fitness or by negative cosmetic effects (Donovan & Leivers 1988).

Death vs non-death

Death has been used widely as the negative outcome in health campaigns (for example, 'Speed kills', 'Smoking kills') (Henley & Donovan 1997; 1999a; 2003; Henley 2002). However, death has some unique characteristics that need to be considered in threat appeals. As death is inevitable the threat appeal should focus either on premature death or on various undesirable attributes of death (slow, painful, etc.). Furthermore, people generally claim to be less affected by threats of their own death and more likely to be affected by the death of loved ones, the effect of their death on loved ones, or causing the death of someone else (Henley & Donovan 1999a; 2003).

Overall then, negative outcomes being considered for inclusion in threat appeals should first be assessed on the above attributes independently of any threat context.

Contingent behaviour complexities

In a threat appeal, adopting a recommended course of action is claimed to protect the audience from the negative outcome. However, the choice of what behaviour to recommend needs careful consideration as there are a number of complexities to consider in constructing the message:

Degree of protection

The recommended behaviour may prevent the negative outcome completely (for example, abstinence from sex, STDs) or, more commonly, the recommended behaviour can only reduce the likelihood of the negative outcome occurring (for example, speed limit compliance and accident likelihood).

'Every 10 kph increases severity of injury'

The Western Australian Office of Road Safety has been running a campaign educating road users about the increased severity of trauma and decreased ability to avoid a crash when the unexpected occurs with every 10 kph increase in speed. This is a more concrete way of demonstrating the effect of speed than a general speed kills type approach, which tends to lack credibility with young male drivers. Furthermore, this approach avoids the common counterargument of this (and other) target group(s) that speed per se does not cause accidents, although they accept that the unexpected can cause crashes.

The lady and pram ad (see below) was very effective in increasing the percentage of young drivers who believed that driving 10 kph slower would reduce their risk of a crash from 76 per cent prior to the campaign to 87 per cent during the campaign.

Asymmetry of effects

The contingent behaviour alternatives are often asymmetrical in delivery of, versus avoiding, the punishment (for example, while abstinence reduces the risk of an STD to zero engaging in sexual behaviour, even unprotected, does not necessarily result in contracting an STD).

Limits on the effectiveness of the contingent behaviour

For many negative outcomes there is some existing base level of likelihood unrelated to the contingent behaviour and for which there are wide individual differences (for example, all individuals have some base level of risk for cardio-vascular disease, regardless of their smoking behaviour).

Quantifying individual risk

Related to the above the overall probability of the negative outcome (base level plus increase due to engaging in the contingent behaviour) for any particular threat appeal is generally unquantifiable for any single individual.

Behaviour target—an increase or a decrease?

A major consideration is whether the focus should be on increasing a desired behaviour (for example, eat more fruit'n'veg, increase physical activities, drive at the speed limit more often, etc.) or on decreasing an undesired behaviour (for example, eat less fat, decrease time inactive, stop speeding, etc.). Learning theory suggests that the choice of whether to increase or decrease a behaviour has implications for the framing of the threat message (see chapter 5).

These contingent behaviour complexities in general lead to major challenges in executing threat appeals. Together they suggest that a major aim of a threat appeal is to increase the target's perceived likelihood of some negative outcome occurring to be significantly above the perceived base level. They also highlight the strategy of focusing on a related contingent behaviour where the main contingent behaviour may not be seen to be particularly efficacious in averting the threat. For example, rather than stressing the likelihood of a collision the Western Australian Office of Road Safety lady and pram ad emphasised the increased likelihood of being unable to stop in time for someone stepping in front of the car for every increase in 10 kph of speed. The ad is filmed from the position of the driver and is in three segments. In the first segment the woman with the pram steps in front and the vehicle easily stops in time. In the second segment the car is travelling a little faster, but manages to stop just short of contact. In the third segment the car is travelling even faster and this time hits the woman and pram; the woman's body hits the windscreen.

Incentive appeals

Incentive appeals can be characterised in the same way as threat appeals only this time compliance with the contingent behaviour produces a positive outcome (figure 4.6).

There are few systematic studies comparing the relative effectiveness of threat appeals versus incentive appeals for the same behaviour for the same target audience (Donovan et al. 1995). However, we would argue that threat appeals are far more effective than incentive appeals where the undesirable behaviour has significant negative health or other outcomes; incentive appeals

Figure 4.5 Office of Road Safety lady and pram ad

are effective where the recommended behaviour has clear positive outcomes and the undesired behaviour has only moderate or low negative outcomes.

It is likely that different individuals will respond differently not only to the two types of overall appeal, but also to different threats and to different incentives. Formative research with the target audience is necessary to identify what

Figure 4.6 Incentive appeals

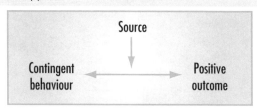

will motivate adoption of the desired behaviour among what proportion of the total population of interest. A recent study by the authors suggests that, for increasing physical activity and fruit'n'veg consumption, threat appeals (that is, stating the negative consequences of non-compliance, such as heart disease, etc.) may be slightly more effective than incentive appeals (that is, stating the positive consequences of compliance, such as increased energy, alertness, etc.).

Gintner, Rectanus, Achord, and Parker (1987) found that people with a higher risk of hypertension (had a parent with hypertension) were more likely to attend a blood pressure screening following a message that emphasised maintaining vigour and wellbeing than following a message that emphasised the severity of the illness.

Framing effects

Consideration of positive versus negative appeals raises the issue of framing in decision making. As used in studies of decision making, framing generally refers to presenting one of two equivalent value outcomes to different groups of decision makers, where one outcome is presented in positive or gain terms and the other in negative or loss terms. For example, a positively framed message might emphasise the benefits to be gained by adopting a promoted course of action (for example, taking a cholesterol test allows assessment of one's risk of heart disease), while the negative frame emphasises the loss of these same benefits if the course of action is not adopted (for example, not taking a cholesterol test does not allow the assessment of one's risk of heart disease) (Maheswaran & Meyers-Levy 1990). Alternatively, a probabilistic outcome might be described in terms of the positive outcome (for example, this medical procedure gives patients a 50 per cent chance of survival) or the negative outcome (for example, in this medical procedure patients have a 50 per cent chance of dying) (Wilson, Kaplan & Schneiderman 1987).

The results of framing studies have been mixed. For behaviours such as breast self-examination (BSE) (Meyerowitz & Chaiken 1987), mammography screening (Banks, Salovey, Greener et al. 1995), exercise (Robberson & Rogers 1998), skin cancer detection (Rothman, Salovey, Antone, Keough & Martin 1993), and smoking (Wilson, Wallston & King 1987) negative framings have tended to result in greater message compliance, at least relative to controls, but not always significantly greater than positive framings.

On the other hand, a positive frame was more effective for promoting exercise as a means of enhancing self-esteem (Robberson & Rogers 1988), parents' use of children's car seat restraints, and for a skin cancer prevention behaviour (Rothman, Salovey, Antone et al. 1993). For surgical procedures positively framed outcomes (probability of success or survival) induced greater compliance than negatively framed outcomes (probability of failure or death) (Wilson, Kaplan & Schneiderman 1987). When the side-effects (the common flu) were framed positively (90 per cent chance of no side effects) or negatively (10 per cent chance of side effects) for a hypothetical new immunisation that protected infants against respiratory complaints such as bronchitis and pneumonia, Donovan and Jalleh (2000) found the positive framing to be superior for low-involved respondents (no infant and not intending to get pregnant), but there was no framing effect for high-involved respondents (had an infant or intended to get pregnant in the immediate future).

Rothman and Salovey (1997), referring to Kahneman and Tversky's (1979; 1982) conclusions with respect to risk aversiveness under positive framing and risk seeking under negative framing, suggest that gain frames would be more effective for disease prevention behaviours (for example, use of sunscreen for skin cancer prevention), whereas loss frames would be more effective for disease detection behaviours (for example, skin examination to detect early cancers). However, our experience over a number of published (for example, Donovan & Jalleh 2000) and unpublished framing studies is that those based purely on variations such as 'taking a cholesterol test allows assessment of one's risk of heart disease' versus 'not taking a cholesterol test does not allow the assessment of one's risk of heart disease' are of little importance.

How much fat is that?

Jalleh and Donovan (2001) suggest that consumers need to be aware of the influence of per cent content labelling on their attitudes and purchase intention. Products with a fat-free label, especially those with less than 90 per cent, might increase their favourable perceptions and purchase intentions relative to their equivalent fat labels. Hence, when consumers are considering buying a product with a positively framed label it is suggested that they take into account the flip side of the label. For example, in assessing mince with a 85 per cent fat-free label consumers need to re-label the product in their mind and ask themselves how they would feel about this product if it were labelled 15 per cent fat before making a purchasing decision.

However, framings of product constituents might be significant. People have more favourable purchase intentions for meat products when they are labelled with the per cent fat-free than when labelled with the per cent fat (Levin & Gaeth 1988; Donovan & Jalleh 1999b). Figure 4.7 shows that this bias exists for 75 per cent fat-free versus 25 per cent fat, 85 per cent fat-free versus 15 per cent fat, and 90 per cent fat-free versus 10 per cent fat. Figure 4.7 suggests that this is because the framing actually affects the perception of fat in the product.

Figure 4.7 Purchase intention and fat/lean ratings by fat/fat-free framing (Jalleh & Donovan 2001)

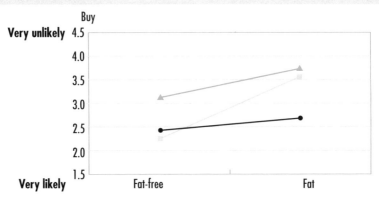

Figure 4.8 Ratings of fat content by fat/fat-free framing (Jalleh & Donovan 2001)

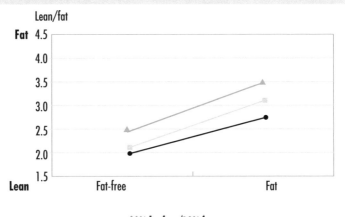

- 90% fat-free/10% fat
- 85% fat-free/15% fat
- 75% fat-free/25% fat

Concluding comments

Communication strategies must not only focus on message content, but also on message execution. Breaking through the clutter is essential. Like the better mousetrap, if nobody knows it's there, it can hardly elicit behaviour change. Message construction must be based on the receiver's initial attitudes, their motivation to process the message, and their ability to do so.

Communication can occur through various media. The good thing about Cialdini's principles of persuasion is that they apply to both interpersonal as well as media channels. And they work.

Threat appeals—and their converse, incentive appeals—constitute the major type of message in most communication strategies aimed at individual behaviour change, whether as consumers, policy makers, legislators, or corporation executives. However, such appeals must be accompanied by the opportunity to adopt the behaviour, preferably in a supportive physical, social, and regulatory environment (see chapter 5).

Overall then, developing successful communication strategies involves two phases (Egger et al. 1993):

Getting the right message
(message content),
and
Getting the message right
(message execution).

Getting the right message involves identifying what message will motivate the target audience to adopt the recommended action (what advertising agency people call 'the hot buttons to push'). It entails ensuring that the message content takes into account the target audience's initial knowledge, beliefs, and attitudes and has the capacity to shift beliefs, attitudes, and behaviour in the desired direction. Formative research with violent men revealed that

- showing the impact of their violence on their or their partner's children was the right message to motivate such men to seek help (see chapter 14)
- showing the minister that there was overwhelming public approval for a domestic violence campaign targeting violent men to voluntarily enter counselling was the right message to gain government approval for the campaign
- showing feminist stakeholders that the messages did not adversely affect victims was the right message to ensure sector support for the campaign.

Egger et al.'s (1993) guidelines for developing communication campaigns

- Establish source credibility by seeking a common point of agreement from which to commence the communication process.
- Increase the salience and intensity of already held positive beliefs and other beliefs that provide a positive context within which to change negative beliefs.
- Link messages that people have potentially negative responses to, to already-held positive beliefs.
- Avoid broaching issues that generate negative responses until prior positive beliefs are firmly established.
- Attempt changes in negative beliefs slowly and in small steps, that is, stay within the target audience's latitude of acceptance—do not make extreme claims.
- Enhance source credibility by presenting apparently even-handed or two-sided approaches that preempt counterarguments that would otherwise distract from the message or lead to rejection of the message.
- Draw explicit conclusions for unmotivated naive audiences; let motivated, knowledgeable audiences draw their own conclusions.

Getting the message right entails ensuring that how the message is presented attracts attention, is believable, relevant, understandable, arouses appropriate emotions, and does not lead to counterargument. The effects of domestic violence on children can be depicted in a variety of scenarios. However, the execution needed to avoid being seen by men to be judging or criticising their behaviour, a perception that would lead to them rejecting the ad's request for them to seek help. Pretesting the ad was essential to ensure message understanding and credibility, as well as ensuring that the perceived tone of the ad did not antagonise men.

This chapter has dealt with a number of aspects relevant to getting the right message and getting the message right, with the emphasis on getting the message right. Chapter 5 provides further frameworks, with an emphasis on getting the right message.

Chapter 5

Models of Attitude and Behaviour Change

Introduction

In this chapter we present a number of models useful for developing campaign strategies. While each can be classified as either motivational, behavioural, cognitive, or affective in emphasis, they all deal with conceptualising the influences on behaviour and hence provide a framework for formative research, strategy development, and campaign evaluation. These models are generally known as 'knowledge–attitude–behaviour' (KAB) models or, more recently, as 'social cognition' models (Norman & Connor 1996; Godin 1994).

Most of these models are based on the assumption that an individual's beliefs about some person, group, issue, object, or behaviour will determine the individual's attitude and intentions with respect to that person, group, issue, object, or behaviour. These intentions, in turn, subject to environmental facilitators and inhibitors, will predict how the individual actually acts with respect to that person, group, issue, object, or behaviour. An understanding of knowledge–attitude–behaviour models provides us with directions for setting communication objectives and for generating message strategies and executions to achieve these objectives. These processes depend on a thorough understanding of the sorts of beliefs that influence attitudes towards the recommended behaviour, how these beliefs and other facilitators and inhibitors influence intentions to behave, and when and how intentions are fulfilled or not fulfilled.

We also present Rogers's broader diffusion model as the major model for understanding how ideas and behaviours diffuse throughout a community. Rogers's model is increasingly being applied in social marketing. Behaviour modification (or applied behaviour analysis) principles are also included to further emphasise that we must translate people's beliefs, attitudes, and intentions into action, and that to do this we must be aware of the necessary environmental factors and skills that will facilitate this translation.

We will briefly describe each of the models most frequently mentioned in the health promotion and social marketing literature (see Egger, Spark, Lawson & Donovan 1999; Egger, Donovan & Spark 1993) before presenting a synthesis

Figure 5.1 The health belief model*

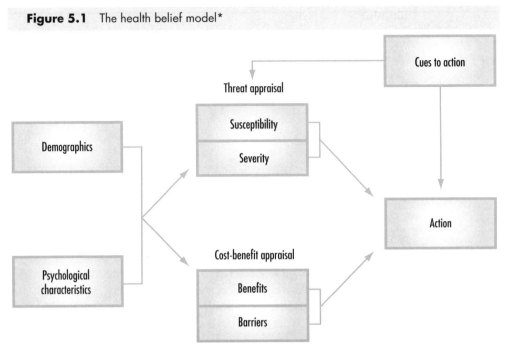

* Adapted from Sheeran & Abraham 1996

of the major variables across all models. A notable omission from this chapter is Prochaska and DiClemente's Stages of Change model; this is covered in chapter 9. A notable inclusion in the chapter is a brief discussion on two concepts generally ignored by these models: morality and legitimacy (Amonini 2001).

The health belief model

The health belief model (HBM) was perhaps the first behavioural model in health education. It was developed in the 1950s by US Public Health Service workers in an attempt to explain participation and non-participation in screening programs for tuberculosis (Becker 1974; Maiman & Becker 1974; Rosenstock 1974a).

The model lists the following factors that are presumed to influence behaviour change in response to a potential health threat:

- the individual's perceived susceptibility to the disease
- the individual's perceived severity of the disease
- the individual's perceptions that the recommended behaviour will avert the threat (and any other additional benefits)
- the individual's perceptions of the costs of and perceived barriers to adopting the recommended behaviour
- the presence of cues to action (internal, such as symptoms; external, such as mass media advertising) that prompt the individual to act.

The HBM states that the recommended behaviour will occur if individuals see themselves as susceptible to a particular health problem, see this problem as a serious one, consider that the benefits of treatment are effective and not unduly costly, and some event occurs to prompt action. These concepts can be applied in reverse where the behaviour under question is not a threat but a promise. For example, performance-enhancing drug usage will occur if athletes see themselves as unable to achieve at their desired level, if achieving at the desired level has considerable rewards, if they consider that drug usage will effectively deliver the required performance without undue side-effects or expense, the drugs are easily available, and perhaps if they learn that a rival is using PEDs. The HBM's explicit inclusion of a cost–benefit analysis (only implied in other models) increases its potential applicability to the sport drug area (Donovan, Egger, Kapernick & Mendoza 2002).

It is also assumed that demographic and psychosocial variables will moderate the above variables.

Hence, individuals are more likely to take up exercise if they consider they are at high risk for diabetes, if they perceive diabetes as a serious disease, if they believe that increased exercise is effective in reducing the risk of diabetes, if they perceive no major barriers or costs (financial, social, or physical) to increasing their level of exercise, and if a friend draws their attention to a physical activity program commencing at a nearby community recreation centre.

As the oldest model the HBM has been used in planning programs in a wide variety of health areas (see Sheeran & Abraham 1996) and has been reviewed extensively (Janz & Becker 1984; Rosenstock, Strecher & Becker 1988). While Janz and Becker (1984) reported that the HBM significantly predicted health behaviours, Harrison, Mullen & Green's (1992) meta-analysis of more strictly selected studies revealed a far weaker effect size. We would suggest that this is because, while the model provides a useful framework for research and for message strategy planning, it is (like many other models) incomplete.

Protection motivation theory

Rogers's (1975) protection motivation theory (PMT) was developed originally as a model of fear arousal to explain the motivational effect resulting from threat communications. The theory assumes that people are motivated to protect themselves from not only physical threats, but also from social and psychological threats (Rogers 1983). PMT also incorporates the concept of self-efficacy from Bandura's (1986) social learning theory.

PMT postulates that individuals undertake two major appraisals when confronted with a threat: a threat appraisal and a coping appraisal (figure 5.2).

As in the health belief model a threat is appraised on two major factors:

■ the perceived severity of the threatened harmful event if it occurs

Figure 5.2 Rogers's protection motivation theory

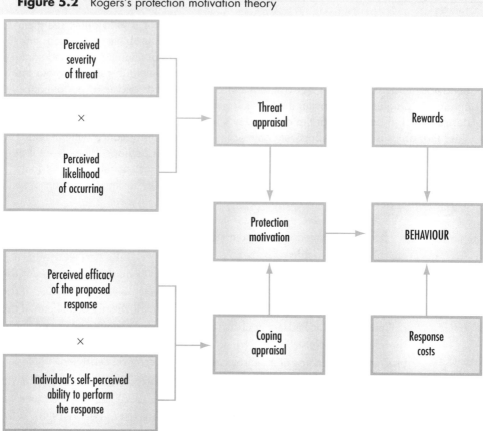

- the perceived likelihood of the threatened outcome occurring if the recommended behaviour is not adopted.

These two factors determine the individual's perceived vulnerability.

The coping appraisal consists of an appraisal of the recommended behaviour on the following two dimensions:

- the perceived effectiveness of the promoted behaviour to avoid or reduce the likelihood of occurrence of the threat (that is, response efficacy)
- the individual's self-assessed ability to perform the recommended behaviour (that is, self-efficacy).

If an individual or an organisation determines themselves to be vulnerable to a threat (for example, a boycott of the company's products), that the recommended behaviour (for example, adopting recyclable packaging) would be effective in removing the threat, and that they are able to carry out the recommended behaviour (that is, the recyclable packaging and technology are available and affordable), then the recommended behaviour is likely to occur. If the threat appraisal is low, either because it is extremely unlikely to occur or not severe enough to worry about, or if the threat is seen to be significant but the recommended behaviour is not seen to be effective or within the individual's or organisation's capabilities (for example, a hostile board of directors), the recommended behaviour will not occur.

The variables in figure 5.2 act to increase the likelihood of adopting the recommended behaviour (coping appraisal) and ceasing the undesired behaviour (threat appraisal). Rogers (1983) later added two further factors:

■ response costs—which act to inhibit adoption of the desired behaviour

■ rewards gained from the undesirable behaviour that facilitate its continuation.

The PMT emphasises the appraisal of threatening or supposedly fear-arousing communications whereas some behaviours might be more effectively motivated, at least for some target groups, by the positive effects or benefits of adopting the recommended behaviour (as noted in chapter 4). For example, many individuals take up and maintain exercise for the positive benefits of exercising (enjoyment, social interactions, feelings of mastery, alertness, etc.) as well as to avoid threatened outcomes of inadequate exercise (avoidance of heart disease, diabetes risk, lose or control weight, etc.) (Donovan & Francas 1990). Hence, a more complete model would include an incentive appraisal, that is, the perceived attractiveness of the positive benefits to be gained by adopting the recommended behaviour. The coping appraisal in this case would be the same as for the threat: whether the recommended behaviour can deliver the promised benefits and whether the individual can perform the desired behaviour.

The PMT has been applied in a number of health areas (see Boer & Seydel 1996), including exercise, alcohol consumption, smoking, breast cancer screening, and STDs (for example, Tanner, Day & Crask 1989; Prentice-Dunn & Rogers 1986; Rippetoe & Rogers 1987; Wurtele & Maddux 1987), and in predicting intentions to engage in antinuclear war behaviours (Wolf, Gregory & Stephan 1986), earthquake preparedness (Mulilis & Lippa 1990), and burglary prevention (Wiegman, Taal, Van Den Bogaard & Gutteling 1992). In general, the concepts of vulnerability and coping appraisal—particularly self-efficacy— have been found to be significant predictors of intention (Boer & Seydel 1996).

Social learning theory

At a basic level learning occurs via a process of reinforcement: behaviours that are rewarded tend to be repeated whereas behaviours that are punished tend not to be repeated. Social learning theorists believe that many learned behaviours depend on social reinforcement (for example, peer pressure influencing taking up smoking) and that new behaviours can be learnt not only by actually experiencing reinforcements, but also by observing reinforcements delivered to others (Bandura 1977b). This is the basis of modelling: adopting behaviours through imitating the behaviours of others. Bandura draws our attention not only to the behaviour per se, but also to the environment in which it takes place.

The power of a model to induce attitude and behaviour change depends on such things as the model's credibility, attractiveness, power, expertise, and empathy with the audience (Rossiter & Percy 1997). It also depends on how clearly and credibly the model's behaviour is seen to be rewarded. Social learning theory is the primary rationale for testimonial type communications and for the modelling of desirable health behaviours in television advertising and entertainment vehicles such as soap operas (see chapter 11).

Bandura (1986) has expanded his social learning theory to a comprehensive social cognitive model. Many of the constructs in this model are similar to those of the health belief model with the addition of the concept of self-efficacy with respect to performing a particular behaviour. Perceived self-efficacy reflects the individual's ability and self-confidence in performing the recommended behaviour. The concept of self-efficacy is perhaps Bandura's major contribution to social cognition models (considered separately as self-efficacy theory by some writers, for example, Godin 1994). Self-efficacy has been found to be a major predictor of outcomes in a large number of studies across a broad range of behaviours and models (as noted above), as well as independently of any particular model (for example, McAuley & Jacobson 1991; Hofstetter, Hovell & Sallis 1990; Schwarzer & Fuchs 1996). It is particularly relevant when considering the use of threat appeals, where it is argued that if an individual experiences high anxiety as a result of the threat but considers themself helpless to avoid the threat, then the maladaptive behaviour (for example, smoking, drug taking, violence) might in fact increase.

The theory of reasoned action

The theory of reasoned action (TRA) is perhaps the most developed of the KAB models and is widely used in social psychology and consumer decision making. It has more recently been applied to a number of health and environmental behaviours (see Conner & Sparks 1995).

Fishbein and Ajzen (1975) proposed that volitional behaviour is predicted by one's intention to perform the behaviour, which, in turn, is a function of attitude towards that behaviour and subjective norms with respect to that behaviour (see figure 5.3). Attitude is a function of beliefs about the consequences of the behaviour weighted by an evaluation of each outcome. Subjective norms are a function of how significant others view the behaviour, weighted by the motivation to conform with each. Hence, an individual might have a positive attitude toward binge drinking but not engage in the behaviour because their football team mates are opposed to it as it affects their chances of winning. Similarly, an individual might have a negative or neutral attitude towards separating glass, paper, and metal in their rubbish, but do so because their children encourage it and all the neighbours are seen to be doing it.

Formative research is necessary to identify all of the relevant beliefs with respect to the consequences of adopting or not adopting the recommended behaviour and whether these consequences are viewed negatively, positively, or neutrally. To accurately predict intentions it is necessary to ensure that all relevant beliefs are uncovered. For example, it might be found that attitudes towards recycling are favourable because only beliefs that were evaluated positively were included, while many beliefs that would be evaluated negatively were unintentionally omitted. Similarly, research is needed to identify all of the relevant others, how these others are perceived to feel about the recommended behaviour, and the extent to which the individual feels motivated to comply with these others. Leventhal and Cameron (1994) remind us that many beliefs might be 'commonsense' or intuitive rather than objective beliefs. Commonsense beliefs are based on people's own experiences and what people see, hear, and feel as they go about their lives. For example, if a smoker feels fit and well, that smoker is far less likely to be influenced by antismoking messages; if people live in areas where certain ethnic groups are associated with crime they are less likely to respond to antistereotype tolerance campaigns.

Fishbein's model introduced two important features. First, the model requires the user to make a clear distinction between attitudes towards objects, issues, events per se and attitudes towards behaving in a certain way towards these objects, issues, events, etc. For example, an individual may have a favourable attitude towards Porsche cars, but a negative attitude towards actually buying one because this would involve borrowing a substantial amount of money at a high interest rate (not to mention, if the purchaser is a male, being the butt of some well-known comments about his anatomy). Similarly, an individual may have a favourable attitude towards condoms per se, but a negative attitude towards actually buying or carrying condoms. Hence, when exploring beliefs and attitudes to predict intentions and behaviour, it is necessary to be precise in terms of whether one is measuring attitudes towards an issue per se (for example, exercise) or attitudes towards engaging in a behaviour (for example, exercising).

Second, the TRA distinguishes between the individual's beliefs related to the object or issues per se and the individual's beliefs about what other people think about the issue and how others think the individual should behave towards the issue (that is, normative beliefs). Hence, the Fishbein model incorporates social norms as an influence on attitudes and behaviour.

Overall then, an individual's intention towards switching from, say, regular-strength beer to a reduced-alcohol beer will be a function of the following.

Attitude

Attitude is measured by first identifying the individual's beliefs about the likely consequences of drinking reduced-alcohol beer, which might be less intoxicating, lead to fewer hangovers, increased alertness, less risk of exceeding .05 if random breath tested, less enjoyment of full-bodied taste, less variety of beer type, less brand imagery; and so on. In research terms individuals are asked to state how likely is it that each of these consequences would occur if they

Figure 5.3 Fishbein and Ajzen's theory of reasoned action

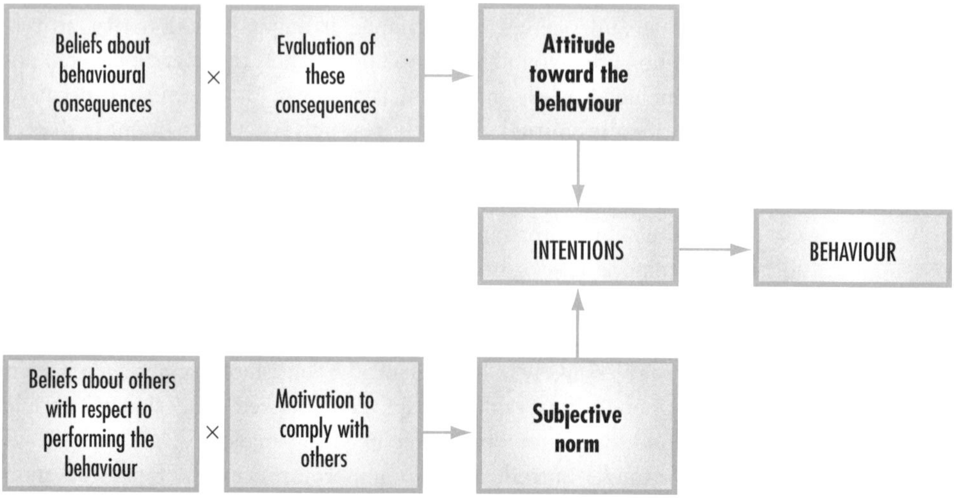

switched to reduced-alcohol beer. This is followed by an evaluation of the beliefs (how positively or negatively consequences such as less hangovers, increased alertness, less taste, etc., are viewed). Attitude, then, is the sum of the likelihood multiplied by evaluation scores.

Social norms

Social norms are measured by first identifying all relevant others (friends, work-mates, family, sporting club mates, etc.) and then establishing how likely it is that each of these would endorse the individual switching to reduced-alcohol beer (normative beliefs). These scores are then weighted by how likely the individual would be to comply with each relevant other (for example, workmates' opinions might be far more important than a spouse's opinion—or vice versa). This last point shows that the behaviour to be predicted should also be defined with respect to situation, particularly in terms of the social environment. An individual might behave quite differently depending on who else is present. Young males often moderate their drinking behaviour in the presence of young women (and stern parents).

Fishbein and Ajzen's model has spawned a number of extensions, most notably the theory of planned behaviour (TPB; Ajzen 1988) and the theory of trying (TT; Bagozzi & Warshaw 1990). The TPB extended the TRA by adding perceived behavioural control—the extent to which the individual perceived the recommended behaviour to be easy or difficult to do.

Both the TRA and TPB have been used quite extensively across a number of consumer purchasing, lifestyle, and health behaviours (particularly smoking, exercise, and STD prevention), with generally good results for all of the major variables in the models in terms of predicting intentions or behaviours (Conner

Predicting binge drinking

Using the theory of planned behaviour as a theoretical framework, a UK study attempted to explore the motivational and attitudinal factors underlying binge drinking and to determine the key predictors of frequency of binge drinking. The TPB variables explained nearly 40 per cent of the variance in frequency of binge drinking, with perceived behavioural control one of the major predictors: more frequent binge drinkers were less likely to believe that their decision to binge drink was under their control (Norman, Bennett & Lewis 1998).

& Sparks 1995; Godin & Kok 1996; Blue 1995; Sheppard, Hartwick & Warshaw 1988).

The theory of trying

The theory of trying (TT) has two major elements of interest. First, the focus is on goals rather than on reasoned behaviour choices in specific situations, hence, TT is directly applicable to most issues in health promotion and social marketing. Second, the theory focuses on trying to achieve these goals (that is, attempting to quit) rather than actual attainment of the goals (that is, successfully quitting). This is a far more realistic focus. For example, rather than attempting to determine the predictors of (successful) quitting we should first determine the predictors of trying to quit. Many studies have failed to show a relationship between attitudes or intentions and behaviours because the behaviours have been defined as successful outcomes (for example, loss of weight, adoption of regular exercise, introduction of policy changes) rather than trying to achieve these goals. Separating trying from achieving also forces the campaign planner to separately consider what leads to trying and what factors then come into play to facilitate or inhibit a successful outcome.

The theory of trying is presented in figure 5.4. The key points in TT are discussed below (Bagozzi & Warshaw 1990). An individual's overall attitude towards trying some behaviour (for example, to lose weight) is a function of three factors:

- attitude towards succeeding and the perceived likelihood (that is, expectation) of success
- attitude towards failing and the perceived likelihood (that is, expectation) of failing
- attitude towards the actual process of trying to lose weight.

Each of the above attitudes is measured by assessing the likelihood of various consequences occurring as a result of succeeding, failing, and engaging in the process, weighted by the evaluation of these consequences. For example, the consequences of successfully losing weight might be feeling healthier, looking better, reduced risk of diabetes, and so on. The consequences of not losing weight might be feeling unhappy, feeling uncomfortable in one's clothes,

Figure 5.4 Theory of trying*

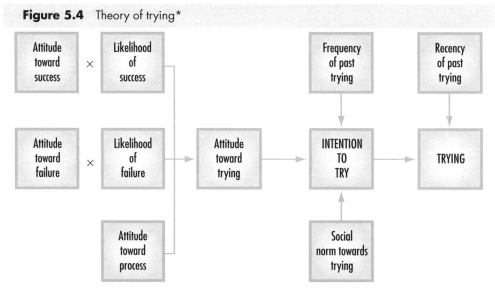

* Adapted from Bagozzi & Warshaw 1990

increased risk of diabetes and heart disease, and so on. Beliefs about the consequences of the process of losing weight might include feeling hungry often,
having to go without the foods one really likes, having to avoid restaurants and
takeaway food, more time in preparation of food, less choice of foods, and so on.
Each of these beliefs is weighted by an evaluation of these consequences and
summed to provide an overall attitude.

An individual's intention to try to lose weight will be determined by:

- their overall attitude towards trying to lose weight as assessed above
- social norms about trying to lose weight (that is, beliefs about important
  others' attitudes towards the individual losing weight)
- the number of times the individual has tried to lose weight before.
  Actually trying to lose weight will be determined by:
- the individual's intention to try to lose weight
- the number of times the individual has tried to lose weight before
- time since the last try.

Bagozzi and Warshaw (1990) showed that their model significantly and substantially predicted trying to lose weight (and was a better predictor than the
TPB) although frequency of past trying was not a significant predictor of trying.
On the other hand, some quitting studies have shown that frequency of past
trying is a significant predictor of attempts to quit and successful quitting.

Cognitive dissonance

Cognitive dissonance is said to occur when the individual holds beliefs that are
inconsistent or when the individual's actions and beliefs are inconsistent

(Festinger 1957). For example, a smoker would experience dissonance if they believed that smoking causes lung cancer; a politician would experience dissonance if they believed that mandatory sentencing unfairly discriminated against lower SES groups and their party was introducing such legislation.

Dissonance is considered to be psychologically uncomfortable and anxiety arousing. The degree of dissonance and hence the degree of discomfort is a function of how strongly held are the various beliefs. Individuals experiencing dissonance are assumed to take steps to reduce this dissonance. This is done by changing beliefs or actions so as to be consistent (for example, the smoker quits), or by changing one set of beliefs (for example, discounting the evidence that smoking causes cancer), or by generating a set of beliefs that overpower the dissonant belief (for example, the smoker thinks of a large number of positives about smoking) (O'Keefe 1990).

Many campaigns are aimed at generating a state of dissonance in the individual, with the recommended behaviour as the means of eliminating this uncomfortable state. Such tactics are particularly appropriate for interpersonal interactions, such as workshops and lobbying. Similarly, forced behaviour adoption can result in attitude changes to be consistent with the behaviour. With respect to compulsory seat belts this has been a desirable outcome. On the other hand, in the politician's situation above, if a conscience vote is disallowed voting for the legislation may lead to a change in beliefs in favour of the legislation.

There has been little published on the use of this model in health and social marketing. However, it is often implied in the strategy of many campaigns and is useful to complement the more comprehensive attitude—behaviour change models.

Theory of interpersonal behaviour

Triandis's (1977) theory of interpersonal behaviour (TIB) (figure 5.5) is similar in many respects to the theory of reasoned action, but has not received much attention outside of psychology and hence little systematic use in health and social marketing (Godin 1994).

The TIB includes two concepts of particular interest not included (or given little weight) in other models: the influence of habit and personal normative beliefs. The inclusion of habit demands that the social marketing practitioner distinguish between new behaviours versus established behaviours. The concept of personal normative beliefs recognises that individuals' morals and internalised values are important predictors in addition to social norms.

Triandis (1977) states that the likelihood of an individual performing a given behaviour is a function of:

- the degree to which the behaviour is already habitual
- intentions to perform the behaviour
- conditions facilitating or inhibiting carrying out the behaviour.

Figure 5.5 Theory of interpersonal behaviour

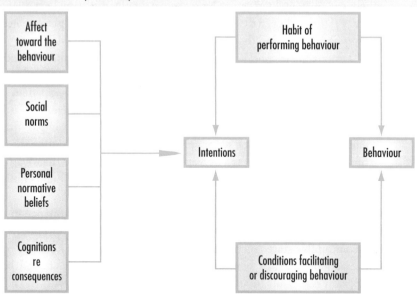

Intentions in turn are influenced by four elements:

- the individual's anticipated emotional response to performing the behaviour (that is, pleasure/disliking; boring/interesting, etc.)
- a cognitive summing up of the positive and negative consequences of performing the behaviour
- perceived social norms and whether that behaviour is appropriate to the individual's social role(s)
- felt obligation to perform the behaviour according to the individual's internalised values.

Hence, an individual could be persuaded to increase their level of physical activity if they had positive expectations—or memories—about the proposed activity, if they considered the benefits outweighed the costs, if social norms reinforced the activity and it was considered appropriate for their age, gender, and social status, and if they considered it the right thing to do. The inclusion of role beliefs is a valuable yet little explored concept. However, the concept may be particularly relevant for stimulating community action on environmental and planning issues. It is likely that many people do not take part in advocacy activities because they see these roles as inappropriate for them.

The Rossiter–Percy motivational model

The Rossiter–Percy model offers specific practical guidelines for developing and executing social marketing messages because of its emphasis on identifying the

Table 5.1 Rossiter and Percy's message strategy model

	Type of motivation	
Type of decision	**Positive**	**Negative**
Low involvement		
High involvement		

appropriate motivations for the target groups as the basis for attitude—and subsequent behaviour—change (Donovan & Owen 1994; Donovan & Francas 1990; Donovan et al. 1995; Donovan 1995a; Donovan & Henley 1997; Henley & Donovan 1998; 2002).

Rossiter and Percy (1987; 1997) classify consumer decision making in terms of two dimensions: the level of involvement associated with the decision (high or low) and the nature of the primary motivations driving the decision (positive or negative). Their framework is shown in table 5.1.

Involvement is defined as the degree of perceived risk—financial, functional, or social—in making the wrong decision and is dichotomised as high or low. Whether a decision is high or low involvement for an individual is determined primarily through qualitative research. High-involvement decision making is inferred by the consumer's extensive prepurchase information gathering efforts so as to reduce the risk of making a wrong decision and the need to be convinced beforehand that they are making the right decision. On the other hand, for low-involvement decisions, consumers can—and generally do—adopt a try-it-and-see attitude before purchase as the consequences of making the wrong choice are insignificant or are perceived as such. These are similar to Petty and Cacioppo's central and peripheral routes respectively (chapter 4)

The adoption of smoking is often a low-involvement decision, whereas the decision to quit is high involvement. In the Rossiter–Percy model the level of involvement largely determines a number of executional rather than message strategy elements. The main implication for communication materials is that executions must be credible for high-involvement decisions, but need only arouse 'curious disbelief' (that is, 'it might be true') for low involvement decisions.

The nature of the motivation largely determines the message strategy. Following Fennell's (1978) analysis of motivations operating in various consumption (or product-use) situations, and imposing an overall drive induction/drive reduction framework from psychological learning theory, Rossiter and Percy (1987) proposed that motivations for behaviour can be classified as either positive (the goal is drive induction or increase), or negative (the goal is drive reduction). For positive motivations the goal is to (temporarily) achieve a positive experience (above 'normal') whereas for negative motivations the goal is to remove or avoid a negative experience and return to 'normal'. The drive

Figure 5.6 Positive versus negative motivations

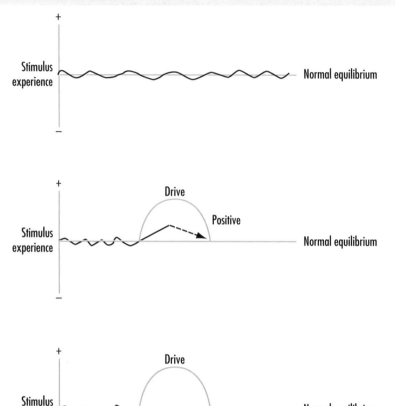

induction and reduction paths of positive versus negative motivations can be illustrated as in figure 5.6.

Rossiter and Percy's motivations and their goal directions are shown in table 5.2. Two positive motives have been added by Donovan et al. (1995): self-approval (note Triandis's personal normative beliefs) and social conformity. The original eight motivations are described more fully in Rossiter and Percy (1987; 1997) and Rossiter, Percy & Donovan (1984; 1991).

Negative motivations relate to actions taken to solve current problems or to avoid future problems. In social marketing the focus is usually on problem avoidance by adopting the recommended behaviour (avoiding air pollution, reducing the likelihood of a crash or the severity of injury, avoiding heart disease, etc.), or problem solution by adopting the recommended behaviour (recycling solves the energy-use problem, reduction of speed limits solves the high-injury problem). Mixed approach–avoidance motives also operate in many areas, including reduced alcohol beers for those wanting to drink alcohol, but not wanting to

Table 5.2   Rossiter and Percy's positive and negative motivations*

Energising mechanism	Goal direction
Negative or aversive origin	
1 Current problem	Solve problem (removal or escape)
2 Anticipated problem	Prevent problem (avoidance)
3 Incomplete satisfaction	Continue search
4 Mixed approach—avoidance	Reduce conflict
Mildly negative origin	
5 Normal depletion	Maintain stable state
Positive or appetitive origin	
6 Sensory gratification	Enjoy
7 Intellectual needs	Explore, master
8 Social approval	Achieve personal recognition, status
9 Personal values*	Act consistent with personal values
Mildly positive origin	
10 Social conformity*	Affiliate

* Adapted from Rossiter & Percy 1997, reproduced with permission of the McGraw-Hill Companies, with the ninth and tenth motives added by Donovan et al. 1995

exceed the legal blood alcohol concentration, low-fat icecream for those wanting the taste but not the calories, and so on. Incomplete satisfaction is also relevant in some areas: air bags for those seeking a safer vehicle, failing to lose weight in one program leading to seeking a more effective weight loss program.

Positive motivations refer to actions taken to achieve an enhanced positive emotional state—usually temporarily because such positive states soon become overbearing, lead to satiation and a return to the normal level. Much unsafe road behaviour is risk taking or sensation seeking behaviour sought for its own sake or to satisfy self-image or social approval needs. In a similar way individuals seek risky thrills on carnival rides or in hobbies like hang-gliding (Craig-Lees, Joy & Browne 1995). While some individuals initiate drug behaviour to cope with anxieties or other personal problems many people initiate drug taking for the expected feelings of enhanced pleasure or excitement. Of course, if the drug becomes addictive, continued use of the drug becomes necessary to solve or avoid problems associated with withdrawal and for the individual just to be able to function normally.

Positive motivations are infrequently targeted in public health messages primarily because most health behaviour adoption for most people has negative motivations. At the same time, the 'If you drink and drive, you're a bloody idiot' campaign approaches an intellectual appeal—'Smart people don't drink and drive'. Adoption of exercise is one health behaviour that many people adopt for positive motivations (for example, to look better, feel more alert, increase social opportunities, compete better, or get stronger) (Donovan & Francas 1990).

We should also distinguish between motives for adoption of a behaviour and motives for continuation of the behaviour. For example, not drink driving or not exceeding the speed limit might be adopted initially to avoid detection and punishment, but if this compliant behaviour leads to feelings of greater relaxation and enjoyment of driving then the compliant behaviour might be maintained for these approach rewards rather than the avoidance rewards. Similarly, exercise may be adopted for weight control and avoidance of heart disease, but after some time, the physical activity per se or the accompanying social interactions may become rewarding in themselves.

It should be noted that positive motivations do not equate to positive benefits. The same positive benefit can result from quite different motives. For example, two drinking drivers might receive positive social reinforcement by their decision to take a taxi rather than drive while exceeding the legal BAC level. However, one individual might have been motivated by the need to avoid social disapproval whereas the other might have been motivated by a desire for approval. Similarly, two individuals might get the same benefit of weight control from exercise, but for one the primary motive was to look better, while for the other the primary motive was to reduce the risk of heart disease.

Another distinction between negative and positive motivations is that, for negative motivations, consumption of the chosen product or performance of the adopted behaviour is largely a means to an end, whereas for positively motivated activities the activity is an end in itself. Speeding is often done for the thrill of the actual behaviour whereas not speeding is done to avoid a penalty. An analgesic is taken not because the analgesic tastes good, but because the analgesic will remove a headache. An icecream is (usually) not eaten to allay hunger pangs, but because the act of consumption per se is enjoyable. As noted above though, it is possible that negatively motivated products or behaviours initially chosen as a means to an end may generate benefits such that they become enjoyable in their own right.

The role of emotions in the Rossiter–Percy model

The Rossiter–Percy model explicitly delineates the role of emotions in message strategy. Motivation is considered to be goal directed (that is, a cognitive component), with emotions being the energising component. Both cognitions and emotions are required for achieving the desired behavioural result. As we know, knowledge is insufficient to achieve behavioural change among many people because this knowledge is unrelated to the underlying motivator for these people. There are two key aspects to the role of emotions in the Rossiter–Percy model:

1   each motivation has its own relevant emotion(s) and it is crucial that communications portray the correct emotion(s)
2   it is the sequence of emotions that is important (for negative motives in particular), not just the arousal of single emotions.

Examples of appropriate emotions (and emotion sequences) are shown in table 5.3.

Table 5.3 Rossiter and Percy's hypothesised relationships linking emotions to motivations*

Negative motives	Emotional sequence
1 Problem removal	Annoyed → relieved
2 Problem avoidance	Fearful → relaxed
3 Incomplete satisfaction	Disappointed → optimistic
4 Mixed approach-avoidance	Conflicted → reassured
5 Normal depletion	Mildly annoyed → content
Positive motives emotional sequence	
6 Sensory gratification	Dull (or neutral) → joyful
7 Intellectual stimulation/mastery	Bored (or neutral) → excited
	Naive (or neutral) → competent
8 Social approval	Apprehensive (or neutral) → flattered
9 Social conformity*	Indecisive (or neutral) → belonging
10 Self-approval*	Conflict (or neutral) → serene, confident

* Adapted from Rossiter & Percy 1997, with the ninth and tenth motives added by Donovan et al. 1995

Emotional appeals

Whereas the emphasis in health and injury prevention campaigns has often been on fear arousal, recent research suggests that a number of emotions other than fear are relevant in social marketing campaign messages (Bagozzi & Moore 1994; Stout & Sego 1994). For example, road safety campaigns in Australia focus on the guilt and remorse experienced by drivers who injure or kill others by their speeding or drink driving (Grey Advertising 1990). Other appropriate emotions for road safety advertising include the following (Donovan et al. 1995):

- *sadness*—at the loss or serious injury of a loved one, the impact on others of the loss or serious injury of a loved one, etc.
- *guilt or remorse*—at having unintentionally caused the loss or serious injury of a loved one, for not having heeded advice that could have avoided the negative consequence, etc.
- *surprise*—at information such as: the dose response relationship between speed and injury, the relationship between speed and distance travelled in a moment's distraction
- *anger*—at the irresponsible behaviours or attitudes of speeding or drinking drivers, etc
- *fear, anxiety*—about the possibility of detection, about the loss or serious injury of a loved one, personal injury, loss of licence, etc
- *shame, embarrassment*—being caught for any offence, but particularly for a socially despised offence, etc
- *acceptance, warmth, love*—for complying with another's request to drive safely, protection of the vehicle's occupants (especially children), etc
- *peace of mind, relief*—at removal of anxiety and tension by compliance.

Morality and legitimacy

Morality refers to the individual's beliefs about whether certain actions are right or wrong, or whether they should or should not take that action. Legitimacy refers to individuals' beliefs about whether laws are justified, whether these laws are applied equally, and whether punishments for transgression are fair (Tyler 1990). The concept of legitimacy applies not just to legislation, but also to rules, regulations, and policies. In general, people are more likely to obey rules that they believe are justified and are enforced in a fair and unbiased manner. With some reflection, and given the use of laws to regulate and influence behaviour, both concepts could have considerable relevance in areas of social marketing. However, they have been largely neglected in social change models, and particularly in public health research and intervention strategies.

This neglect is surprising given the historical links between health and (religious) morality (Thomas 1997) and the fact that Fishbein's theory of reasoned action originally included the concept of moral or personal norms (Fishbein 1967; Fishbein & Ajzen 1975). Triandis (1977) included personal normative beliefs, but his model has attracted little attention in health and social interventions. Furthermore, legislation is widely used to regulate a broad range of activities such as driving behaviours, underage alcohol and tobacco consumption, drug use, land degradation and toxic waste disposal, lighting fires in forests, littering behaviour, physical abuse, child abuse and neglect, and so on. Hence, it is important to assess people's perceived legitimacy of the laws and the authorities behind the laws in these areas.

Norman and Connor (1996) found only a few studies that incorporated measures of moral norms within the public health domain. Such studies include explaining altruism and helping behaviour such as donating blood (Pomazal & Jaccard 1976; Zuckerman & Reis 1978) and intentions to donate organs (Schwartz & Tessler 1972). Other studies have found measures of moral norms to be predictive of recycling behaviour (Vining & Ebreo 1992; Allen, Fuller & Glaser 1994), eating genetically produced food (Sparks, Shepherd & Frewer 1995), buying milk (Raats 1992), using condoms (Godin & Kok 1996) and committing driving violations (Parker, Manstead & Stradling 1995).

Few public health and public policy campaigns have considered the use of moral or legitimacy appeals. In Australia moral norms have been considered in the context of road safety behaviours (Donovan & Batini 1997; Homel, Carseldine & Kearns et al. 1988) and in the use of performance-enhancing drugs in sport (Donovan & Egger 1997; Mugford, Mugford & Donnelly 1999). Donovan (1997) included an individual's personal morality in his model of factors that influence underage drinking, but carried out no empirical studies. However, to our knowledge, no Australian (or overseas) school, community, or mass media campaigns targeting substance use have been explicitly based on morality concepts or have included components on legitimacy. The USA has used legitimacy in some contexts: 'Buckle Up. It's the Law.'

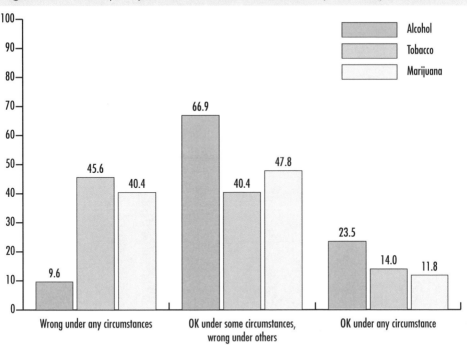

Figure 5.7 Moral perceptions of alcohol, tobacco, and marijuana use (per cent)

Noting the strong body of research supporting the empirical relation of moral reasoning development to criminal behaviours (see Tyler 1990; 1997) and behaviours such as delinquency, honesty, altruism, and conformity (Blasi 1980), Amonini (2001) looked at youths' perceptions of the morality of alcohol, tobacco, and marijuana use and the legitimacy of the laws governing the use of these substances. She found strong relationships between alcohol, tobacco, and marijuana use and youths' perceptions of morality and legitimacy (figures 5.7–5.10).

Figure 5.7 shows that many young people do consider alcohol and tobacco use to be moral issues. At least three out of four respondents considered the use of alcohol (76 per cent), tobacco (86 per cent), and marijuana (88 per cent) as morally wrong under some or any circumstances. Respondents tended to be less accepting of tobacco and marijuana use than of alcohol use; nearly half of the students thought tobacco (46 per cent) and marijuana (40 per cent) use were wrong under any circumstances, but only one in ten (10 per cent) thought drinking alcohol was wrong under any circumstances.

Figures 5.8–5.10 show the relationship between overall perceptions of morality and tobacco, alcohol, and marijuana consumption respectively. It is clear that young people who see substance use as morally wrong under any circumstances are far less likely to use these substances—and vice versa. A greater proportion of non-current cigarette smokers (57 per cent) compared to current

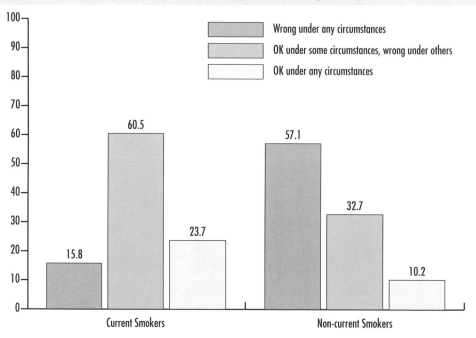

Figure 5.8 Moral perceptions of tobacco by tobacco use (per cent)

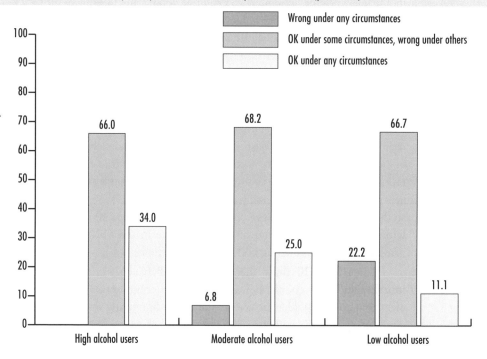

Figure 5.9 Moral perceptions of alcohol by alcohol use (per cent)

Figure 5.10 Moral perceptions of marijuana by marijuana use (per cent)

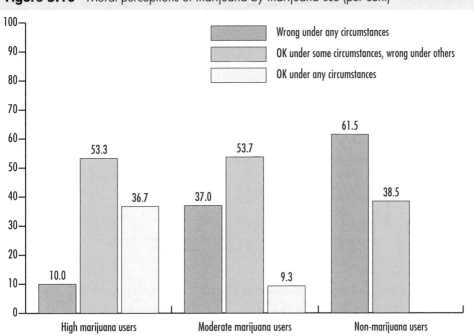

smokers (16 per cent) thought smoking was wrong under any circumstances. Conversely, more current smokers (60 per cent and 24 per cent) compared to non-current smokers (33 per cent and 10 per cent) thought smoking was all right under some or any circumstances, respectively ($\alpha = 0.00$).

Similarly, none of the high alcohol users and only 7 per cent of the moderate alcohol users indicated drinking was wrong under any circumstances, compared to 22 per cent of the low alcohol users, and a greater proportion of non-marijuana users (62 per cent) compared to infrequent (37 per cent) and frequent users (10 per cent) indicated that 'using marijuana is wrong under any circumstances'.

Amonini (2001) suggested that interventions, including student discussion of the moral issues surrounding substance use (and abuse), may prove effective in postponing or even preventing substance use, particularly tobacco and marijuana consumption, or reducing excess use of these substances.

Diffusion theory

Everett Rogers first published his book *Diffusion of Innovations* in 1962. The concept has been readily adopted in commercial marketing (to predict new product adoption) and widely used in developing countries (for example, adoption of agricultural methods and public health measures), but has only in the past 10 years or so attracted much attention in the public health area in developed countries. Although the model is more of a process or stage model, it is

Figure 5.11 Diffusion of innovations

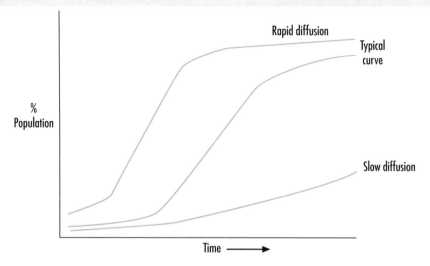

included here for its concepts related to the characteristics of innovations that facilitate and inhibit adoption.

Rogers (1995, p. 5) defines 'diffusion' as 'the process by which an innovation is communicated through certain channels over time among the members of a social system'. Diffusion theory applies to both planned and unplanned diffusions and to both desirable and undesirable innovations (for example, the rapid adoption of the cocaine variant crack in the USA). Figure 5.11 shows the rate of diffusion of three innovations. From the social change practitioner's point of view one of the major issues is how the rate of adoption of the new idea, product, or behaviour can be accelerated. Figure 5.11 shows that many innovations take off at about the 20 per cent adoption mark when, according to Rogers (1995, p. 12), 'interpersonal networks become activated so that a critical mass of adopters begins using an innovation'.

Each of the four main elements in diffusion—the innovation, communication channels, time, and the social system—will be discussed in turn.

The innovation

An innovation is an idea, product, or practice that is perceived as new by the adopting population, that is, it need not be objectively new. The main area of study here is on the attributes of the innovation that influence its rate of adoption.

Relative advantage

If the new object or practice is clearly seen to be better than the old it will be adopted more readily. Relative advantage can be assessed in a variety of ways, including convenience, economy, prestige, and time. Email is much faster than postal mail; automated rubbish trucks are perceived to be more economical than manned trucks.

Compatibility

The more the new object or practice is consistent with current values and past experiences the more readily it will be adopted. Family planning and STD prevention practices face this attribute in countries where cultural and religious values are opposed to them. Automatic teller machines are incompatible with many people's desire for personal interactions.

Complexity

New practices and ideas that are easy to understand are more readily adopted than those that are difficult to understand or that require special skills and training. User friendly software was a major factor in the rates of adoption of office and home computers.

Trialability

Being able to trial a new product or practice reduces the risk of the new product not delivering the promised benefits and allows the adopter to learn about the innovation before adoption. New grains can be trialled in limited agricultural plots. Copy machines were initially placed in offices and the owners were charged on a per copy basis. The more a product or practice can be trialed before purchase, the greater the rate of adoption.

Observability

The more the innovation—and its results—are visible, the greater the rate of adoption. Observability provides greater exposure as well as stimulating social discussion. Mobile phone adoption was clearly helped by visibility of use—and clear demonstration of effectiveness in communication.

Communication channels

Mass media channels are the most effective way of creating awareness for a new idea, product, or practice, whereas interpersonal channels are the most effective way of getting the target audience to accept and adopt the new idea (Rogers 1995). This applies particularly to where the change agent and the target group have the same background, social status, or similar values (Cialdini 1984). Rogers states that a major impediment to most planned social diffusions is that the change agent and the target are quite dissimilar (heterophyllous). Tupperware's use of party hosts to sell products to their friends is a very good example of acknowledging that persuasion occurs best between people of similar interests. Similarly, Indigenous youth prefer Indigenous people to deliver alcohol and other health messages (Donovan et al. 1997c).

Interpersonal influences

The California 'Stop AIDS' project began with a series of group discussions to inform the development of messages for a media campaign. However, on following up group participants on another matter the researchers noted that participants volunteered that their beliefs and attitudes about negotiating safe sex and their safe sex practices had changed dramatically as a result of participation in the group discussions. Hence, the planned media intervention was dropped and the funds expended on recruiting gay men to run more and more focus groups. Men in the early groups were asked if they would like to lead a similar group. Those interested were given a brief training in group moderation, further information about HIV/AIDS, and so on. This led to the SafetyNet© program: inhome parties modelled on the Tupperware party, to educate gay men about safe sex (AIDS Action Committee 1989).

The importance of interpersonal networks in the diffusion process is one of the most important concepts of the diffusion process and hence for community development interventions.

Time

Time can be noted on an individual basis in the sense of the time taken to move from awareness, through persuasion, to decision, and adoption. Some decision processes are relatively brief; others may take several months.

Time also can be considered in the sense of some people adopting the innovation soon after its introduction (early adopters) while others only adopt after the vast majority have adopted (laggards). In general, five groups are noted: innovators (the first 2–3 per cent), early adopters (the next 10–15 per cent), the early majority (the next 30–33 per cent), the late majority (the next 30–33 per cent), and the laggards (the final 17–20 per cent). Effort expended on identifying the innovators and early adopters can result in a more efficiently planned diffusion.

Finally, as shown in figure 5.11, the rate of adoption can vary from very rapid to quite slow.

The social system

The social structure also influences the rate of adoption. Variables here include the extent to which communication channels exist, the presence or absence of strong opinion leaders, the prevailing social norms and their variation between parts of the system, whether the adoption decision is an individual one or must involve collective decision making or a single authority's decision, and whether adoption of the innovation has desirable and undesirable consequences, not just for the individual but also for the social system as a whole. Rudd (2003) analyses how health policies diffuse through to general practice, given the nature of general practice and the attitudes and beliefs of GPs about their role in the health system. Social system factors appear particularly important in developing countries and, for example, in Indigenous communities in Australia.

Table 5.4	Behaviour modification strategies	
	Procedure-following behaviour	
Consequence type	Deliver consequence	Remove consequence
Good/pleasant	positive reinforcement (increases response)	negative punishment (decreases response)
Bad/unpleasant	positive punishment (decreases response)	negative reinforcement (increases response)

Behaviour modification–applied behavioural analysis

The terms 'behaviour modification' and 'applied behaviour analysis' are generally interchangeable. We will primarily use the term 'behaviour modification', which is defined as 'the systematic application of principles derived from learning theory to altering environment–behaviour relationships in order to strengthen adaptive and weaken maladaptive behaviours' (Elder, Geller, Hovell & Mayer 1994, p. 128). Behaviour modification is based on the assumption that behaviour is determined by environmental antecedents and consequences. Hence, interventions are designed on the ABC model—antecedents, behaviour, consequences (Elder et al. 1994; Geller 1989).

Many social marketing campaigns, particularly in road safety and public health, are aimed at decreasing undesired behaviours: do not drink and drive, do not exceed .05 if driving, reduce speed, eat less fat, quit smoking, reduce alcohol consumption, and so on.

At the same time, other campaigns are aimed at increasing desired behaviours: switch to light beer if drinking and driving, eat more fruit'n'veg, be smoke-free, walk to the bus stop/up the stairs/to the shop, and so on. The question in many situations therefore is whether the emphasis should be on increasing the desired behaviour or on decreasing the undesired behaviour. For example, for targeting obesity in children should we focus on reducing the time spent watching television and playing video games (that is, reduce inactivity) or focus on increasing the children's level of physical activity? Regardless of the answer the lesson from behaviour modification/applied behavioural analysis is that different strategies are appropriate for increasing behaviours versus for decreasing behaviours. This is particularly important for message strategies in communication materials and for direct behavioural interventions.

Beginning with the goal of increasing a behaviour or decreasing a behaviour, table 5.4 delineates two methods for increasing a behaviour (reinforcement strategies) and two ways of decreasing a behaviour (punishment strategies). Each depends on whether the consequence is delivered (positive) or removed (negative) as a result of the behaviour occurring.

Reinforcement—increasing a behaviour

There are two ways of increasing a response.

- *Positive reinforcement*: the behaviour is followed by a pleasant consequence (for example, group socialising after exercise).
- *Negative reinforcement*: the behaviour is followed by removal of an unpleasant situation (for example, headache and tension gone after meditation).

Punishment—decreasing a behaviour

There are two ways of decreasing a response.

- *Positive punishment*: the behaviour is followed by an unpleasant consequence (for example, speeding is followed by a fine).
- *Negative punishment* (or response cost): the behaviour is followed by removal of a pleasant situation (for example, drink driving is followed by a loss of licence and hence limitations on mobility and socialising).

Two other processes are also relevant:

Extinction

A behaviour will decrease if previously applied positive consequences are discontinued or barriers prevent their being obtained. For example, walking may decrease if aesthetic features of the environment are removed or friends are no longer available to walk with. Blood-donating behaviour will decline if donors have to visit a central location rather than donating at the worksite.

Response facilitation

A behaviour will strengthen or reemerge if a punishment or response cost is discontinued. For example, an athlete may revert to using performance-enhancing drugs when the level of random testing is reduced or speeding behaviour returns after speed camera usage declines.

In designing interventions, formative research is necessary to determine what are the appropriate reinforcers and punishments for the intervention targets. For example, Egger's GutBusters® program for men emphasised the looking good benefit of weight loss and increased physical activity rather than health benefits. Rossiter and Percy's motives provide a framework here; some people may be motivated primarily by social recognition rewards, others by financial incentives, still others by gifts. Young males fear the loss of their driving licence more than the threat of physical harm to themselves.

Feedback on positive results, such as number of accident-free days in a workplace, is an important reinforcer. Advocates should remember that, as well as writing to politicians and policy makers they wish to persuade, they should also write with reinforcing messages to those already onside, thanking them for their support.

Another lesson from behaviour modification is to identify the reinforcers of the behaviours we wish to reduce or eliminate. Such an understanding is liable to lead to more sustained change if attempts are then made to either substitute benign reinforcers or take away the need for the reinforcers in the first place. For example, much alcohol and drug abuse is related to escaping from reality.

While rewards and response costs can be instituted in practice (lower insurance premiums for non-smokers, loss of driver's licence for unsafe drivers), punishments are more difficult to introduce in non-legal situations. However, all of the above strategies can be depicted and modelled in communication materials. As noted earlier, threat appeals (positive punishment and response costs) are widespread in social marketing.

Most of the above deals with the behaviour–consequence link. Interventions can also facilitate the desired behavioural response by looking at the antecedent–behaviour link (Elder et al. 1994; Geller 1989):

- environments should be designed to make the behaviour change easy, such as worksite exercise rooms and showers
- reminder signs can be very effective; a 'Take the stairs' sign placed near a lift increased use of the stairs dramatically; 'Belt up' signs at carpark exits increase seat belt usage
- opinion leaders, experts, and celebrities can be used to demonstrate the behaviour or wear clothing promoting the behaviour
- target individuals can be encouraged to make public commitments to adopt the desired behaviour
- educational materials with behavioural tips are also useful; quitting smokers are encouraged to identify environmental cues that trigger smoking and to remove them
- education sessions should include interactive demonstrations rather than just passive lecturing (Tell them and they'll forget—Demonstrate and they'll remember—Involve them and they'll understand).

While some planning models include a number of the above concepts (for example, Green & Kreuter's (1991) PRECEDE–PROCEED model; see chapter 13), there has been limited systematic integration of behaviour modification concepts into social marketing programs. Geller (1989) provides an integrative example for environmental issues, while Elder et al. (1994) provide a number of examples of the concepts in practice.

Synthesising the models

It is clear that many of these models have similar concepts, but that no one model includes all relevant concepts. We advocate a pragmatic, eclectic approach, selecting concepts from each of the models depending on which are more or less applicable to the behaviour in question.

Assume an adult is at risk for diabetes Type II. The above models suggest the following questions need answering to develop appropriate interventions.

1 *What is the individual's perceived likelihood of contracting diabetes, given no change in their current behaviour?*

   What beliefs or perceptions underlie this perceived likelihood?

   If the perceived likelihood is unrealistically low, what sort of information, presented in what way, and by whom, might increase this likelihood?

     What is their knowledge of the causes of diabetes?

2   *What is the individual's perceived severity of contracting diabetes?*

     Is this realistic? If not, what sort of information, presented in what way, and by whom might change this perception?

3   *What is the individual's attitude toward adopting the recommended alternative behaviours such as a change in diet or adoption of exercise?*

     Are some behaviours more acceptable than others? Why?

     What are the perceived benefits of continuing the risk behaviours?

     What are the perceived benefits and the disbenefits of the alternative behaviours?

     What social and physical environment barriers inhibit adoption of the recommended dietary and exercise behaviours? What facilitators exist?

4   *What is the individual's perceived likelihood of averting the threat if the recommended behaviours are adopted?*

     If this is low, on what beliefs is this perception based? What information might change this perception?

5   *What are the individual's beliefs about their ability to adopt the recommended behaviours?*

     On what beliefs are these efficacy perceptions based?

     Is skills training required?

     What intermediate goals can be set to induce trial?

6   *What appear to be the major motivations that would induce trial of the recommended behaviours?*

     Are positive benefits (feelings of wellness, increased capacity for physical activity) more motivating than negative benefits (avoidance of disease) for some individuals or groups and vice versa for others?

7   *What are the individual's main sources of information for health?*

     Who are their major influencers?

     Who might be additional credible sources of information and influence?

8   *How does the individual's social interactions, including their extended family, club memberships, employment, and homecare role influence their health beliefs and behaviours?*

9   *Does the individual exhibit any personality characteristics that might inhibit or facilitate the adoption of healthy behaviours?*

10 *What are the individual's perceptions of social norms with respect to the recommended behaviours?*

     Does the individual see the recommended behaviours as compatible with their social roles and self-image?

11 *What are the individual's perceptions of the morality of non-compliance with the recommended behaviour and consistency with internalised values?*

12 *On a broader scale, what is the extent of GPs' knowledge of diabetes risk factors and their willingness to undertake preventative measures with patients exhibiting these risk factors?*

13 *What factors exist in the individual's social, economic, work, and physical environments that facilitate and inhibit attendance at diabetes screening?*

14 *What factors exist in the individual's social, economic, work, and physical environments that facilitate and inhibit healthy eating and exercise habits?*

15 *What are health bureaucrats' knowledge of diabetes and their attitudes towards allocating funds to prevention?*

High five: the words of the experts

In a rather remarkable summit meeting, the US National Institutes of Mental Health managed to bring together Albert Bandura (social cognitive learning theory), Marshall Becker (health belief model), Martin Fishbein (theory of reasoned action), Harry Triandis (theory of subjective culture and interpersonal behaviour), and Frederick Kanfer (theory of self-regulation and self-control), in Washington DC in October 1991. The objective was to distil from all these individuals' models implications for developing AIDS interventions (Fishbein et al. 1991).

The five theorists decided on a set of eight variables that predict and explain behaviour: intention, environmental constraints, ability, anticipated outcomes (or attitude), norms, self-standards, emotion, and self-efficacy (see text).

Behavioural scientists have now generally come to the following set of principles that guide the framework for interventions (Fishbein et al. 1991; Elder et al. 1994).

For an individual to perform a recommended behaviour

- they must have formed an intention to perform the behaviour or made a (public) commitment to do so
- there must be no physical or structural environmental constraints that prevent the behaviour being performed
- the individual must have the skills and equipment necessary to perform the behaviour
- the individual must perceive themselves to be capable of performing the behaviour
- the individual must consider that the benefits and rewards of performing the behaviour outweigh the costs and disbenefits associated with performing the behaviour, including the rewards associated with not performing the behaviour (that is, have a positive attitude towards performing the behaviour)
- social normative pressure to perform the behaviour must be perceived to be greater than social normative pressure not to perform the behaviour
- the individual must perceive the behaviour to be consistent with their self-image and internalised behaviours (that is, morally acceptable)
- the individual must perceive the behaviour to be consistent with their social roles
- the individual's emotional reaction (or expectation) to performing the behaviour must be more positive than negative.

In general, Fishbein et al. (1991) consider that the first three are necessary and sufficient for behaviour to occur. Hence, if a violent man has formed a strong intention to call a helpline about his violence, if a telephone is easily accessible, and if the call can be made in private and with assured confidentiality, it is likely that the behaviour will occur. The remainder of the above variables primarily influence intention or facilitate or inhibit translating the intention into action.

Concluding comment

The models described in this chapter apply equally to beliefs and attitudes about the behaviours of interest as well as the beliefs and attitudes about the social and political issues related to those behaviours. Hence, these models are useful not only for developing campaigns to promote healthy behaviours, but also for developing advocacy campaigns.

Chapter 6

Research and Evaluation

Introduction

Research and evaluation require specialist technical expertise. This chapter aims more to facilitate interaction with such experts rather than impart research skills. After distinguishing between qualitative and quantitative research and presenting some of the major qualitative research methods (after Close & Donovan 1998) we describe the research framework of the US National Academy of Sciences (Coyle, Boruch & Turner 1989) as an overarching framework for research and evaluation. The emphasis will be on qualitative research because this is where strategy development comes from and where there is perhaps least understanding. Given that much of the application of social marketing is in public health we then define the public health research concepts of prevalence and incidence, describe epidemiological studies, and note how to interpret logistic regression odds ratios, one of the major tools in public health research. Given that much formative and experimental research measures behavioural intentions as the dependent variable, we also comment on the relationship between intentions and behaviour, concluding with a brief discussion on research in Indigenous and culturally and linguistically diverse (CALD) communities.

Qualitative versus quantitative research

The most common distinctions made between quantitative and qualitative research are as follows (much of the following is based on Close & Donovan 1998).

- Qualitative research is designed to identify, describe, and explain people's points of view, whereas quantitative research is designed to measure how many people hold each of these points of view.

■ Qualitative research methods consist of semistructured, open-ended questioning techniques, in which the responses are subject to varying degrees of interpretation, whereas quantitative research methods consist mostly of structured, closed-ended questioning techniques, in which there is little variation in degrees of interpretation.

Qualitative research attempts to identify the different attitudes people hold and to explore how these attitudes were formed. It probes the influence of factors such as people's values, past experiences, sources of information, peers, family, the media, and sociocultural institutions on the development of these attitudes and their expression in behaviours. It generates grounded theories or hypotheses about the relationships between these variables and behaviours, which can be tested in further qualitative research, but more likely via quantitative research methods. The nature of such relationships is based on the interpretation of the researcher. Such an understanding provides clues as to what type of interventions would be most effective (whether persuasion could be effective whether legislation would be accepted, whether education alone would be sufficient, etc.).

The major qualitative techniques are focus groups, paired interviews (especially for children and adolescents), individual depth interviews (IDIs), and ethnographic methods such as participant and non-participant observation. The validity of qualitative research findings is largely determined by the skill of the interviewer. Hence, it is essential that properly trained indepth interviewers and focus group moderators be used to gain benefit from the research and to avoid incorrect strategies that are based on misinterpretation of qualitative data.

Much of qualitative research questioning is open-ended (see box; note that the interviewer asks neutral questions, avoids leading questions, and is completely non-judgmental. This is very important in areas such as health and social policy where people might give socially desirable answers.)

Quantitative research attempts to determine what proportions of the population hold the various attitudes and behave in certain ways. It attempts to iden-

Qualitative versus quantitative research methods

	Qualitative	Quantitative
Questions	Semi-structured	Structured
Answers	Open-ended Paraverbal Non-verbal Non-response	Closed-ended (answer categories, rating)
Interviewer	Interactive	Passive
Interviewee	Participant	Respondent
Analysis	Descriptive (basic) Inferential (advanced)	Statistical Descriptive, with some inference
Sample Size	Small (can replicate to increase reliability)	Usually large
Data Sampling Unit	Points of view	People, households, buying units

Example of open-ended questioning*

Q *What is it you like about attending a festival movie?*

A Well, it's very different from going to an ordinary movie.

Q *In what way is it different?*

A It's more of a special event ... You look forward to it more, and there's more excitement in the crowd.

Q *How do you mean?*

A I think there's a greater sense of expectation in the atmosphere and that the movie is going to be different from the ordinary run-of-the-mill Hollywood types.

Q *How do you mean 'different'?*

A I'm a bit of a movie fan, so I'm interested in different directors, how screenplays appear and things like the camera work. Some of the festival movies are interesting because they include a lot of techniques you wouldn't see otherwise.

Q *You also mentioned a different atmosphere at festival movies. What did you mean?*

A There's an extra buzz 'cos you feel part of the festival ... like being a member of a special group—and you know the movie possibly wouldn't get here ordinarily, so you feel that you're seeing something that a lot of other people won't get to see.

Q *Tell me a little more about feeling part of the festival?*

A Well, I suppose I don't go to many what you might call highbrow things like the theatre and ballet, but many of my friends and other people I know do. Going to a festival movie makes me feel like I am getting a bit of culture and gives me something in common with these other people—I can join in their conversations about what's going on during the festival.

Note that as the above questions are open-ended different interviewers might have followed up different aspects of the first response and hence got different data. In addition, people can interpret the above statements differently. Two researchers' conclusions might be as follows.

* Close & Donovan 1998

Qualitative data: same data, possible different interpretations

Researcher A

This person primarily attends festival movies because they are seen to be far more enjoyable than mainstream movies, and because the festival offers them a chance to be among the first—or only—local people to see the particular movies. It is this opportunity of a more interesting somewhat exclusive experience that is the primary motivation.

Researcher B

This person primarily attends festival movies because their desired self-image, and the image they want to project to others, includes being seen to be interested in cultural events. However, they have little interest in and rarely attend any live performance event, but they do like going to movies. Hence, the festival—because of its cultural image and the person's perceptions of the sorts of people who attend festival events—provides an opportunity to bolster their desired self-image in a way that fits with what they already enjoy doing.

tify and quantify using statistical methods, the extent of relationships between the identified points of view, and sorts of factors listed above. Quantitative research is associated primarily with survey methods and experimental research, especially randomised control trials. Quantitative methods—such as regression, factor analysis, and correspondence analysis—also allow the exploration of the (mathematical or statistical) relationship between variables.

Main qualitative research methods

Qualitative research methods originated from psychology and are most associated with probing people's psyches for hidden motivations and underlying psychodynamics. Much of the early qualitative research emphasised the uncovering of such motivations, as popularised in Vance Packard's book *The Hidden Persuaders* and, in research circles, by Ernest Dichter's *Handbook of Consumer Motivations*. These days, the emphasis has shifted to more of a phenomenological observation approach, that is, using qualitative research to learn how people talk about, think about, and feel about various products, services, and issues, rather than delving into deep Freudian or Jungian (or whoever's) interpretations of what people say.

The two main qualitative research methods are

- individual depth interviews (IDIs)
- focus group discussions.

Individual depth interviews

IDIs are one-on-one, usually face-to-face interviews, lasting anywhere from 45 minutes to several hours. This sort of minimum time is required to allow the interviewer to establish trust and rapport with the respondent so that the respondent feels comfortable in revealing the information sought, some of which might be very personal.

The interviewer has a list of topics to cover, but there is no requirement to stick to the order. In fact, good interviewers use the respondent's answers to

Qualitative research is used when

- little is known about the area
- there is a need to know how attitudes are formed
- there is a need to identify motivations
- there is a need to understand how motivations are relevant
- there is a need to learn the language of the target audience

and for

- exploring reactions to communication materials, merchandise, and interventions
- observing interaction among peoples
- piloting questionnaires
- generating new ideas
- but NOT pretesting ads for go–no go decisions.

IDI topic outline

- What issues in your neighbourhood and suburb concern you most? List, and for each one, probe why.
- Which of these issues, if any, would you attend a community meeting on if there were going to be any local council policy changes? Probe and explore why for each reason mentioned.
- How useful do you think these sorts of community meetings are? Do you think that local government takes notice of what people say? Does the state government? Who do you think they listen most to?
- Are you aware of any instances in your suburb or anywhere else where the residents got organised and overturned a government decision? What was it? Why were they successful?
- Last community event attended—if any: Probe all details: who went with, expectations, and whether or not fulfilled.

follow up and explore issues rather than sticking to a rigid sequence. Part of an IDI topic or question outline for a survey attempting to explore what motivates people to attend (or not attend) community issues meetings is shown in the box above.

Laddering or benefit chaining questioning

One questioning procedure that is very useful, even in brief interviews, is called laddering (or benefit chaining). Benefit chaining attempts to go beyond first responses to identify end benefits and beyond the physical or tangible attributes to determine what benefits these attributes give.

For example, low fat is a physical attribute of an icecream, but the end benefit sought by the consumer might be weight loss, or weight control, or less likelihood of heart disease, or being able to eat an extra piece of cake. Benefit chaining is useful to identify the different benefits sought by different types of consumers. In fact, benefits sought is a major way of segmenting some markets.

Here are two examples from Close and Donovan (1998) of a laddering question interchange, in which the physical attribute 'strong' is benefit chained to establish psychological end benefits.

Q *What brand of coffee do you drink?*

A Maxwell House.

Q *Why do you drink Maxwell House?*

A Because it's strong coffee.

Q *What's good about strong coffee?*

A It keeps me awake.

Q *And why is that important/what's good about that?*

A I get more work done.

Q *And why is that important/what's good about that?*

A My productivity rating looks good to my manager.

Qualitative techniques

- Focus groups (mini, standard, extended)
- Individual depth interviews

- Point-of-use, point-of-purchase interviews
- Participant observation
- External observation

- Projective techniques (associative, TAT, picture sorts, shopping lists)
- Laddering or benefit chaining
- Imagery generation
- Cognitive response measures (including emotion measures)

Q And why is that important/what's good about that?

A I get praised and it improves my promotion prospects.

Q And why is that important/what's good about that?

A I feel good about myself. I feel like I'm achieving my goals.

One can imagine the sort of television commercial that might result from this interview: busy office, ambitious yuppie working into the night, a jar of Maxwell House prominently displayed on the work desk, an approving boss smiling in appreciation as the yuppie leaves the office, yuppie looking pleased as Punch.

On the other hand, the interview might go like this for someone else.

Q What brand of coffee do you drink?

A Maxwell House.

Q Why do you drink Maxwell house?

A Because it's strong coffee.

Q What's good about strong coffee?

A I just love the taste and smell of coffee. So the stronger, the better.

Again, one can imagine the sort of television commercial that might be developed to reach this segment type: terrific visuals of rich brown coffee beans pouring into a giant Maxwell House coffee jar. Cut to mug of steaming, rich brown coffee being held in someone's hand. Pull back to show person enjoying the (presumably) rich aroma, then sipping the coffee. A satisfied 'Mmmm ...'

If the question were about physical activity and the person said they like going for a run, the line of questioning would attempt to elicit what was liked— and why.

Q What sorts of things do you like about going for a run?

A I love the feeling of freedom and being alone.

Q What's good to you about being alone?

A I can concentrate on my breathing and get really relaxed once I hit my rhythm.

Q *And what's good about that? What do you get from that?*

A For that period of time I'm somewhere else, I'm totally oblivious to all my day-to-day problems. It's a complete escape.

Q *And what's good about that?*

A Afterwards I feel renewed, energetic, and enthused. It's a great feeling.

Focus group discussions

Focus groups generally consist of

- six to nine individuals (that is, a manageable number so everyone can join in)
- people who are selected because of their relevance to the research objectives
- people who sit around and talk about the topic of interest under the guidance of a group moderator
- people who generally work from a topic outline in the same way as for IDIs
- a structure in which the questioning should be flexible rather than rigidly following a sequence of questions.

With the permission of the group members (see the Market Research Society of Australia's Code of Professional Behaviour) the groups are usually audio and/or videotaped for later analysis. They may also be videotaped for the client to watch or, at some research companies' premises, may be viewed directly via a one-way mirror.

Participants are served refreshments and are currently paid from $30 to $50 for attending.

Focus groups (or just group discussions) are the most used (and, some would argue, misused) technique in qualitative research. They were originally called focus groups because the usual procedure was to discuss broad issues and then focus in on the particular area of interest. This probably stemmed from the psychological approach, in which the clinician, quite appropriately, attempted to place a person's problem in the total context of their lives rather than treat the problem as an isolated issue.

This broad-to-specific approach is appropriate for much of what qualitative research is used for now. For example, to more fully understand a person's physical activity or eating habits, it is useful—some would say essential—to first get an overview of people's leisure and work activities in general, which would include understanding also their family and other institutional involvements. If we want to understand mothers' food choices for their children we need to understand what it is like bringing up children in general. Concerns for nutrition often take second place to convenience and what the child will readily accept. When mum is busy getting the family dinner, a Mars bar (this is not a paid placement) or packet of Smith's crisps (ditto) served up in front of the television at least promises some peace, however temporary. This broader approach allows a better understanding of wider sociocultural influences on motivations and behaviour.

On the other hand, group discussions are often used to get reactions to specific things such as brochures, advertisements, packaging, new products, piloting questionnaires, etc. In these cases the group usually focuses on the specific task from the beginning.

Where do these group participants come from?

Most research companies either keep databases of people who have previously expressed their willingness to take part in consumer research groups (perhaps when they have taken part in a street or home interview), or recruit via cold calling at random from telephone directories, or sometimes place ads on the radio or in community newspapers.

Sometimes researchers will approach organisations (sporting or social clubs, for example) and offer the organisation an incentive if the organisation can supply a number of people who fit the desired demographic or other characteristics. Such groups are called affinity groups and there is some disagreement among researchers as to their value. While they do have their uses, in general we recommend against using affinity groups—unless the research objective is to understand the role of that particular organisation in its members' lives and in the issue at hand.

In health and social policy areas most of the time we are dealing with general population groups. However, we are frequently dealing with professionals: service providers, policy makers, funders, carer support groups, etc. These can be recruited from staff lists, often with the assistance of the client, or they are identifiable in the area under study. Organisations also provide access to their clients for research purposes (with the permission of the client) (for example, people receiving income support).

Group and IDI recruiting

Ensuring the appropriateness of the people selected to participate in the groups or IDIs is the single most important aspect of qualitative research. Hence, a screening questionnaire is administered to potential participants to ensure that they fit the required characteristics.

The research objectives determine the overall characteristics of people required. For example, if the aim is to determine what differentiates full-strength beer drinkers from mid-strength beer drinkers and what promotional or other incentives (if any) might be used to get full-strength drinkers to switch to mid-strength, groups should be chosen on the basis of current consumption—perhaps two groups of mid-strength drinkers (to find out why they switched) and then two groups of full-strength drinkers to assess reaction to the motives and benefits identified in the mid-strength groups. Henley and Donovan (2002), to study people's motivations to change and the decision processes they went through during these changes, recruited two groups of people who had made a

Screening questions for recruiting by attitude to discuss Aboriginal issues

How do you feel about the following issues?
- Are you in favour of, against, or have no feelings either way about Aboriginal land rights?
- Are you in favour of, against, or have no feelings either way about a treaty with Aboriginal people?
- Are you in favour of, against, or have no feelings either way about a formal apology being given to those called the stolen generation of Aboriginal people?
- Those answering 'against' to any two of these go together
- Those answering 'in favour' to any two of these go together
Those in between can form a third grouping.

deliberate decision in the past 6 months to do more exercise and had done so, and two groups comprising people who had made and carried out a deliberate decision to eat more healthily.

A number of other aspects are important for group recruiting in particular. One of the most important relates to the homogeneity of the group. Group studies show that the more homogeneous the group (that is, the more the group members have in common), the better the group interaction and individual member participation. Hence, as far as possible—and depending on the research objectives—groups should be homogeneous with respect to age categories, gender, and, especially where costs of activities are important (for example, discussing leisure and recreation pursuits), income or socioeconomic status (SES).

Attitudes should be a major criterion for recruiting. For example, in recruiting groups to talk about Aboriginal issues, including reconciliation, Donovan Research (Donovan 1992a) used a set of questions to identify those negative and those positive towards Aboriginal issues (see box). Screening this way allowed far more negative attitudes and beliefs to be expressed by participants as they realised they were among like-minded people than when this was not the case.

Screening criteria can be dynamic

In a series of group discussions on parenting and the place of children in society Donovan Research (Donovan & Francas 1987) first screened potential group members on dimensions such as children or no children, children's ages, SES, single- versus two-parent household, and step-parent household. Early groups revealed that the way many parents dealt with their children was related to

Group homogeneity breeds individual security

The more homogeneous the group, the more group members feel they are in the company of others like themselves. This sense of familiarity breeds security and a freedom to express their feelings without fear of being misunderstood or being unduly criticised.

their own childhood. Later groups were then recruited on this question: 'Would you describe your childhood as happy or unhappy or mixed?'. (Pretesting showed a reluctance of people to admit their childhood was unhappy, hence the 'mixed' category.) Those reporting a mixed childhood were grouped together. In a striking display of homogeneity providing a sense of security and lowering inhibitions, in the groups that followed, these participants revealed childhood incidents that were not mentioned in the earlier groups. Once participants began to reveal negative events in their childhood and realised that most others in the group had experienced similar events, the events revealed became even more personal and shocking. In one group of upper SES women with a 'mixed' childhood three admitted (in a male-moderated group) to being sexually abused as a child by a family member; in a lower SES group (same moderator) four admitted to being sexually abused as a child.

Exclusions from groups

Nothing stops a free discussion more than someone in the group declaring themselves—or being seen by the others to be—an 'expert' in the area. It is common practice in commercial research to exclude from groups people working in the advertising, public relations, marketing consulting, and market research industries because these people may have knowledge about the issue that consumers in general would not have and because they may be more interested in the research process than in participating as a consumer. Other exclusions are based on the topic. Thus, dentists and their families would be excluded from groups on toothpaste. In the health and social policy areas care must be taken to exclude those working in the areas under study when recruiting general population groups. For example, teachers should be excluded from groups on parenting (do a group of teachers together), nurses, doctors, etc., from general population groups on health, psychologists, counsellors, etc., from groups on mental health, bureaucrats working in that particular area, and so on. And remember in the recruiting questionnaire to ask not just for people's current occupation, but also for their previous occupations.

When to use focus groups and when to use IDIs

For most issues and most occasions focus groups are the preferred method. Focus groups have a clear time—and therefore cost—advantage (it is quicker to interview eight people at a time than conduct eight separate interviews). The group participants also benefit from the group dynamics.

IDIs are useful when the issues involved are so sensitive that people may not want to discuss them in front of others (for example, sexual or personal hygiene issues), when the type of person is difficult to get to come to a group (for example, busy executives, shift workers), or when the issues are unique to individuals and require time to elicit (for example, personal history type probing).

Research fads: 'Smile! You're on candid camera.'

An increasingly common technique today is for researchers to photograph the target group as they go about their daily lives, where they hang out, where they work, their entertainment venues, etc. In some cases members of the target group are given the cameras and asked to take the photographs themselves, delivering them later to the researchers. As is often the case this new technique is increasingly being used without real consideration of what is being measured. Nevertheless, it can provide valuable additional data about the language and lifestyles of target groups for those clients who never make the time or effort to observe their target groups.

The use of photographs probably stems from Zaltman's metaphor analysis technique (ZMET: Zaltman's Meta Elicitation Technique, Zaltman & Coulter 1995), whereby respondents are asked to select from magazines and newspapers pictures that illustrate their metaphors for the product being studied in advertising research and bring these pictures along to a group discussion or IDI.

In our experience, if the groups are carefully recruited with respect to homogeneity issues, are run by a skilled moderator, and have a careful step-by-step introduction to the specifics of the issue, then even very sensitive issues are quite readily discussed in groups.

While focus groups are still the major qualitative technique in both commercial and social marketing, other methods are proving useful, particularly in providing convergent validity. Discreet observer and participant observer techniques are increasingly being borrowed from anthropology and sociology as techniques to increase our understanding of behaviour and its influencers. These kinds of techniques range from rubbish analysis, to hidden cameras observing television audience behaviour, to street gang participation. In many cases though, it simply means objectively observing the behaviour under study, attempting to construct behaviour patterns, and making inferences about the relationships between beliefs, attitudes, motives, and behaviour. Observational methods are particularly useful for studying the influence of social factors on behaviour.

From our point of view qualitative research is essential in determining overall strategies, with a mix of qualitative and quantitative methods useful for determining the viability of identified strategies and quantitative indicators best for revealing outcome effects.

Research and evaluation framework

Following Egger, Donovan and Spark (1993) we consider the US National Academy of Sciences' research framework to be helpful in conceptualising research questions. Although the framework was developed for the development and evaluation of media campaigns the principles apply to any type of intervention. Coyle et al. (1989) delineate four types of evaluation designed to answer four questions:

1 *Formative research*   What type of intervention would work best?
2 *Efficacy trials*   Could the campaign actually make a difference if implemented under ideal conditions?
3 *Process evaluation*   Was the campaign implemented as planned?
4 *Outcome evaluation*   What impact, if any, did the campaign have? Did it make a difference?

Formative research: What is likely to work best?

Formative research informs the development of interventions, products, and communication materials. It answers questions such as:

- What strategies could be used to motivate violent men to voluntarily seek help to stop their violence?
- Can media advertising be used to change racist stereotype beliefs?
- What approach would be most effective in stimulating concern about heart disease in rural Indigenous communities?

Formative research needs to identify and explore reaction to the various means of achieving the stated objectives (violent men entering counselling programs, changes in stereotyped beliefs, increase in knowledge of CVD risk factors, and uptake of preventive actions). It should explore not just the targeted individuals' attitudes, beliefs, and behaviours, but also the social context, structural facilitators and inhibitors, and the roles and views of all relevant stakeholders with respect to potential alternative interventions.

Formative research methods can include quantitative research, such as surveys, literature reviews, and epidemiological analyses for background data and for generating ideas and hypotheses. However, the most valuable formative research uses face-to-face qualitative methods with all relevant stakeholders where the reactions to potential interventions and their components can be gauged both directly and indirectly. Focus groups and IDIs allow the exploration of reactions, particularly possible ways of overcoming negative reactions. Qualitative research with country residents, for example, suggested that a media campaign could be successful in influencing people's attitudes towards Aborigines and employment, but would not be successful if it was simply seen as 'the government' showing positive images of Aboriginal people without some rationale. Hence, the campaign was sourced to the local Aboriginal corporation and was focused around an Aboriginal Employment Week (Donovan & Leivers 1993).

Similarly, focus groups or small-scale surveys could be used to assess attitudes towards and potential purchase of water flow-controlling products, and what message strategy would be appropriate to reinforce, create, or alter attitudes and behaviours with respect to such devices. Matters of price, aesthetic design, and impact on water flow would all need to be considered, including attitudes of manufacturers and retailers. Similarly, survey or desk research might reveal that many members of a campaign target audience have limited literacy. Hence, if

Using paid advertising to counter racist stereotype beliefs: formative research

In an attempt to adopt prevention strategies, Western Australia's Equal Opportunity Commission wanted to assess the potential for a mass media-based campaign to change discriminatory practices against Aboriginal people in three areas: access to employment, housing, and entertainment venues. A regional city was selected for the feasibility study.

Formative research consisted of focus group discussions with non-Aboriginal residents and small business operators, IDIs with key informants (for example, local government councillors, police, headmasters, etc.), and individual and group interviews with key members of the Aboriginal community. The qualitative research indicated that campaigns targeting housing rental discrimination and access to entertainment venues would not be successful (few would rent a home to an Aboriginal family; there was no support for neighbours who would, and public housing was seen to be readily available anyway; no one considered there was any discrimination with respect to access to hotels and nightclubs).

On the other hand, seeking employment was admired, as were employers willing to give Aborigines an opportunity. Furthermore, discriminatory attitudes were found to be based largely on underestimates of the numbers of Aborigines in paid employment and the length of time Aborigines stayed in a job. Hence, a media campaign was considered feasible to address these misperceptions.

self-help materials were to be produced they would need to be supplied on audiocassette in addition to any printed materials.

Coyle et al. (1989) recommend four processes in the formative stage of a communication campaign: idea generation, concept testing, setting communication objectives, and copy testing. These are discussed and elaborated below to encompass interventions in general, although the emphasis will be on the communication elements of interventions.

Idea generation

This relates to identifying potential ways of addressing the identified problem given available resources. It explores what overall strategy or type of intervention could be effective, what sort of products could be necessary, and what message strategy could motivate the desired attitude and behaviour changes. For example, to generate political support for tobacco control measures the British Medical Association came up with the idea of publishing a document showing how many people died from smoking-related diseases in each parliamentary constituency (Lewis, Morkel & Hubbard 1993), a tactic successfully copied by Western Australian antismoking advocates. Another example is the Domestic Violence Prevention Unit in Western Australia, which thought that violent men might call an anonymous helpline for counselling (Donovan, Paterson & Francas 1999f). The Department of Transport in Western Australia thought people might drive less if they received a personalised approach and were given information about public transport (James 2002).

Concept testing

Concept testing is an iterative process that attempts to assess which of the ideas generated in phase one are viable. It focuses on getting the right message, product, or tactic. While qualitative research is the primary tool for idea generation, quantitative survey research is often carried out to confirm that acceptance of the final concept is generalisable to the total target population and acceptable to all stakeholders. Laboratory style experiments also can be used to test different concepts by exposing different but matched groups to different concepts and then comparing the groups' reactions.

Concept testing takes the idea to the target audience, either in a general way or in some concrete form, which may be a prototype if it is a product, a printed message if it is a communication, or a plan outline if it is a more comprehensive intervention.

When developing the GutBusters® weight loss program for men, testing of alternative components revealed that appeals to body image (that is, waist loss rather that weight loss) were likely to be more effective than health claims alone. The concept of measuring waist:hip ratio was also appealing to men, with the provision of a tape measure in the GutBusters kit (Egger & Mowbray 1993; Egger, Bolton, O'Neill & Freeman 1996).

The *Freedom from Fear* campaign recently explored three communication strategies for motivating violent men to call the Men's Domestic Violence Helpline: the potential loss of their partner and children, the negative impact of the violence on their children, and a demonstration of the remorse that often follows a violent episode. Concept testing assessed whether these themes would have an impact, and, given the necessity to choose only one theme (resources were limited to only one theme), which of these themes would have most impact on most of the target audience. This level of testing did not necessarily require any stimulus materials—it was based on the exploration of men's beliefs and attitudes in qualitative research (Francas & Donovan 2001).

Development of communication objectives

Given the outcome of the above two processes the next step is the development of a set of communication and behavioural objectives, that is, a statement of knowledge, beliefs, and attitudes desired to be brought about in the target audience so as to lead to the desired behaviour change (see chapter 12). This then becomes the starting point for the development of communication materials and strategies for promotion of the campaign. In the case of advertising and publicity this would form the basis of the brief given to the advertising or public relations agency.

Pretesting

Getting the right strategy is essential for success, whereas executing the strategy right determines the degree of success. This stage generally applies only to testing specific products (Quit Kits, water controllers, STD packs) or specific communication materials (press kits, advertisements, brochures, slogans). Products can be tested in groups or individually (depending on the product), or placed in people's homes for a specified time.

Copy testing is the name commonly given to testing advertising and other communication materials. Given that there are a number of ways in which a message can be executed (graphically, with high emotion, type of music, quick cuts or extended scenes, etc.), pretesting is designed to maximise the possibility that the approach taken is likely to be the most effective under the circumstances. Copy testing involves exposing a test audience to a draft of the message (for example, an advertisement, press release, pamphlet, or video presentation) and evaluating the potential success of that message in achieving the communication objectives.

With respect to the *Freedom from Fear* concepts noted above, say, each could be executed in a variety of ways. One way to demonstrate the potential loss of family could be to show a child enacting various scenarios with dolls in a doll house: with her dolls the child mimics a man and a women arguing, followed by the female doll packing a suitcase and leaving the doll house with two child dolls. Another way could be to show a man coming home to an empty house, showing the emotions on his face as he pulls out empty dressing table drawers and looks at family photos left behind.

Testing concept executions clearly requires stimulus material and executions are often developed in a series of group discussions. However, where a go–no go decision is required with respect to, say, launching a television ad, printing a brochure, or producing a radio ad, or, as is often the case, in choosing between several different concept executions, the final testing of alternative executions is best carried out using quantitative methods (Rossiter & Donovan 1983). Quantitative copy testing involves exposing the material(s) to carefully screened members of the target audience and, where appropriate, comparing their responses to those of a similarly selected control group who are not exposed to the material(s).

Involving agency creatives in developing communications

With respect to developing concept executions for social marketing campaigns it is highly desirable that behavioural scientists and experts in the content area be involved in the development of materials with the agency creatives and other professionals. It is insufficient to simply provide the advertising or public relations agency with just a written or verbal brief. In the commercial world ad agency personnel often take a 'tour of the factory', talk to the frontline sales

One example of this was when developing advertising for the National Tobacco Campaign, group meetings were arranged for the agency creatives to meet with the medical specialists who dealt with smoking-related diseases as well as with behavioural science professionals working in the tobacco control area. These meetings also resulted in advertising creatives visiting the specialists' laboratories. The results were the dramatic artery, stroke, and lung ads that have been adopted and adapted now in several overseas jurisdictions (Canada, New Zealand, USA [Massachusetts] and Singapore) (Hassard 1999).

people, or at least observe focus group discussions with the company's customers. For social marketing areas it is even more crucial for agency personnel to take a tour of the factory as many issues will be initially completely alien to them. It is also of great assistance to creatives in that the best ideas are based on a sound understanding of the issue.

Copy testing: what to measure

The following kinds of measures are usually taken after exposing people to campaign materials, although specific measures will vary by the type and objectives of the material(s):

- the thoughts and feelings generated spontaneously by the material
- the extent to which the message is correctly understood
- the extent to which the message is credible
- the extent to which the message is seen to be personally relevant, important, and useful
- the extent to which the message motivates the recommended action
- the extent to which the audience sees the recommended action as effective and themselves capable of performing the action
- likes, dislikes, and specific confusions in the material(s)
- where appropriate, the extent to which the presenter or models in the materials are credible and relevant as role models to the target audience

Focus groups with New South Wales drinkers and drivers concluded that appeals to responsibility and concerns for safety were insufficient motivation for drinkers to avoid driving, but that a more personalised approach involving embarrassment if caught and arrested could be effective. But how could this be executed?

John Bevins, Australia's pioneer creator of advertising in social marketing campaigns, accompanied the police as they arrested drink drivers to explore this embarrassment aspect further. The result was the award-winning 'Under 05 or under arrest' television ads showing the humiliation of apparently otherwise law-abiding, middle-class people undergoing the process of being arrested: having tie and shoe laces removed, being placed in a police dock, etc. (Egger et al. 1993).

Using copy testing: are big production budgets necessary for creating effective road safety advertising?

The success of the Victorian Traffic Accident Commission's (TAC) comprehensive multicomponent road safety strategy focused international attention on the dramatic but costly television advertisements used by the TAC in Australia. This raised the issue of whether costly ads were necessary to achieve this level of impact. Based on standard advertising copy testing measures (Rossiter & Percy 1997) we developed a set of measures to assess the relative effectiveness of twelve road safety ads varying in production costs from $15 000 to greater than $250 000. The twelve ads covered four road safety behaviours (speeding, drink driving, fatigue, and inattention) and included a variety of executional types within and across behaviours. One ad in each of the four behaviours was an expensive Victorian TAC ad ($200 000 or more).

Just under 1000 appropriately screened motor vehicle driver's licence holders were recruited via street intercept methods and randomly allocated to one of the twelve ad exposure conditions. The results showed that while the two best performing ads were highly dramatic TAC ads showing graphic crash scenes, these were also the most expensive ads to produce and, being 60 seconds and 90 seconds in length, the most expensive to air. In several cases 30 second, low-cost talking heads testimonials performed equally as well as their far more expensive counterparts. We concluded that big production budgets may not be necessary to create effective road safety advertising (figure 6.1; Donovan, Jalleh & Henley 1999d).

- where appropriate, the extent to which any metaphors or analogies in the ads are credible and relevant.

While the top scoring ads in figure 6.1 for inattention and fatigue were also the most expensive this was not the case for speeding and drink driving ads, where ads costing as little as $20 000—$50 000 performed as well as their counterparts costing in excess of $200 000.

Efficacy testing: Can it work and can it be improved?

Efficacy testing is what is called 'test marketing' by commercial marketers. Test marketing of new products, sales promotions, retailer agreements, distribution channels, or advertising campaigns is often carried out in a limited geographical area that does not involve excessive risk or cost, and in a sample of a population with similar characteristics to the larger target audience. During the test period surveys are carried out and sales figures recorded in the area. Efficacy testing usually involves comparing a test with a control area and may include assessments of measures such as calls to a hot line, sales of products, enquiries, etc. Diagnostic surveys measure awareness of, beliefs about, and attitudes towards the intervention. If results are positive, the intervention is then introduced in all the company's markets. The Hunter Valley region of New South Wales and Adelaide in South Australia are often used as commercial test markets.

Figure 6.1 Ad impact on behavioural intentions as a driver*

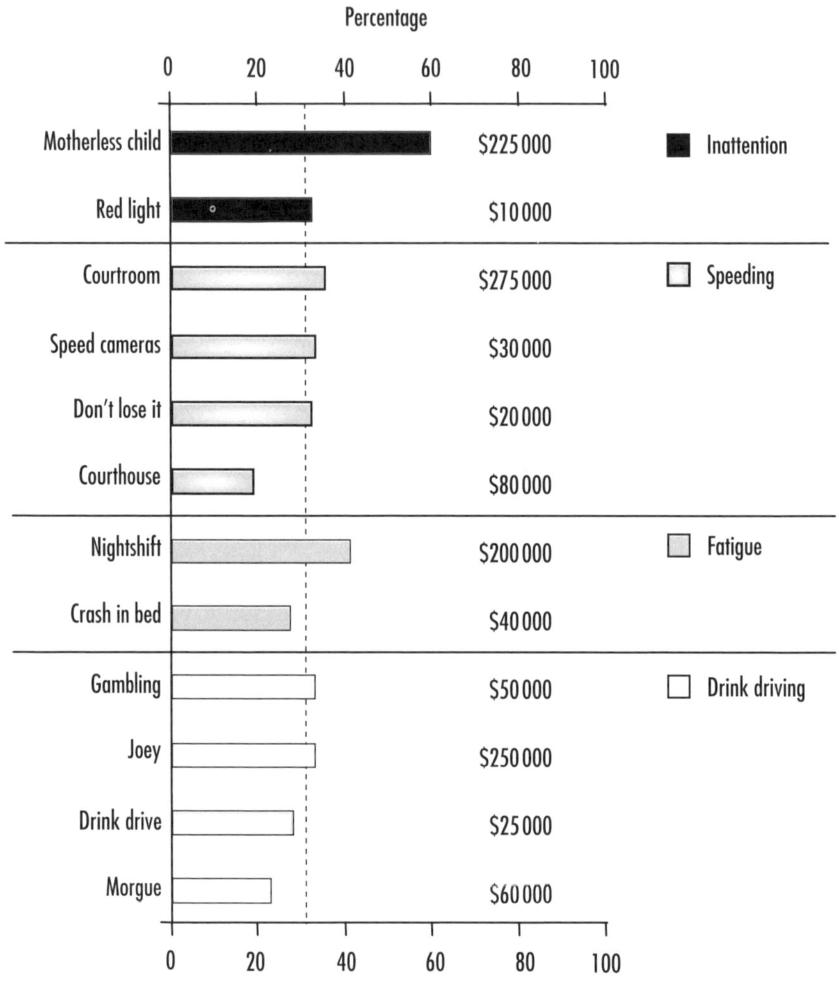

* Donovan et al. 1999d

Efficacy testing is designed to measure whether an intervention could work if it was implemented optimally, but under real world rather than laboratory type conditions. However, other than some school-based and worksite interventions, efficacy testing appears to be infrequently carried out in health and social marketing, usually because of time and budget restraints. One example that the first author was involved in while at the Centers for Disease Control (CDC) involved prerecruiting people to watch a particular news program on one or other television station for a number of nights. People were randomly assigned to a program that was to air an AIDS ad or to a control program that was to contain no AIDS ads. The viewers were not told the purpose of the research. Pre–post surveys showed a significant increase in the proportion of people in the

Using paid advertising to counter racist stereotype beliefs: efficacy research

This project was designed to assess the viability of using mass media to change racist stereotype beliefs. Formative research suggested that this could be done under certain conditions (see box, p. 133). Implementing the campaign in one country town and conducting a pre–post survey of people's beliefs about Aborigines and employment constituted an efficacy test of the concept of assessing the viability of using mass media to change racist stereotype beliefs. Given the successful outcome in Bunbury (see chapter 11) the approach was further tested in Kalgoorlie and Port Hedland. Unfortunately, as with so many other social issues, funds were never made available to launch the campaign on even a statewide basis, let alone a national basis.

exposed group spontaneously mentioning AIDS as an 'important national issue', but no such increase in the control group (Siska, Jason, Murdoch, Yang & Donovan 1992).

Process research: Is the campaign being delivered as proposed?

Process measures are collected during or at the end of an intervention. The questions these measures are designed to answer is whether the intervention was implemented as proposed, whether the intervention reached those it was intended to reach, if not, why not, and what immediate impact the intervention had on beliefs, attitudes, and behaviours related to both implementation and to the intended outcomes. Aspects of concern for media-based or supported campaigns are recognition, recall, and impact of the message strategies. Process research methods can range from personal interviews to recording of target audience demand for information, materials, etc. The *Freedom from Fear* domestic violence campaign in Western Australia relied on paid advertising to reach violent men and encourage them to call a men's domestic violence helpline. Telephone surveys were carried out at various intervals during the campaign to assess whether violent and potentially violent men were aware of the campaign, whether they understood the advertising messages, and whether they were aware of a helpline for men to call about domestic violence. Calls to the Men's Domestic Violence Helpline were also monitored as a function of media weight. The proportion of violent men calling the Men's Domestic Violence Helpline who accepted an offer of counselling is also a process measure as it indicates the skill of the telephone counsellors in encouraging violent callers to undergo long-term counselling.

Do intentions predict behaviour?

Much formative research and efficacy testing measures (shifts in) attitudes and behavioural intentions. A common query to researchers who present their pre-test data to program managers, is 'How valid are intentions as predictors of actual behaviour?' Most of the research in this area comes from consumer behaviour studies. These have generally shown a good correlation between what people say they will do and what they actually do in terms of consumer purchases. Reviewing a number of market research studies Urban, Hauser and Dholakia (1987) suggest a reasonable weighting for responses on a five point scale would be as follows.

Response	Weight
Definitely will	0.7
Probably will	0.35
Might or might not	0.1
Probably won't	–
Definitely won't	–

Hence, if we presented people with a weight loss program and asked how likely they would be to enter the program within the next month (the more specific the timeframe, the more accurate the prediction) the predicted uptake—all other marketing factors being in place—would be as follows.

Response	Per cent	Weight	Likely uptake
Definitely will	15	0.7	10.5
Probably will	28	0.35	9.8
Might or might not	33	0.1	3.3
Probably won't	13	–	–
Definitely won't	11	–	–
Total	26		

Note the key statement—***all other marketing factors in place.*** All of these estimates assume 100 per cent awareness of the service, ease of access, availability, and so on. Estimates must take these factors into account for assessing actual demand.

Just what behaviour are we trying to predict? One of the major reasons why attitudes and intentions sometimes turn out to be poor predictors of behaviour is that we have measured the wrong behaviour. This occurs in two ways:

■ first, for many behaviour changes it is trial that we want to predict not successful adoption (trying to quit smoking versus quitting smoking—'Do you intend to try and quit in the next month?' versus 'Do you intend to quit in the next month?')

■ second, for many targeted messages there are intermediate steps that an individual will go through before trying or adopting the behaviour (for example, 'Do you intend to seek more information about quit smoking courses?' versus 'Do you intend to quit?').

Figure 6.2 Continuous tracking involving n = 50 interviews weekly, summed over a 3 weekly moving total

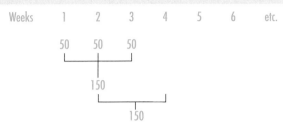

Continuous tracking

One of the most recent and fast-growing process evaluation methodologies is called 'continuous tracking' (Sutherland 1993). Continuous tracking was initially designed to track advertising campaigns and that is still by far its major use. However, the methodology can be used to monitor any set of inputs (intervention variables) and outputs (dependent variables).

Continuous tracking (or continuous information tracking—CIT) is designed to monitor campaign effects as a function of campaign activities on a weekly basis. In a continuous tracking program interviewing is carried out continuously throughout an extended period. Although clearly desirable it is prohibitively expensive to track the effects of a campaign with a weekly sample size sufficiently large to justify looking at each week's data separately. To overcome this and yet still provide a continuous monitor of changes the data are collected on a weekly basis and then combined using a moving average roll, as depicted in figure 6.2 above.

In typical CIT projects between fifty and 100 interviews with appropriately screened members of the target audience are carried out each week (spread across the 5 week days), summed over two or three weekly moving totals, and correlated against weekly campaign activities. The aim is for each moving average point to be based on a minimum of 100–150 respondents. One key benefit of this method is that it smooths out random variation that can seem important but be irrelevant. The major limitation is that it makes it difficult to see the true impact of one-off events of short duration. This can be overcome, if budgets permit, by increasing the weekly sample size to do away with the need to roll the data.

Continuous tracking data can be collected via any of the commonly used quantitative data collection techniques (door-to-door, street intercept, telephone, or self-completion mail questionnaire). Given the small daily interview samples probability-based household face-to-face interviewing would be prohibitively costly. Telephone offers the advantage of a more representative sample relative to the cost-equivalent face-to-face intercept interview. However, face-to-face intercept interviewing offers the important advantage of being able to present stimulus material to respondents (ad telestills or other campaign materials). Hence, when measuring ad recognition by telephone care must be taken to ensure that the verbal description of the ad provides sufficient cues to enable an accurate measure of whether the respondent has been exposed to ('seen') the ad.

Continuous tracking of consumer measures allows direct assessment of campaign effects by observing differences between campaign on and campaign off periods, and by being able to observe any immediate or delayed effects of specific events. An added advantage is that the data are inherently suitable for plotting graphically so that relationships between campaign effects and campaign activities (for example, advertising TARPs) may be clearly visible without recourse to sophisticated inferential statistical techniques. A target audience rating point (TARP) is a standard measure of the weekly volume of television advertising weight scheduled to reach the target audience. TARPs are a multiple of the percentage of the target audience reached by (exposed to) the campaign and the average number of times (frequency) a target audience member is exposed to the advertising. Hence, TARPs data are somewhat ambiguous in that 240 TARPs may represent 80 per cent of the target audience reached with an average frequency of three, or 60 per cent reached an average of four times, and so on. (In most cases advertisers attempt to reach at least 80 per cent of their target audience over the first 2 weeks of a campaign.) In spite of this ambiguity TARPs data have been found to be reliably related to various campaign effects (Brown 1985; Sutherland 1993).

A major benefit of CIT is that it encourages experimentation with various media weights to assess optimal expenditure of funds. Over time the relationship between TARPs levels and advertising impact can be measured, as can differences between creative approaches. For example, by varying media weights during the course of a campaign (or over different campaigns), thresholds above which there are diminishing returns—and below which there is a nil effect—can be established for various campaign effects. Similarly, a good indicator of advertisement effectiveness—advertising cut-through, the extent to which an advertisement is recalled when respondents are asked to remember, say, recent tobacco advertising—may plateau beyond some threshold of TARPs and may require some minimal TARPs level to even register.

Further advantages of CIT over pre–post surveys include the following.

Reduction of timing biases

In pre–post surveys the results may be influenced by the actual timing of the survey fieldwork, especially if some uncontrolled event (media item or publicity, severe weather conditions, pricing fluctuations, etc.) occurs prior to either survey wave. Ongoing data collection not only identifies major confounders, but also tends to smooth out the effect of minor uncontrolled events.

Ability to capture unforeseen events

Because interviewing is being carried out across an extended period (often 12–40 weeks) it provides the opportunity to measure the impact of specific events, whether planned or unplanned (policy announcements, media publicity, etc.). The impact of such events on attitudes and beliefs is picked up in the course of the regular tracking process rather than requiring a separate *ad hoc* survey.

Integration

CIT has the ability to integrate a range of campaign inputs (advertising, PR activity, significant events, related initiatives, etc.) and campaign outputs (awareness, attitudes, telephone calls, sales behaviour). This integrated analysis can provide an understanding of which inputs (or combinations of inputs) are most effective in influencing the desired outputs.

Another major feature of CIT is that one can identify dependent variables that vary directly and contemporaneously with media weight or type of campaign activity (for example, calls to a Quitline), and those that vary as a function of cumulative campaign activities (for example, changes in some attitudes and beliefs).

Continuous information tracking involves the ongoing monitoring of media activity and the simultaneous measurement of the following five variables.

1   Processing impact of the various communications per se (advertisement recall and recognition, message take out, etc.).
2   Changes in salience or awareness of the topic in question (for example, tobacco as a significant health issue).
3   Changes in knowledge of or beliefs about the topic (beliefs about damage caused by smoking, beliefs about benefits and disbenefits of smoking, etc.).
4   Changes in overall attitudes or disposition towards the issue (overall attitude to smoking, quitting, smoke-free areas, etc.).
5   Changes in behaviour or intentions (switching to lower tar, amount consumed, attempted quitting or intentions to attempt to quit, encouraging a smoker in the same household to quit or not smoke in the dwelling, etc.).

Figures 6.3a–6.3c present some typical results for continuous tracking studies.[1] Figure 6.3a shows spontaneous ad recall for ads related to speeding. Recall (or cut through) is clearly related to advertising weight and is highest for the woman and pram ad. The ad focuses on the time allowed for action and the braking distance needed to stop when an unexpected event occurs.

The action takes place from the point of view of a driver. A woman pushing a pram steps onto the road in front of the driver.

In the first scene the driver is travelling slowly and stops easily, in the second scene the driver is travelling faster and just manages to stop inches from the woman and pram, in the third scene the driver is travelling faster still and this time the woman is hit and flung against the windscreen which is shown shattered and bloodstained. The main aim of the ad is to convince drivers that driving at 10 kph less has a marked effect on reducing the likelihood of a crash and the severity of injury if there is a crash.

---

1   Road Safety Speed Advertising Tracking (provided by NFO Donovan Research and the Office of Road Safety; see Batini & Farley 2001)

Figure 6.3a Tracking of road safety speed advertising campaign

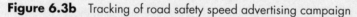

Figure 6.3b Tracking of road safety speed advertising campaign

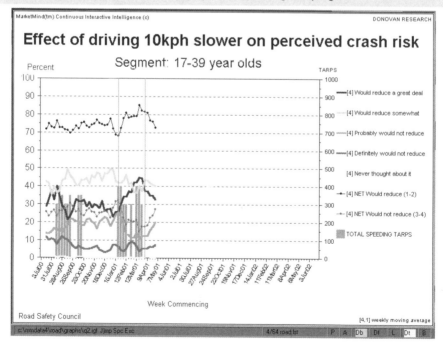

Figure 6.3c Tracking of road safety speed advertising campaign

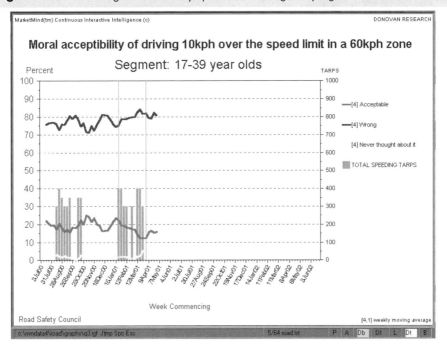

Figure 6.3b shows that although this belief is increasing slowly over the months of the campaign it is still influenced by advertising presence: the proportion agreeing with this belief declines when the advertising goes off air. These data demonstrate the importance of a continual media presence, even for well-established beliefs and attitudes.

Figure 6.3c shows that perceptions of the morality of driving 10 kph over the limit in a 60 kph zone (note the links between the messages) have steadily increased over time, but this measure is not as weight-sensitive as the above two measures.

Outcome research: Did it work?

Outcome or impact measures are designed to assess whether, and the degree to which, a media initiative or media campaign has achieved what it set out to do. Short-term effects are usually called 'impact measures' and these include intermediary objectives such as changes in beliefs, attitudes, and some behaviours. Longer-term effects are called 'outcome measures'. These can be determined by a number of means, each with advantages and disadvantages. Most require pretest and posttest measures to evaluate the effect of the intervention.

The outcome effectiveness of many health promotion campaigns in terms of morbidity or mortality may not be known for many years. For example, the

Table 6.1a   Using projective techniques to measure attitudes

Pocket money expenditure lists	
List 1	**List 2**
Movies	Movies
Icecreams and lollies	Cigarettes
Saving for a record or cassette	Ice creams and lollies
Comic	Saving for a record or cassette
Batteries	Comic
Video games	Batteries
Hamburger	Video games
	Hamburger

Table 6.1b   Using projective techniques to measure attitudes

	No cigarettes on list (n = 382)	Cigarettes on list (n = 240)
Someone I would (would not) like	45.0	26.5
Attractive (unattractive)	46.6	35.0
Unpopular (popular)	26.7	36.8
Troublemaker (well-behaved)	59.4	87.4
Smart (foolish)	33.8	13.5
Outgoing (shy)	83.3	89.7
Grown up (childish)	30.6	29.1

*Donovan and Holden 1985

outcome of the 'Slip, Slop, Slap' campaigns on skin cancer may take 10–20 years to be apparent in morbidity and mortality rates for skin cancers.

Similar statements apply to Quit campaigns and lung cancer and dietary fat campaigns and heart disease. Hence, these campaigns should be evaluated in terms of intermediate measures such as beliefs and attitudes, and behavioural measures such as sun protection behaviours, presenting for screening, maintenance of non-smoking, dietary habits, and sales data such as per capita sales of sunscreen, cigarettes, and foods containing a high percentage of saturated fat.

In a study carried out on the mid north coast of New South Wales the main intervention objective was to encourage older people to eat more high fibre bread. Sales audits were taken of laxative sales from pharmacies in the town and these showed a 50 per cent decline in laxative use over a 3 month intervention period accompanied by a 60 per cent increase in bread sales (Egger, Wolfenden, Pares & Mowbray 1991). Other relevant sales audits, depending on the objectives of the intervention, may be condom, food, cigarettes or liquor sales, fitness centre memberships, or chlamydia tests carried out (France, Donovan, Watson & Leivers 1991)

Using projective techniques to measure attitude

Projective techniques are very useful research tools and can be applied in qualitative and quantitative research. Projective techniques involve presenting ambiguous stimulus material (thought bubbles, pictures, ink blots, etc.) to people and asking them to interpret the situation. It is assumed that they project their own thoughts and feelings in their response. Projective techniques are useful when respondents are unable or unwilling to respond to direct questioning or where direct questioning may yield socially desirable responses or be subject to demand characteristics.

One of the major challenges in tobacco control is that younger children appear to be opposed to smoking (sometimes vehemently so), but at around the age of 12–14 years they abandon these beliefs and take up smoking. Why is this so? One reason may be that children are not as negative about smoking as we think, but might simply be giving socially desirable responses to questions about smoking, especially when the questioners were adults. In an effort to assess whether this was the case we adapted a classic projective technique in marketing, the shopping list (Haire 1950). After an introduction and sample exercise about how people form impressions of other people, 8–10 year old schoolchildren were given either one or the other of the two lists shown in tables 6.1a of what a hypothetical boy or girl their age spent their pocket money on. The only difference was that one list in table 6.1a contained cigarettes. The children were asked to write a description of this hypothetical boy or girl and then rate them on the bipolar scales in table 6.1b. No attention was drawn to any of the items on the lists. The results show that the child spending pocket money on cigarettes was viewed far more negatively than the other child. The projective technique allowed us to rule out that negative attitudes to smoking were due to demand characteristics.

Research concepts in public health

Research methods in public health are based on the disciplines of epidemiology and biostatistics.

Epidemiology can be defined as the study of the distribution and determinants of the frequency of disease. Frequency refers to quantifying the occurrence or existence of disease. Distribution refers to how the disease is distributed in populations, for example, geographically, by age or gender, and over time. Determinants refer to identifying why the disease occurs more or less frequently in one group than another. A determinant is not necessarily a cause, but might be an enabling factor.

Epidemiology does not generally deal with identifying cause per se, but with what the lawyers might call 'probable cause' (tobacco company lawyers excepted, of course). Thus, if lung cancer rates are considerably higher among smokers than non smokers and this relationship (relative risk) holds across age, gender, national, and occupational groupings, then the more confident we can be in assuming that smoking is a probable cause of lung cancer.

Of course, there are many variables that we need to control for, especially where lifestyle and environmental factors could interact. For example, smokers are more likely than non-smokers to use alcohol and other drugs, smokers are more likely than non-smokers to work in blue-collar occupations (at least these days) and hence more likely to be exposed to industrial pollutants at the work-place, even in their places of residence. It is crucial that these covariates are controlled for before coming to any conclusion about the influence of smoking on lung cancer rates.

Biostatistics covers the statistical tools used in biomedical sciences. These methods allow the determination of the significance of differences between frequency measures in different subpopulations, measures of absolute and relative risk, and measures of association between variables and outcomes.

Measures of disease frequency

Prevalence and incidence are two basic ways of describing the frequency of occurrence of disease in a population.

Prevalence

Prevalence is the proportion of the population with the disease at a certain point in time (existing cases). It is expressed as per cent per 1000, per 100 000, etc. Prevalence is related to the onset of a disease and recovery. For example, outbreaks of curable infectious diseases are characterised by an initial rapid rise in prevalence followed by a decline as the disease runs its natural course through the population and diseased people recover. Because prevalence indicates neither when the people initially got the disease nor which previously diseased people subsequently recovered or died it is not a good measure of the overall rate or the risk of getting the disease.

Incidence

Incidence refers to how many new cases of a disease occurred in a population during a specified interval. It is usually expressed as number of new cases per unit time per fixed number of people (for example, number of new cases of cancer per 10 000 people in 1 year). Because of the restriction to new cases, the population in which the incidence is measured is restricted to those who are susceptible to getting the disease during the observation period (for example, for some infectious diseases lifetime immunity can be established and so those who had been immunised should be excluded from the population under study). This restricted population is typically called the 'at-risk population' because they are at risk of getting the disease. For this reason incidence is often also called 'risk' because it reflects the likelihood of a person in the population of

Figure 6.4 Types of study designs in epidemiology

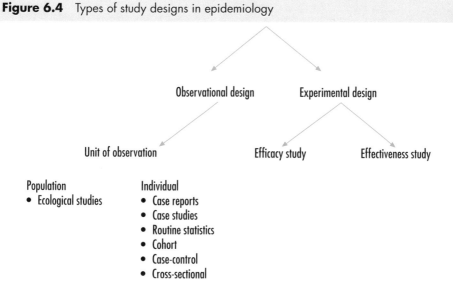

interest getting the disease within a certain period (including one's lifetime; 'lifetime risk'). Incidence is important in allowing researchers to study the impact of harmful exposures or preventative interventions on the occurrence of disease because it does not depend on the length of disease course or its fatality.

Types of study designs

Studies in epidemiological and medical and public health research are usually classified into two main categories: experimental and observational designs (Lilienfeld & Lilienfeld 1980) (see figure 6.4). In observational studies the investigator merely observes the existing situation. In experimental studies the investigator intervenes by manipulating exposure and other factors and then observing the outcome. Experimental studies are usually referred to as intervention studies.

Experimental research enables researchers to determine the causal relationship between variables. Descriptive research simply describes the population of interest on a number of variables, such as attitudes and behaviours, and perhaps the correlations between these and factors such as sex and age. Descriptive research can infer, but cannot confirm, causality.

Experimental (intervention) studies

There are two main types of experimental studies: efficacy and effectiveness. Studies of efficacy determine results under ideal conditions, whereas studies of effectiveness determine results under typical conditions. An example of an experimental study is the randomised clinical trial in which a representative sample of subjects is randomly allocated to one of several groups, each group receiving a different treatment or intervention. Measurements are made immediately following

Correlation and causality: Does smoking cause lung cancer?*

It might be noted that smokers constitute only 28 per cent of all Australians but 85 per cent of Australian lung cancer patients. If there were no causal link between smoking and lung cancer smokers should constitute only 28 per cent of all lung cancer patients.

However, there might be a third factor that causes lung cancer. For example, far more smokers than non-smokers might work in mines and other worksites where the air contains toxic irritants. Smoking may be associated with higher alcohol and junk food consumption. Hence, statistical methods such as logistic regression are used to explore all associated factors to determine whether, when all other factors are kept constant, the relationship between lung cancer and smoking still remains. However, while correlational evidence can be used to infer causality final proof of causality depends on experimental data from the laboratory showing how the constituents of tobacco actually cause cancer.

* After Close & Donovan 1998

treatment or later, or they are followed over time until some event occurs. For example, a representative sample of early stage breast cancer patients are given surgical treatment and then randomised to receive chemotherapy or no chemotherapy. The patients are followed over time until death. Relative survival rates are used to assess the efficacy of the chemotherapy.

Observational studies

Observational studies can be categorised according to the unit of observation: population or individual. The most common observational studies in which the unit of observation is the population are called 'ecological' studies. In an ecological study average rates of disease are compared with average levels of exposure to a particular agent (for example, national heart disease rates versus national average consumption of dietary fat).

The main types of observational studies where the unit of observation is the individual are as follows.

Cohort

A representative sample of subjects is selected (the cohort) and followed over time to see if and when a certain event occurs. For example, a representative sample of coal miners may be followed for the development of respiratory disease. Cohort studies are used to obtain information on incidence rates.

Case control

A representative sample of subjects with a particular characteristic (the cases) and a representative sample of subjects without the characteristic (the controls) are obtained. Information is then compared concerning antecedent factors in the two groups. For example, a sample of spine-injured motor vehicle casualties and a sample of non-spine-injured motor vehicle casualties are obtained. Details of the accident (for example, wearing seat belt) are then compared.

Cross-sectional

Measurements or observations are made on a random sample of subjects selected from a defined population at a given point in time. Cross-sectional surveys are used to obtain information on the prevalence of specified characteristics in the population and subpopulations.

Odds ratios and logistic regression

A common way to compare disease rates in different populations and subpopulations is to calculate risk rates or risk ratios, for example, the risk rates among smokers and non-smokers of contracting lung cancer or the risk rates among men versus women of contracting colorectal cancer.

Regardless of the type of epidemiological study the data can be presented in 2×2 contingency tables of disease status versus exposure status.

		Disease status	
		Diseased	**Not diseased**
Exposure	Exposed	a	b
Status	Not exposed	c	d

The proportion a/(a+b) estimates the risk of disease among the exposed, while c/(c+d) estimates the risk of disease among the unexposed. The ratio of these is the relative risk (RR) of one group relative to the other:

$$RR = a(c+d)/b(a+b).$$

Consider the results of a cohort study on lung cancer outcomes and smoking status.

		Disease status		
		Lung cancer	**No lung cancer**	**Total**
Exposure	Smokers	28	209	228
Status	Non-smokers	7	458	465
		35	667	683

The risk of lung cancer among smokers would be 28/228 = 0.123. The risk among non-smokers would be 7/465 = 0.015. The RR for smokers versus non-smokers is the ratio of these two risks:

$$RR = 0.123/0.015 = 8.2$$

That is, smokers are approximately eight time more likely than non-smokers to contract lung cancer.

If the above table represented the results of a case-control study it would be inappropriate to calculate relative risk because the number of cases would be determined by the investigator and not necessarily represent prevalence in the total population. In this case odds ratios are another way of comparing prevalence or incidence scores where the point of reference is exposure status rather than disease status. In the example above the odds of being a smoker (that is, exposed) in those with lung cancer is a/c (28/7 = 4.0); the odds of being a smoker in those without lung cancer is b/d (209/458 = 0.46). The odds ratio (OR) for being a smoker in those with lung cancer (the diseased group) compared to those without is the ratio of these two odds and therefore estimated by

$$OR = ad/bc = 28 \times 458/7 \times 209 = 8.7$$

This means that lung cancer sufferers are 8.7 time more likely to be smokers than non-smokers.

Where the frequency of events is rare, that is, the number of diseased relative to the total number of cases is very small (as in the above example), then ORs are similar to—and often used as—estimates of relative risk.

The odds ratio describes the relative likelihood of different groups having a disease (in a cohort study), being a substance user or excess user (in a cross sectional survey), being exposed to some risk factor (in a case-control study), or achieving some impact threshold in an intervention trial. The reason why OR is popular in epidemiology is because it may be estimated from many different study designs. ORs can be calculated for any studies, whereas relative risk ratios are not appropriate for case-control studies and other studies in which the sample sizes of the exposed/non-exposed or diseased/non-diseased are chosen by the investigator rather than occurring by chance in the population. Hence, most studies, especially case-control and cross-sectional studies, report ORs. Cohort and randomised control trials more commonly report relative risk and risk differences respectively.

The above examples illustrate crude odds ratios, in which possible confounders are not taken into account (age, gender, etc.). Regression is the use of one variable (the independent or explanatory variable) to predict the value of an associated variable (the dependent or response variable). Logistic regression allows the prediction of the dependent variable holding a number of other variables constant, with the strength of the association expressed as an odds ratio for binary comparisons (smoker versus non-smoker, sufficiently physically active to obtain health benefits versus insufficiently active, agrees with a questionnaire item versus disagrees with the statement, drinks six or more standard alcoholic drinks a day versus drinks five or less standard alcoholic drinks a day, and so on). Hence, another reason why odds ratios are so popular and why one of the most common data analyses in the public health literature is the reporting of odds ratios via logistic regression.

With respect to significance, odds ratios (and relative risks) are usually presented with their 95 per cent confidence intervals (CIs). (A confidence interval is a range of values within which one is confident the true value of the measure of association is contained.) Confidence intervals that do not include 1.0 represent a significance level of 0.05, that is, less than one chance in twenty that the result is due to chance.

Using logistic regression and odds ratios to identify predictors of marijuana use

Amonini (2001) administered a comprehensive questionnaire to approximately 600 14–17 year olds. The questionnaire was based on Donovan's (1997) model of substance use. It measured marijuana, alcohol, and tobacco use and included a large number of items measuring factors such as personality dispositions, parental relationships, and parental supervision, and, for each substance, perceived morality of use, perceived social benefits, harmful health effects, and perception of the laws governing use.

Table 6.2 shows the results for the personality measures for marijuana use versus non-use. The single factor model shows the crude or unadjusted odds ratios for each variable regardless of its correlation or relationship with any other variable. These show that young people with a high tolerance of deviance are almost five times (4.99) more likely to be marijuana users than non users and those with a medium tolerance of deviance are over twice as likely (2.21) compared to those with a low tolerance of deviance (1.00). Similarly, greater risk-seeking disposition and greater psychological reactance are related to increased marijuana usage. On the other hand, a greater risk-aversive disposition and greater religiosity are associated with decreased marijuana usage, for example, those with high religiosity are one-tenth as likely (0.11) and those with medium religiosity are approximately half as likely (0.49) to be marijuana users than those with low religiosity.

As there may be sex and age differences with respect to these personality variables and marijuana use, the next column calculates odds ratios with sex and age held constant. The odds ratios remain essentially unchanged in this sex-and-age-held-constant model. The third column calculates odds ratios controlling for all factors. That is, the results represent the extent to which each variable is independently related to marijuana use. This model shows that all of the personality variables except risk-aversive disposition remain significant predictors of marijuana use, at least at the 'high' level:

- young people with a high tolerance of deviance are three times (3.01; CI 1.28–7.09) more likely to be marijuana users than non-users
- those with a high risk-seeking disposition are eight times more likely (8.16; CI 2.67–24.93)
- those with medium risk-seeking disposition nearly three times more likely
- those with high reactance are 6.59 times more likely (CI2.02-21.53)
- those with high religiosity are one-tenth as likely (0.09; CI 0.03-0.26) to be marijuana users than those with low religiosity.

Research in Indigenous communities

There has been a long history in Australia of research in Indigenous communities, unfortunately, not always—or even often—to the benefit of the communities

Table 6.2   Personality measures for marijuana use versus non-use*

Individual factors	Logistic regression odds ratios for current marijuana use (base: non-use)				
	Single factor model (SFM)	SFM with sex and age	All construct variables	p value	Confidence interval
DEMOGRAPHIC					
Sex					
Male	1.00	1.00	1.00		
Female	0.62**	0.61**	0.61	0.06	0.36–1.02
Age					
14 years	1.00	1.00	1.00		
15 years	1.59	1.66	1.66	0.17	0.80–3.47
16 years	2.33*	2.38*	2.38	0.02	1.14–4.97
17 years	1.75	1.72	1.72	0.15	0.81–3.63
PERSONALITY					
Tolerance of deviance					
Low	1.00	1.00	1.00	0.04	
Medium	2.21*	2.21*	1.78	0.14	0.83–3.83
High	4.99*	4.59*	3.01	0.01	1.28–7.09
Risk-seeking disposition					
Low	1.00	1.00	1.00	0.00	
Medium	3.83*	3.66*	2.98	0.03	1.08–8.23
High	10.87*	11.23*	8.16	0.00	2.67–24.93
Risk-aversive disposition					
Low	1.00	1.00	1.00	0.20	
Medium	0.76	0.80	0.67	0.28	0.32–1.40
High	0.21*	0.22*	0.49	0.08	0.22–1.08
Psychological reactance					
Low	1.00	1.00	1.00	0.01	
Medium	3.85*	3.63*	2.33	0.05	0.99–5.53
High	7.14*	6.71*	6.59	0.00	2.02–21.53
Religiosity					
Low	1.00	1.00	1.00	0.00	
Medium	0.49*	0.55*	0.49	0.04	0.25–0.96
High	0.11*	0.11*	0.09	0.00	0.03–0.26

* Amonini 2001

Measuring impact evaluation via odds ratios

Jalleh, Donovan, Clarkson, March et al. (2001) conducted a quasi-experimental field study to assess the impact of a Healthway-sponsored mouthguard campaign on behavioural change. The campaign was conducted among junior competition rugby union and basketball players, with Australian Rules footballers serving as control. On one day early in the season (pre), all players participating in the three sporting codes were inspected for mouthguard wearing onfield prior to commencement of the game. A similar inspection of all players was carried out in the last rounds prior to the finals (post). Table 6.3 shows the proportion of players wearing a mouthguard pre and post campaign for the three sports. Logistic regression was used to assess the significance of the impact of the campaign on mouthguard usage. The variables included in the model were type of sport, pre–post campaign, and the interaction of these two variables.

Table 6.3 Field study on mouthguard-wearing campaign

	Pre (%)	Post (%)	OR	95 % CI
Competition				
Rugby union	77	84	1.57	1.22-2.02
Basketball	23	43	2.55	2.04-3.18
Australian rules football	72	73	1.05	0.84-1.30

The odds ratio for the pre–post campaign coefficient for rugby union is 1.57 with a 95 per cent confidence interval of [1.22, 2.02]. This suggests that the use of mouthguards post campaign is estimated to be 1.57 times more than pre campaign and we are 95 per cent confident that the prevalence odds ratio comparing post- to precampaign mouthguard usage for rugby is between 1.22 and 2.02. As the 95 per cent CI for OR does not include 1.0 the observed difference in rates is not likely to have occurred by chance.

under study. Nevertheless, the last 10 years or so has seen an improvement in areas such as the involvement of Indigenous people in these research efforts, feedback of results to the communities, and research that provides skills training and potentially sustainable effects in the communities. There is still a long way to go however, with Indigenous researchers still in short supply and high demand.

Researching Indigenous communities presents special challenges to non-Indigenous people, especially those with an emphasis on hypothetico–deductive methodological approaches (as distinct from those with more of a phenomenological approach). Relative to other Indigenous peoples', Australian Indigenous culture appears to be very complex. Concepts of manners, interpersonal styles, use of language, and importance attached to clock time are vastly different, leading not only to unreliable and invalid research data, but also to misunderstandings on a grand scale between communities and politicians and bureaucrats. Donovan and Spark (1997) provide a discussion of many of these issues, particularly as they pertain to survey research in Indigenous communities. Drawing on

Donovan and Spark (1997) suggest a number of issues to be aware of when conducting survey research in traditional Indigenous communities. These include:
- direct questioning is inconsistent with traditional culture
- information gathering is an exchange process in indigenous culture
- the importance of the concept of privacy
- English is the second, third, or even fourth language for many people in remote communities
- concepts of numeracy, intensity, and specificity need special consideration
- the concept of time is viewed very differently from the way Europeans view time
- interpersonal interaction styles are very different from European ways
- the need for interaction with the community before and after the research phase
- community composition and sampling implications.

their experience in such research they provide a number of personal guidelines for individuals involved in Indigenous research.

One of the implications from Donovan and Spark (1997) is that questionnaires not only need to take into account the above guidelines from the point of view of the respondent, but should also be mindful that the interviewer is likely to be an Indigenous person for whom English is a second or third language. Hence, the questionnaires need to be very clearly set out, easy to follow, and be jargon-free. Donovan and Spark (1997) recommend visual illustrations wherever possible to facilitate communication. Figures 6.5, 6.6a, and 6.6b show visuals used by Spark (1999) in assessing health needs in remote communities.

Randomised control designs versus diffusion methodology for indigenous community research

A common methodology in whole-community (or settings) intervention research in non-Indigenous communities is the random assignment of communities to conditions (schools, worksites, towns, hospitals, etc.). However, given the fluctuating composition of Indigenous communities—especially remoter communities—this is simply not feasible, although many have tried (for example, Spark 1999) and many continue to attempt to obtain random or convenience samples within communities to compare intervention effects between communities. This approach is also often hampered by insufficient sample sizes being available to assess real but minimal effects.

One Indigenous researcher (Owen 2002) is proposing a diffusion methodology approach to assess the impact of a heart-health education intervention in Indigenous communities. Owen's project, like many others, involves community workshops as a major intervention component. Owen's workshop attendees will learn about heart disease and risk factors and cover topics such as ways of healthier food purchasing and preparation, the importance of physical activity,

Figure 6.5 States of health

Read this story before Questions 8, 9, 10 and 11.

There is a hill and on one side there are people who are <u>healthy and strong</u> in their bodies and on the other side are people who are <u>sick and weak</u> in their bodies.
In the middle are people who are <u>just okay</u> - not very sick, but not with good health either. Half way down one side are people who are a fair bit strong and healthy. Half way down the other side are people who are a bit sick.

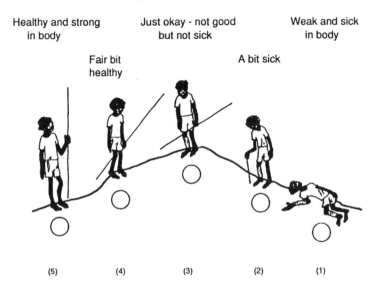

Figure 6.6a Fatty foods and heart troubles

How much does eating **TOO MUCH FATTY FOOD** like take-away pies, chips and deep fried chicken, cause **HEART TROUBLES?** (Tick one circle or dot)

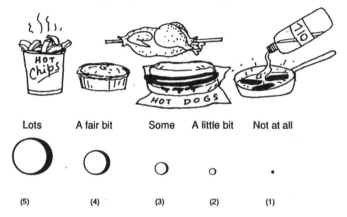

Figure 6.6b Sugary foods and diabetes

Does eating too much SUGAR cause diabetes? (Tick one circle or dot)

Lots	A fair bit	Some	A little bit	Not at all
⬤	◯	○	∘	·
(5)	(4)	(3)	(2)	(1)

and the need to stop smoking. Owens proposes to ask workshop attendees to nominate up to five individuals in their community who are at risk of heart disease and with whom they come into regular contact. These individuals will then be interviewed immediately after the workshops and then 6 months later, to assess the impact of the intervention.

Personal guidelines for research in Indigenous communities*

- Remember, you are a guest of the community. Act with the same sensitivity as you would to your host in any non-Aboriginal, semiformal situation. Announce your arrival to the community office before proceeding to contact individual members or groups.
- Be polite, courteous, and respectful, especially to elders and other people of importance in the community.
- Do not be pushy. Wait until you are invited to enter a house, to join a group, or to participate in any activity.
- Be honest, open, and natural. Do not be condescending or sycophantic. Do not contrive to appear Aboriginal. You will gain more respect by being a whitefella who is making a genuine effort to understand the way of life in remote Aboriginal communities.
- Be patient. Be prepared to visit the community prior to the commencement of the study and to spend long periods of time in the community. Be prepared to spend time establishing rapport before asking your questions. Allow respondents plenty of time to respond.

* Donovan & Spark 1997

Concluding comments

This chapter has covered a broad variety of topics—but that is the nature of research in social marketing. The main points to remember are these:

- qualitative research is essential for strategy development
- good qualitative researchers are not easy to find
- pretesting ideas, materials, methods, and measures is necessary to ensure that the program has a good chance of success
- process and impact evaluation are crucial both for answering whether and why the program did or did not work and for justifying further program activities
- innovation in research ideas and methods is as important as innovation in program design and implementation.

All in all, think of research as an investment and evaluation as a tool for improvement rather than a tool for judging.

Chapter 7

Ethical issues in social marketing

Introduction

In this chapter we explore what we mean by ethical social marketing behaviour and take a brief look at some of the major ethical theories that have influenced our current way of thinking. Ethical decision making will be illustrated through a case study.

Ethics and marketing

People like to joke that the concept of an ethical marketer is an oxymoron. But this is a serious issue, one that is being given serious attention by social marketers, as evidenced in the recent publication of *Ethics in Social Marketing*, edited by Andreasen (2001).

Marketing as an activity has been accused of being unethical in a number of ways (Murphy & Bloom 1990): creating greed and dissatisfaction, misleading because it does not give the full picture of a product, manipulative because it persuades people to buy things they do not need, and a waste of valuable resources that could be spent in better causes (it is said, for example, that the global Coca-Cola marketing budget could make a real difference to worldwide child poverty). Marketing is accused of focusing on selected target markets—often those that are wealthy or privileged—and neglecting others. Conversely, other marketers, such as the tobacco companies and alcohol marketers, are accused of targeting vulnerable audiences such as children, teenagers, and socioeconomically disadvantaged groups. Marketing is accused of being intrusive in that television advertisements enter our homes and disrupt our leisure time, while billboards distract our attention on the road. Social marketers need to be mindful of all these ethical issues.

In addition it has been argued that social marketers should be held to even higher ethical standards than commercial marketers because there is a greater potential for harm if social marketing practices are unethical than when commercial marketing practices are unethical (Murphy & Bloom 1990). Also, as

Can social marketing be used to achieve unethical aims?

This question occasionally appears on the social marketing listserver, usually as a warning that we have to be careful that unscrupulous people, such as political parties, issue organisations, or even hate groups might use social marketing to influence people's beliefs, attitudes, and behaviours with respect to achieving their own ends. However, the question suggests a view of social marketing as just a bag of techniques. From our perspective social marketing is, by definition, the application of marketing principles and tools for the common good. In simple terms the answer to the above question is 'no', but marketing per se, as a set of tools and techniques, can be applied to any advocacy or persuasive task—ethical or otherwise. As we consider that social marketing is, by definition, concerned with ethical goals, the primary concerns for social marketers are whether their methods are ethical and whether the relative allocation of resources is ethical.

social marketing is usually funded by governments (taxpayers) or non-profit organisations (charitable donations) the way the funding is used is a matter of public trust and should be subject to scrutiny at the highest ethical standards (Andreasen 2001).

People who view a social marketing campaign as unethical are likely to reject both the campaign itself and the campaign message. The result would be worse than doing nothing. It has been shown that even expert members of the public, including professors of ethics, have difficulty in separating the ethics of a social idea from the ethics of marketing the social idea (Lusch, Laczniak & Murphy 1980). This can have an adverse effect in two ways. If the social idea is seen by some as unethical, for example, gay rights, then it can reflect on the social marketer even if the marketing techniques used are ethical. Similarly, if the marketing techniques are seen as unethical, such as offering misleading or incomplete information, this can have an adverse effect on the public's response to a social idea which itself is ethical (Lusch et al. 1980). Early antismoking ads in Australia had to be modified because of exaggerated claims, thus providing the tobacco industry with some support for its claim that the link between smoking and health was exaggerated and not proven.

What do we mean by 'ethics'?

The word 'ethics' is used in the broad sense to denote a moral philosophy or to refer to a system of moral or value judgements. It is the study of what people ought to do or feel they ought to do.

When we talk about ethics we are often talking about what feels morally right. There may or may not be a legal issue involved. Often, when there is a legal issue, our way is clearer. It is against the law to manufacture and sell illegal drugs and most people would agree it is unethical to do so. But while it is legal to manufacture and sell cigarettes not everyone would agree that it is ethical to do so. On the

We know that something feels unethical when we feel a sense of shame thinking about it. It is useful to ask yourself two questions when contemplating a potentially unethical act:

1 How would I feel if my boss, friends, peers, a journalist, or even my mother found out about it?
2 How will I feel about it tomorrow or next year? These two questions represent the external and internal referents for what is ethical.

Making ethical decisions on the basis of external sources is called 'moral heteronomy' (Benn 1988). There are two external sources of information about what is ethical: the law and cultural mores. Laws are created by society, specifically by those chosen to do so, such as politicians. There are sanctions for laws breached. Mores are also agreed upon by society, often supported by religious teachings and cultural traditions. Some mores are also laws (for example, 'Thou shalt not kill'), but not all (for example, 'Honour thy father and thy mother'). When you ask yourself how the people around you would regard your action you are referring to external referents.

Making ethical decisions on the basis of internal moral judgments is called 'moral autonomy' (Benn 1988). The concept of autonomy is central to ethical thought. When you ask yourself how you would feel about your action you are making an internal reference to the self. This form of ethical reasoning is more highly prized by ethical philosophers than the external reference of moral heteronomy. For example, German philosopher Immanuel Kant believed that it was only by making rational and autonomous moral decisions that individuals could fulfil their greatest potential.

Ethical theories

A full exploration of ethical theory is beyond the scope of this book, but we discuss some of the major influences on ethical thought in our present-day society.

To Greek philosopher Aristotle (384–322 BCE) ethics was the study of virtue. Virtue was seen to be the quality that falls between two extremes, 'the golden mean'. For example, between the two extremes of cowardice and foolhardiness lies the virtue of courage (Patterson & Wilkins 1991). Ethical behaviour was seen to depend on the character of the person who performed the act. A virtuous person could perform ethical acts. To be virtuous, a person had to be of good character and had to think about their behaviour and apply reason to their choices. This is a 'non-consequential' view of ethics, that is, the act is ethical because of the nature of the person who performs it not because of any good consequences that may follow from it.

MacIntyre (1999) stated that there are two fundamental virtues: integrity and constancy. Both of these virtues set limits on how much we adapt to different situations. Integrity means that we maintain some values across all social contexts. Constancy means that we maintain values through time with 'an unwavering directedness'. Without these virtues we become compartmentalised, a divided self, holding many—sometimes conflicting—values that change according to the roles we are required to play.

Most religions hold a basic moral principle that is believed to have been handed down by God or from nature. Within the Judeo-Christian beliefs this principle is 'Do unto others as you would have them do unto you'.

In the eighteenth century another non-consequentialist, Kant (1724–1804), contributed the philosophy of the categorical imperative, which states that an act itself is ethical if, through reason (logical thought), we would will that it be made a universal law and if it emerges from a respect for humanity and from a determination to do no harm to others or to give help to others. Kant's philosophy can be summed up as the Golden Rule: 'Do unto others as you would have them do unto you.'

John Stuart Mill (1859; 1991) contributed the consequential theory of utilitarianism, in which an act is ethical if the consequences of the act are good, regardless of whether the person who performs the act is a good person (as Aristotle would have it) or whether the act was chosen for the right reasons (as Kant would require). Good consequences are those that produce the greatest happiness for the greatest number of people. Central to this theory is the egalitarian concept that everyone's happiness is equally important (Patterson & Wilkins 1991). However, Mill's theory has been criticised for promoting a simplistic view where the end justifies the means or where the welfare of some members of society is sacrificed for the benefit of the majority. In any case, any attempt to measure the relative amounts of happiness that will arise from different acts will be open to debate.

Two other philosophers, W. D. Ross and John Rawls have had a major impact on our current way of thinking about ethics. Ross (1930; 1963) advocated an 'ethic of prima facie duties': fidelity, gratitude, beneficence, non-maleficence, and self improvement. Later, Rawls's theory of justice (1971) asserted two principles of justice: maximum freedom for all and the distribution of wealth so that the poorest members of society would be as well off as possible, or at least not further disadvantaged. Both of these ideas have been criticised, Ross's for being unable to advise which of his prima facie duties should take precedence over another, and Rawls for advocating unfair taxation. However, they do offer alternatives to classical utilitarianism that have been absorbed to some extent into our current accepted way of thinking about ethical behaviour.

Another important ethical approach is libertarianism, which derives from the philosophy of John Locke (1690; 1961) who recognised that all people have negative rights (for example, the freedom to be free from outside interference) as well as positive rights (for example, the right to certain benefits supplied by others). A proponent of libertarianism, Robert Nozick (1974), argued that we have a right to a say in the important decisions that affect our lives. Individuals are entitled to make informed decisions about their lives without unnecessary interference. This entitlement to negative rights such as life, liberty, and property (in the broadest sense) requires that we exercise our rights only as far as they do not infringe the rights of others. This concept is particularly relevant to social marketers, who may be asked from the libertarian point of view to justify their wish to interfere in the decisions that people make, such as whether to smoke, to ride a motorcycle without a helmet, or to practise unsafe sex.

other hand, some would feel that, while it is illegal to use cannabis, usage is not a moral issue but rather one of personal choice (Amonini & Donovan 2001).

Through ethics we attempt to come up with a system of rules based on commonly agreed values. Unfortunately, the complexity of human experience means that we can never come to an absolute agreement about what is ethical. Instead, we hold some general rules and then apply reason to each new situation. The debates over abortion and euthanasia are good examples of divergent thinking on ethical issues.

Ethical organisations

It can be argued that organisations as well as individuals have moral responsibility and that problems arise when the organisational values are inconsistent with external morality or with the individual's own values (Tsahuridu & McKenna 2000). The individual might abdicate personal ethical responsibility, seeing it as the duty of the organisation to make the appropriate ethical decisions. The extreme example of this is the action of soldiers during wartime: 'I was only obeying orders.' In such a case the individual is acting out of moral anomie, the absence of moral reasoning.

People often feel they have little choice but to go along with their organisation's decisions or give up their job, for example, a health-conscious, non-smoker working for an ad agency that handles the account of a cigarette company. However, people's choices may influence organisational mores as more marketing professionals take a stand to work only for clients they see as ethical (Hornery 2000). On a small scale, advertising agencies have been set up in Australia offering their services to clients with, for example, a commitment to community-focused advocacy (Social Change Media, Sydney) or to clients who make a positive contribution to the environment or social good (Cicchianni Malone Advertising Designers, Sydney) (Hornery 2000).

On a larger scale there is an increasing concern that multinational corporations should accept moral responsibility for the way their profit-driven decisions impact on the welfare of groups and individuals (Amba-Rao 1993). The Body Shop is an example of a company that has adopted a policy of corporate responsibility, which includes measuring social and environmental outcomes as well as financial outcomes (Robertson 1999). On the other hand, Nestle was forced by a consumer boycott to address the ethical issues involved in selling their product in the developing world. This led to the adoption of a formal Code of Marketing for Breastmilk Substitutes (Post 1985).

Another difficult ethical question for the social marketer occurs when government organisations elect to run a social advertising campaign essentially for political capital. For example, a 'Just Say No' (to drugs) campaign that is not even supported by a helpline is clearly not a well-thought-out campaign. We also know that some messages can backfire and increase feelings of rebellion in the target market. Is it ethical for the social marketer to contribute to a campaign that clearly will not be effective? Is it sufficient to voice objections? Only individuals can decide how far they are prepared to compromise their principles in the face of practical considerations such as keeping a job and more strategic considerations such as keeping a job in which they might later be able to make a valuable contribution to a social cause.

Nike and non-consequentialist thinking

There are two main schools of ethical thought: consequentialist and non-consequentialist. For the consequentialist school the ethical choice produces favourable consequences. This includes the theory of utilitarianism that ethical choices produce the greatest good for the greatest number of people. This would be the argument social marketers would use to defend their use of market segmentation, focusing limited resources where they are most likely to have the greatest good effect even though this might mean that some needy segments, such as hard-core addicts, are neglected. The non-consequentialist school of thought holds that ethical behaviour is not determined by results, that some behaviours are intrinsically good. The social marketer who argues that hard-core addicts should be included in the target market may be arguing that this is the ethical course of action even if it is not cost-effective. Social marketers with a strong commercial marketing background appear, for the most part, to subscribe to the consequentialist school, whereas those with a public health or community action background may be more likely to subscribe to the non-consequentialist school.

An interesting example of non-consequentialist thought occurred when students were shown a Nike ad advocating the message that girls who play sports suffer fewer negative and more positive events in their lives. The words included 'If you let me play … I will like myself more. I will have more self-confidence. I will suffer less depression … I will learn what it means to be strong. If you let me play sports.' The only evidence that Nike sponsored the ad was a single Nike swoosh symbol. Many students discounted any value in this message. Their antagonism arose from believing that Nike uses cheap labour in the developing world. The students' ethical thinking was non-consequentialist and goes back to ancient Greece: if the source is not seen as good, then anything that comes from it is tainted; only virtuous people can make virtuous decisions.

In May 2001 Dr Richard Smith resigned as professor of medical journalism at the University of Nottingham following the university's decision to accept UK£3.8 million from British American Tobacco. The money was designated to establish an international centre for the study of corporate responsibility. As editor of the *British Medical Journal* Dr Smith conducted a poll of readers. He asked two questions: Should the money be returned? and, if not, Should he resign as a professor at the university? There were 1075 respondents and their viewpoint on the first question was fairly unequivocal: 84 per cent thought the university should return the money. Agreement on the issue of resigning was less clear: 54 per cent voted for resignation if the money was not returned. In his letter of resignation Dr Smith acknowledged that the readers were divided over whether it was better to dissociate himself entirely or stay in the organisation to continue arguing the case. He said he had decided to resign 'both because I said I would do what the *BMJ*'s readers said I should do and because I've argued so strongly that the university shouldn't have taken this money' (Ferriman 2001).

Ethical principles

In today's Western society ethics has come to mean making rational choices between good and bad, deciding what actions can be morally justified, and, when faced with several morally justifiable choices, determining which is the most desirable (Patterson & Wilkins 1991). Downie and Calman (1994), considering ethical decisions in health care, concluded that the following four ethical principles be used as a rule of thumb to guide decision making:

- *the principle of non-maleficence*: do not harm others physically or psychologically
- *the principle of beneficence*: give help to others when they need it
- *the principle of justice*: treat everyone fairly and equally
- *the principle of utility*: make choices that produce the greatest good (or happiness) for the greatest number of people.

In line with libertarian ethical theory we would add a fifth consensus principle:

- *the principle of non-interference with the liberty of others*: allow everyone the freedom to exercise their fundamental rights as long as they do not infringe upon the rights of others.

Fundamental concept of autonomy

The basis of all these ethical principles is the assumption that we ought to respect people as autonomous beings, that is, with dignity, rights, and equality, who can make rational decisions for themselves about what is right for them (Rawls 1971; Dworkin 1988; Downie & Calman 1994). Ethical dilemmas invariably arise when this assumption of autonomy is questioned. Social marketing ethical decisions are likely to arise in situations involving a person who is not fully autonomous, for example, when the person is unborn (when the issue is abortion), an addict (when the issue is smoking or drug abuse), or a prisoner (when the issue is voting rights).

William Smith (2001), a social marketing practitioner, lists a number of moral principles that are particularly relevant in the context of social marketing.

- *Truth*: Are we being entirely truthful? Is there some exaggeration or inaccuracy or omission?
- *Privacy*: Are we invading the privacy of any group of people or revealing information about people that is not appropriate?
- *Modelling*: Are we inadvertently modelling antisocial or undesirable behaviours?
- *Morally offensive*: Are we demonstrating or encouraging behaviour that society finds offensive?
- *Fair and balanced*: Are we being fair to all groups?
- *Stereotyping*: Are we inadvertently perpetuating inappropriate or harmful stereotypes?

Increasing child adoption rates

The ethics of using marketing techniques to increase child adoption rates was raised on the social marketing listserver after a CBS *60 Minutes* program (9 January 2000) (Andreasen 2000; 2001). To increase adoption rates the children attended adoption fairs where prospective parents were able to talk directly with them and have an idea of their personalities and interests. The adoption fairs were supported by other marketing techniques such as brochures and websites.

Some of the ethical concerns were:
- would the children feel like property rather than autonomous beings?
- would the experience harm them in any way?
- would they feel even more rejected if they were not placed after attending one of these fairs?

In a way that recognises their autonomy, their ability to make rational choices for themselves, two of the children who had been placed were asked what they thought of the process. They said that although they cried after each fair they weren't picked from they believed they had 'to hang in there' because this was their best chance of eventually being placed. This comment from some of the children relieves us of some of our ethical concern (though we might wonder what response we would get from children who have still not been placed). But we agree with Andreasen's (2000) caution that 'We need constantly to ask whether using our powerful tools in certain areas—especially where kids are involved—meets tests of fairness and lack of harm'.

An interesting alternative communication strategy emerged from the list server discussion. It was suggested that many people who would like to adopt a child think they are ineligible when it is quite likely that they are eligible. Factual information about eligibility criteria could improve adoption rates without risking any harm to children (Black 2000). When one strategy feels unethical it is always worth asking the question: Is there an alternative strategy that could achieve the same result that feels more comfortable ethically?

- **Protecting children**: If our programs are going to be seen by children are they appropriate for their age?

  Smith (1999) cautions that such questions cannot be used as a simple ethical scorecard, assigning equal weight to each and achieving a minimum score before proceeding with a campaign. Ethical dilemmas occur when principles collide, such as the need to be truthful and the requirement to respect privacy. It is often difficult to decide whether one principle should take precedence over another. Smith (1999; 2001) makes the important point that any ethical decision is contextual. Several factors, and the ways in which they interrelate, need to be considered.

- *The actor* or provider, usually a government agency or non-profit organisation. How similar is the actor to the audience? What are the actor's motives? If there are several motives, are any in conflict? There is the potential for conflicts to occur in joint ventures where one partner may be profit-driven.

- *The offering* or product, the idea that is being sold, such as immunisation, blood donation, quit smoking. Ethical products are safe, accessible, and not too costly in terms of psychological as well as financial costs.

Ethical behaviour checklist

Laczniak and Murphy (1993, pp. 49–51) recommend that a checklist of eight questions be used to assess whether an action is ethical. The eight questions are paraphrased below.

1 Is there a law against it?
2 Is it contrary to accepted moral duties, including fidelity, gratitude, justice, non-maleficence, and beneficence?
3 Is it contrary to any special obligations of the organisation?
4 Is there any intention to cause harm?
5 Is it likely that major harm will result?
6 Is there a better alternative that would result in greater benefits?
7 Are any rights likely to be infringed, including property rights, privacy rights, and inalienable consumer rights including right to information, to be heard, to have a choice, and to have a remedy?
8 Is anyone left worse off and, if so, is this person already disadvantaged?

If the answer to any of the eight questions is 'yes' the action should be reconsidered.

- *The act* or program itself, how truthful it is, how fairly it represents people.
- *The context* in which the act will occur, when and where the communication will take place. There are different ethical problems if the context is within a school or in mass media, for example.
- *The audience.* What are the demographics of the intended and any unintended audiences. Does the intended audience have the resources to understand and act on the communication? Who else may see the communication and think it has relevance to them, particularly when using mass media?
- *The consequences*, intended and unintended, for both audiences. If the consequences are beneficial does that make the campaign ethical, even if it was less than truthful? Does the end justify the means, as the utilitarians believe?

Contextual ethicists argue that ethical decisions have to take into account the full cultural and historical background of all those involved and that this is especially important in today's multicultural societies (Thompson 1995). This leads us to the difficult question of moral cultural relativism: Can any act be defined as ethical if a society deems it to be? An example would be the extermination of the Jews in Nazi Germany. In the past, many behaviours that are now no longer acceptable, such as slavery, have been justified. Who is to say that some of our present-day behaviours will not later be judged as unethical? In the relativist mire it is difficult to see how anyone can be sure that an act is ethical. Thompson (1995) answers this problem by appealing to the concept of moral autonomy, that the added difficulty presented by relativism should make each individual reflect carefully on their own beliefs and behaviours. This process of individual moral reasoning needs to include an informed understanding of the historical and cultural reasons why past societies may have adopted different ethical standards than those adopted today.

Codes of behaviour

The word 'ethics' is also used in a specific way to describe a code of behaviour. Many professional organisations have a code of ethics (or code of conduct; see the Australian Marketing Institute's Code of Ethics in the box below). Members of such organisations agree to abide by their professional code of ethics. For example, a fundamental aspect of marketing codes is the concept of a voluntary and fair exchange, of mutual benefit to both parties. If the exchange is unfair, that is, if it benefits one party at the expense of the other, or if the consumer is coerced by false or misleading information, the practice is seen to be unethical. Codes of ethical conduct can only give broad guidelines. Social marketers face many choices that may not be specifically covered by the code where they have to make a decision about what is ethical.

AMI code of professional conduct

1 Members shall conduct their professional activities with respect for the public interest.
2 Members shall at all times act with integrity in dealing with clients or employers, past and present, with their fellow members and with the general public.
3 Members shall not intentionally disseminate false and misleading information, whether written, spoken or implied nor conceal any relevant fact. They have a duty to maintain truth, accuracy and good taste in advertising, sales promotion and all other aspects of marketing.
4 Members shall not represent conflicting or competing interests except with the express consent of those concerned given only after full disclosure of the facts to all interested parties.
5 Members in performing services for a client or employer, shall not accept fees, commissions or any other valuable consideration in connection with those services from any other than their client or employer except with the consent (express or implied) of both.
6 Members shall refrain from knowingly associating with any enterprise which uses improper or illegal methods in obtaining business.
7 Members shall not intentionally injure the professional reputation or practice of another member.
8 If a member has evidence that another member has been guilty of unethical practices it shall be their duty to inform the Institute.
9 Members have a responsibility to continue the acquisition of professional skills in marketing and to encourage the development of these skills in those who are desirous of entry into, or continuing in, the profession of marketing management.
10 Members shall help to improve the body of knowledge of the profession by exchanging information and experience with fellow members and by applying their special skill and training for the benefit of others.
11 Members shall refrain from using their relationship with the Institute in such a manner as to state or imply an official accreditation or approval beyond the scope of membership of the Institute and its aims, rules and policies.
12 The use of the Institute's distinguishing letters must be confined to Institute activities, or the statement of name and business address on a card, letterhead and published articles.
13 Members shall cooperate with fellow members in upholding and enforcing the code.

Do more good than harm ...

Favor free choice ...

Evaluate marketing within a broad context of behavior management [giving consideration to alternatives of education and law] ...

Select tactics that are effective and efficient ...

Select marketing tactics that fit marketing philosophy [that is meeting the needs of consumers rather than the self-interests of the organisation] ...

Evaluate the ethicality of a policy before agreeing to develop strategy.

* Rothschild 2001, pp. 35–6

Criticism of social marketing as paternalistic

As we have seen the concept of autonomy is central to ethical thinking. One criticism that is often levelled at social marketing is that it does not treat people like autonomous beings, rather, it takes a paternalistic approach. Paternalism is the attitude that says people need to be protected from self-inflicted harm in the way that a father or mother protects a child (Downie & Calman 1994). 'Nanny state' is another term that has come to be used in reference to government regulation and social marketing. Knag (1997, p. 405) makes a distinction between old-style, authoritarian paternalism, which chastised the individual with the use of laws and sanctions, and a newer maternalism or nanny state, which smothers the individual with 'education and therapy (or rather, propaganda and regulation)'.

The implication is that social marketers tell people what they should and should not do as if they were children being supervised by a nanny. At the extreme people may be afraid that 'social marketing could ultimately operate as a form of thought control by the economically powerful', a view expressed by some participants in a survey of attitudes towards social marketing (Laczniak, Lusch & Murphy 1979). The question was raised in an American state legislature debate on mandatory seat belt laws: 'Where [do] we draw the line between the nanny state and the freedom of the individual to make sensible decisions?' (Bayer 1992). In New Hampshire, USA, they answered this question by rejecting such legislation. Wearing seat belts and motorcycle helmets is not compulsory in New Hampshire where the state motto is 'Live free and die'.

One argument that is often quoted to justify paternalism in safety contexts is that the economic costs of allowing unsafe behaviour have to be borne by the community. Dworkin (1988) dismissed this argument pointing out that the costs of wearing a helmet and surviving a motorbike accident could be far greater than the alternative.

Some degree of paternalism by the state is necessary and often desirable because people are not entirely self-reliant in every circumstance (Mead 1998).

For example, the government requires credit card companies to print interest rates on statements so that consumers are properly informed; it requires people to provide for their own retirement, as well as requiring children to be vaccinated (Mead 1998). These examples of paternalism are acceptable in part because they apply to all members of society. The criticism of paternalistic social marketing is that it is often paternalistic towards a selected group of people, such as smokers, or those considered unable to make competent decisions. Being selected out in this way can create a backlash resulting in counterproductive responses so that an intervention could end up doing more harm than good.

In *The Rise of the Nanny State* Holt (1995) argues that governments are extending the range of their regulatory powers, restricting free markets, and intruding into areas of personal responsibility, all under the guise of acting in the public good. Wikler (1978) considered the case for stronger government intervention by weighing the pros and cons of an interesting strategy: the introduction of a fat tax that would require citizens to be weighed and pay a surcharge if they were overweight. He concludes that this paternalistic interference would not be justified because there are other ways—through education and therapeutic efforts—to appeal to the risk-taker's autonomy.

A real concern is that when people are treated like children they become like children, retaining their desires and appetites but abdicating responsibility for their individual choices to the state (Knag 1997). An example would be smokers who declare that they will continue to smoke until the government bans smoking (Brown 2001). One way that social marketers can overcome the perception of paternalism and maternalism is to design campaigns so that the audience views the message as informative rather than directive.

Health promoters argue that many behaviours they wish to change are not entirely voluntary (O'Connell & Price 1983). For example, it is argued that an individual's choice to smoke or to drive fast has already been manipulated by commercial interests. Thus, they argue that health promotion efforts are intended to reduce ignorance and restore true personal autonomy—the ability to make fully informed and rational choices (Smith 1992). Support for this claim was found in a study of the effects on young people of smoking scenes in films (Pechmann & Shih 1999). The researchers found that young viewers were positively influenced to smoke by seeing smoking scenes in films, but that this effect could be nullified by showing an antismoking advertisement before the film.

Moral imperialism

Another criticism of social marketing on a more global scale is that of 'moral imperialism' (Brenkert 2001). The criticism is that social marketing promotes the paternalistic attitude of Western society towards other cultures, particularly those in developing countries. We (in the West) see issues such as birth control and safe sex to prevent the spread of AIDS as being in the interest of the developing country. However, many issues could be culturally sensitive, for example, advocating the use of condoms in a South American country with a strong Catholic tradition. Many issues are resisted on the basis of culture and religion,

Who determines what is the social good?

As discussed in chapter 1 we propose that social marketers use the United Nations Universal Declaration of Human Rights as the fundamental reference when determining what issues represent the social good. As an external ethical referent this Declaration has been debated and is agreed by many to reflect the most highly regarded, basic values of our society. It provides a benchmark against which finer ethical questions can be measured. It enshrines rights of freedom, equality, privacy, and education, all of which are fundamental concepts in social marketing.

The thirty Articles can be read in full at the Office of the High Commissioner for Human Rights' website at <http://www.unhchr.ch/udhr/>, but here we list some of the most relevant Articles.

Article 1   All human beings are born free and equal in dignity and rights. They are endowed with reason and conscience and should act towards one another in a spirit of brotherhood. (That is, the right to autonomy.)

Article 2   These rights apply to everyone. No distinction shall be made on any basis.

Article 3   Life, liberty and security of person.

Article 7   Equal before the law and entitled to protection against discrimination.

Article 11   Presumed innocent until proved guilty according to law in a public trial.

Article 12   No one shall be subjected to arbitrary interference with his privacy, family, home or correspondence, nor to attacks upon his honour and reputation.

Article 18   Everyone has the right to freedom of thought, conscience and religion.

Article 19   Everyone has the right to freedom of opinion and expression.

Article 21.2   Everyone has the right to equal access to public service in his country.

Article 21.3   The will of the people shall be the basis of authority of government.

Article 26.1   Everyone has the right to education.

for example, female circumcision and women's rights in Muslim countries. Social marketers have to be mindful that everything they do involves imposing values onto people who may not share those values and who may have good reason for not wanting to share them (Dann 1998).

Brenkert (2001) analysed the special ethical problems faced by international social marketers. Some of the problems identified by Brenkert are that they may not be citizens of the country in which the project takes place and may not hold the same cultural values. They may also have more power and resources than the people to whom the social marketing effort is directed. Brenkert concluded that social marketers should recognise that not all apparently harmful values should be challenged or can feasibly be changed. Further, inherent in the use of persuasion as a means to the social marketing end is the responsibility to ensure that non-compliance must be a real option for those who are being persuaded. People must be informed what behaviour change is being attempted and why, and should have reason to trust the people who are attempting to effect the change (Brenkert 2001).

Criticism of power imbalances in social marketing

It can be said that the primary ethical issue in social marketing is the problem of power (Laczniak et al. 1979). The group with the most financial power or strongest political support is likely to be able to impose its values on groups with fewer resources. At the same time stronger groups are more able to resist political or government power. For example, in 1986 the Singapore government initiated a campaign to encourage graduate mothers to have more children. The purpose was to increase the population and to produce a more intelligent populace. It created controversy and was resisted by the educated people to whom it was directed (Teo 1992).

One of the major issues facing government departments is determining the priority needs of numerous and diverse stakeholders. In the context of road users, for example, it may be difficult, even when there are major environmental and health benefits to be gained, to assign limited resources to groups such as pedestrians and bicyclists when the majority of road users are private and commercial drivers.

One way in which an imbalance of power becomes potentially unethical is when alliances are formed between powerful corporations and non-profit organisations and causes. Corporations are increasingly choosing to spend money on cause-related marketing rather than giving donations to charitable organisations. In this way the corporation has some control over how the money is spent and how much publicity is received for the donation.

A difficulty may arise when the commercial partner's interests appear to be inconsistent with the social partner's. For example, a Hong Kong charity, Caritas Integrated Service for Young People, was criticised for accepting money from the Tobacco Institute of Hong Kong for the purpose of running twenty antismoking programs targeted at young people (Kwok 2000). Similarly, a

Kellogg's Kids Help Line

An example of successful, mutually beneficial cause-related marketing in Australia is Kellogg's sponsorship of the Kids Help Line, a free, confidential, counselling service for 5–18 year olds. It began in 1998 as a $50 000 onpack promotion and developed into an ongoing, multimillion dollar partnership. The Help Line reports handling approximately 60 000 calls per year, calls that would otherwise have gone unanswered <http://www.kellogg.com.au/06/03/0603.asp>.

Kellogg's market research indicated that, within a month, the Kids Help Line was regarded by the majority of Australians as the most respected charity in Australia (Burbury 1999). Despite these mutual benefits it must be remembered that cause-related marketing is 'profit-motivated giving' (Varadarajan & Menon 1988, p. 58), in which the commercial partner has the balance of power.

campaign in the USA to combat domestic violence and offer support to abused women was funded by the Philip Morris family of companies (Forbes 2000).

Some people have said that the tobacco industry has no role to play in preventative health care. In Canada the University of Alberta turned down an offer of $500 000 from a tobacco manufacturer and the University of British Columbia has adopted a policy of refusing all tobacco company sponsorship (Sibbald 2000). On the other hand, the Universities of Toronto, McGill, and Calgary have all accepted funding from Imasco Ltd, which owns Imperial Tobacco. The University of Calgary used the money to help establish a Faculty of Nursing Learning Centre (Sibbald 2000). A utilitarian ethicist would say that the end justifies the means and might even ask the question: Is it ethical *not* to accept this money and run these valuable programs? Our view is that if the primary aim of the tobacco marketer's donation is to promote corporate or brand awareness or to improve the image of the tobacco company, then it is unethical to accept the funds as it clearly contributes to the promotion of tobacco: the ultimate end would be harmful.

Before making an ethical decision it is always worth considering whether there are, in fact, only two choices. In the above examples two choices are evident:

1   take the money and run the prevention program
2   refuse the money and do not run the program.

However, as in many ethical dilemmas, there is usually a third possibility: that is,

3   obtain the money to run the program from a different source.

Social alliances can be a very successful strategy for both partners. However, there is an unfortunate consequence of the trend towards partnerships that is discussed by Andreasen and Drumwright (2001). Causes that are perceived as attractive, such as breast cancer, receive greater support and exposure, whereas unattractive causes, such as AIDS, receive less support and exposure. They explain that breast cancer is seen as attractive because it affects a large number of people, is unpredictable, is not associated with undesirable behaviours, and is not necessarily fatal, while AIDS is unattractive because it is associated with drug use and male homosexuality. Even within the cause of breast cancer there are more partners keen to be associated with the more attractive activities of research than with the more mundane aspects, such as providing transport to screening for disadvantaged groups. Andreasen and Drumwright (2001, p. 107) cautioned that social alliances can be driven by a market mentality, in which causes are supported because they are appealing, or not unappealing, in preference to causes that have a greater need of support but are less appealing.

This focus on popular versus unpopular causes is not confined to corporate alliances; governments too are inclined to allocate health funds to areas seen to be (or assumed to be) popular with voters and to neglect more worthy areas that are not seen to be popular with voters. (An Australian health minister was alleged to have said that he could not persuade cabinet to support prostate screening because 'it's not sexy', meaning 'not popular' with the masses.)

Criticism of unintended consequences

Ethical social marketers need to consider the possible unintended consequences of their actions. One unintended consequence of social marketing is the risk of increasing the prevalence of victim blaming. Victim blaming is the tendency people have to attribute people's illnesses, injuries, unemployment, or other disadvantaged state to deficiencies under their personal control (laziness, no will power, absence of interest in 'good' practices, etc.) (Lee, Campbell & Mulford 1999). Victim blaming occurs in a variety of contexts, such as child pedestrian injuries (Roberts & Coggan 1994), domestic violence (Fawcett, Heise, Isita-Espejel & Piack 1999) and AIDS. One criticism that was levelled at Australian AIDS campaigns was that they increased the likelihood of blaming the victim of AIDS for being gay or a drug user (Dr Tom Carroll, Commonwealth Department of Human Services and Health, New South Wales, personal communication, May 1995).

It is important to address the possibility that a social marketing message may increase risk by normalising behaviours that would not be advocated otherwise. For example, some people are concerned that AIDS prevention campaigns advocating condom use may be inadvertently conveying the message that promiscuous sex is acceptable (Brown & Singhal 1993). Similar concerns are voiced that harm-reduction strategies, such as needle exchange schemes and provision of injecting rooms, may send the wrong message that drug use is acceptable (MacCoun 1998).

Another unintended consequence can occur if the message is subverted by hard-core target markets so that negative role models become perceived as positive. For example, in Australia, many people identified with Norm, the popular couch potato character of the 'Life! Be In It' campaign, with little if any resulting impact on their levels of physical activity. More recently, an attempt has been made to subvert the successful 'Drink and drive—you're a bloody idiot' slogan by adding, 'Make it home—you're a bloody legend'.

Interesting illustrations come from the field of edutainment. It was thought that the American sitcom *All in the Family* would promote tolerance through the

Unintended consequences

A 10-year-old boy cries in the night. His mother goes in to comfort him. He says he is crying because 'Daddy's going to die of lung cancer'. Her son had seen a Quit smoking advertisement showing a boy his age attending his father's funeral after the father has died from a smoking-related illness. The son had no way to resolve the anxiety raised by the advertisement; he couldn't quit smoking himself because he didn't smoke and he couldn't make his father quit (Henley & Donovan 1999b).

By being aware of potential consequences appropriate action can be taken to minimise the effects, such as scheduling television advertisements in the late evening when children are less likely to see them.

Ethical social marketing research

Many of the issues researched in social marketing are often highly sensitive. Surveys on domestic violence, child abuse, smoking, drug abuse, etc., could all arouse in the respondent a degree of anxiety and the need for further information or help. It is standard practice in social marketing research to offer respondents appropriate helpful literature to take away with them at the end of the interview, such as a Quit pack, or leaflet on cancer prevention. It is also necessary to be able to give out telephone numbers, email and website addresses for helplines and other counselling services.

satirical depiction of the bigoted character of Archie Bunker. Instead, it appeared that viewers who were already prejudiced identified with Archie Bunker and their prejudices were reinforced (Brown & Singhal 1993). Similarly, the Indian government produced a soap opera, *Hum Log* (*We People*), intended to improve the status of women. One of the characters, Bhagwanti, was intended to be seen as a negative role model, demonstrating subservient behaviour that was rewarded with abuse. The producers intended people to see Bhagwanti as an argument for women's equality. In fact, 80 per cent of women viewers saw her as a positive role model, embodying traditional female values; many men said they thought India needed more women like Bhagwanti (Brown & Singhal 1993).

Another potential unintended consequence is that the message might have an adverse affect on people outside the target market (Henley & Donovan 1999b). For example, is it ethical to use the threat of premature wrinkles caused by smoking to try to persuade young women to quit when this same message could lessen the self-esteem of people who already have wrinkles (Kirby & Andreasen 2001)? We might reasonably decide on a utilitarian approach here—the end justifies the means—because the harm to wrinkled people is outweighed by the greater good done to the young women.

Similarly, it is essential to consider the effect of a campaign on people for whom it may trigger unwelcome associations. For example, a campaign targeting child abusers will inevitably trigger painful memories in children and adults who have suffered and continue to suffer abuse. It is unethical to run such a campaign without ensuring beforehand that helplines and counsellors are aware of the likely increase in demand and are able to resource the increased demand.

Case study

Freedom from Fear, **domestic violence prevention campaign**

The following case study illustrates some of the numerous ethical issues that can confront the social marketer and these are discussed using the ethical principles explained earlier. The case study is Western Australia's *Freedom from Fear* campaign targeting male perpetrators of domestic, intimate partner, violence (Donovan, Paterson & Francas 1999f), which is discussed fully in chapter 14. The main innovation of this campaign was to offer male perpetrators and potential perpetrators free counselling services to help them voluntarily change their behaviour. Rather than threatening imprisonment and other legal sanctions the campaign focused on amplifying feelings of guilt and remorse in perpetrators by emphasising the effects of violence on children. This was a universally relevant message. Perpetrators who did not have children still responded to this message, many of them recalling their own experience of violence as children.

Ethical question: Can we ensure that the campaign will not cause physical or psychological harm?

Extensive formative research ensured that the ad messages would not adversely impact on victims and children, especially victims' children. Relevant stakeholders, including women's groups, police, counsellors, and government departments were consulted throughout the development stage. Child psychologists were used in testing the ad concepts with victims (including child victims) and children of victims and abusers. Although the ads were to be scheduled in adult time it was still regarded as crucial that any child who saw the ad would not experience clinical stress. The concepts were also tested to ensure that children did not take away the message that they should encourage their fathers to call the helpline as this might have put children in greater danger. Other checks included assessing the extent to which the ads appeared to be an unwarranted attack on men in general and whether the ads appeared to condone violence towards women under any circumstances.

Confidentiality was a major issue; many of the callers to the helpline were admitting a criminal act. Anonymity was assured and callers were not pressed to give their name. When a referral to counselling was not possible the helpline counsellors asked the caller to nominate an address to which they could send educational self-help booklets and audiocassettes.

Ethical question: Does the campaign give help where it is needed?

There was a need to address the potential criticism that the campaign helped the perpetrator at the expense of the victim and that these resources would be better used in providing help for victims and their children. This was done by keeping the focus on *Freedom from Fear*. The ultimate aim was to address the women's need to be free from the fear of violence long term by providing counselling to the perpetrator as distinct from encouraging women to seek legal sanctions, such as restraining orders, which do not necessarily reduce the fear. New counselling programs for women and children were also funded by the state government.

Ethical question: Does the campaign allow those who need help the freedom to exercise their entitlements?

Women and children are entitled to lives free of abuse. The campaign is contributing to their ability to claim this entitlement. The ultimate goal of the campaign is that they should be free from fear. In addition, in this non-coercive approach the male perpetrators are being given the freedom to choose whether they seek counselling and a practical means of doing so.

Ethical question: Are all parties treated equally and fairly?

It would be unethical to raise hopes and motivation to change unless sufficient resources were available and accessible over a sufficient time period. This is nominally a 10-year campaign that receives substantial funding from the state government. The resources include a helpline that is staffed by specially trained counsellors as well as government-subsidised counselling programs. These programs are provided in twelve locations throughout Western Australia, six of them in regional areas. Given Western Australia's geography it was recognised that access to counselling programs would necessarily be limited in remote areas but it was hoped to extend access in later phases of the campaign. Meanwhile, self-help materials could be sent to any location. Access to programs was provided in non-working hours and the helpline was staffed day and night.

It was decided that all materials and programs would be provided free to ensure that no financial barrier existed or could be rationalised as existing at any income level. Again, the focus was on the victim; it was important that victims of low-income perpetrators would not be disadvantaged.

Ethical question: Will the choices made produce the greatest good for the greatest number of people?

To date, the campaign has received 12 500 calls and approximately 2500 men have been referred to counselling. Initial estimates are that it costs about $2500–$3000 per referral to the completion of the counselling program. The utilitarian view is that this compares favourably with the cost, approximately $50 000, of treating one victim of domestic violence, including the costs of police, medical, courts, welfare, and potential income loss. There is also the increased freedom from fear experienced by hundreds of women and children whose partners have voluntarily sought counselling.

Ethical question: Is the autonomy of the target market recognised?

This campaign holds that many male perpetrators are fully autonomous, responsible for their actions, and able to voluntarily choose to change their behaviour. The campaign acknowledges that the perpetrator who genuinely wishes to change his behaviour has a right to treatment and to be treated with dignity in this treatment.

Concluding comments

Social marketers need to ensure the highest ethical standards in promoting social causes. There is great potential for doing harm if social marketing practices are unethical. Ethical practice can be achieved by asking a few simple questions before proceeding with a campaign and keeping them in mind throughout the life of the campaign. The questions are designed to alert marketers to issues relating to basic, shared ideas about what is held to be right, fair, and just in our society. These questions refer to the principles of non-maleficence (doing no harm), beneficence (doing good), justice (fair and equal treatment), and utility (providing the greatest good to the greatest number). Social marketing campaigns that fail to recognise the autonomy of a target market are justly criticised for being paternalistic. Fundamental to all ethical questions is the assumption that all people deserve to be treated as autonomous beings.

Chapter 8

The Competition

Introduction

This chapter analyses the competition from three main perspectives:

1 defining the competition
2 monitoring the competition
3 countering the competition.

Given the importance of early childhood development for later adolescent and adult behaviours, of special interest is the competition for kids. The targeting of children has gone from virtually non-existent in the early 1950s, through specific targeting of child products, to the more recent all-out drive to inculcate consumption values among children as the dominant cultural values. While this has not yet reached the same level as in the USA (where there is a growing backlash; Walsh 1995) there are signs that it is increasing rapidly in Australia and deserves urgent attention.

Defining the competition

Competition and the principle of differential advantage

This principle refers to an analysis of the marketer's resources versus those of the competition, with the aim of determining where the company enjoys a differential advantage over the opposition. The aim is to focus the company's resources on products or markets that exploit this differential advantage. A differential advantage could be held in technology, human resources, markets, or financial backing.

Commercial organisations, as part of their strategic planning process, regularly carry out **SWOTC** analyses—audits of the organisation's **s**trengths and **w**eaknesses, identification of **o**pportunities, **t**hreats facing the organisation, and analysis of their **c**ompetitors. The monitoring and understanding of competitive activity is sometimes to emulate or follow such activity, while in other cases the aim is to preempt or counter competitors' activities.

Threats—existing and emerging—should get particular attention. This requires monitoring changes and potential changes in the various environments noted in chapter 3, particularly technological, economic, and political changes. The aim is to brainstorm how to turn these threats, wherever possible, into opportunities or at least take steps to minimise the impact of the threats. For example, rather than seeing the fragmentation of media channels as a threat to mass campaigns it may be seen as an opportunity to provide more tailored messages to various subgroups.

Defining the competition in social marketing

In commercial marketing the competition for a particular product or brand is generally defined as those alternatives that meet the same basic needs or compete for the same resources. Red Rooster Chicken's competitors are not just KFC and other fast-food chicken suppliers, but are all fast-food suppliers such as McDonald's and Pizza Hut. Competing products are those that can be substituted for the organisation's product, that is, functional alternatives. For example, if icecream is not available, frozen yoghurt can be chosen for a family dessert. If Pizza Hut is closed, takeaway Chinese can be substituted. For convenience foods, choices between the various alternatives are not based just on the taste of the various products, but also on price, variety of offerings, convenience of location, opening hours, and associated promotion incentives (for example, free Coke with every pizza). Competition is based on the total bundle of benefits consumers are seeking in fast food: affordable, quick and easy to obtain, liked by the whole family, robust packaging for the takeaway journey, options for different tastes and appetite sizes, and so on.

For high-priced items such as a motor vehicle the competition might not be the various car manufacturers, but what else can be purchased for that amount of money (for example, home extensions, an overseas holiday, a home entertainment system, or a boat).

Thus, there are clearly defined competitor entities at the brand level (Red Rooster versus KFC) and the product category level (all fast-food entities). There are also competitive forces that may affect the whole product category or some entities more than others: a trend towards growing beards would impact all men's razor suppliers and the introduction of computers led to the demise of typewriters (these broader competitive forces have been discussed in chapter 3).

Defining the competition is not as simple for health and social marketers although the basic definition of all those alternatives that meet the same basic needs or compete for the same resources still applies. For example, many non-nutritious snack foods offer convenience, low price, good taste, and a fun image. To compete, healthy snack foods must satisfy these same needs—or introduce 'new' needs (see chapters 4 and 5). In fact, introducing new needs is a common tactic in social marketing, as we are often promoting products that do not provide equivalent functional benefits to those we wish to replace, or only some, often at a substantial psychological or dollar cost.

Nevertheless, the lesson from the notion of functional alternatives is that when we look at our competition we must look for the benefits people are getting from their undesired behaviours and then devise strategies to substitute other benefits or show how the same benefits can be met by the desired behaviours. Similarly, we can identify and then highlight the disbenefits people see in their current undesirable behaviours and show how these can be avoided by adopting the desired behaviour.

Categorising the competition in social marketing

While they are not necessarily mutually exclusive we propose the following categories to assist in designing strategies to monitor and counter the competition:

- competitors clearly defined in terms of any use of their products (no safe level of tobacco use, some illicit drugs, leaded petrol, some forms of asbestos, etc.)
- competitors defined in terms of excess use or abuse of their products (some illicit drugs, alcohol, guns, motor vehicles, gambling, etc.)
- competitors defined in terms of sociocultural beliefs and values that inhibit the uptake of healthy behaviours (attitudes to birth-control inhibiting contraception, machismo attitudes inhibiting condom use and facilitating the spread of AIDS) or affect the health of the planet in general (materialism, consumption as lifestyle)
- competitors defined by beliefs and values that create conflict in society (for example, racist organisations, fundamentalist religious organisations, terrorist groups)
- competitors defined by beliefs and values that have negative consequences for many while benefiting a select few (global corporations, privatisation of government services, armaments suppliers, media organisations).

Table 8.1 indicates who are the primary target groups for each of these categories of competition. For product competitors, where there is no safe level of consumption, our goal may be to drive the product marketers out of business and reduce consumption to zero. Our primary targets are individuals and, where companies are unlikely to be cooperative, governments for legislation.

For excess use or abuse competitors the aim is to ensure responsible use or consumption by individuals and responsible marketing by corporations. Our primary targets are individuals and, where they are likely to be cooperative, product manufacturers and marketers. Public servants are a primary target for product regulation and governments for relevant legislation in the absence of corporate cooperation. For example, food manufacturers and (some) alcohol

Table 8.1 Type of competition and targets for change

Type of competition	Primary targets			
	Individuals	Corporations	Public service	Government
Unsafe product	xxxxx	xxx	xxx	xxxxx
Excess	xxx	xxxx	xxx	xxxxx
Sociocultural	xxx	xxxxx	xxxxx	xxxxx

marketers appear approachable with respect to product modifications and responsible marketing, whereas tobacco marketers are not.

In the domain of beliefs and values our goals are to neutralise (by any ethical means) those beliefs and values that cause harm to members of a society or inhibit achievement of health and wellbeing. In such cases our primary targets are the decision makers in corporations (including media owners and publishers), the policy makers in bureaucracy, or the law makers in government. Whether the primary target is the corporation (for voluntary cooperation) or the government (for legislative compliance) will depend on the specific issue. For hate websites government regulation and legislation are deemed essential. On the other hand, responsible reporting would be negotiated with the media with respect to issues such as suicide, celebrations involving alcohol, and sexual issues.

There are of course beliefs and values associated with product and excess use competitors. In fact, many sociocultural beliefs and values support the continuation of unhealthy lifestyles and behaviours that inhibit community wellbeing. For example, tolerance of alcohol as an integral part of celebrations facilitates adolescent binge drinking, and female slimness in the media facilitates bulimia and anorexia. On a broader scale, beliefs about a subservient role of women in society facilitate sexual and physical violence against women, beliefs that economic factors have priority inhibit community welfare allocations, insufficient acknowledgement of environmental influences enhances victim blaming and inadequate allocation of resources to structural change. All of these are competitive forces that must be taken into account.

While health and social change organisations face competition from these external competitors they also face internal competition for available resources (for example, the National Heart Foundation, cancer councils, and Diabetes Australia all compete for donations and grants; government departments such as Family and Children's Services and Ageing Care compete for budget allocations). The emphasis in this chapter is on external competitors; however, the lessons should assist organisations compete (or cooperate) for available resources.

'I'd like to see that'

What we would like to see is the various NGOs with similar goals carrying out joint SWOTC analyses so that the different organisations could then carry out complementary or synergistic rather than overlapping or even contradictory campaigns.

Monitoring the competition

Commercial organisations monitor their competitors' activities via qualitative and quantitative research assessing consumers' perceptions of their competitors' products and corporate image vis-à-vis their own. Competitors' annual reports, press releases, advertising, building activity, public tenders, and employment notices can all be monitored to gain an insight into competitors' activities. Independent reviews in trade magazines and the business media also provide information about competitors' activities.

Similarly, in social marketing all of the above sources provide useful information. However, in most cases, the most valuable information comes from the competitors' public marketing and promotional activities, supported, wherever possible, by internal documents outlining the company's strategies and target groups.

Analysing the messages contained in alcohol advertising (social success; see below), looking at the sports that tobacco companies sponsor (motor racing—thrills and glamour), and monitoring product placement in entertainment vehicles (cool images, fashion) provides a wealth of information about the benefits offered by these products. A study of alcohol advertising and promotion, for example, can assist in understanding appeals to young males. Similarly, advocacy groups need to monitor industries such as the tobacco industry and attempt to preempt anticipated industry moves.

The media are often singled out as one of the major factors influencing people's attitudes and values with respect to products, consumption, and lifestyles (Pollay 1986; Hovland & Wilcox 1987; Strasburger 1993). Media includes paid advertising, how and what news is reported, movies, television programs, lifestyle magazines, radio talkback, websites, and so on.

Advertising makes a specific contribution to a consumption-based society. Advertising portrays what products and brands are associated with what lifestyles, what socioeconomic status, what attitudes to life, and, consequently, how we can adopt and maintain a particular self-image by purchasing and consuming

Toys R not always harmless fun

Barbie gets a credit card

Monitoring the competition includes keeping a close eye on toy marketers. In keeping with the early commercialisation of children, Cool Shoppin' Barbie comes with a MasterCard. She chirps 'Credit approved' when her MasterCard is put into Mattel's toy cash register. There are fears that such a no-limit card might encourage irresponsible spending among children and could lead to youngsters accepting credit cards from banks while too young to fully understand the consequences (Associated Press 1998).

The tanning doll: Cancer educators in the UK are up in arms about a French doll that takes only a minute in the sun to tan. The doll comes with a beach bag, towel, deckchair and fake suntan lotion. Cancer educators believe that the kids will get the message that it is safe to sunbathe and try and get as tanned as their doll. With skin cancer cases on the rise in Britain, these educators are 'not amused'. (Williams 2001).

appropriate products (Cushman 1990). Social commentators claim that advertising has particular influence on the young, especially regarding which brands or product categories are in or cool (Twitchell 1996). Advertising also models for young people what various product categories are used for.

We will look at just a few examples here, with an emphasis on monitoring what appears in the media.

Body image and eating disorders

Eating disorders affect about 2–3 per cent of people, 90 per cent of whom are women (Hay 1998). It is likely that the images of women portrayed in fashion magazines and advertising, particularly of beauty products, has a lot to do with this. Advertising in particular uses sexuality and physical attractiveness to sell products, particularly to girls. Thinness is also emphasised as the ideal standard for women, although fashion models weigh almost 25 per cent less than the average female and supermodels' slimness represents just 1 per cent of women aged 18–34 (Mediascope 2000a). It is not surprising then that in an American survey of Grade 5–12 girls 69 per cent reported that magazine pictures influenced their idea of body shape and 47 per cent wanted to lose weight because of magazine pictures (Field, Cheung, Wolf et al. 1999).

Unfortunately, all this leads to women reporting dissatisfaction with their body size; girls dissatisfied with their bodies diet more and are more prone to eating disorders (Mediascope 2000a). Controlling weight is also a factor often mentioned by young women as a reason for smoking (Carter, Borland & Chapman 2001)

What we need to do is monitor the sizes of women appearing in advertising and on the fashion, entertainment, and celebrity pages of magazines. This, coupled with research showing the influence of these images on young girls' and women's dissatisfaction with their body image and the link between such dissatisfaction and eating disorders, would provide the evidence needed to undertake

---

For women and fashion, size does matter—small is beautiful

Five years ago, the ideal female body shape was a size 10. In life, in shopfronts, and on *Friends* that ideal was reduced to a size 8, which in turn was shrunk to size 6. Now the ultimate fashion statement lies in a woman convincing herself she does not exist at all: size 0. Replacing the sizing regime (8 to 16) with an 0–6 range—as local designers are now doing—is ostensibly about making the average woman feel better about buying clothes. Downsize a single number on a label, and overnight the customer who was a self-conscious size 14 is into reassuring single digits.

Trouble is, this ploy to make women feel smaller than they actually are occurs at a time when what was regarded as slim is now seen as plump. In the mid 1990s, the upmarket American department store Saks retrenched Frances, a tall, size 10 mannequin who had put in 20 years of unstinting service, and replaced her with Frannie, a stringy size 8. According to a report in The Australian Magazine last weekend, in 1950 a shop dummy's average hip measurement was 86.5cm. By 1990 this had dropped to 79cm, even though the average woman's hip measurement had grown to 94cm.

Neill 2001

advocacy with editors and advertising agencies. Such lobbying has proved effective in other areas: the proportion of women with a deep tan has declined substantially in young women's magazines in Australia (Chapman, Marks & King 1992; McDermott 2001).

Tobacco

Tobacco litigation in the USA provided antitobacco activists with unprecedented access to internal tobacco company documents. These documents have provided evidence with respect to the tobacco industry's knowledge—yet public denial— of the ill health effects of tobacco, their deliberate marketing to children, covert PR campaigns to discredit passive smoking research, using low-tar cigarettes to delay or deter quitting, aggressive moves into developing countries, and their role in large-scale cigarette smuggling (ASH 2000). The evidence for their targeting of underage youth is particularly compelling (for example, Perry 1999). A UK report provides further evidence of the tobacco industry's marketing tactics from an analysis of the tobacco industry's main UK advertising agencies (Hastings & MacFadyen (2000).

All of these documents provide substantial evidence for lobbying government to increase controls over the marketing of tobacco and the regulation of the industry per se. VicHealth Centre for Tobacco Control's (2001) *Blue Chip* document provides a very good summary of the evidence for regulation of the tobacco industry in Australia.

Monitoring the tobacco industry's new products, advertising, sponsorship, and promotional activities is essential
- to ensure that the industry is not contravening promotional regulations
- to ensure that the industry is not exploiting loopholes or legitimate activities
- to develop counter strategies.

Since the ban on advertising the tobacco industry has constantly looked for ways to circumvent the ban. Hence, studies are regularly conducted to monitor

Figure 8.1 Sly endorsement

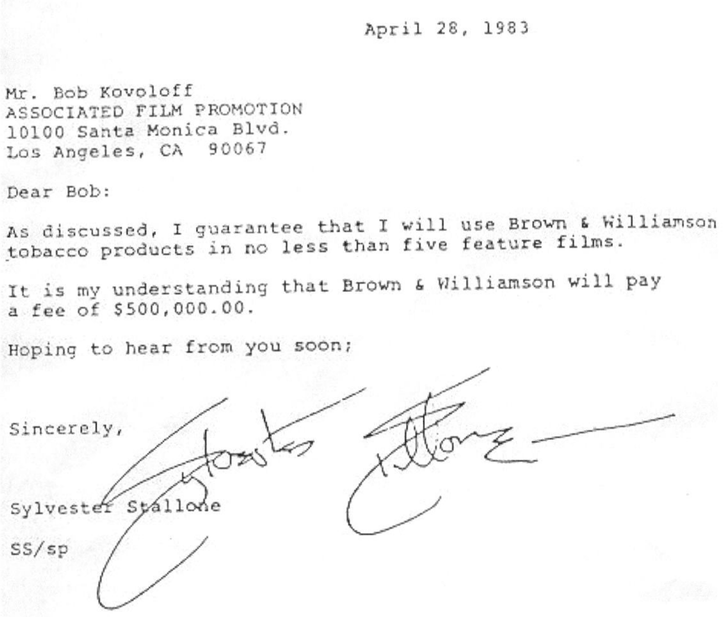

```
                                              April 28, 1983

Mr. Bob Kovoloff
ASSOCIATED FILM PROMOTION
10100 Santa Monica Blvd.
Los Angeles, CA  90067

Dear Bob:

As discussed, I guarantee that I will use Brown & Williamson
tobacco products in no less than five feature films.

It is my understanding that Brown & Williamson will pay
a fee of $500,000.00.

Hoping to hear from you soon;


Sincerely,



Sylvester Stallone

SS/sp
```

the incidence of tobacco in the major media (magazines, newspapers, movies, internet sites, popular music, television programs). Studies in Australia show that movies popular with young people in the period 2000–01 included 51 minutes of smoking in 11 hours and 56 minutes of film (Donovan, Weller & Clarkson, 2003). Given that 90 per cent of this portrayal showed smoking in a positive or normative light this is equivalent to 104 x 30-second tobacco promotions. Similar studies in Australia (Clarkson, Donovan, Giles-Corti & Watson 2002) and the USA (Roberts, Henriksen, Christenson & Kelly 1999; Roberts, Christenson, Henriksen & Bandy 2002; Glantz 2002) indicate that tobacco incidents are increasing in popular movies and elsewhere.

Tobacco companies are also targeting women in various ways. Philip Morris assists domestic violence groups and Philip Morris and RJ Reynolds sponsor various women's organisations in the USA, including the National Women's Political Caucus and the Centre for Women Policy Studies (Eaton 2001; WHO 2001). Similarly, tobacco companies have sponsored various African-American organisations while at the same time targeting blacks with specific brands. In 1990, after much pressure, RJ Reynolds dropped its Uptown brand that targeted inner-city blacks; it also dropped plans for its Dakota brand, which was to target young, blue-collar women (Cooper-Martin & Smith 1994).

A number of internet sites of unknown origin have appeared that promote tobacco to youth and women (see figures 8.3 and 8.4). There is some suspicion that tobacco companies might be behind some sites.

Tobacco and alcohol feature in children's animated films

One might think that children's animated films (the very symbol of young children's entertainment) would be free of tobacco and alcohol use, except perhaps in rare circumstances. Not so. Of fifty such films reviewed, 56 per cent portrayed one or more incidences of tobacco use and 50 per cent included alcohol use. Good and bad characters were equally likely to use tobacco or alcohol. However, the most frequent tobacco portrayals were of cigars (59 per cent) rather than cigarettes (21 per cent); wine (60 per cent) dominated the alcohol incidences, followed by beer (32 per cent). While these distributions suggest the use of alcohol and tobacco in character development none of the films included any verbal messages about negative health effects. Given the influence of modelling on behaviours and that character development can occur without alcohol and tobacco there is no reason for inclusion of alcohol and tobacco use in children's animated films (Goldstein, Sobel & Newman 1999).

Journalists are a good source of information about industry marketing tactics. Moor and Rice, writing in South Australia's *Adelaide Advertiser*, report that in Australian nightclub bars women dressed in Alpine colours (turquoise and white) have been selling discounted Alpine cigarettes and that Alpine cigarettes have been made available free to patrons to sample. They also report that

Figure 8.2 Bogart leads the pack

SMOKER'S HOME PAGE

For the TRUE Smokers

This page was created for the recognition of a community spirit between smokers - all very different people - like the one that has grown on alt.smokers. It is also intended to provide resources, facts and other fun stuff related to the great pasttime of smoking. It is dedicated to all the TRUE smokers in the world, so please let us know what you'd like to see here!

WARNING! This page may be hazardous to anti-smokers' blood pressure. Quitting now may greatly reduce your chances of moral outrage.

Continue

Figure 8.3 The Smoking Section

The Smoking Section

Hi! You've entered The Smoking Section, an art museum that pays tribute to women. It is our belief that women should not be degraded as stupid people, or sex toys, or anything sexist, but rather, women should be treated with respect, like real ladies. This art exhibit shows how honorable women can be, for when a woman smokes, she is showing everyone around that she is intelligent, sophisticated, and ladylike. Most of all, she is saying that she knows what she is doing.

Feel free to click on any of the thumbnails to view the entire picture. And enjoy your visit to The Smoking Section.

Figure 8.4 Jenny's Teen Smoking Page

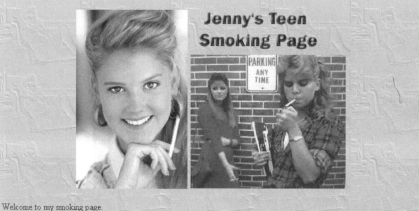

Welcome to my smoking page.

I'm a 17 year old lesbian girl who smokes close to 1-1/2 packs a day. I have been smoking since I was 13 when my girlfreind Kelly asked me to smoke because it would make me look sexier. I recently swithched to Misty light 120's. I used to smoke VS 120's and still do sometimes.

I started this page because I think smoking is sexy and I hate all the anti-smoking bullshit I get. I'm also very interested in being politically incorrect, thats one of my main fucking reasons for starting the page.

Thanx to everyone who sent me pics.

Unfortunatly I can't put nudes on my webpage. Sorry.

This page will continue to grow as long as you keep sending me more pics of pretty teens 12-18 Please no cigar pics or pics of adult women. I really like getting several pics of the same girl even if she's not smoking in some of them.

Sign My Guestbook. You can also View My Guestbook.

You can send me pics and stories, or just write me at jenny.g@usa.net

Philip Morris is apparently providing dance parties and nightclubs with free go-go dancers dressed in corporate colours. The company's primary target appears to be young women, particularly rave partygoers. Furthermore, in 2000 Moor and Rice linked the wavesnet domain to Philip Morris via its advertising agency, Mojo. Mojo at that time was the agency for Alpine and wavesnet was an internet company set up to run a national fashion competition (and build up a database of clients) (Moor & Rice 2000).

Alcohol

In Australia alcohol consumption is very much guided by cultural forces (Pettigrew 2000). Movies and television entertainment programs commonly portray alcohol consumption as a normal part of life, usually depicting alcohol as a mood-altering substance that serves as an aid to socialising and as a stress reducer (Smith, Goldman, Greenbaum & Christiansen 1995; Dorfman & Wallack 1996; Wallack, Grube, Madden & Breed 1990). A content analysis of a systematic sample of fifty programs on British television showed 80 per cent included reference to alcohol, with a reference occurring on average every 6 minutes (Smith, Roberts & Pendleton 1988); the incidence is even higher on soaps. A content analysis of alcohol portrayal in British soap operas revealed, on average, a visual or verbal reference to alcohol every 3.5 minutes (Furnham, Ingle, Gunter & McClelland 1997). None of the British programs contained any messages about the potential harmful effects of alcohol.

In contrast an Australian study of the most popular shows in 1989 revealed a reference to alcohol on average about once every 20 minutes (Noble, Martin, Ford et al. 1990). However, the duration of the incidents was not measured. As in the UK study the incidence was higher in soaps than other program types. A later study showed that alcohol drinking acts per hour had not changed much from 1990 to 1997 (approximately 3 per hour), although overall incidence had declined from 11.6 per cent of scenes to 3.4 per cent of scenes over six popular serials (Parsons, Rissell & Douglas 1999). However, some shows emphasise alcohol more than others: *Big Sky* had 6.5 drinking acts per hour in 1997 (Parsons et al. 1999); in a current Australian soap targeted at young people (*The Secret Life of Us*) approximately 25 per cent of scenes appear to contain alcohol (Roberts 2002).

Beer advertising in Australia (and elsewhere) has generally focused on the conviviality and camaraderie attainable via beer consumption or on beer as an appropriate and normal reward for hard work (Pettigrew 2000; Parker 1995). Noble et al. (1990) identified 155 television ads for alcohol in the week they studied, 47 per cent being beer ads. They reported that 35 per cent of the ads suggested that alcohol would contribute to social achievement and 54 per cent that alcohol would contribute to sporting achievement. They noted that while beer ads were associated with sporting success spirits ads (32 per cent of all ads) associated spirits with sexual or physical intimacy. These same distinctions can be seen in alcohol advertising today (see Jones & Donovan 2001; 2002).

> ## Don't like the taste of alcohol? Try an 'alcopop' or gelatin shot
>
> American public health advocates are complaining about what they call 'starter brews' aimed at entry-level consumers who do not like the taste of alcohol. Malt-based brews include personalised brands such as Mike's Hard Lemonade, Hooper's Hooch, and Jed's. Teens agree that the products appear designed for them (underage drinkers) rather than adults and to ease them into more traditional alcoholic beverages. The sweet, lemonade taste is what primarily attracts teens to try them (*BoozeNews* 2001).
>
> Similarly, packaged gelatin shots (Zippers), in flavours such as Rum Rush, Vodka Splash, and Tijuana Tequila are causing concern because they look like the Jello snacks popular with kids (Lyderson 2002).
>
> In Australia Jones and Donovan (2001) found that a major attribute promoted by the UDL vodka-based mix that many underage young people saw aimed at them, was that it was 'easy to drink'.

Alcohol sites on the internet appear to have been particularly designed to appeal to youth. The USA-based Center for Media Education (CME 1998) examined seventy-seven beer, wine, and spirit websites found through search engines, links from other sites, or through articles in the trade press. The sites were examined for the following features:

- use of cartoons, personalities, language, music, or branded merchandise popular in youth culture or which would be particularly attractive to college or high school-aged students
- offers of contests, interactive games, online magazines (e-zines) geared to youth, created virtual communities or chat rooms, or sponsored youth-oriented music or sports events.

CME found that 62 per cent of all sites, including 82 per cent of beer sites, 72 per cent of spirits sites, and 10 per cent of wine sites, contained at least one element considered by CME to be appealing to youth, with most sites using approximately three elements. The most common youth appeal elements identified were cartoons or motion video (53 per cent beer sites, 62 per cent spirit sites), branded merchandise (75 per cent beer sites, 28 per cent spirits sites), and games or contests (43 per cent beer sites, 45 spirits sites), youth-oriented language or slang (43 per cent beer sites, 41 per cent spirits sites), and use of sound or downloadable sound (39 per cent beer sites, 34 per cent spirits sites). As in advertising in general beer and spirits sites appeared much more appealing to youth than wine sites.

Carroll and Donovan (2002) examined six Australian websites representing the alcohol beverage categories of beer, spirits, cider, wine, liqueurs, and alcoholic sodas: Carlton Cold, Jim Beam, Strongbow, Wicked Wines, Midori, and Sub Zero. A number of these sites used features appealing to children and adolescents (interactive games, music downloads, competitions, etc.) and, in general, contained a number of features inconsistent with the content and spirit of the Australian Voluntary Alcohol Beverages Advertising Code. We concluded that web marketing practices should be covered by similar codes as apply to advertising in general (regardless of their shortcomings).

'Kapow!' to PowerMaster

Heileman's Colt 45 dominated the American malt liquor market in the 1980s (malt liquor has a higher alcohol content than regular beer and a higher market share in low-income neighbourhoods). However, Heileman was losing volume overall and badly in need of a new product. Along came PowerMaster, 31 per cent stronger than Colt 45 and 65 per cent stronger than regular beer. The product was clearly aimed at inner-city blacks. The US Surgeon-General described the brewer's plans as 'socially irresponsible' and the Bureau of Alcohol, Tobacco and Firearms withdrew approval for the PowerMaster name because of its implied reference to alcohol strength. Heileman withdrew the product, although it had spent US$2 million on research and marketing for the brand (Cooper-Martin & Smith 1994). Heileman executives were clearly blind to the alcohol marketing environment in the USA at the time (academics aren't the only ones living in ivory towers).

Prejudice

Examples of negative stereotyping of ethnic groups, blacks, women, the elderly, people with disabilities, and other marginalised groups abound in the media and will not be laboured here (Bryant & Zillmann 2002). Negative portrayals do not appear only in the popular media. A content analysis of advertisements in medical journals found that relative to men, women were negatively portrayed, rarely being shown in technical jobs but often in provocative poses and as complainers, among other things (Hawkins & Aber 1988).

Racism in particular appears alive and well throughout the world. A Ford advertisement featuring line workers from its Dagenham plant in the UK featured a number of black employees. However, when the ad ran in Poland (and later by mistake back in Britain), the black and brown faces and hands had been altered to white and one employee's beard and turban had been removed. Apparently, the changes had been made to suit local tastes. Clearly, Ford did not feel that Poland would react positively to people of colour (*Economist* 1996).

The internet has been readily adopted by American hate groups, with numbers rising sharply in recent years, including an increase in Ku Klux Klan branches. Many of these sites appear to be targeting children with interactive games (the objective of one is, apparently, to lynch a black man) (Liu 1999).

Internet hate sites also target children

The Alabama-based Southern Poverty Law Centre reported that the number of hate groups active in the USA was 537 in 1998, up from 474 in 1997, and that white supremacist hate sites on the internet increased from 163 in 1997 to 254 in 1998. These sites allow American hate groups to not only target disgruntled youth and laid-off blue-collar workers in the USA, but to reach millions around the globe.

A more recent report by the Simon Wiesenthal Centre documents more than 1400 internet hate sites, with 120 more appearing just after the report was released. Many attract children by offering crossword puzzles and video games—with racist themes.

Figure 8.5   Healthier heart ad

Start the day
with a healthier
heart.

New to Australia, Heart Plus combines the great taste of reduced fat milk with omega-3. This nutrient is known to assist in the functioning of the cardiovascular system by lowering blood triglyceride (fat) levels and helping maintain a regular heartbeat. And just one 250ml glass of Brownes Heart Plus gives you 95% of a suggested daily intake of this © &™ NHF 1998 used under licence.

valuable nutrient. Heart Plus is also rich in vitamins C and E, antioxidants that help your body use omega-3 nutrients more efficiently. Folate and vitamins B6 and B12 help promote good blood flow through your arteries by lowering harmful levels of homocysteine. And of course, it's low in both fat and cholesterol. So, when you make Brownes

Heart Plus part of a life that includes a balanced diet and regular physical activity, you can drink milk to your heart's content. For more infomation please phone the customer service line on 1800 675 484 or visit the website at www.heart-plus.com.au **Heart Plus. The low fat milk with omega-3.**

We need to be continually on the lookout for how various groups are portrayed in advertising, movies, and television programs in particular.

Countering the competition

Countering the competition is of course what this whole book is about. Nevertheless, this section serves to introduce several strategies and tactics either not covered elsewhere or covered in more detail later (especially chapters 9, 10, and 11). As indicated in chapter 1 meeting the competition requires strategies aimed at

Figure 8.6 The Heart Foundation tick

The Heart Foundation's Tick Program helps people choose healthier foods that are lower in fat, saturated fat, and sodium (salt). Many are also higher in fibre and calcium, and have less sugar. All foods are independently tested and assessed against strict nutritional guidelines before getting the Tick of Approval. Random testing is carried out on the Tick products throughout the year to ensure that they always meet the strict nutrition guidelines.

1   the end consumer's beliefs, attitudes, and behaviours
2   those with the power to modify products and services
3   those with the power to enact legislative and environmental changes that facilitate or enforce the desired end behaviour.

From another perspective we can target unhealthy or undesirable products and behaviours and attempt to find acceptable healthy or desirable substitutes, and we can target environmental aspects that facilitate desirable and inhibit undesirable behaviours. In fact we commonly need to do all of these.

Examples of product alternatives

There are numerous examples of products that have been modified to make them more healthy or less risky to users. Many of these changes have been brought about by consumer demand (that is, manufacturers have seen a potentially profitable market segment for a particular product). Others have been brought about by lobbying manufacturers and others by legislation following intensive advocacy.

Food and beverage products abound in such variations as low fat, high fibre, sugar free, cholesterol free, saturated-fat free, vitamin boosted, and low alcohol variations. Recent examples are Kellogg's folate-rich breakfast cereals, the cholesterol-lowering spread Pro-activ, and Brownes Dairy's Heart Plus milk. Unfortunately, the healthier alternatives are often more expensive than the regular product (for example, Heart Plus milk is approximately 40 per cent more expensive). The National Heart Foundation's tick of approval makes it easy for consumers looking for healthy alternatives. In some cases manufacturers and commercial food preparers have been persuaded to replace saturated fats with polyunsaturated or monosaturated fats.

There are also environmentally friendly (or more so than others) cleaning products, products in recyclable packaging, and ozone friendly aerosol packs.

Motor vehicle manufacturers tout their vehicles' environmental friendliness and safety features and, after much advocacy and against opposition from the oil, lead, and chemical industries (Isaacs & Schroeder 2001), petrol is now lead-free.

In a variation on this theme and in an attempt to make desirable branded products more affordable to low-income youth, Hakeem Olajuwon, an NBA basketball star, worked with Spaulding to develop a shoe that sells for US$35 (compared to Nikes or Reeboks at around US$120) (CNAD 1997). Whether this will stop poor youth stealing the more expensive shoes from stores or other kids remains to be seen. Nevertheless, it is a step in the right direction.

Examples of behavioural alternatives

For many social marketing campaigns we are concerned with behaviours other than purchasing and consumption of products and services (safer driving, tolerance, good parenting practices, physical activity, interacting positively with neighbours, lobbying, etc.). Similarly, many food preparation (cutting off fat) and cooking behaviours (less overcooking) result in more nutrition with the same foods.

Consider positive parenting practices, such as rewards for good behaviour, discussion with the child, time out, and diversionary tactics. These are competing with smacking, yelling at, and denigrating the child. The parent's end goal is the elimination or reduction of bad behaviours and the maintenance of good behaviours. However, for many parents, smacking and yelling are quicker and easier ways to get an immediate stop to the bad behaviour, while rewards, discussion, and diversion are more time-consuming methods requiring more (cognitive) effort and are methods that many parents do not know how to go about (everybody has the skills for smacking and yelling). Campaigns can show parents how to use these methods, convince them that the end goal will be reached better by these methods, and that they are effective in the short term. While extra care is needed in messages attacking negative parenting practices, the disadvantages of such can be pointed out (for example, a tantrum resulting from smacking which is only exacerbated by further smacking—as many supermarket shoppers can attest to).

Similarly, alcohol consumption serves many motives, providing many benefits to young people in particular with respect to lessened social inhibitions, increased feelings of wellbeing, and enhanced social and sexual interactions. However, excess alcohol consumption can sometimes preclude these benefits and result in considerable disbenefits the following day. Rothschild (1997) described a program at the University of Wisconsin to combat binge drinking by offering appropriate alternative, non-alcoholic activities and venues for students, such as keeping the recreational facilities open late on weekends and having an all-night, non-alcoholic dance club. Given that intoxication reduces a drinker's ability to make sound decisions while drinking, forward planning is essential to control alcohol consumption. Hence, Health Department of West-

For hot chips, size does matter*

Surveys in New Zealand have shown that changes in deep-frying of hot chips practices could have a significant impact on fat intake from this fast-food source. Similarly, changes in chip thickness would also have a significant impact. Interestingly, 89 per cent of chain outlets used thin chips (6–10 mm), while 83 per cent of independent outlets used thicker chips (12 mm or more).

* Morley-John, Swinburn, Metcalf & Raza 2002

ern Australia campaigns urge drinkers to eat a big meal beforehand, plan to stay over if a long night's drinking is likely, appoint a skipper before the event, or plan to drink lower-alcohol drinks.

Campaigns aimed at increasing people's levels of physical activity compete with a variety of forces. They compete first and foremost with job and family commitments, sedentary entertainments, and all other leisure activities for the individual's time. They also compete with alternative modes of transport and all other labour- and time-saving devices (automatic opening doors, escalators and lifts, the car, etc.). They further compete with entrenched beliefs that only vigorous activity is likely to be of any benefit, that exercise can only be done via an organised activity that requires costly equipment or clothing or both, and beliefs that other healthy activities such as a good diet, no smoking, and moderate drinking more than compensate for minimal exercise.

Little wonder then that physical activity levels in Australia are either steady or decreasing, that obesity is on the rise, and that physical activity campaigns have had little impact (albeit they are underresourced and not comprehensive). Current campaigns have attempted to show how people can build an increase in physical activity into their daily lives via walking to get to public transport, taking the stairs instead of lifts and escalators, doing heavy gardening and housework, and walking for leisure. In fact, the National Physical Activity Guidelines for Australia begin with an attempt to reframe how people look at physical activity: 'Look at movement as an opportunity, not an inconvenience' (Egger et al. 2001).

Advocacy for environmental and structural change

Advocacy research has long been used by public health and other social policy-oriented organisations to support approaches to politicians to achieve legislative and policy change. Alarmed by Philip Morris's introduction of the more affordable fifteens packets of cigarettes accompanied by a teenage-oriented advertising campaign referring to how easy they might be to hide ('Alpine 15s. They fit in anywhere'), Wilson, Wakefield, Esterman, and Baker (1987) carried out a brief survey of children smokers and adult smokers. Although Phillip Morris claimed the packs were not targeted at children the survey showed that 57 per cent of children who smoked had bought a pack of fifteens in the past

Attacking alcohol ads that reinforce sexist attitudes towards women

On the premise that sexist advertising contributes to a social context conducive to violence against women the California campaign 'Dangerous Promises' pressured the alcohol industry to change the way in which they depicted women in their ads. After receiving a lukewarm response from brewers and spirit makers (but a positive one from wine marketers) to proposed additions to alcohol advertisers' codes of ethics, the campaign produced controversial billboard counterads under the banner of 'Consumers to stop sexist advertising'. One ad read: 'Bloodweiser, King of Tears—Selling Violence Against Women' (a play on 'Budweiser—King of Beers). The aim was to attract media attention to these ads, some of which the billboard companies refused to run—hence generating more publicity. They also established good relationships with journalists, supplying them with background data with respect to the relationship between violence, alcohol, and sexist attitudes along with numerous examples of sexist ads (such data and visuals making the journalists' jobs easier). Alcohol advertising featuring women decreased markedly in San Diego County, the brewers agreed to reconsider the code of ethics changes, and the spirits trade association agreed to an additional code dealing with sexism in advertising (Woodruff 1996).

month compared to only 8 per cent of adult smokers. This information resulted in regulations being changed in all Australian states to prohibit small packs (Chapman & Reynolds 1987).

More recently, to support information arising from tobacco company documents, several research studies have provided evidence of a causal link between tobacco company marketing and youth smoking (Biener & Siegel 2000; Botvin, Goldberg, Bitvin & Dusenbury 1993; MacFadyen, Hastings & MacKintosh 2001; Pierce, Choi, Gilpin et al. 1998). These sort of data assist antitobacco advocates in lobbying government to restrict tobacco marketing practices. Chapman and Wakefield (2002) provide a good history of tobacco control advocacy in Australia.

Although not common in Australia (the exceptions being Billboard Utilising Grafittists Against Unhealthy Promotions [BUGA UP] and early antitobacco activists), grass roots movements have been successful in the USA. Perhaps this is because such movements are less necessary in Australia, where governments have traditionally played a far greater pro-active role than in the USA in all areas of public life, and especially in public health and safety areas. (Unfortunately, this is lessening now as we will note later.)

Isaacs and Schroeder (2001) describe how two women had an enormous impact on public policy—and no doubt on public attitudes—to drink driving in the USA. In 1978, after a drunk driver ran over and killed a teenager in her home town a woman called Doris Aiken founded Remove Intoxicated Drivers (RID). Two years later Candy Lightner formed Mothers Against Drunk Driving (MADD) after her daughter was run over and killed by a drinking driver. The media took to the women's stories and the women took to the media and the road, resulting in hundreds of media stories and the energising of antidrunkdriving activists throughout the USA who formed local chapters of RID, MADD, and Students Against Driving Drunk (SADD). Activists provided victims' services, lobbied government officials, and monitored the courts. Between 1981 and 1985 state legislatures passed 478 laws to deter drunk driving; Congress passed legislation to provide extra funds to states that enacted stricter drunk-driving laws, and in 1984 tied federal highway funds to a minimum drinking age of 21 years (Isaacs & Schroeder 2001).

Marketing education

One of the tactics employed by early antitobacco advocates in Australia when tobacco advertising was legal was to educate schoolchildren to analyse tobacco advertising (today we would call it deconstructing). Philip Rubenstein, a former ad agency person, used to lead such sessions in South Australia. It was thought that if children were taught to recognise the ad creator's tactics they would be less vulnerable to their effect. However, we are not aware of any convincing evidence that this is the case. Our own qualitative research over a number of commercial and social marketing projects, suggests that target audiences can be aware of the advertiser's strategy and simultaneously be persuaded by it (for example, 'I know he's being paid to do the ad, but I still think he makes it cool', 'They are trying to say that drinking [such and such a brand] makes parties more fun—and drinking does').

Goldberg and Bechtel (undated) developed and tested a five-session intervention that analysed alcohol advertising (ADSMARTS). While the intervention showed a slight negative shift in attitudes towards beer advertising and a slight decrease in normative perceptions (how many students their age drink alcohol at least monthly), there was no shift in intentions to drink alcohol in the immediate future. Nevertheless, we can see little harm and potentially some good in teaching schoolchildren to analyse tactics in advertising and promotion.

Industry self-regulation: An oxymoron?

Industry self-regulation is often promoted by industries themselves as the ideal solution rather than government interfering in the marketplace. However, too often self-regulation appears to be adopted simply to deflect government action and is more honoured in the breach. Nevertheless, many marketers do adhere to their own ethical and self-regulation codes of conduct. With respect to body image women's magazine editors in the UK agreed in 2000 to exclude images of very thin models from their magazines (Womersley 2000).

A number of studies have concluded that alcohol advertising encourages young people to drink and reinforces drinking habits (Hastings, MacKintosh & Aitken 1992; Wyllie, Zhang & Casswell 1998; Grube & Wallack 1994). The strong association of alcohol and sport, particularly beer advertising, is reflected in studies showing higher levels of consumption among physically active males versus less active males (Faulkener & Slattery 1990). Australian breweries

Table 8.2	Relevant sections of the AANA code

Advertisements shall:

2.1 not portray people in a way which discriminates or vilifies a person or section of the community on account of race, ethnicity, nationality, sex, age, sexual preference, religion, disability or political belief;

2.2 not present or portray violence unless it is justifiable in the context of the product or service advertised;

2.3 treat sex, sexuality and nudity with sensitivity to the relevant audience and, where appropriate, the relevant program time zone;

2.5 use only language which is appropriate in the circumstances and strong or obscene language shall be avoided;

2.6 not depict material contrary to prevailing community standards on health and safety.

sponsor AFL teams and Bundaberg Rum is a major sponsor of the Wallabies rugby union team. Hence, it is important to monitor alcohol advertising to ensure that responsible consumption is portrayed, especially in advertising. Given the link between alcohol consumption and youth health, restrictions on alcohol advertising have increasingly become an issue for debate around the world (Jones & Donovan 2002). Some countries rely on governmental regulation, whereas others, including Australia, utilise a system of industry self-regulation. But is it working in Australia?

Jones and Donovan (2002) examined eleven alcohol advertising complaints (relating to nine separate advertisements) that were lodged with the Advertising Standards Board (ASB) by members of the general public between May 1998 and April 1999. Eight marketing academics (expert judges) were given copies of the ads and the Australian Association of National Advertisers' Code of Ethics (table 8.2 above) and Alcoholic Beverages Advertising Code (see box below). Without knowing the ASB's rulings they were asked to judge whether the advertisements breached any of the clauses of the two codes. The ads were similarly assessed by a group of second-year advertising students (student judges).

A majority of the expert judges perceived breaches of the codes for seven of the nine advertisements (table 8.3). For all nine of the advertisements, a majority of the university students felt that each of the ads was in breach of one or more of the Codes. The ASB had ruled that none of the ads breached any of the Codes. Most of the AANA breaches related to inappropriate sexual portrayals. Most breaches of ABAC related to mood effects and alcohol contributing to social or sexual success.

The ad for Finlandia Vodka is an animated television ad. The action takes place in a nightclub and is set to dance music. It shows varying scenes:

- a female disc jockey clad in a tight-fitting dress approaches the music desk and plays a record
- a woman crawls along the bar counter toward a man; he holds his T-shirt up, she strokes his lower belly in a downward direction (toward his belt) and then grabs his (vodka) drink from him
- two women are shown dancing together and then kissing on the lips
- a man admires a scantily clad woman drinking a bottle of Finlandia Vodka; the man and woman then proceed to dance intimately together.

The Voluntary Alcohol Beverages Advertising Code (ABAC)

Advertisements for alcohol beverages must:

a) present a mature, balanced and responsible approach to the consumption of alcohol beverages and, accordingly-

   i) must not encourage excessive consumption or abuse of alcohol;

   ii) must not encourage under-age drinking;

   iii) must not promote offensive behaviour, or the excessive consumption, mis-use or abuse of alcohol beverages;

   iv) must only depict the responsible and moderate consumption of alcohol beverages;

b) not have a strong or evident appeal to children or adolescents and, accordingly-

   i) adults appearing in advertisements must be over 25 years of age and be clearly depicted as adults;

   ii) children and adolescents may only appear in advertisements in natural situations (eg, family barbecue, licensed family restaurant) and where there is no implication that the depicted children and adolescents will consume or serve alcohol beverages; and

   iii) adults under the age of 25 years may only appear as part of a natural crowd or background scene;

c) not suggest that the consumption or presence of alcohol beverages may create or contribute to a significant change in mood or environment and, accordingly-

   i) must not depict the consumption or presence of alcohol beverages as a cause of or contributing to the achievement of personal, business, social, sporting, sexual or other success;

   ii) if alcohol beverages are depicted as part of a celebration, must not imply or suggest that the beverage was a cause of or contributed to success or achievement; and

   iii) must not suggest that the consumption of alcohol beverages offers any therapeutic benefit or is a necessary aid to relaxation;

d) not depict any direct association between the consumption of alcohol beverages, other than low alcohol beverages, and the operation of a motor vehicle, boat or aircraft or the engagement in any sport (including swimming and water sports) or potentially hazardous activity and, accordingly-

   i) any depiction of the consumption of alcohol beverages in connection with the above activities must not be represented as having taken place before or during engagement of the activity in question and must in all cases portray safe practices; and

   ii) any claim concerning safe consumption of low alcohol beverages must be demonstrably accurate;

e) not challenge or dare people to drink or sample a particular alcohol beverage, other than low alcohol beverages, and must not contain any inducement to prefer an alcohol beverage because of its higher alcohol content; and

f) comply with the Advertiser Code of Ethics adopted by the Australian Association of National Advertisers.

The Advertiser Code of Ethics, developed by the Australian Association of National Advertisers and referred to within the ABAC, also states, inter alia, that advertisements

- shall treat sex, sexuality and nudity with sensitivity to the relevant audience and, where appropriate, the relevant program time zone; and
- shall not depict material contrary to prevailing community standards on health and safety.

The advertisement concludes with a still shot of three bottles of Finlandia Vodka and the words 'Play Dirty, Drink Pure' superimposed on the screen.

The ad for Bundaberg Rum was a radio ad with the following script:

> You go to the dentist for a check up and he ends up doing more construction work than the Sydney Olympics … Do you? … (a) Go back to work speaking like the elephant man? (b) Dribble all over your boss? or (c) Stick to a liquid diet and have a Bundy and cola for dinner? See, you can solve anything with a Bundy and cola.

There is a clear discrepancy between the expert judges and members of the ASB with respect to interpretations of the codes of practice. Given that these marketing academics were not biased against alcohol advertising and self-regulation, it appears that ASB members may lack objectivity (or expertise) in their assessments of complaints. This failure to replicate the ASB's decisions questions whether ethical responsibility is being met by the self-regulatory system for alcohol advertising. Studies such as these can be presented to marketers and advertisers to pressure them to pay greater attention to relevant codes of conduct.

The most recent advertising self-regulation issue in Australia appears to have been solved very amicably and, in relative terms, very quickly. A number

Table 8.3 Expert judges' analysis of code breaches of alcohol ads*

		Expert Judges	
		Number reporting a breach (n = 8)	Main clauses(s) breached
36/98 & 88/98	Bimbagden Estate wines	6	2.3 AANA (4), C ABAC (3)
186/98	Scrumpy Jack cider	6	2.5 AANA (5)
257/98 & 15/99	Antipodean wine	7	2.3 AANA (7)
268/98	Finlandia Vodka	8	2.3 AANA (6) C ABAC (3)
269/98	Strongbow cider	1	–
324/98	Strongbow cider (animated)	2	–
73/99	Fourex Bitter beer	5	2.3 AANA (4)
81/99	Bundaberg Rum	6	2.6 AANA (3) C ABAC (6)
94/99	Tooheys New beer	6	2.1 AANA (6)

* Jones & Donovan 2002

of individuals and organisations became concerned that car advertising appeared to increasingly portray unsafe driving behaviours, as well as placing undue emphasis on their vehicles' acceleration, power, and agility in traffic. There was no advertising code that specifically covered motor vehicle advertising (although one could argue that AANA 2.6 would cover these aspects), and advertising agencies and vehicle manufacturers initially opposed any such code. However, after pressure from bodies such the Royal Automobile Clubs (especially in Western Australia), state road safety organisations, federal politicians, and motor vehicle manufacturers agreed to comply with a code drawn up largely by road safety advocates. And all this in less than a year's activities.

Kids are kids right? Wrong. Kids R Cu$tomer$!

The blurb on James U. McNeal's (1992) handbook on marketing to children (*Kids as Customers*) can hardly repress its delight at the opportunity provided by kids in the USA: '$9 billion of their own spending money and an influence over $130 billion of their parents' and carers' spending' (and that figure is much greater in 2003). But wait, there's more! Licking its lips in anticipation of even more goodies the book goes on to say that, as future customers, children will control even more dollars and that McNeal 'shows business how to cultivate today's children into loyal customers'. 'What's more,' says the jacket, as if the billions of dollars at home are not enough, 'McNeal urges business not to overlook the potential of … foreign children.'

McNeal's book is touted as 'the indispensable marketing handbook for companies marketing to four-to-twelve year-olds'. That's right, 4 year olds. 'Retailers, advertisers, product designers, and market researchers will all benefit from McNeal's extensive research.' But will the children?

McNeal's subject index lists one entry on 'Ethics in marketing to children' (p. 20), where we read:

> This brings up one more warning of sorts. Kids are the most unsophisticated of all consumers; they have the least and therefore want the most. Consequently, they are in a perfect position to be taken. While it is difficult to market to them successfully, as observed above, it is equally difficult to market to them ethically. Safeguards must be in place every step of the way.

We did find other references to ethical practices in the book (for example, p. 128 refers to the packaging of bubble gum to look like chewing tobacco and snuff as an unethical practice). Unfortunately, McNeal's book is pretty short on what these safeguards could be and there is no substantive discussion on any ethical issues. Perhaps this simply reflects the amoral view of the market, marketers, and marketing professors.

Figure 8.7   Adbusters—fighting back

Well, the marketers have certainly taken McNeal's and others' words to heart, pouring millions of dollars into advertising and promotions, including traditional media as well as product placement, the internet, and tie-ins with movies and fast-food chains in particular (McNeal 1992). For example, the major toy crazes of Pokemon, Cabbage Patch Kids, and Tamogotchis have all been assisted by fast-food promotions; in 1996 Disney and McDonald's signed a 10-year global marketing agreement (Schlosser 2001). Not satisfied with promotion in the public domain major marketers are turning to schools to promote their products. And marketing consultants are cashing in by specialising in this area. School Marketing Partners developed a school lunch menu to promote Fox's movie *Anastasia*. The November menu features an Anastasia game (actually, an ad for the movie) and a come-on to buy Anastasia toys from Shell service stations (Orwall 1997).

The introduction of Channel One in 1990 in American schools appears to have been the foot in the tent. Channel One places television and VCR equipment in schools. In return, the schools ensure that students watch Channel One programming where each telecast contains two minutes of ads for major youth marketers. But wait, there's more! Schools are then drawn into Channel One promotions with major advertisers, with teachers and principals acting as promoters, handing out coupons for JC Penney blue jeans and Subway sandwiches, or helping kids prepare ads for Snapple (an apple juice drink), design vending machines for Pepsi, or sign petitions for Reebok (Lex 1997). Lex (1997) reports that in 1991 only 2 per cent of public schools sold branded fast food, but by 1997 this figure was 13 per cent—and growing, in spite of federal nutritional guidelines and sometimes higher prices.

Competition for kids: school as battleground

Advertising and promotion to kids in schools in North America is big business for the corporations involved and can be a strikingly successful fundraising strategy for the schools. It has diversified from corporate sponsorships of sports, music, and facilities to include advertising posters in school hallways and on school buses, exclusive beverage deals, corporate classroom teaching materials, cafeteria franchises, exclusive vending machines, computer lab screensavers, and educational television programming interspersed with commercial ads (Schlosser 2001; Aidman 1995; Salkowski 1997).

Ads appear in the sports stadium, gymnasium, cafeteria, hallways, school buses, on textbooks, and even in the toilets (Chaika 1998). In an innovative deal even the rooftops of schools in the Dallas–Fort Worth airport flight path were targeted so that passengers would see ads for Dr Pepper (a bottled drink) as they flew over (Schlosser 2001).

Generally, the businesses involved are soft drink manufacturers, fast-food franchises, clothing and shoe companies. Deals have also been made with restaurants, hotels, and telecommunication organisations. Schools are not keen to accept advertising from companies involved in political, religious, alcohol, tobacco, or sex products (Chaika 1998). However, violent R-rated movies have been increasingly advertised in student newspapers, a practice criticised by the Federal Trade Commission following the 1999 Columbine High School shootings (Molnar & Reaves 2001).

But it is clearly not all crass commercialisation. In a project testing screensaver promotions, companies were asked to design their ad around an inspirational message to be approved by a panel of educators and parents. Pepsi's ad, 'Develop a thirst for knowledge', was approved, whereas a fast-food ad with a picture of a hamburger and the slogan 'Hungry? Get the taste now!' was rejected (Salkowski 1997). So reassuring.

The growth in this market has been substantial over the last decade despite some controversy, argument, and opposition. In 1999 the Ontario School Bus Association issued a policy statement arguing that external advertising on school buses could reduce the uniquely recognisable and conspicuous appearance of school buses, thereby putting children at risk (Ontario 1999). The Consumers Union in Canada issued a major report in 1998, *Captive kids: A report on commercial pressures on kids at school*, in which they highlighted a number of disturbing trends, among them the following.

- *The use of biased corporate sponsored educational materials in schools*. An examination of 200 examples of corporate education materials and programs found that 80 per cent were biased in favour of the sponsor's products or views. For example, Proctor & Gamble sponsored an educational packet that taught that disposable nappies are better for the environment than cloth nappies. They did not advise that they had commissioned the study that produced these results. Proctor & Gamble has since stopped production of the kit.
- *Requiring whole schools to participate in corporate-sponsored contests*. Such a whole school contest occurred at Greenbriar High School in Georgia. A prize of $500 was offered by Coca-Cola for the best marketing idea. The students, wearing T-shirts, arranged themselves to spell out the word 'Coke' and were photographed from a crane. One of the students in the letter 'C' suddenly revealed a T-shirt that said 'Pepsi' and was promptly suspended from the school. His suspension provided fuel for the debate on the appropriateness of such corporate activities (Schlosser 2001).

A similar fate befell Jennifer Beatty who chained herself to the metal mesh curtains of her community college's oncampus McDonald's. Beatty was protesting about McDonald's labour, marketing, and environmental practices and was banned from the college as a result (Lydersen 1998). McDonald's apparently has quite a financial stake in the college, having built the college's student centre (the McDonald's Student Centre—complete with golden arches) and leased a restaurant in the centre. This financial stake might explain why the college administration cracked down on student protests against McDonald's (Lyderson 1998).

Activists ('culture jammers' such as Adbusters; see urinal ad from Campaign for Commercial Free Schools) are attempting to counter the trend in North America. For example, Arizona State University has a Commercialisation in Education Research Unit, which gathers and publishes statistics on corporate intrusion into education. They report that the number of citations of commercialisation in the media increased from approximately 1000 in 1990 to nearly 7000 in 1999/2000, declining to approximately 5500 in 2000/2001 (Molnar & Reaves 2001). The authors hope that this represents a decline, but acknowledge that it may also represent people coming to accept what they see as the inevitable. As they put it, 'Cash-strapped administrators accept, sometimes solicit, and increasingly defend commercialising activities as means of making up budget shortfalls and financing everything from computers and musical instruments to art supplies and staff training' (Molnar & Reaves 2001, p. 5). Given the money involved it is not surprising that schools succumb to such overtures. Pepsi has an exclusive vendor deal in Denver schools that is expected to generate $5.4 million for the schools over the next 5 years (Schwartz 1998). The real problem comes when the school's income is tied to the quantity of the product sold, which is the basis for some deals. How can such schools not encourage consumption?

Until schools are adequately financed it will be very difficult to counter the trend. It has been suggested, perhaps disingenuously, that teachers could use this opportunity to teach media literacy so that children are less vulnerable to influence (Chaika 1998). As we noted above, this may help, but it is certainly no answer to the problem.

Australian schools for sale?

Corporate involvement in schools in Australia appears to be limited to sponsorship, primarily of sports teams, musical programs, and the provision of additional facilities. It would appear that schools here are not yet under as much pressure as those in the USA from major corporations, although loose legislation appears to offer the opportunity for similar intrusions. For example, the *School Education Act 1999* (WA) 'enables limited access to sponsorship and use of advertising in government schools. In general, the involvement of the business community in education is perceived as an advantage provided educational goals and values are not compromised and students are not exposed to commercial exploitation.' However, 'commercial exploitation' is not defined. On the other hand, in response to the Act, the Western Australia Department of Education prepared a policy document that appears reasonably restrictive. It allows advertising and sponsorship that is 'consistent with the generally accepted values, purposes and goals of government school education', and states that

> It is the intention of the Act, regulations and this procedure that participation in advertising and sponsorship will not generate pressure on children, parents or schools to purchase particular goods or services, subscribe to particular beliefs or attitudes or pursue particular courses of action.

Education departments in each state broker major sponsorships. For example, the School Sport 2000 Foundation in New South Wales is sponsored by Dairy Farmers, NRMA, Sydney Markets, WIN, and NBN television. Smaller sponsorships are negotiated by individual schools. Until now most approaches have been by local firms and decided on an individual basis by the school, for example, a local business providing stationery to a school in return for an acknowledgment in the school newsletter. The extent of controversy so far has included whether a sponsorship provided by a local hotel in a country town was sending the wrong message to kids about alcohol consumption (Western Australia), or a wine producer wanting to sponsor primary school sports jumpers could be acknowledged in the newsletter but not have their logo on the team jumpers (South Australia).

The education department in each state has a general policy on advertising and promotion in government schools that is used by schools as a reference. Where grey areas exist the schools may approach the department for advice. As noted above, the policies in most states require promotion to be consistent with the values and goals of government education. However, the concept of consistency is open to interpretation. McDonald's sponsorship of a school music program, such as Musica Viva in New South Wales, appears acceptable (Lamont 1996), but not the inclusion of a fast-food franchise in the school, which could be seen as inconsistent with the goals of healthy lifestyle.

Consistency or appropriateness is considered in relation to the product, the company's marketing strategies, its public image, and its impact on environment (Australian Capital Territory policy). Policies also include statements that students should not be exploited commercially and should not be pressured to purchase products, that product endorsement should not be sought as a condition of sponsorship, and staff should not benefit personally from any sponsorship deals. Some policies specify that academic debate should not be limited. For example, the New South Wales policy states that the sponsorship 'must not compromise the professional standards and ethics of teachers, nor limit academic debate in the classroom'. Others specifically exclude companies associated with undesirable products, such as tobacco, alcohol, sex, armaments, and gambling. For example, Victoria specifically excludes gambling companies as a response to approaches made to schools by gambling companies in that state.

One compromise from South Australia illustrates the Consumers Union principle that sponsorship should not require whole-school involvement: junior cricket clinics were sponsored by Milo (owned by Nestle), but there was some concern expressed by parents about Nestle's environmental record. The principal made the decision to continue the program, but to allow parents the right to exclude their children if they felt strongly about the issue. This is not really a solution though, as the children might be deprived of participation.

Jazzybooks, a promotion strategy that has been highly successful in the UK, has recently moved into Australia. Jazzybooks are exercise books that are provided free to participating schools. In Australia the colourful covers depict ads for Telstra's 1800 Reverse service and Planet X. Advertisers are asked to promote positive messages relating to self-esteem and achievement (Callaghan 2001). Hence, Planet X, associated with extreme sports, has the slogan 'Extreme achievement'. The media pack states that the covers will be sponsored by reputable companies, charities, and government agencies.

In 2001 Jazzybooks claimed to have over 900 schools in the program in Australia, which meant they would have been reaching 400 000 primary and high school children. They also claimed to have 'high ad recall and sharp sustained increases in brand awareness, brand imagery, product usage and propensity to purchase' largely due to the 3 month life of the exercise books (over one term) in an uncluttered environment (Jazzybooks Media Pack).

Internal competition

Finally, a word about internal competition. Competition can also come from government and political party policy. Government departments charged with social change are continually forced to compromise programs because of government policy. The highly successful Western Australian media advertising-led *Freedom from Fear* campaign targeting male perpetrators of domestic violence was initially questioned by the incoming Labor government, apparently because the incoming government preferred a community action approach. Furthermore, the *Freedom from Fear* campaign had been an initiative of the Liberal government that preceded this Labor government.

Privatisation

Privatisation is possibly today's major competitor to achieving major changes in the social determinants of crime, ill health, and social distress. Privatisation involves a move away from community responsibility (via government-funded programs) and an increasing tendency towards individual responsibility with, arguably, the most deleterious impact on the disadvantaged in society. Predatory corporations who lobby government to yield what many consider core areas of government to the private sector represent real competition for many government departments. In Australia in recent years this has seen areas such as public transport, prisons, energy, roads, flight terminals, and road transport taken over by the private sector. At the same time we have seen increasing pressure on schools, police, universities, and hospitals to raise funds from the private sector—via sponsorship and other fundraising—to remain viable. While the airforce has never had to have a lamington drive to raise funds for a new fighter plane, school principals are having to spend more and more of their time on financial management rather than their core business of education.

Would a privatised police service put the same value on domestic violence and child abuse prevention as a government service does? Would there be the same cooperation between a private police service and welfare organisations? Would a private service focus on convictions rather than prevention as a key performance indicator? What are the implications for social marketing of community policing and neighbourhood watch? Would householders be more inclined or less inclined to cooperate with a profit-motivated police service?

Figure 8.8 Do covers sell books or does sell cover books?

In short, there are many implications of privatisation, and not just directly for government departments or units charged with social change. For example, what are the implications for health department campaigns within privatised prisons where there may well be a cost incurred by the prison corporation? A major task for social marketers—as we define them—is to use social marketing to ensure that governments retain what are considered the core functions of government that ensure the health and wellbeing of its citizens.

Competition for the cops: What will happen to the game 'Cops and robbers'?

While private detectives such as Sherlock Holmes, Larry Kent, and the men from the renowned Pinkerton Agency have been around for some time, few citizens would ever have expected that their local copper might some day be an employee of a major corporation rather than a public servant. The growing reality, however, is that this may well be the case—and the cops are worried. Retiring Western Australian Assistant Commissioner Doug McCaffery warned that the Western Australia Police Service needed to protect its turf from security firms that offered the government a cheaper option: 'The police service is going to have to work hard to make itself competitive so it remains a viable option for the government' (Harvey 2001). In fact, the police have already virtually conceded the business-to-business area of policing to the private sector, with private security firms being primarily responsible for crime prevention in industry. Gated housing communities will be the next to have private security (as in the USA).

In Swedish writer Mankell's bestselling serial killer thriller this exchange takes place between a couple of senior cops in Sweden.

> There's a rumour going round that staff numbers are going to be cut back on Saturday and Sunday nights.
> That won't work. Who's going to deal with the people we've got in the cells?
>
> Rumour has it that they're going to take tenders for that job from private security companies.
> Security companies?
> That's what I heard.
>
> Mankell 2000, p. 20.

Concluding comments

Social marketers must continually identify and monitor their competition. This is essential to understand why our target audiences are engaging in undesirable ways, as well as to mount advocacy campaigns, where relevant, against corporations marketing undesirable products and organisations promoting undesirable ideas. Monitoring means more than just looking at marketing tactics. Industry manufacturing and preparation practices must also be monitored. Unfortunately, little government-funded research is directed towards this aim, although there are signs that the importance of such data is now being increasingly recognised.

Our major area for competition is children. In this chapter we have emphasised the schoolroom as the place where we must draw the line against commercialism. We do not want in Australia to have the fast-food giants running school tuckshops and university canteens. We do not want principals and teachers acting as sales and commission agents for marketers. We do not want school textbooks (like McGraw-Hill's) that use brand names such as Nike, Burger King, and Oreo in its math problems, or free samples of Prego spaghetti sauce for measuring viscosity, or samples of candy that gush when bitten so children can discuss the process needed to make such candies (Peters 1999). We do not want children assuming that commercial consumption is all of, rather than just a part of, life—or, in the extreme, life itself, as in this paraphrase where professional sport's values have also declined, 'Branding isn't everything. It's the only thing'.

But commercialism is only one of the competitors for children. Competition for kids to become healthy citizens comes also from the family, community, and socioeconomic conditions in which they are born and nurtured. And here we compete with government and major institutional forces. Most social marketers face competition for resources from other social marketers and competition from political and ideological forces in government and the bureaucracy. Hence, as Andreasen (2002) discusses, perhaps social marketers need to be doing a lot more marketing of social marketing.

Overall, most commercial products operate on three aspects: making a product or service

- attractive
- affordable
- available.

Hence, we need to counter on all three of these aspects—whether by education, motivation or legislation—as well as remember that before people will adopt our recommended behaviours they must have

- motive
- opportunity
- ability.

Thus, meeting the competition can also involve skills training for the target group and ensuring that the environment actually provides opportunities for expressing the desired behaviour.

Chapter 9

Market Segmentation and Target Marketing: the principle of selectivity and concentration

Introduction

Market segmentation—the division of the total market into relatively homogeneous but distinct segments, and target marketing—the selection and concentration of marketing resources on one or more of these segments, together constitute one of the most important principles of marketing (Lunn 1986; Piercy 1991; Kotler 1989): the principle of selectivity and concentration. This principle follows naturally from a focus on consumer or client needs since it acknowledges that

- different subgroups exist in a population
- the differences occur on a variety of dimensions
- different strategies and approaches are necessary to reach, communicate with, or motivate different subgroups.

This last point is crucial: unless the segments respond differentially to different elements of the marketing mix there is no point in segmenting (Rossiter 1987).

Differences may occur in three ways:

1 *locating* or reaching members of the target segment: different target audiences may be reached by different channels, inhabit different geographical areas, or attend different types of entertainment
2 *communicating* with members of the target audience: different target audiences may have different values, attitudes, and lifestyles and hence, different communication styles may be necessary to attract their attention and establish rapport
3 *motivating* members of the target audience: different target groups may be motivated to achieve the desired behavioural reaction by different factors.

For example, lower SES groups may be more avid watchers of television soap operas and reality television shows than upper SES groups, but a message about (child) immunisation can be communicated in the same style and tone of language to both and both may be motivated by the same factor (protection of their children). In this case we need only select different media vehicles to reach the

Table 9.1 Bases for market segmentation

Demographic	Age, sex, income, education, religion, ethnicity, occupation, family life cycle
Geographic	State, region, city size, density (urban, suburban, rural, remote), climate, local government area, postcode, census collector's district
Psychographic	Values, lifestyle, personality
Sociodemographic	Social class
Epidemiological	Risk-factor status
Behavioural	Frequency, intensity, regularity
Attitudinal	Positive, neutral, negative
Benefits sought	Varies by issue (for example, avoid disease, sensory enjoyment, peace of mind, etc.)
Readiness stage	Prochaska's stages of change

different groups. In other cases we may need different ways of communicating to appeal to different groups and their motivations to comply may be quite different.

Commercial organisations spend a great deal of resources identifying and determining which segments will be most profitable for them. Not surprisingly then, market segmentation and target marketing are emphasised in virtually all literature defining or describing social marketing and its application to public health campaigns (Hastings & Haywood 1991; Egger, Donovan & Spark 1993; Donovan & Owen 1994; Andreasen 1995; Manoff 1985; Novelli 1984; Lancaster, McIlwain & Lancaster 1983).

Market segmentation and target marketing involve three phases (Kotler 1989):

1 *dividing* the total market into segments and developing profiles of these segments

2 *appraising* each segment and *selecting* one or more segments as target markets

3 *developing* a detailed marketing strategy for each of the selected segments.

Market segments can be described or profiled in many ways (see table 9.1), with market researchers continually seeking better ways to delineate segments that respond differentially to different elements of the marketing mix. Regardless of the base(s) chosen for the initial segmentation (for example, age and sex), the segments are also usually described or profiled on as many other variables as possible so as to better understand the chosen segment(s). That is, we may segment teen smokers by age (13–16 years, 17–19 years) and sex, but then, within each segment, we could further segment by employment status and attitude to quitting. We could then profile the different subgroups on their leisure activities (type of music preferred, indoor versus outdoor orientated, passive versus active leisure pursuits, etc.), and so on.

For health promotion campaigns, target groups often are described in terms of risk factor status (smokers, the obese, the inactive, heavy drinkers, diabetics, etc.), or demographic groupings that epidemiologically appear at higher risk for

Segmenting kids

Carolyn Heath, of kids marketing consultancy Logistix Kids, suggests segmenting children according to their stages of development when planning how to communicate with and motivate kids (Ligerakis 2001):

- sensory: 0–2 years
- perceptual: 3–7 years
- analytical: 8–12 years
- reflective: 13–16 years.

Those interested in children's beliefs about health and morality use a similar demarcation, all based on Piaget's longstanding cognitive development stages.

the health issue in question (blue-collar groups for smoking, sedentary occupations for physical activity, Aborigines for diabetes, street kids for hepatitis C, etc.). While acknowledging that resources often dictate the choice of such broad target segments, in this book we focus on what we consider two of the most useful ways for segmenting target populations for social marketing campaigns: attitude—behaviour segmentation (after Sheth & Frazier 1982) and stage of change segmentation (after Prochaska & DiClemente 1984). These methods should be applied even where resources are limited since both direct the social marketer to a better understanding of the beliefs and attitudes of their target groups. However, before continuing, a brief word on psychographics—beware.

Psychographics

One popular method in the marketing and advertising area is the psychographic or lifestyle approach. In this procedure respondents answer a number of attitude, belief, and behaviour questions (usually fifty to 100), some general and some specific to the issue in question. Cluster analysis is then used to group respondents who respond similarly to the items and discriminant analysis is used to determine which items best differentiate the resulting clusters. The psychographic approach has appeal because, compared to traditional demographic segment descriptions such as 'married, 2.5 children, aged 30–45, lower-middle socioeconomic level', psychographic segments list descriptions such as 'outgoing, active in community activities, enjoys physical activities rather than reading, prefers barbecues rather than dinner parties, etc'. Furthermore, psychographic segments are often given catchy segment titles such as 'swinging singles', 'elderly adventurers', or 'sensitive New Age man'. The green profilings (see box below) also demonstrate the intuitive appeal of psychographic segmentation. We take the view that psychographics are useful in communicating with segments, but the basic segmentation should be on dimensions that inform how to motivate the different segments.

The main problem with psychographic and other lifestyle and attitude–interests–opinions (AIO) segmentations is that the groups are not particularly

> ## SKIN CANCER
> ## HAVE YOU BEEN CHECKED?
>
> The [suburb] LIONS CLUB has organised a FREE skin cancer screening. Specialists from the LIONS CANCER INSTITUTE will be available to examine people who feel they are at risk of having skin cancer.
>
> If you are 16 years of age or older and have or had one or more of the following:
> * a family member who has a malignant melanoma
> * five or more moles (not freckles) on your arms
> * moles or skin cancers removed
> * a mole or freckle that is changing in size or colour
> * fair skin that burns rather than tans
> * blistering sunburn as a child
> * any inflamed skin sores that do not heal
>
> then please phone [telephone number] to make an appointment.
>
> Venue: ....
>
> Date: ....
>
> If you are concerned but cannot attend the screening on that date, please express your interest with the LIONS CANCER INSTITUTE and see your family doctor.

In an attempt to increase the appropriateness of attendees at free skin cancer screening clinics, the Lion's Cancer Institute in Western Australia ran ads like this one (see chapter 6) (Katris, Donovan & Gray 1996).

exclusive, in fact, there is considerable overlap between them. For example, 70 per cent of cluster 'A' might agree with the statement 'I prefer visiting natural wilderness areas to man-made entertainments such as Sea World' versus 35 per cent of cluster 'B' agreeing with the statement—a statistically significant difference. Nevertheless, 35 per cent of cluster 'B' do share this characteristic of cluster 'A'. Attitude–behaviour and other segments (described below), defined specifically with respect to the targeted behaviour, are at least mutually exclusive with respect to the primary bases of segmentation.

Perhaps unfortunately, many health organisations appear to be seduced by the intuitive appeal of lifestyle segmentation. However, what the USA National Cancer Institute's consumer health profiles (see box) lack are the reasons why people in these clusters do or do not engage in screening behaviour.

The National Cancer Institute's (NCI) consumer health profile*

Two segments: 'Golden Ponds' and 'Rustic Elders'

Similar demographics: Retired couples, high school education, US$20 000–$27 000 (household income), blue-collar/service workers.

Similar health behaviours: need mammography screening, rely on Medicare or Medicaid.

Different leisure and media habits:

Golden Ponds	**Rustic Elders**
Enjoy indoor gardening	Enjoy camping
Contribute to PBS	Enjoy rodeo
Read *Modern Maturity*	Read hunting mags
Subscribe to cable television	View outdoor advertising

Implications: Both Golden Ponds and Rustic Elders need mammography screening messages, but different appeals and channels should be used to communicate to residents in these two clusters.

* National Cancer Institute 1982

Sheth and Frazier's attitude–behaviour segmentation

Sheth and Frazier (1982) present a model of strategy choice based on the concept of attitude–behaviour consistency or discrepancy (see table 9.2). They provide a systematic procedure not only for describing various target segments in terms of attitude and behaviour (the diagnosis), but also suggest a strategy for achieving behaviour change within each of the defined segments (the prognosis). Population surveys are necessary to determine the proportions falling into

The green consumer: behavioural clustering

Soutar, Ramaseshan, and Molster (1994) cluster analysed a sample of Western Australian respondents with respect to their types of pro-environmental purchasing behaviours rather than attitudes (for example, purchased environmentally friendly products or from companies with pro-environmental reputation, purchased products in recyclable packaging or refillable packaging, purchased biodegradable products, environmentally friendly constituents, removed extra packaging instore, purchased in bulk to avoid packaging).

They found five clusters as follows:

- group 1 (22 per cent) was least engaged in pro-environmental purchasing
- group 2 (21 per cent) was primarily concerned with waste avoidance
- group 3 (20 per cent) was primarily concerned with pro-environmental constituents
- group 4 (16 per cent) was primarily concerned with waste and constituents
- group 5 (21 per cent) engaged in all types of pro-environmental behaviours.

Soutar et al. (1994) then attempted to profile these groups against environmental attitudes, general values and demographics. However, there were few meaningful results, no doubt because of the considerable overlap in behaviours between several of the groups.

Green consumers: attitudinal and behavioural clustering*

Using a number of attitude and behaviour items the Roper Organisation delineated five consumer segments in 1992 with respect to attitudes and behaviours towards waste disposal, recycling, the environment, and conservation in general:

- 'true-blue greens' (20 per cent): hold positive attitudes towards pro-environmental issues and behave accordingly; they are opinion leaders, trend setters, high SES— professionals, executives.
- 'greenback greens' (5 per cent): will pay higher prices for ecologically friendly products; intellectually concerned, but not activists, and have busy lifestyle.
- 'sprouts' (31 per cent): some tendencies in pro-environmental direction, but not strong
- 'grousers' (24 per cent): express pro-environmental support, but rationalise their lack of green behaviours; object to higher prices and tend to blame others for environmental problems
- 'basic browns' (35 per cent): least active group; most socially and economically disadvantaged group, they don't believe individuals can make a difference.

* Ottman 1993

each of the segments. The segments should also be profiled in terms of their demographics, media habits, lifestyle variables, risk factor profiles, and other relevant health beliefs and attitudes.

According to Sheth and Frazier when attitudes and behaviour are consistent and in the desired direction (cell 1), a reinforcement process is required to sustain the desired behaviour. This can be done by reinforcing the attitude, reinforcing the behaviour, or both. For example, non-smoking teenagers should be continually reminded of all the reasons why they do not smoke, adult non-smokers can be reinforced by insurance premium discounts, non-smokers should continue to congratulate smokers for quitting, road safety campaigns should offer feedback that the campaigns have successfully reduced crashes, etc.

Where people hold positive attitudes towards, but do not carry out, the desired behaviour (cell 3) an inducement process is required. These can be aimed at minimising or removing organisational, socioeconomic, time, and place constraints. This could include actions such as providing change rooms at the worksite to facilitate lunchtime or before and after work exercise, providing discounts to non-working mothers to attend a gym during off-peak hours, visiting worksites for blood donations, and so on. In short, making it easier for the positive attitude to be translated into action.

In some cases the behaviour is being performed but the attitude is negative (cell 2). This may occur where a partner insists on a particular behaviour or where the behaviour is temporarily mandatory. In these cases, rationalisation needs to occur to shift the individual into the positive Cell 1. Information on the benefits of the behaviour need to be communicated, along with reinforcement.

Where attitudes are negative and the behaviour is not being performed (cell 4) behavioural confrontation (for example, restrictions on the behaviour) or

Table 9.2   A typology of strategy mix for planned social change*

		ATTITUDE	
		Positive	**Negative**
Perform		**Cell 1**	**Cell 2**
		Reinforcement process	Rationalisation process
		(a) behavioural	Attitude change
		(b) psychological	
DESIRED BEHAVIOUR			
Don't perform		**Cell 3**	**Cell 4**
		Inducement process	Confrontation process
		Behaviour change	(a) behavioural
			(b) psychological

* Sheth & Frazier 1982

psychological confrontation (for example, hard-hitting television ads, face-to-face counselling) may be necessary.

The particular components of each of these overall approaches will depend on the beliefs underlying the overall attitudes towards the desired behaviour, along with an understanding of physical, social, and structural facilitators and inhibitors. For example, some people who feel positive towards increasing their levels of physical activity may simply be lazy, others may lack nearby safe facilities, and others may have too many family and work demands to have the time.

In much of our work we include a neutral category on the attitude dimension (see table 9.3) as there are many situations for which people do not have a view one way or the other. It represents the more realistic strategy of attempting to move people first from a negative to neutral, then, from neutral to a positive position rather than from a negative to a positive position in one step. We also often include two or more levels of the desired behaviour as there are quite distinct existing gradations of desired and undesired behaviour for many issues (physical activity levels, alcohol frequency or amount, regular versus occasional intimate partner violence, degree of water and energy conservation, degree of recycling, etc.). That is, the behavioural segmentation can be done either with respect to the desired behaviour or the undesired behaviour.

Table 9.3   Extended Sheth–Frazier segmentation model

Attitude	Behaviour		
	Strongly perform desired behaviour	**Moderately perform**	**Do not perform desired behaviour**
Positive	Cell 1	Cell 4	Cell 7
Neutral	Cell 2	Cell 5	Cell 8
Negative	Cell 3	Cell 6	Cell 9

The nature of the segments also allows a determination of whether mass media messages are an appropriate and cost-effective method for influencing the different segments. For example, segments 4 and 7 in table 9.3 are far more likely than segment 9 to respond to a media campaign and segment 9 probably requires a totally different approach. However, even in this case, mass media may be used to increase that target group's awareness of the issue.

A stage approach to segmentation

A segmentation model directly applicable for many areas of behaviour change derives from James Prochaska's clinical work with cigarette and drug addiction (Prochaska & DiClemente 1984; 1986) and the transtheoretical model of behaviour change. This model now forms the fundamental basis of some social marketing frameworks (Andreasen 1995).

The stages of change concept divides the total target segment (for example, all smokers, all non-exercisers), into subsegments depending on their stage in progression toward adoption of the desired behaviour (quitting; taking up exercise).

Prochaska's stages are:

1 *precontemplation*—in which the individual is not considering modifying his or her unhealthy behaviour

2 *contemplation*—in which the individual is considering changing an unhealthy behaviour, but not in the immediate future

3 *preparation*— in which the individual plans to try to change the unhealthy behaviour in the immediate future (that is, in the next 2 weeks or appropriate timeframe)

4 *action*—the immediate (6 month) period following trial and adoption of the recommended behaviour and cessation of the unhealthy behaviour

5 *maintenance*—the period following the action stage until the unhealthy behaviour is fully extinguished

6 *termination*—when the problem-behaviour is completely eliminated, that is, 'zero temptation across all problem situations'.

As in the Sheth–Frazier model, Prochaska and DiClemente claim that individuals at different stages of change would have different attitudes, beliefs, and motivations with respect to the (desired) new behaviour. Hence, different treatment approaches and health communication strategies may be necessary for individuals in the different stages of change. There is some support for these claims over a variety of areas (see Prochaska, Velicer, Rossi et al. 1994b for an analysis of twelve health behaviours), but particularly smoking (Prochaska, Velicer, DiClemente & Fava 1988; DiClemente, Prochaska, Fairhurst et al. 1991), nutrition (Curry, Kristal & Bowen 1992; Campbell, Symons, Demark-Wahnefried et al. 1998), and exercise (Marcus & Owen

1992; Marcus, Rakowski & Rossi 1992; Oman & King 1998; Prochaska & Marcus 1994).

Prochaska, Norcross, and DiClemente (1994a) describe nine activities or processes of change that individuals use to proceed through the stages of change:

- *consciousness raising*—increasing awareness about the problem
- *emotional arousal*—dramatic expressions of the problem and consequences
- *self-reevaluation*—reappraisal of the problem and its inconsistency with self-values
- *commitment*—choosing to change and making a public commitment to do so
- *social liberation*—choosing social environments that foster or facilitate change
- *relationship fostering*—getting help from others, professional or otherwise
- *counterconditioning*—substituting alternatives
- *rewards*—administering self-praise or other positive experiences for dealing with the problem
- *environmental control*—restructuring of the environment to reduce temptations and opportunities.

The earlier processes are experiential but, once the commitment is made, the processes are primarily behavioural. The transtheoretical model also incorporates the notion of decisional balance: that an evaluation of the costs (cons) and benefits (pros) of making the change varies over the stages, with cons outweighing pros in precontemplation, pros outweighing cons in the action stage, and crossing over occurring during contemplation.

Prochaska's concept is similar to marketing's buyer readiness segmentation, which states that, at any particular point in time, the market can be described in terms of those unaware of the product, those aware of the product, those informed about the product, those interested in the product, those motivated to buy the product, and those who have formed an intention to buy the product (Kotler 1989). The implications of this are that marketing objectives and strategy will vary according to the relative proportions of the total market in each of these different stages.

Egger, Donovan, and Spark (1993) and Donovan and Owen (1994) have suggested the potential utility of the stage model as a segmentation base in health promotion and social marketing. They delineated the various communication and behavioural objectives at the different stages, as shown in table 9.4.

Donovan and Owen (1994) claim that mass media health promotion campaigns are most influential in the precontemplation and contemplation stages (by raising the salience and personal relevance of the issue), of moderate influence in the preparation stage (by reinforcing perceptions of self-efficacy and maintaining salience of the perceived benefits of adopting the recommended behaviour), and of least influence in the action and maintenance stages where beliefs and attitudes are well established and where socioenvironmental influences are greatest.

Table 9.4   Campaign objectives and relative influence of mass media campaigns by stages of change*

PROCHASKA Stages Media	Communication objectives	Behavioural objectives	Mass media influence
Precontemplation	Raise awareness of issue, personal relevance	Seek further information	High
Contemplation	Increase personal relevance, build response efficacy	Form an intention to try	Moderate–high
Preparation	Build self-efficacy, reinforce reasons for trial	Trial	Moderate
Action	Reinforce reasons for adoption; maintain motivational and efficacy support	Adoption	Low
Maintenance	Maintain reasons for adoption	Maintain new behaviour	Low

* Donovan & Owen 1994

Prochaska and DiClemente's stages of change concept has been readily adopted by health promoters and social marketers (for example, Andreasen 1995; Booth, Macaskill, Owen et al. 1993; Donovan & Owen 1994; Egger, Donovan and Spark 1993; Maibach and Cotton 1995). However, for any marketing segmentation base to be meaningful it must be shown that the different segments respond differentially to some aspects of the communication and marketing mixes directed at the segments. Hence, the utility of the stages of change approach in social marketing is dependent on evidence that individuals in the various stages of change do respond differentially to elements of the social marketing mix. While a number of studies have shown differences between individuals in the different stages of change, much of this has been directed towards the implications for counselling and educational interventions (DiClemente, Prochaska, Fairhurst et al. 1991; Marcus, Rakowski & Rossi 1992; Marcus, Selby, Niaura et al. 1992; Booth, Macaskill, Owen et al. 1993).

Donovan, Leivers, and Hannaby (1999e) tested three antismoking ads and analysed the results for precontemplators, contemplators, and those in the ready for action and action stages. Figure 9.1 shows a significant relationship between the stages of change and the perceived relevance of the ads and figure 9.2 shows a significant relationship between the stages of change and the ads' impact on intentions to quit or cut down the amount smoked. These results support the utility of the stages of change as a segmentation variable.

Prochaska's stages of change concept is widely used but perhaps not always properly understood, especially with respect to the various processes applicable to each of the stages (Whitelaw, MacHardy, Reid & Duffy 1999). Nevertheless, regardless of whether or not one adopts Prochaska's recommended intervention processes for the various stages, the model is very useful simply as a segmentation method for formative research and targeting. For example, the Western Australian *Freedom from Fear* campaign targets 'men who are aware of their problem

Figure 9.1   Perceived personal relevance of Quit ads by smokers' stage of change*

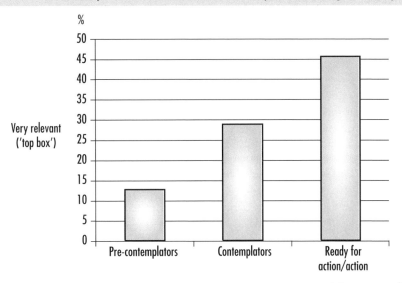

* Donovan et al. 1999e

Figure 9.2   Impact of Quit ads on the likelihood of quitting or cutting down by smokers' stage of change*

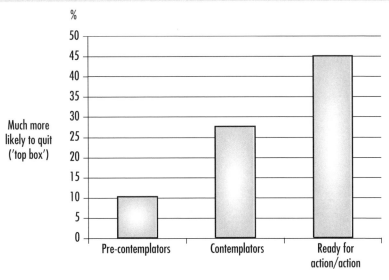

* Donovan et al. 1999e

and want to change', that is, in stages terminology, violent men in the contemplator and, especially, the ready for action stages (Donovan, Francas, Paterson & Zappelli 2000; see chapter 14).

- Sensation seeking is a personality trait associated with the need for novel, complex, ambiguous, and emotionally intense stimuli and the willingness to take risks to obtain such stimulation.
- People with a high tendency to seek sensation are much more at risk for use of a variety of drugs.
- Based on research with high-sensation seeking teens, antimarijuana public service announcements were developed for high-sensation seeking adolescents and televised in three counties.
- Spots were placed in programs that were watched by high-sensation seeking adolescents.
- Teenagers were surveyed before and after the campaign. The results were analysed for high-sensation versus low-sensation-seeking teens.
- All three campaigns resulted in significant reductions in marijuana use in high-sensation-seeking adolescents. Usage did not change among low-sensation seekers.

* Palmgreen, Donohew, Lorch et al. 2001

Selecting target audiences

Having delineated the various segments, the next step is to select one or more segments on which to concentrate. The commercial marketing literature offers only broad criteria as to how to select between segments. Similarly, with the exception of Andreasen (1995) and Donovan, Egger & Francas's (1999a) TARPARE model described here, little exists to assist public health practitioners to select segments where limited resources require some prioritising.

For commercial marketers segment size appears to be the primary determinant, although it is clear that other criteria need to be taken into account, such as the intensity of competitive activity directed at each segment, the range of products and services already available to each segment, the ease of geographically reaching each segment for tangible product delivery, access to the target segments via media channels for message delivery, and the price sensitivity of different segments. These criteria provide a starting point for the TARPARE model.

The TARPARE model (from Donovan et al. 1999a)

TARPARE is a useful and flexible model for understanding the various segments in a population of interest and assessing the potential viability of interventions directed at each segment given limited resources. The model is particularly useful when, as is usually the case, there is a need to prioritise segments in terms of available budgets.

TARPARE is generally applied after a number of segments have been identified within a particular area of interest. That is, given a Sheth–Frazier attitude-behaviour segmentation, such as that in table 9.3, or a Prochaska segmentation (that is, precontemplators, contemplators, and preparers for action), the TAR-PARE model evaluates the various segments on the following criteria.

- **T:** *The Total number of people in the segment.* In general, the greater the number of people, the greater the priority of the segment. This criterion is particularly important for mass interventions where small percentage shifts in large proportions of the population yield substantial benefits (for example, reductions in driving speed and severity of injury; cholesterol shifts (Rose 1985; 1992).

- **AR:** *The proportion of At Risk people in the segment.* This includes a number of factors: an assessment of what proportions of the segments are classified as low, medium, or high risk with respect to the issue under consideration, an assessment of associated risk factors, and an assessment of expected benefits of risk reduction in the segment. For example, the proportion of heavy smokers might be greatest among blue-collar males aged 25–35 years, but 36–50-year-old blue-collar male smokers might have higher obesity levels, lower levels of physical activity, and a higher incidence of diabetes. The proportion in each segment classed as at risk (high or moderate) and whose behaviour, if modified, would provide the greatest reduction in health costs can be calculated or estimated. In general, the greater this proportion the greater potential return and hence the higher the category's priority.

- **P:** *The Persuasibility of the target audience.* This refers to how feasible it would be to change attitudes and behaviour in the segment. In general, the more persuasible the more likely an intervention can be effective and the higher the priority. Segments with a higher proportion of members neutral or positive to the desired behaviour would have a higher priority than segments with a high proportion vehemently opposed to the desired behaviour change.

- **A:** *The Accessibility of the target audience.* This refers to how easy it is to reach each segment via mass communication or other channels, such as worksites, community centres, entertainment venues, schools, and other institutional settings. The more accessible the target audience the more likely an effective outcome and the higher the priority. This measure should take into account cost per thousand data for media activities. For example, a target audience may be accessible, but the necessary media may be expensive.

- **R:** *Resources required to meet the needs of the target audience.* This involves assessing the financial, human, and structural resources needed to service the segment. This refers to the extent to which interventions can be directed towards each segment with current services and facilities versus the need for additional resources. For example, various segments might be motivated to engage in increased physical activity by a particular campaign, but this may require new programs or facilities to meet this demand (for example, indoor running tracks, heated swimming pools).

- **E:** *Equity.* This refers to the need for inclusion of social justice considerations. Groups such as Indigenous people and homeless teenagers might constitute a very small proportion of the population, but for equity reasons warrant special programs.

The TARPARE model was originally developed as a qualitative assessment and can be usefully applied as such. The model can also be represented as a weighted multi-attribute model, in which each segment's overall score is the weighted sum of its scores on each of the attributes where the weightings reflect the relative importance of each attribute:

$$\text{Segment priority} = f\ (T.w_t + AR.w_{ar} + P.w_p + A.w_a + R.w_r + E.w_e)$$

where w_i represents the weight attached to each factor and

T = total number in segment
AR = % at (high) risk
P = persuasibility
A = accessibility
R = additional resources required
E = equity factor

T and **AR** require epidemiological data, **P** requires an estimate based on attitudinal research, **A** requires a knowledge of media and entertainment habits and other lifestyle characteristics, **R** requires an analysis of existing resources and a survey of consumer preferences, and **E** requires a knowledge of policy as well as the practitioner's own ethical considerations. These factors can be measured quantitatively through surveys and questionnaires or qualitatively through such processes as focus groups. However, even with quantitative data on these attributes, the assignment of weights remains subjective and dependent on the values of the practitioner.

TARPARE example: selecting a target segment for a physical activity campaign (after Donovan et al. 1999a)

Based on the Sheth–Frazier segmentation shown in table 9.5 (Donovan & Owen 1994, reprinted, by permission, from R.J. Donovan & N. Owen, 1994, 'Social marketing and population interventions', in *Advances in exercise adherence*, edited by R.K.Dishman, Champaign, IL, 276), a quantitative analysis is shown in table 9.6 for selection of target segments for a physical activity campaign.

In this example each of the criteria are given equal weights and each criterion is scored 1–5, with 5 indicating a high-priority score, 3 indicating medium, and 1 indicating a low-priority score. For example, 5 for At Risk would indicate a substantial proportion of high-risk people in the segment, 1 for Resources would indicate that resources would be stretched to achieve campaign objectives in that segment, 3 for Equity would indicate a medium-strength argument for inclusion on equity grounds, and 4 for Persuasibility would indicate that a large proportion of the segment could be classed as contemplators or ready for

Table 9.5 Exercise attitude–behaviour segmentation*

	Attitude to exercise	
Exercise behaviour	Positive (%)	Neutral/Negative (%)
Exercise at or near level sufficient for maximal cardiovascular benefits (high actives)	11	3
Exercise at light/moderate level for some cardiovascular benefits ('medium actives')	35	19
Little or no exercise (inactives)	16	16

* After Donovan & Owen 1994

change (that is, high persuasibility). A number of sources are available to assist in assigning scores (Corti 1998; Egger, Donovan & Corti 1998).

Scores for each segment are summed to indicate a priority ordering. With no weighting this application ranks inactive positives top priority (23), followed closely by inactive neutrals/negatives (21), and medium active positives (20). Unweighted scores often yield small differences between groups.

Applying weights that reflect practitioners' values, organisational policies, and available resources generally yields clearer differences between segments. For example, to reflect a desire for maximal benefit for the greatest number with relatively little audience resistance we would apply the following weights to segment size, at risk status and persuasibility, and leave all other criteria unweighted:

- 4 to segment size (w_t)
- 3 to at risk status (w_{ar})
- 3 to persuasibility (w_p) (total of 10).

Applying these weights the top two segments are more clearly separated from the others:

- inactive positives: 50
- medium-active positives: 49
- inactive neutrals/negatives: 42
- medium-active neutrals/negatives: 39
- high-active positives: 33
- high-active neutrals/negatives: 27.

Depending on the situation other criteria may be added. For example, in times of crisis, such as with infectious disease outbreaks, a further criterion of *Urgency* may need to be applied, that is, the extent to which action is necessary or opportunistic in the immediate short term or whether timing is not a crucial factor. For example, a marked increase in the presentation of dengue fever cases would require an immediate public education campaign of mosquito breeding control and bite prevention to prevent an epidemic.

It is likely that different organisations will have different views on the weights they consider appropriate to each of the criteria. Some organisations may have a mass population emphasis, others might emphasise social justice considerations, and others might emphasise those most at risk regardless of segment size.

Also, we have demonstrated here only an additive choice model. It may well be that some decision makers may use quite different decision models (Hawkins, Best & Coney 1995). Some organisations might, for example, first eliminate any target group below a certain size, then eliminate any group scoring low on accessibility and persuasibility, then rank those remaining on social justice needs.

Andreasen (1995) suggests six factors to be taken into account when deciding resource allocation:

- segment size
- prevalence in each segment of the problem under consideration
- severity of the problem in that segment
- ability of the segment to cope with the problem (termed 'defenselessness', p. 186)
- reachability
- responsiveness (that is, 'probable willingness to listen', p. 186).

Three of these are directly comparable with TARPARE: size, reachability (accessibility), and responsiveness (persuasibility). Andreasen's defenselessness has some similarity with our equity factor and his prevalence and severity factors have some overlap with our at risk factor. Andreasen has no factor comparable to TARPARE's resources factor.

TARPARE was developed for application within a risk area, as in the above examples. However, it may also be applied between risk areas. For example, a health agency with sufficient funding for only one campaign may need to decide which of a set of programs should be given priority: for example, promotion of safe sex practices among teenagers, medication compliance among asthmatics, increasing physical activity among retired people, or smoking cessation and alcohol reduction among women attempting to become pregnant or in the early

Targeting opinion leaders

We may sometimes wish to select opinion leaders for formative research or to analyse survey data by. Here is a useful ten item agree/disagree scale (in Weimann 1991).

I usually count on being successful in everything I do
I am rarely unsure about how I should behave
I like to assume responsibility
I like to take the lead when a group does things together
I enjoy convincing others of my opinions
I often notice that I serve as a model for others
I am good at getting what I want
I am often a step ahead of others
I own many things others envy me for
I often give others advice and suggestions

Table 9.6   TARPARE model for choice of target group for physical activity campaign*

Target group	Size (% adult population)	At risk status	Persuasibility	Accessibility	Resources	Equity	Total score (unweighted)
High active positives	2 (11)	1	5	5	1	1	15
High active neutrals/ negatives	1 (3)	1	4	5	2	1	14
Medium-active positives	5 (35%)	3	4	4	2	2	20
Medium-active neutrals/ negatives	3 (19)	3	3	4	3	2	18
Inactive positives	3 (16)	5	4	4	4	3	23
Inactive neutrals/ negatives	3 (16)	5	1	3	5	4	21

*Donovan et al. 1999a

stages of pregnancy. Models such as TARPARE may be used to determine which of these areas should be given highest priority or, as in Andreasen's (1995) approach, the proportion of resources to be allocated to each.

Overall, the model provides a disciplined approach to target selection and resource allocation, and forces consideration of just what weights should be applied to the different criteria and how these might vary for different issues (HIV/AIDS interventions, antismoking campaigns, exercise promotion, parenting interventions, domestic violence campaigns, etc.), or for different objectives (increases in knowledge, changes in habitual behaviours, attitude formation or change, political lobbying, etc.). Focusing attention on the TARPARE criteria and attempting to apply these to the various segments can lead to a greater understanding of the various segments and their relative viability regardless of which segment is selected.

Cross-cultural targeting

With the recent exception of some Indigenous campaigns it has been common practice in Australia and elsewhere to simply translate mainstream campaign materials into the languages of major migrant and ethnic groups in the community (for example, the Commonwealth's recently launched families antidrug campaign) and/or to simply place campaign messages in the ethnic media. This is understandable given limited resources, the number of language groups in the community, and the small numbers in many of these groups. It would be far too expensive to carry out formative research with every language group and develop culturally specific campaign services and materials for each group. Furthermore, where there are similar motivations relevant to the desired behaviour across cultures, this may not be necessary.

However, where resources are available, it is far more effective to develop campaigns that recognise cultural differences. This is especially crucial where the underlying motivations are different and where the ability of the message to

Tailoring

In using the term 'tailoring', Pasick et al. (1996) not only lessen objectification of the target groups, but also exemplify a consumer orientation in that the same core service or product is to be delivered, but tailored or modified so as to enhance acceptability, uptake, and impact in each target group.

attract attention and engage the audience depends heavily on culturally specific components.

Based on their work in developing interventions for increasing breast and cervical cancer screening among various ethnic groups in Northern California, Pasick, D'Onofrio & Otero-Sabogal (1996) provide a model for developing interventions for specific target ethnic groups (which they term 'tailored' rather than 'targeted' interventions). They suggest research to identify the cultural dimensions relevant to the specific issue and that these rather than broader cultural dimensions should be taken into account when developing interventions. For example, they identified *fatalismo*, a fatalistic outlook in Hispanic culture that engenders a pessimistic view on curing cancer and acts to inhibit screening uptake. Similarly, Vietnamese people were reported to be inhibited by the superstition that 'if you look for cancer, you will find it'.

The first author's research with Indigenous Australians suggests that traditional views on death due to 'magic' (perhaps for some transgression) may act as a barrier in traditionally oriented remote communities to accepting death due to heart disease and other lifestyle diseases. Similarly, the more collectivist nature of Indigenous culture indicates that apart from a greater emphasis on community involvement in intervention design and implementation, there also needs to be greater emphasis on how the community benefits from the intervention, rather than on just individual benefits.

Pasick at al (1996) suggest that there has been too much focus on the broadly defined racial or ethnic group (Vietnamese, Greek, Muslim, Chinese, etc.) and insufficient awareness of cultural dimensions specifically relevant to health. In this sense, 'culture' not only includes values, beliefs, and traditions, but also the living environment, opportunities or lack of for healthy behaviours, and opportunities or lack of for cultural expression. For example, the vast disparity in living environment conditions between Indigenous communities and non-Indigenous communities in Australia indicates that at least the implementation of interventions must be tailored to local conditions.

Pasick et al. also suggest that a focus on the specific dimensions often reveals far more similarities between groups than differences. In this sense they note that socioeconomic status is a significant determinant of health that often elim-

Cultural tailoring

Interventions, strategies, messages, materials that conform with specific cultural characteristics that directly influence behaviour and health (Pasick et al. 1996).

Figure 9.3 Relative Importance of culture in developing interventions for ethnic groups*

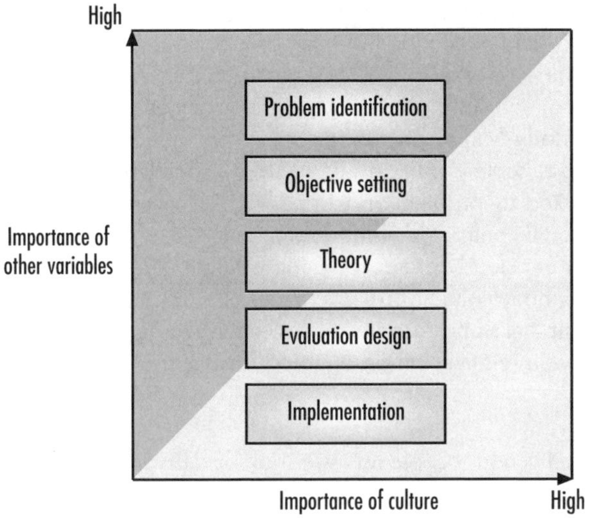

* Adapted from Pasick et al. 1996

inates differences between racial or ethnic groups. Similarly, the differences between subgroups of an ethnic group are sometimes greater than between different ethnic groups. Donovan, Mick, Holden, and Noel (1997c) found that, with respect to alcohol issues, urban Indigenous youth were in many ways more similar to lower SES non-Indigenous youth than they were to remote community, more traditionally oriented Indigenous youth. They also suggested that remote community Indigenous youth overall may be more similar to non-Indigenous youth than they are to Indigenous adults in their traditionally oriented communities.

Using a five-phase intervention model of problem identification, objective setting, theory, evaluation design, and implementation, Pasick et al. proposed that the extent of cultural tailoring required depended on the relative importance of cultural versus other variables in each of these phases. Their model is shown in figure 9.3, where the angle and location of the line is established by research. In the lower shaded area cultural factors are more important; in the upper unshaded area other factors are more important.

In their study of underage drinking, Donovan et al. found a number of differences between Indigenous youth in urban settings and Indigenous youth in remote communities (for example, interest and participation in traditional ceremonies, English literacy and use of traditional language) as well as commonalities (for example, family and kinship ties and obligations, interest in Indigenous celebrities, music preferences) that had implications for underage alcohol interventions. They also listed differences and commonalities between Indigenous youth and non-Indigenous youth in general (see box). With respect to these differences Donovan et al. concluded for Indigenous youth that

Differences between Indigenous and non-Indigenous youth*

- Greater cash resources among non-Indigenous youth.
- Higher literacy and education levels among non-Indigenous youth.
- Less direct exposure to alcohol abuse among non-Indigenous youth.
- Greater educational and employment opportunities available to non-Indigenous youth, particularly with respect to remote youth.
- Non-Indigenous society primarily marked by social drinking; Indigenous society primarily marked by problem drinking.
- Indigenous youth confronted with racism.
- Indigenous youth clearly prefer Indigenous health workers, but accept non-Indigenous people who gain their trust.
- Greater kinship links and responsibilities among Indigenous youth; greater face-to-face contact with relatives on an ongoing basis.

* Donovan et al. 1997c

- Indigenous people are essential for delivery of alcohol messages to Indigenous people
- the language used should be clear and simple English or the traditional language should be used
- alcohol messages should include or even emphasise negative social effects (violence, lack of money for food and other necessities, etc.) as well as health and performance effects, and, in remote areas, be linked to traditional culture
- for remote communities with licensed premises, interventions should be concurrently aimed at alcohol availability within the community.

On a broader scale they emphasised the importance of increasing educational and employment opportunities as well as campaigns aimed at lessening racism.

Overall, in Pasick et al.'s framework, Donovan et al. (1997c) concluded that the problem identification, objective setting, and theoretical models for under-

Similarities between Indigenous and non-Indigenous youth*

- Similar interests in music and sports, especially in salient celebrities.
- Hanging around focal points (for example, shopping centres).
- Sources of alcohol—parents' supplies, older siblings, friends.
- Drinking behaviours—mostly quick consumption, binge drinking.
- Types and brands of alcohol drunk.
- Occasions of drinking—parties (when parents absent)
- Places of drinking—parks, bushland.
- Strong peer bonding and other developmental features (establishing identity, conflict with adult rules, wanting to assert independence, self-consciousness in dealings with the opposite sex, etc.).
- Similar self-reported reasons or benefits of drinking, although boredom is more important in remote Indigenous communities.

* Donovan et al. 1997c

Figure 9.4 Relative importance of culture in tailoring alcohol interventions for Indigenous youth*

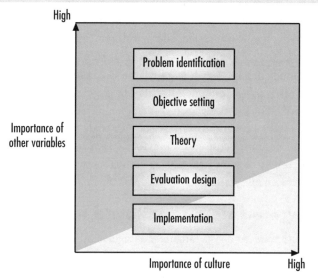

* Donovan et al. 1997c

age drinking are largely independent of cultural differences, especially for Indigenous urban youth at school. However, they concluded that cultural differences are important in expressing the content of the intervention materials and are crucial for implementation. This is depicted in figure 9.4.

Donovan et al. concluded that the similarities suggested that

- similar alcohol-related beliefs and behaviours need to be targeted for both Indigenous and non-Indigenous underage youth
- adult sources of alcohol need to be controlled for both
- intervention components with respect to entertainment and sport apply to both and can include many common elements (in some cases the same Indigenous and non-Indigenous celebrities can be used for both groups)
- intervention components dealing with deconstructing alcohol brand images (and marketing images in general) can include the same brands
- programs aimed at remaining within the peer group but not participating in drinking need to be included in both
- recreational programs need to be targeted to both—and particularly at the 14–17 or 15–17 age group who are 'too old' for what they consider 'childish' activities, but 'too young' to be admitted to adult venues or activities.

Individual tailoring

Prior to mass communications, personal selling was a major factor across all product and service areas, especially in non-urban areas. The travelling salesman was part of the landscape and is written into folklore. Similarly, prior to the advent of self-service supermarkets and hypermarkets, personal selling was paramount, even for commodities and packaged goods. The best salespeople then—and now—were those who first established a good knowledge of their customer, identifying both their specific and general needs. Little wonder that mass advertising was called 'salesmanship in print' by one of the first advertising legends, the copywriter John E. Kennedy (Lasker 1963; 1987).

Good salespeople, while selling the same product to every customer, tailored their pitch to the idiosyncrasies of each individual customer. Hence, the roominess of a Ford stationwagon could be emphasised for golf bag and buggy, children's bassinette and toys, dog space, or trade tools and equipment, depending on the potential customer's previously established needs and lifestyle. While there might be some or even a great deal of overlap each individual received a customised sales pitch.

Targeted versus tailored messages

As we have seen above targeted messages are designed for a segment of the population based on a characteristic or set of characteristics shared by members of the segment (occasional smokers, upper SES people opposed to refugees seeking asylum, 14–24 year old females with bulimic tendencies, etc.). Tailored messages are designed for one specific individual based on prior assessment of the individual (Kreuter, Farrell, Olevitch et al. 2000).

The advent of computers and interactive technology has stimulated the development of tailored messages; individual information can be entered and analysed and the customised message constructed and delivered in the one session.

The information required of the individual consists of a beliefs, attitudes, and behaviour questionnaire based on some model(s) of attitude—behaviour change and, increasingly, on what stage of change the individual is in. The programmer—and here's the rub—then matches the individual's responses with a number of predeveloped messages that incorporate the individual's information. Obviously, the potential effectiveness of the tailoring will depend on the nature

Not quit altogether yet?

Having answered a questionnaire about recent quitting attempts, smoking behaviour, family characteristics, etc., our trying-to-quit smoker might receive the following message: There are a lot of rugby events being televised at the moment and the times when the games are close seems to be when you find it hardest to resist the urge for a smoke. Remember this next time and make sure there are no cigarettes in the house before settling down to watch a match and that you have a packet of those peppermint lollies you like. Your daughter Molly turns 11 in 3 months time. That's a crucial age for kids to start experimenting with smoking, so the sooner you quit the better for her and for you. For a detailed, easy to follow guide to developing tailored communications for delivery by computer, see Kreuter et al.'s (2000) *Tailoring Health Messages: Customising communication with computer technology*, published by Lawrence Erlbaum.

and quality of the information entered and the validity of the model used by the programmer to generate information based on the questionnaire data. If tailored messages do not work better than non-tailored messages in a particular instance (and there have been plenty of those), it does not mean that the concept of tailoring is not valid; we simply might have not done it properly. Overall though, Kreuter et al. (2000) provide evidence that, in general, tailored messages do outperform non-tailored messages, but not always and not always by much (for example, Bernhardt 2001). As would be expected, studies are now moving towards the type of tailoring that seems to be most effective.

Concluding comments

The principle of selectivity and concentration and its ramifications constitute one of the most important concepts in marketing and hence in social marketing. It derives directly from a consumer orientation and is plain common sense. However, the usual situation is that social marketers do not have the resources to develop campaigns and specific intervention components for all target groups, no matter how they are defined. Nevertheless, given a culturally neutral message, one can ensure that different target groups can be reached and served by astute media channel and media vehicle selection, along with strategic location and delivery of services. Similarly, it is relatively simple to develop materials that contain the style of language and visual symbols of different target groups without altering the basic information provided. Where the target groups differ in basic motivations or require different products and services, then different campaigns or programs must be developed for optimal effectiveness.

Various segmentation bases in table 9.1 can be used for strategic planning at an organisational level (assigning responsibilities to different sections for different geographic areas, different age groups, occupational groups or genders, etc.). However, at the program planning level, the segmentation must be on the basis of the targeted behaviour and the target group's attitudes and beliefs with respect to that behaviour. It is knowledge of the attitudes and beliefs about the behaviour that indicates what intervention strategy is most appropriate for each group and that allows us to develop the relevant motivational messages for behaviour change. In many cases social marketers identify key influencers to lobby or at whom to direct campaigns. This may range from targeting women to persuade their men partners to undergo more frequent health checks, opinion leaders to publicise screening programs, or local political leaders and political advisors for policy and legislative changes. This is segmentation at an organisational planning stage. All people within these groups should then be segmented according to their attitudes and current behaviours with respect to the issue in question.

The Sheth–Frazier model is a direct application of this approach, while the stage-of-change categories assume a simultaneous application of the attitude

More jargon: 'signalling' versus 'tailoring'

Signalling refers to an executional style—graphic symbols, content and formatting—that appeals to a specific audience (for example, the quick-cuts visual style of MTV that appeals to young audiences). Tailoring refers to customising offerings based on prior knowledge of the audience's interests.

and behaviour dimensions. Both can be applied to the same issue, although in practice, one or other appears more appropriate.

The stage-of-change approach appears most appropriate for addictive and habitual health-related behaviours (from whence it was derived), and those health behaviours where there is a long period of adoption and where people see considerable barriers or disbenefits of adoption of the desired behaviour (for example, physical activity, food habits, weight control, smoking).

The Sheth–Frazier framework seems to be more useful for health behaviours where very few are beyond the precontemplation stage (for example, reducing alcohol consumption), for non-addictive health behaviours (for example, screening behaviours), and non-health behaviours (such as antiracism, public transport, recycling, and water conservation).

The Pasick et al. framework appears useful in determining to what extent mainstream interventions need to be modified for different ethnic groups. This requires considerable formative research to identify not just the broad cultural dimensions that need to be taken into account (which are often already known anyway), but also, more importantly, those specific to the issue in question. It is important to remember that these include not just cultural values, but also all aspects of culture, including living conditions and economic and educational status.

By way of turning full circle the advent of interactive technology combined with mass communication delivery channels has enabled the development of messages customised to individuals on a mass scale. Health professionals have been quick to pick up on this development, with promising results but still some way to go. There are clearly opportunities to take this approach further in a variety of social marketing areas, but we must be careful not to let the technology drive

Dear valued customer ... versus Dear Dr Henley ...

Personalising messages is a common technique in database direct marketing. The marketer knows that people are more likely to open and read a personally addressed message than a generic one. Health professionals are also beginning to realise this: immunisation reminder cards that are personally addressed get a greater response than those simply addressed 'Dear parent'. Personalisation should not be confused with tailoring.

the agenda; it is the tailoring that is important, not whether the messages are delivered by computer. The successful TravelSmart project referred to earlier and presented in more detail in chapter 14 used tailored messages (or what they call 'individualised marketing') without the aid of any sophisticated software.

Chapter 10

The Marketing Mix

Introduction

In this chapter we discuss one of the fundamental principles of marketing, the marketing mix or the 4 Ps in a social marketing context. The 4 Ps as identified by McCarthy (1960) are **P**roduct, **P**lace (or distribution), **P**rice, and **P**romotion. In chapter 2 we discussed the Principle of Customer Value as referring to the sum total of the benefits provided by the mix of these Ps. While many writers have attempted to widen the number of Ps (for example, Partnerships, Politics, and Persuasion) this chapter will focus on the traditional 4 Ps and a fifth P (**P**eople) for services marketing. Given that many health and welfare products are services, lessons from services marketing are essential in social marketing—although largely overlooked.

The marketing mix

The marketing mix, or the 4 Ps, covers the main areas in which decisions are made so as to maximise value to the customer. Although we discuss these elements in turn it is important to recognise that the marketing mix refers to the blending of all four such that they complement each other in an integrated marketing effort. For example, products with a high price are accompanied by extensive advertising and promotion that attempt to justify the higher price, either objectively or subjectively, via appeals to sensory attributes, social status, or lifestyle. Borden first used the term 'marketing mix' in 1953 to compare marketing to the process of baking in which appropriate ingredients in the correct proportions are blended (Sargeant 1999). As stated earlier, the total value of a particular perfume to the customer is determined not only by its fragrance, but also—and arguably more so—by its packaging, brand name, brand positioning (that is, brand image), price, and the image of the outlet from where it is purchased.

- Product is defined as 'anything that can be offered to a market for attention, acquisition, use, or consumption that might satisfy a want or need. It includes physical objects, services, people, places, organisations and ideas'

236

Western Australian Positive Parenting campaign*

The Western Australian Family and Children's Services campaign promotes positive parenting techniques, given evidence that an 'encouraging parenting style' is associated with substantially lower rates of mental illness in children (Silburn, Zubrick, Garton, Gurren et al. 1996). An encouraging parenting style involves using encouragement rather than criticism and rewards rather than punishments. The Positive Parenting campaign was designed to assist parents in gaining mastery of the encouraging parenting style. It built on existing skills to help parents manage their children's behaviour effectively at different stages in their development. The total marketing mix was designed to demonstrate and convey the positive effects of good parenting styles, such as happy family relationships, rather than the negative consequences of poor parenting, such as child abuse and domestic violence.

* Henley, Donovan & Moorhead 1998

(Kotler, Chandler, Brown & Adam 1994, p. 260). Concepts of design, branding, product variation, and packaging relate to product.

- **Place** (otherwise called 'distribution') is the process of making the product available to the consumer, including the network or channel of organisations that may be involved as well as the activities they perform. Concepts of logistics, retailing, and wholesaling relate to place. Place also includes access factors such as opening hours, availability of public transport, availability and ease of parking, wheelchair access, etc.

- **Price** is the total of monetary and non-monetary costs exchanged when purchasing a product or service or adopting a practice or idea. This involves financial concepts such as availability of credit terms, discounts, and EFTPOS availability, and psychological costs such as embarrassment (in a gym setting), withdrawal symptoms (smoking cessation), or peer derision (choosing a low-alcohol beer). Time and effort costs are also included (which can be reduced by other elements of the mix such as making the product easily obtainable and trialable).

- **Promotion** is the mix of activities undertaken to create awareness of the product and its benefits and to persuade the consumer to purchase. Promotion includes advertising, direct marketing, personal selling, sponsorship, sales promotion, and public relations.

- **People** refers to those people actually involved in the delivery of services and who interact with the customer. Interpersonal skills are important in all areas where staff interact with customers, including supermarket checkouts. However, along with relevant knowledge and expertise, interpersonal skills are arguably far more important in the sorts of sensitive areas involved in much social marketing.

Each of these elements of the marketing mix needs to be tailored to individual market segments. The product can be modified for different segments, the place may be different for different segments, the monetary and non-monetary costs may be perceived differently by different segments, the most effective promotion strategy may vary according to the segment, and different types of staff may be appropriate for different segments.

An awareness of the marketing mix concept provides public health and social change practitioners with a structured framework for considering all of these aspects when planning campaigns, many of which are often overlooked by non-marketers (and even by many marketers). We will discuss each of the Ps in turn.

Product

In commercial marketing, the product generally refers to the tangible product purchased by the consumer (for example, a DVD player, a wristwatch, perfume) or the service provided (for example, a haircut, a university degree, tree lopping, tax return lodged). In some cases, a mix of tangible products and services is purchased as when a landscape architect supplies the trees, ornamental ponds, and the overall design. In the following discussion we will use the term 'product' to include services.

However, as we noted in chapter 2, the principle of customer value emphasises that products and services are purchased not so much for themselves, but

---

The Stanford Heart Disease Prevention Program*

The Stanford Heart Disease Prevention Program was an early (1970s) attempt to apply social marketing principles in a real-life field setting to sell the idea of heart disease prevention to a community. The success of this health promotion effort was largely due to the careful consideration given to each aspect of the campaign, including the marketing mix. The mix was identified as follows.

Product: Information about risk factors in heart disease and tangible products and services such as heart-healthy recipe books and quit smoking classes comprised the product. The product line was complex, including different products for different segments of the target audience, depending on their age, ethnicity, and needs.

Place: The distribution strategy aimed to maximise the opportunities people had to receive and process the campaign's information and obtain the tangible products. They used media channels, health professionals, community organisations, and commercial organisations such as pharmacies and bookstores to distribute the message.

Price: They recognised that there would be monetary and non-monetary costs (time, social support, and psychological costs) in adopting the heart-healthy message.

Promotion: Promotion strategies included mass media, direct mail, and community events. The program produced a 1-hour television special called, *Heart Health Test*. The number of viewers was significantly increased by targeting areas with a direct mail promotion that encouraged people to watch the show. They also wrote to teachers asking children to encourage their parents to watch the show (an early example of using 'pester power' in a good cause).

* Solomon 1984

Product development gone mad—chocolate-coated carrots!

Reminiscent of the sweetening of medicines to get kids to take them, the Wacky Veg range of vegetables was launched in 1997 by Iceland Foods, UK, and backed by the Cancer Research Campaign. The product range includes chocolate-flavoured carrots, cheese-and-onion flavoured cauliflower, pizza-flavoured sweet corn, and baked bean-flavoured peas. The products are intended to increase children's consumption of vegetables after research indicated that mothers had become reluctant to cook vegetables that wouldn't be eaten. No artificial additives were used. Extensive testing with parents and children (aged 5–13 years) indicated the likelihood of good results. However, the range was delisted within a few months following poor sales and some bad publicity (Murray 1997; Saxelby 1997; 'Too wacky veg' 1997).

for the benefits they provide to the buyer (Lancaster 1966). You may recall Charles Revson's (of Revlon Cosmetics) statement that 'In the factory we make cosmetics; in the store we sell hope', and Levitt's more mundane example that, although people may buy a quarter-inch drill, what they want is a quarter-inch hole (Kotler 1988, p. 243).

A concept that ties these two concepts (customer benefits and the marketing mix) together is Kotler's (1988) concept of the core product, the augmented product, and the actual tangible product.

The core product is the underlying benefit that the consumer is obtaining by buying a product or service or by adopting a practice. For computers the core product might be better management decision making; for the practice of leaving a certain number of trees in a paddock the core product might be continued crop productivity through avoiding salinity; for a facial and manicure the core product might be feeling better about oneself. In the above examples the 'tangible' or 'observable' products are the computer, the behavioural practice, and the facial and manicure.

The augmented product involves the buyer's total consumption system. It includes any additional services and benefits that supplement the actual product. For computers this involves aftersales service, training, warranties, associated software, a widespread consumer user network, and so on. For a facial and manicure this may involve the presence of music, advice on skin care, the availability of tea and coffee.

In the promotion of physical activity the core product might be a longer, healthier life through cardiovascular disease-risk reduction, the actual product might be an aerobics class, and the augmented product might include a creche, off-peak discount rates, clean hygienic change rooms and a complimentary towel. In a weight loss program the product may be augmented with incentives, rebates, weigh-ins, social support, and newsletters (Wilson & Olds 1991).

For dengue fever prevention the actual product might be a brochure on tips for reducing mosquito breeding and the practice of ensuring that containers around the premises are emptied of water; the core product is avoidance of dengue fever and continued good health. The augmented product (if there is

> ### Augmented product—carpooling guaranteed ride home*
>
> A survey indicated that 36 per cent of commuters in Atlanta, Georgia, would be much more likely to sign up for a vanpooling scheme if they were assured of a guaranteed ride home in an emergency. Federal funding of US$10 000 was put into an innovative campaign that included this guarantee: cab fare or a rental car would be provided free of charge for someone who had to return home for an emergency. Twenty-four employers in forty-five worksites agreed to participate in the scheme. There were fears that people would abuse the provision, but that is not what happened. Interestingly, although everyone wanted the guarantee, only about 1 per cent had actually used it after a year and a half.
>
> * Ledford 1999

one) might be a free sample of insect repellent and a discount voucher for window and door screening.

As noted above different target audiences might be seeking different core products (that is, benefits) from the same actual product (or behaviour). For example, some people take up exercise to avoid specific health problems, such as heart disease, while others may do so to maintain their mental health or to enjoy social interactions. Similarly, health behaviours might be promoted as delivering benefits other than health benefits if that is what is required to motivate purchase. For example, Egger and Mowbray (1993) report that many men are motivated to 'lose their gut' in the GutBusters program so as to improve their appearance (and hence, self-esteem) rather than to gain health benefits.

For most social marketing programs the core product relates to the health and wellbeing of the individual, community cohesion and strength, and reduced dollar and human costs associated with preventable morbidity and premature mortality.

For many social marketing campaigns the actual product is not a tangible product and may not involve tangible augmented products either. If tangible products are available, often they are not necessary for core product purchase. Thus, most smokers quit smoking without calling a quitline, enrolling in a quit smoking program, or using quit tapes or instructional booklets.

Product considerations in social marketing

Product considerations in social marketing differ from commercial marketing in a number of ways (Rothschild 1979; Bloom & Novelli 1981; Chen 1996). These differences can make formulating a product strategy in social marketing much more difficult than for goods and services.

- *Inflexibility*: commercial marketers generally have the option of redesigning their product to make it more appealing to consumers. For example, they can change its colour, shape, design, or add extra features. The social product is much less flexible. For example, the social product idea 'Don't drink and drive' involves not drinking beyond a very specific limit, a blood alcohol level of .05 in Australia.

- *Intangibility*: tangible goods exist in space and time. Intangible services exist in time but not space, though they may have observable outcomes (for example, a new hairstyle, a bank deposit). Many social marketing products are concepts or ideas that are intangible in a different way; they do not exist in space or time but, rather, in our consciousness. This applies particularly to prevention of problem behaviours (as distinct from cessation of problem behaviours). For example, the not smoking actual product consists of a negative attitude to smoking. Similarly, tolerance campaigns attempt to instil positive beliefs about diversity and respect for others—which may never have an opportunity for behavioural expression.

- *Complexity*: social products are often far more complex than consumer goods and services, requiring as they do high levels of information processing. Whereas the commercial marketer can focus on just one benefit of a product, the social marketer may be required to convey multiple benefits as well as being honest about any possible negative effects. For example, the decision to immunise a child could be far more complex than decisions relating to the child's clothing or haircut. Complex information may need to be conveyed to a target market with poor literacy and education. For example, an oral rehydration product was sold in Honduras as a tonic for infants when research showed that Honduran mothers did not understand the concept of dehydration. As most mothers were not able to read, the label showed how to mix the product in four pictures (Rasmuson 1985 and Smith & Pereja 1981, cited in Chen 1996).

- *Controversial*: social products are often quite controversial, particularly for some segments of the target market. For example, the Western Australian *Freedom from Fear* campaign targeted male perpetrators of violence, arousing controversy among some women who believed that funding should only go to victims of violence, and among some men who believed that female perpetrators should also be targeted. For some people, some social marketing messages can be seen as an attack on their personal liberty (for example, early opposition to the concept of random breath testing, gun owners' opposition to gun control, especially in the USA).

- *Weak personal benefits*: in commercial marketing the individual consumer usually obtains the product's benefits, but for some social products the benefits are obtained by society. An individual may perceive the personal benefits of individual action to be quite weak. Examples of such social products are recycling, energy and water conservation, and not littering. Marketing social products with weak personal benefits requires that people believe in the notion of collective efficacy, that the recommended behaviour will achieve meaningful benefits for all if a majority of people are persuaded to adopt the behaviour (Bonniface 2002).

- *Negative frame*: social products often recommend the cessation of a behaviour, such as smoking, and the message may sound negative. Social

Figure 10.1 Pedometer

marketers have recognised the latter and often frame recommendations as positive statements: 'Quit' for 'Stop smoking', 'Respect yourself' for 'Stop drinking to excess', 'Work safe' for 'Stop working dangerously', and 'Keep Australia beautiful' for 'Don't litter'. However, in many cases it is appropriate to use a negative sounding message: 'Eat less fat', 'If you drink and drive, you're a bloody idiot', 'Child abuse—no excuses, never, ever'. Generally, we would recommend using threats where the objective is to cease or reduce a behaviour and incentives where the objective is to adopt or increase a behaviour (see chapter 5).

The product mix in social marketing

Another important product concept in commercial marketing is the concept of a company's product mix, the overall assortment of products offered and how they complement each other. The cancer foundations or councils in Australia have an extensive product range, from sunscreens (in various packs and sizes) to hats to sunglasses (a very wide range of styles) and umbrellas (see below). In Rockhampton's physical activity campaign, the ads emphasise the variety of ways (the product mix) people can achieve the goal of '10 000 steps' per day (Mummery & Schofield 2002; Brown, Mummery, Eakin et al. 2002). People who register receive a log book to help them plan how to gradually achieve the goal of 10 000 steps per day and can purchase a discounted pedometer (augmented products).

This concept is clearly related to the concept of market segmentation. For example, in promoting physical activity, different ways of meeting physical activity targets sufficient to provide health benefits must be available for different target groups. Hence, incidental activity is promoted to those who are time-limited (or think they are), walking clubs are promoted to mothers of school-aged children and seniors' groups, and the concept of cumulative benefits from short periods of moderate-intensity physical activity is promoted to those who would otherwise not see any benefit in these short periods. Computerised quit

Figure 10.2 Poster for Rockhampton's 10 000 Steps a Day campaign

programs are essentially a product mix in which different program components are applied to smokers in the different stages of change.

Branding in social marketing

The American Marketing Association has defined a brand as 'a name, term, symbol, or design, or a combination of them, intended to identify the goods or services of one seller, or group of sellers and to differentiate them from those of competitors' (Sargeant 1999, p. 97). Key characteristics of a brand are that it should be memorable, recognisable, easy to pronounce, distinctive, and able to convey the product's benefits and appeal (Kotler, Roberto & Lee 2002) (hence, the 2002 Western Australian 'Find Thirty' campaign to increase physical activity by incorporating 30 minutes of activity in most days). The brand's logo is particularly important to visually draw attention to the brand and portray an

How does your brand rate?*

Modern	Neither	Old fashioned
Amateurish	Neither	Professional
Working class	Neither	Upper class
Cool	Neither	Uncool
Active	Neither	Passive
Weak, timid	Neither	Strong, powerful
Friendly	Neither	Unfriendly
Bright, bubbly	Neither	Dull, sombre

* The attributes used would be based on the brand's or campaign's desired attributes or communication objectives

appropriate image, as exposure to the logo is often the most frequent type of contact people will have with the brand.

However, branding is more than just naming a product or campaign; it is developing brand attributes that are expressed in all areas of the marketing mix. A common phrase in the commercial literature is that of 'brand personality'—the set of human characteristics associated with a brand (Aaker 1997, p. 347). After much multivariate analysis, Aaker (1997) distilled a large number of traits down to five dimensions: sincerity (for example, honest, genuine), excitement (for example, daring, imaginative), competence (for example, reliable, efficient), sophistication (for example, glamorous, romantic), and ruggedness (strong, outdoorsy). Any cigarette brands come to mind?

Branding was originally restricted to manufactured products, but recent years have seen a trend towards branding primary products also (for example, Harvey beef), with branded fruit and vegetables such as Sunkist oranges and Queensland bananas reportedly returning 60 per cent higher profits than unbranded produce (Kotler et al. 1994).

While many social marketing campaigns have always been strongly branded (for example, Quit, The Drug Offensive, *Freedom from Fear*, the Victorian TAC's road safety advertising), recent years have seen a stronger emphasis on branding in the social marketing literature and in practice. With some notable

Branding gone mad?

On 17 April 2001 the social marketing listserver reported that the following excerpt appeared in the 9 April 2001 edition of *Advertising Age*:

Secretary of State Colin Powell is making the branding of the State Department a ... goal of his administration, and has named former J. Walter Thompson Co. Chairman Charlotte Beers assistant secretary of public diplomacy.

Secretary Powell is quoted as saying earlier that year: 'I am going to bring people into the public diplomacy function of the department who are going to change from just selling us in the old USA way to really branding foreign policy ... branding the department, marketing the department, marketing American values to the world, and not just putting out pamphlets.' Maybe he should have talked to George W. about what attributes he wants the brand to have.

Figure 10.3 Branded 10 000 steps

'10 000 Steps'
The campaign to increase physical activity in Rockhampton in Queensland is aptly branded in terms of the specific target people set for themselves: '10 000 Steps'.

exceptions what has been lacking, however, in Australian (and elsewhere) social marketing campaigns is the evaluation of the brand's attributes. The Australian government's Drug Offensive brand has been monitored against its youth target audience and found to be relevant and credible (Carroll 2001; Carroll, Taylor & Lum 1996).

Branding is now being adopted enthusiastically by sporting and arts organisations, the non-profit sector (Feder 1998), and by health and other government authorities involved in social marketing (for example, see CDC's branding exercise in Kirby 2000). For non-profits branding is seen to have considerable benefits for fund-raising.

However, what many are calling branding (for example, Colin Powell's statement) has previously been called 'corporate image'. By branding an organisation

Branding sun protection– the Cancer Foundation of Western Australia*

The Western Australian Cancer Foundation's SunSmart campaign encourages the adoption of sun protection behaviours such as sitting in shade, wearing long sleeves, using sunscreen, staying out of the sun in the middle portion of the day, and wearing a hat and sunglasses. The Cancer Foundation also has an extensive merchandising division which sells sun protection products through retail outlets and via catalogue, including:
- swimwear and clothing
- sunscreens in a range of sizes, including zinc sticks in different colours, with Barbie and Thomas the Tank Engine sunscreens for children
- cosmetics such as foundation with UV filters and SPF 15+ lipstick
- Hats and bicycle helmet covers
- Sunglasses and sunglass accessories (cases, straps and cleaning cloths)
- umbrellas, driving sleeves, pram covers, and cabanas.

Figure 10.4 Cancer Foundation of Western Australia, *Summer Catalogue*, 2002–03

(such as CDC) what is really meant is establishing the desired image (positioning) of the organisation in stakeholders' minds.

One consideration for government-funded campaigns is the inclusion of the state or commonwealth logo as well as the campaign brand. Most governments require that their logo also be included. However, government branding of a campaign could reduce source credibility with a sceptical target audience. For example, some young people may not find the information contained in a government antimarijuana campaign credible because of the government's prohibition agenda (Perman & Henley 2001). Often the solution is to include the government logo but as small as possible and in a non-intrusive way.

In the Positive Parenting campaign, the core product is the benefit to children of improved mental health under an encouraging parenting style and a better relationship between parent and child The actual product consisted of practical information on how to develop the skills needed to carry out positive parenting practices. The campaign communication objectives included encouraging the belief that parenting is not an innate, natural skill but a skill that can be learnt, and that rewards can be just as effective, if not more so, than punishments. The campaign wanted to encourage the attitude that asking for help in parenting is OK and that the Family and Children's Services (the selling organisation) is approachable and friendly. These attitude shifts were supported by a new logo and change of name for the government organisation.

Figure 10.5   Positive Parenting campaign poster

The actual product included a number of printed and video products and services targeted to parents, teenagers, professional carers, and other intermediaries. The products included magazines, parenting videos, and parenting courses.

* Henley, Donovan & Moorhead 1998

Place

Consistent with a consumer orientation, place (or distribution) decisions in commercial marketing basically refer to ensuring and facilitating accessibility to the product for all target segments. Place decisions involve matters such as physical distribution, number and type of outlets, opening hours, availability of public transport, availability and ease of parking, atmosphere in outlets, and other environmental aspects such as cleanliness.

Commercial marketers are well aware that, at least for fast-moving consumer goods, the more widely available the product the greater the sales. Vending machines are an example of making products such as cigarettes, snacks, and beverages available 24 hours a day in locations other than retail outlets to make the most of impulse purchasing and increase their ability to reach target groups that might otherwise not be reached (for example, shift workers in some locations, underage smokers).

Hence, where social marketers have tangible products or services, the same principles of making access easy apply. While some people are prepared to

Figure 10.6 Signposting the 10 000 Steps

expend time and effort to donate blood others are not and will only do so if the organisation comes to them. Safe sex campaigns should ensure that condoms are available not just in pharmacies, but also in supermarkets and, especially for young people, in the neighbourhood 7/11 type stores and petrol station minimarts. Even more so, it is essential that condoms are available in vending machines in nightclubs, pubs, and bars where young people congregate to play the mating game. This not only ensures ready access at times of need but also avoids the problem of embarrassment inhibiting purchase in retail situations. A distribution strategy of placing condom vending machines in places frequented by young people was used successfully in Portland, Oregon, to reduce embarrassment and increase convenience (Frankenberger & Convisser 1995).

One innovative place strategy in the USA involved the cooperation of gay bar owners. As homosexual males are at high risk of venereal disease, owners of gay bars were asked to allow a small lab to be set up in a private area in the bar to allow screening tests to be conducted there (Brehony, Frederiksen & Solomon 1984). Similarly, drink-drive campaigns visit public bars inviting drinkers to take a breathalyser and to accept information on safe drinking levels (Pozzi, James, Kirby & Cassells 1996).

Place also includes the ambience of the physical environment (many social service locations are distinctly uninviting) and facilities available (toilets and

Shopping for a mammogram

Since 1997 in the USA women have been able to pop in for a mammogram while shopping at Nordstrom department stores. The centres are run by hospitals but feel more like health spas as they offer fluffy white robes, music, and coffee. There is usually further added incentives such as a cosmetic gift bag, free facial, hand massage, or makeover. If there is going to be a bit of a wait women are provided with beepers so they can shop while waiting for their turn ('Cosmetics on 1' 1997; 'Checkup' 1999; 'New motivation' 2000).

   This concept has been adopted in Australia. In May 2000 David Jones announced a partnership between BreastScreen New South Wales and the Royal Hospital for Women to set up the Rose Clinic at the Elizabeth Street store in Sydney. The clinic offers mammography screening, bone density tests, and blood pressure checks (*Retail therapy* 2002). This place strategy has a major impact on non-monetary perceived costs of time and effort.

change rooms). If we want people to use public transport more we need to ensure that the train carriage, bus, tram, and ferry interiors are clean, bright, and cheery, that the seats are reasonably comfortable, and that handrails are easily accessible if one is standing. We also need to ensure people's security while on the vehicle and while at the pick up points.

   Privacy considerations are important for many government and NGO welfare services and safety considerations are always important. Encouraging people to walk for health benefits requires that their local area not only have smooth paths (to avoid tripping and falls) and protected street crossings (to avoid being hit by motor vehicles), but the area should also be well lit at night and free of muggers.

   The 10 000 Steps campaign in Queensland uses signposts (see figure 10.6) to not only promote the campaign, but to also facilitate walking goals by providing distances between various points.

   Social marketers are also interested in making it harder—or less convenient—for the consumer to continue undesired behaviours. For example, a prevalence of no-smoking venues makes quitting smoking easier and also makes continuing to smoke more difficult. Public health advocates attempt to reduce access to cigarettes by banning cigarette vending machines in areas where underage children have unsupervised access and, in the case of alcohol in rural and remote communities, by restricting hours of opening and the quantity and type of alcohol that can be purchased.

Intermediaries

It is often useful or even necessary to employ intermediaries to distribute the product through a channel or network. In social marketing, intermediaries may be teachers, employers, community groups, parents, general practitioners, pharmacists, other health professionals, and so on.

One complexity in social marketing is that the intermediaries in the distribution network are often much harder to control than paid intermediaries in commercial marketing (Shapiro 1990). For example, while they may be positively inclined towards the campaign messages, they may have their own ideas about how the message should be communicated, to whom, and when. Another difficulty is that the social marketing intermediaries may need to receive some training before being fully capable of delivering the product. This applies even to otherwise well-trained professionals. For example, GPs are often the first to admit that they lack skills in lifestyle counselling in areas such as smoking cessation, alcohol reduction, diet modification, and physical activity uptake. A survey of American doctors' attitudes to physical activity showed that, although 91 per cent encouraged their patients to become more active, only 3 per cent had training in exercise physiology; most (78 per cent) felt there was a need for more training in medical school on the medical aspects of exercise (Williford, Barfield, Lazenby & Olson 1992). Similarly, a survey of Western Australian doctors found that family practitioners felt able to give general advice on physical activity but were not confident that they could give specific advice (Bull, Schipper, Jamrozik & Blanksby 1995).

Early attempts to involve general practitioners in helping their patients quit smoking were not successful, partly because many GPs were smokers themselves and did not know the best ways to quit (Bloom & Novelli 1981). This is similar to today's situation with Indigenous health workers among whom smoking rates are as high as in the general Indigenous community (Murphy & Mee 1999; Roche & Ober 1997). Many GPs also appear reluctant to raise alcohol issues with their patients (McAvoy, Donovan, Jalleh et al. 2001). Nevertheless, general practitioners are an attractive channel for distributing health messages because they are associated with strong source credibility.

However, non-traditional intermediaries are being used to deliver information to specific target groups. A UK project to improve sexual health and reduce HIV transmission in ethnic minority groups worked with community entities such as shopkeepers, hairdressers, and taxi drivers to distribute health education materials, condoms, and advice (King 2001). In developing countries similar community points have been used, such as brothels, etc. (WHO 2000).

In using intermediaries we need to remember the marketing concept and the idea of exchange. In short, we cannot expect youth workers, forestry workers, GPs, and pharmacists, say, to help out without providing something in return and making their involvement as easy as possible. For example, the New South Wales DrinkLess project that encouraged GPs to assess their patients' drinking habits provided doctors with a questionnaire on a laminated sheet, a quick and easy scoring method, a single page laminated sheet for diagnosis and behavioural suggestions, and a wallet-size booklet on tips for reducing consumption to give to at-risk patients. Considerable formative research with GPs and practice staff was undertaken to develop the intervention so that it involved the least amount

Doctors prescribe physical activity

Bull and Jamrozik (1998) conducted a study in Western Australia to explore whether general practitioners could help inactive patients become more active. Doctors gave sedentary patients verbal advice on increasing their physical activity levels and then mailed out an information booklet to the patient within 2 days of the visit. Patients were asked to report their activity levels by mail survey at 1, 6, and 12 month intervals. At each follow-up there was a significant difference between the percentage who reported being active in the intervention group compared to the control group, leading to the conclusion that this simple and cost-effective place strategy could be effective.

A further study was conducted in New South Wales to see whether inactive people would increase their activity levels if they were given a written prescription for physical activity by their general practitioners (Smith, Bauman, Bull, Booth & Harris 2000). Patients were allocated to one of three groups: written prescription only, written prescription plus a booklet mailed to their home, and control group. People were asked to report their physical activity levels at the first interview, after 6–10 weeks, and after 7–8 months. There was some improvement at the 6–10 week follow-up in the group who received both prescription and booklet, though this had not been sustained by the time of longer term follow-up. However, even modest gains such as these could become significant if adopted as a population strategy (Smith et al. 2000).

of time and effort on the part of the practice (Wutzke, Gomel & Donovan 1998).

Emerging technologies: computers–kiosks

Health professionals may not always be the most appropriate distributors of health advice. Prochaska and colleagues have shown that computer-based expert systems can be effective change agents (Prochaska 1997; Ruggiero, Redding, Rossi & Prochaska 1997; Grimley, Prochaska & Prochaska 1997; Pallonen, Velicer, Prochaska et al. 1998). They found that participation rates over time can remain high, that is, people are more likely to continue going back to an interactive computer program than to a health professional, particularly when they have not yet managed to succeed in making the desired change. Further, computer programs will sustain high fidelity of implementation compared to systems that rely more on human performance, that is, they do not get tired of saying the same things and they do not get despondent if the patient is not successful. This could be an advantage when attempting to disseminate proven educational programs in school. Computers, unlike teachers, would not be tempted to shorten, skip over sections, or alter the material (Pallonen et al. 1998).

Ruggiero et al. (1997) used an interactive computer program to encourage pregnant smokers at varying stages of change to quit smoking. The multimedia computer program was easy to use (had touchscreen data input) and gave clear, immediate feedback with customised graphics. A surprising 67 per cent of the women said they would have used the computer program in preference to receiving one-on-one counselling from a health professional. This suggests that the use of computers would be widely accepted as well as highly cost-effective. One of the reasons given for the preference was that many of the women (55 per cent) felt that they would be more candid with the computer than with a person (Ruggiero et al. 1997). In other instances it may be useful to complement a counsellor's role with computer-aided elements (Grimley et al. 1997).

Kiosk/Computers can provide a convenient place strategy. They could be placed in doctors' waiting rooms, in health clinics, hospitals, or in other settings such as bars, shopping malls, or schools. The convenience factor would need to be balanced with sensitivity to the target market however. Winzelberg, Taylor, Sharpe et al. (1998) found that participants in a multimedia intervention to reduce unhealthy eating reported feeling self-conscious using the computer program in a public arena, especially as there were audio components and colourful screens that could attract unwanted attention. There is a need to determine where the optimal locations are for such kiosks. A study by Nicholas, Huntington and Williams (2002) looked at twenty-one kiosks in pharmacies, hospitals, information centres, and doctors' surgeries. Their data suggest that information centres perform best, followed by hospitals. Surgeries performed less well, with the authors suggesting that people may be inhibited by the close proximity of others and that searching for health information may not be seen as appropriate when they are about to ask their doctor to answer their health questions. A project in Far North Queensland among several Indigenous communities is piloting such kiosks, where the kiosk modules are focused on specific issues relevant to the communities, such as diabetes and alcohol. Early pilot findings suggest that the kiosks need to be marketed as much to local health administrators and professionals as to consumers, a finding not dissimilar to experiences in non-Indigenous health settings (Gillespie & Ellis 1993).

Helplines

Telephone helplines are a common means of making information or a service (for example, counselling) accessible to those geographically unable to visit an outlet and those unable or unwilling to visit a service during working hours. Telephone helplines can be simple prerecorded messages or provide an interactive service. They have a number of advantages:

- they allow dissemination of information to large numbers of self-selected people, yet they can also provide a highly personalised service
- they are convenient and private (almost everyone has easy and affordable access to a telephone and helplines are often free of charge)
- they can be staffed 24 hours
- they also offer a degree of anonymity (Anderson, Duffy & Hallett 1992).

Most of the time helplines are reactive, that is, they simply respond to people's requests for information. However, it may be useful to consider the proactive potential of helplines. For example, the US National Cancer Institute's Cancer Information Service has adopted a policy of referring callers, where

Anonymity of helplines

The helpline staff at the Cancer Foundation of Western Australia noticed that almost all the men who called in response to an advertisement inviting men to call a helpline number for advice on prostate cancer referred to 'that ad' or 'that thing in the paper', without mentioning the condition itself (Wharton 2001).

appropriate, to clinical trials or to mammography screening. They also recommend that helplines be used as a research tool, for example, to assess the efficacy of campaigns with different minority groups (Anderson et al. 1992).

However, one of the major problems for helpline operators is achieving the right balance between demand and supply for crisis services. It is expensive to have a large bank of counsellors sitting idle, but it can be disastrous if suicidal or assault victims in need of trauma counselling cannot get through because 'all our operators are busy'. This was the problem faced by the *Freedom from Fear* campaign (see chapter 14).

Internet helplines are an alternative to telephone helplines and seem to offer even more anonymity. They are proving popular with boys, who are less likely than girls to use telephone helplines, although concerns have been raised by groups such as the Samaritans and Childline that the internet is unregulated (Beenstock 1999).

A variation on the above is where the helpline calls the person. Automated calling systems are now being tested—similar to automated sales systems—where people respond by pressing the buttons on their phone if they want to hear all or parts of a message.

Peer selling

Although Avon salespeople included worksites and other organisations where women congregated as sales targets, it appears that we have Tupperware to thank for the rapid adoption of peer selling (including pyramid selling) by sellers of such products as cosmetics, vitamins and health supplements, lingerie and sex aids, and household cleaning products.

The SafetyNet program that grew out of the StopAIDS project mentioned in chapter 5 is modelled on the Tupperware method. The party is led by a trained facilitator who is gay. Such peer-led groups are effective because the informal setting allows communication of a personal nature, the relaxed atmosphere conveys positive feelings about safe sex, peer group members can share their concerns with each other, and specific information can be easily adapted to suit ethnic or otherwise different social groups. Evaluations showed significant changes in partygoers' intentions to use safe sex (AIDS Action Committee 1989).

An Indigenous PhD student at the University of Western Australia uses Heartaware parties in an attempt to teach healthy eating and food-preparing habits to Indigenous people. The host is asked to invite friends and relatives to a lunch get-together. Prior to lunch the group is given a brief talk on heart disease and risk factors. The student and a local nutrition worker then prepare lunch, explaining how the foods they chose and how they prepared the food lessen the risk of heart disease (Owen 2002).

A variation on this tactic is used frequently by tobacco and alcohol marketers to target young people. Individuals are paid by the tobacco and alcohol marketers to attend and mingle at parties, bars, and nightclubs and distribute cigarettes or offer to buy those around them a drink (see chapter 8).

Price

In commercial marketing, price usually refers to monetary costs incurred when purchasing goods or services. However, non-monetary costs are also involved in the purchase of commercial products. For example, there may be time costs involved in test driving a new car or travelling to a particular outlet, effort costs in switching to a new bank, and psychological costs in trying a new brand of sports shoe.

Price in social marketing includes monetary costs, but most costs for most campaigns involve time, effort, physical discomfort, and psychological costs. Adopting a regular exercise routine may involve monetary costs such as purchasing appropriate clothing or necessary equipment, admission fees, travel costs, and babysitting costs. However, the major costs may relate to time and the lost opportunity to engage in other desired activities, perhaps effort and physical discomfort, and even social embarrassment (for example, a person with little sense of rhythm attending an aerobics class, an overweight person joining a group of slim walkers).

In general public health promoters attempt to reduce the monetary costs of compliance by providing subsidised or free services (for example, the Western Australian government subsidised children's bike helmets), but overlook or minimise the inhibiting effect of other costs. For example, the physical discomfort cost of nicotine withdrawal is one of the high costs involved in quitting smoking, along with foregoing the comfort of a cigarette in anxious situations, but this was rarely acknowledged in early antismoking campaigns. Similarly, targeting young males to drink low-alcohol beers may involve considerable psy-

Taxing cigarettes encourages quitting

There is a clear correlation between the cost and the consumption of cigarettes (Chambers, Killoran, McNeill & Reid 1991). Recently, the American Academy of Family Physicians called on governors in the USA to help them discourage smoking by raising tobacco taxes on the basis that, for every 10 per cent increase in the price of cigarettes, adult smoking is cut by 3–5 per cent and teenage smoking by 7 per cent (Bullock 2002). A 1988 study (Godfrey & Maynard 1988) similarly found that adult smoking was cut by 5 per cent for every 10 per cent increase in price.

Pricing water conservation

The Sydney Water Board switched to a user-pays system in 1993 as a way of encouraging water conservation. In return for a flat rate of 65 cents per kilolitre consumers were offered a benefit: the abolition of an $80 per annum special environment levy. It was expected that most consumers would pay more in the first year or two before they adjusted to a reduced consumption level but that subsequently the flat rate cost would reduce demand (Della-Giacoma 1993). It was hoped that the subsequent reduced demand would obviate the need for the building of a new dam—hence, considerable capital savings and reduced environmental impact.

Similar thinking is behind transport departments encouraging less use of motor vehicles—less capital road works for the department and better for the environment (see chapter 15).

chological costs (derisory comments from others, for example) as well as foregoing feelings of relaxation associated with mild intoxication.

Recycling programs, with distinctive bags or bins for different products (papers, bottles, cans) attempt to reduce the time and effort costs of sorting and storage of recyclable materials. Kerbside pick-up eliminates the time and effort of delivering to recycling stations, and is piggybacked onto household rubbish collection to minimise forgetting and limiting effort to one occasion in the week.

Strategies to increase the monetary cost of undesirable behaviours can be used by social marketers to good effect. For example, Chaloupka (1995) found that college students' decisions to smoke and the number of cigarettes they smoked were highly sensitive to price, more so than adults', leading to the conclusion that substance use and abuse is reduced, especially among younger people, by policies raising the price of licit and illicit substances.

In social marketing contexts costs are usually short-term and certain, whereas benefits are often long-term and less certain (Weinstein 1988). For example, the physical withdrawal costs of giving up smoking are immediate and certain, whereas the health benefits, such as reduced risk of lung and throat

Cheaper low-fat snacks sell

Commercial pricing strategies can be an effective way to increase compliance with a social marketing objective. One study (French, Jeffrey, Story, Hannon & Snyder 1997) examined the effect of reducing the price of low-fat snacks in nine vending machines selling low-fat and regular food. At the baseline low-fat snacks made up 25.7 per cent of total sales. During the 3-week intervention, when prices of low-fat snacks were reduced by 50 per cent, their sales went up to 45.8 per cent of total sales. After the intervention, when prices had returned to normal, sales dropped back to 22.8 per cent. In a larger study (French, Jeffrey, Story et al. 2001) similar effects were found for both adolescent and adult populations (vending machines in secondary schools and at worksites). Prices were reduced by 10 per cent, 25 per cent, and 50 per cent, resulting in increases in sales of low-fat snacks of 9 per cent, 39 per cent, and 93 per cent respectively.

cancer, are long-term and a matter of probabilities. Many social marketing health campaigns stress the long-term benefits without fully addressing the short-term costs (Weinstein 1988).

Pricing of community services—Who should pay?

Governments' push towards privatisation and a user pays philosophy can serve to maintain and even exacerbate inequities that already exist in society with respect to access to transport, education, recreation, and health care. Crompton (1981) provides a useful discussion of pricing in the public sector. He delineates four major functions of pricing in the delivery of community services:

- equity
- revenue production (governments can increase their revenues by charging for previously uncharged services)
- efficiency (charging for services can reduce unwarranted demand, discount pricing can be offered in low demand times to encourage shifts in demand)
- income redistribution (general taxation revenue used to supply services free to disadvantaged groups).

We are interested here primarily in equity.

The equity issue raises questions of who should pay and what share according to benefits received. If benefits are received exclusively by users, then this can be considered to have the characteristics of a private service and the total cost should be borne by the user (for example, private parking stations). If the user benefits, but the wider community (non-users) also benefits, then the user should pay a certain amount and the community should subsidise the cost (for example, public transport reduces air pollution). Where all members of a community benefit and there are no feasible ways of excluding some members from using the service (for example, schools, police), then costs should be borne totally by the tax system. The question for our society is where various services will be placed. Toll roads are now becoming common in Australia, tertiary fees have been introduced, entrance fees to some national parks are charged, energy is being privatised, security companies are proliferating, and so on. The danger is that we will reinforce already existing discrepancies between the quality of life of those with high incomes and those without. Those who can afford toll costs will have less travel time than those who cannot. While tolls may encourage the use of public transport, this depends on public transport being available. Many workers will be disadvantaged by tolls.

Do local government swimming pools benefit the whole community or just users? Is there a differential benefit in low versus high SES areas? If they reduce delinquency and improve the health and wellbeing of otherwise disadvantaged groups should they be free or heavily discounted in some areas?

Related to this discussion are those studies that attempt to assess how much people would pay for certain benefits, such as reduced pollution, reduction of

Western Australian Positive Parenting campaign: price and place*

In the Positive Parenting campaign the costs of adopting the idea of positive parenting were primarily non-monetary. Time, effort, and energy were required to seek out further information, read the printed materials, or watch the videos and then practise the recommended positive parenting strategies. Psychological costs of embarrassment were involved in asking for help; parents might be reluctant to go to a government department and ask for help parenting their children in case they are labelled potential child abusers.

Figure 10.7   Western Australian Positive Parenting campaign

Many of these costs were reduced by the place strategy. Instead of expecting people to come in to the government office building to obtain information, this product was brought to the target market. Information was made available in local libraries, by direct mail, on the internet, and via a helpline. However, reminiscent of early health promotion shops in shopping centres, the department opened a number of parenting information centres in shopping malls. The centres are colourful, inviting, and convenient, they reduce time and effort costs as well as embarrassment costs.

* Henley, Donovan & Moorhead 1998

logging in forests, electric cars, and other environmental gains. The general result is that when isolated as a specific user cost many are reluctant to pay more. However, if the cost is borne by the whole community there tends to be more support for more costly alternatives that have environmental benefits.

Promotion

The promotion mix involves a variety of methods, including advertising, sales promotion, sponsorship, publicity and public relations, free merchandising (giveaways) and personal selling. It may involve mass media, localised media, outlet point-of-sale materials, instore promotions, promotions and incentives to

'In NY and LA, a party's not just a party any more, it's a PR opportunity'*

Similar to peer selling and the fashion event marketing of tobacco companies is the phenomenon of private parties and weddings being sponsored, even handing out goody bags. So far the trend appears to be confined to PR savvy people and socialites. However, the breweries in Australia appear to be getting in on the act by providing cheap or free beer to various groups' functions.

* Brown 2002

intermediaries, internet sites, cross-promotions with other organisations, and so on. Given that promotion is generally covered in other chapters (in particular chapters 11 and 12), it is covered only briefly here. Personal selling is covered under its own P—People—in the next section.

Perhaps one area that social marketers could consider more is that of sales promotions. Whereas advertising and other communication modes are intended to primarily impact on beliefs and attitudes, sales promotions are intended to act directly on behaviour (Rossiter & Percy 1997). By offering a free sample, discount or gift, sales promotions are intended to generate an intended purchase earlier than it might otherwise take place, encourage purchase of a greater quantity, or—and of most interest to us—induce trial in previously resistant audience members, perhaps by making the perceived value of the purchase greater than the perceived costs, or at least greater than the costs of one trial. That is, sales promotions are often targeted at other brand loyals to at least trial the discounted brand. However, with some exceptions (see box below), the usual sorts of sales promotions, such as competitions, have not worked particularly well in attracting people to cease undesirable behaviours. Sales promotions in our language are 'incentives' or 'facilitators'. Offers to pick people up to take them to vote or to a community meeting, or a week's free trial at a gym, or free passes to Adventure World or Movie World for all those enrolling in a parenting course, would all fall into the category of sales promotions.

Another area that has always challenged social marketers is how to utilise the concept of point-of-sale advertising and promotions as in the commercial area. Road safety authorities attempt to use radio ads during drive time that ask the driver to look at their speedometer; ads on a Friday and Saturday evening

'Quit and Win' contest: using sales promotion in social marketing

In 2002 ninety-eight countries participated in the Quit and Win smoking-cessation contest, organised by the National Public Health Institute in Finland and supported by the World Health Organization. In Taiwan alone more than 23 000 smokers took part, agreeing to stop using all tobacco products for at least 1 month. Contestants' claims were verified with a test to see if they were tobacco-free. A 93-year old, Hsu Tuan, who had been a chain smoker for 75 years, gave up smoking forty cigarettes a day to win the top prize (Chang 2002).

Praise the Lord and Pass the Fruit n' Veg*

The US National Cancer Institute's '5-a-Day for Better Health Program' encourages people to eat 5 or more daily servings of fruit and vegetables. A randomised delayed-control intervention with 50 Black churches in North Carolina yielded a significant and substantial increase in fruit and vegetable consumption in the intervention churches. The multi-component intervention was indeed just that, involving tailored bulletins to individual participants, monthly updates, serving fruit and vegetables at church functions, distributing a cookbook, showing members how to modify their favourite recipes to be more healthy, training lay advisors, involving local grocers and promoting local produce, and having the pastors promote the project during services.

* Campbell, Demark-Wahnefried, Symons et al. 1999

remind drivers of the number of drinks to remain under .05 and the chances of being RBTed. Similarly, Healthway's DrinkSafe sponsorship asks the venue to strongly advertise low-alcohol beers at the point of sale.

What we call attempting to intervene at the point of decision making, Kotler et al. (2002, p. 308) refer to as 'Just in time' promotions—strategies that target the audience at the moment they are about to make a choice between the undesirable behaviour and alternate behaviours. For example, an individual about to order a meal may be influenced to make healthy choices by the Heart Foundation tick against certain menu items. Similarly, a good place to promote the message that infants should lie on their backs to sleep would be on the front of babies' nappies.

Another of Kotler et al.'s (2002) suggestions is that smokers who express a wish to give up could be encouraged to slip a photo of their child or children under the wrapper of their cigarette packet. However, this requires the cooperation of the smoker. Health authorities in Australia are attempting to have graphic images of ill health effects placed on cigarette packs as is required in Canada. A Canadian study of the impact of the warnings found that 44 per cent of smokers said the new warnings increased their motivation to quit, 21 per cent said that on one or more occasions they decided not to have a cigarette because of the new warnings, and 18 per cent said they had asked for a different pack to avoid a particular warning. In addition, 48 per cent of non-smokers said the new warnings made them feel better about being a non-smoker (intl-tobacco mailing list 2002). What social marketers need to do is become more innovative in reaching our target audiences at the point of decision making.

Because in many cases our product is information-based (even though the information is intended to lead to behaviour change) promotional channels and place factors often overlap. That is, pharmacists and pharmacies are both media through which we deliver messages as well as the pharmacy being a tangible location where the information products are available. The point is not to get hung up on what is place versus what is promotion in these cases (as did the social marketing listserver on 'what is a product' in October 2002). The main

Figure 10.8 Western Australian Positive Parenting campaign

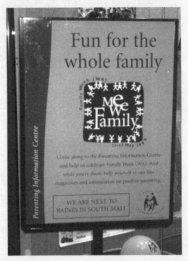

Two of the television advertisements used in the Positive Parenting campaign were called 'Teach your children well' and 'Accentuate the positive'. Some of the messages were 'Praise works wonders', 'Try not to threaten', 'Catch your children being good', 'Set limits and stick by them', 'Credit where credit's due', 'Be firm but fair', 'You can't control everything'.

These messages were also promoted through: radio and print advertising, publicity, a website, a Parenting Line, a magazine, a series of booklets (Living with Babies/Toddlers/Children/Teenagers, and one for teens: Living With Parents!), family weeks, sponsorship, and merchandise.

* Henley, Donovan & Moorhead 1998

point is simply to ask the question: What are the best ways to reach and impact the target audience? A good example of place merging with promotion through partnership is shown above.

People

People factors are important in all organisations, whether for-profit, not-for-profit, or government departments. Regardless of their role in the organisation the staff with whom the client interacts are generally the most important in generating attitudes towards the organisation. For example, a friendly, pleasant, and helpful receptionist in an organisation (often lowly paid and undervalued) can make a substantial contribution to an organisation's image and repeat business. More importantly, there would be little point in spending substantial funds on a campaign to encourage people to use public buses if the bus drivers were rude, unfriendly, and reluctant or unable to give people information about the service.

Cookin' chitlins for littluns*

Background

A severe form of diarrhoea was affecting African-American infants in Atlanta. The bacteria causing the illness was *Yersinia enterocolitica (YE)* associated with the preparation of a traditional African-American dish, chitterlings or chitlins, which is made out of pork intestines. Although identified in 1989 and followed by traditional health education materials, a 1996 review showed that infants were still getting sick and some were dying, especially following Thanksgiving and Christmas holidays when this dish was traditionally served.

Formative research

Focus groups and interviews were conducted with members of the community about how they prepared the chitterlings, what chitterlings meant to them culturally, and what hygiene practices they used. Some women washed the chitterlings during the cleaning process while others preboiled the chitterlings before cleaning. Laboratory cultures (and the researchers' own experience) showed that the preboiling method eliminated the bacteria. As part of their research the social marketers joined their participants in taste tests of chitterlings prepared each way to be sure they could honestly claim that preboiling made no difference to the taste.

Product

The product was the practice: 'Preboil your chitterlings for 5 minutes before cleaning and cooking as usual.' The primary target market was identified as older African-American women because these women were likely to prepare the chitterlings and likely to have the care of babies in extended families. One difficulty was that many in the target market did not associate infants' illness with chitterlings (infants did not often eat chitterlings but were exposed to the bacteria by being in the kitchen during preparation).

Price

Costs included the change to traditional cultural practices, the idea that preboiling would 'boil in the dirt', that it involved extra work up front, and that it would make a difference to the taste. These were countered by explaining that many traditional African-American grandmothers had been using the preboil method in their families for generations, that taste tests showed no difference in taste, that it made the whole process faster overall, as well as safer for children, and that there would be no need to exclude babies from the kitchen for extended periods (so childcare problems could be avoided). (The previous health education intervention had recommended removing children for many hours without taking into account the inconvenience or high cost of childcare in such a situation. The preboil method meant that children only had to be removed for a few minutes.)

Promotion

Brochures, flyers, cartoon stickers, and public service announcements as well as news releases and television news features were used. Two intermediary target markets were identified—health care providers and community leaders—and special materials were developed for each of these segments.

Place

Grocery shops were targeted to place flyers at point of sale next to the chitterlings. As many of the primary target market were churchgoers and as churches were seen as a trusted source, clergy were asked to distribute leaflets at church or with newsletters. Leaflets were available in doctors' waiting rooms as well as those of women and infant clinics and hospitals. As well as using mass media, gospel radio talk shows popular with the target market were used, with grandmothers explaining their traditional way of preparing chitterlings using the preboil method.

Outcome

A noticeable difference in the number of hospital admissions was seen after just the first Christmas holiday.

The marketing mix elements are summarised in table 10.1, from Peterson and Koehler (1997), showing how they are determined separately for the primary target market and for intermediaries.

* Peterson & Koehler 1997

The relevant factors for staffing are selecting the right people for the job and training to ensure that they do the job right.

There are three main factors relevant to all people's tasks:

- interpersonal skills
- product knowledge skills
- process skills.

The degree to which each is required depends on the job requirements. For example, a supermarket checkout person is required to have minimal interpersonal skills (be friendly, pleasant, polite) and virtually no product knowledge (with 10 000 products in the store how could they?), but the task requires competence in processing skills with respect to use of the bar code technology, cash register, EFTPOS, and bagging.

Other jobs will require more extensive skills in all of these areas, especially product knowledge in retail and industrial organisations (for example, new car and computer salespeople), and interpersonal skills in service areas, including defusing client anger and dealing with problems when the process is disrupted. Process knowledge and skills appear particularly important in government welfare areas.

In social marketing, especially where we are dealing with the underprivileged and disadvantaged, staff need to be patient and understand their clients' needs. Cultural and sensitivity training may be needed. For people already suffering from low self-esteem, a sense of helplessness, and a feeling of being just a number, even innocent gestures may be misinterpreted and lead to a disturbance.

Many social marketing programs involve volunteers and lay helpers. However, most of their training appears to be in the content area in which they are helping rather than in dealing with the target audience as customers. Training in interpersonal skills is equally important.

Table 10.1 Summary of target segment and focused interventions*

Target population	Product	Price	Promotion	Place
Chitterlings preparers Primarily older African-American women in metro Atlanta	**Message** Pre-boil chitterlings before cleaning	**Perceived barriers** Change from traditional technique Perceived change in taste Extra 5 minutes of up-front work **Perceived Benefit** Community ownership as source of technique Taste test showed no change in taste Faster/easier overall Safer for children Child care issues avoided	**Cartoon flyers** Walk-by eye-catching **Flyer/bulletin insert** Short read: problem and community solution **Brochure** Full info for interested readers **News release** PSA: Public service announcements Newspaper articles Radio talk show TV news spots Focus on new problem with a simply community solution	**Grocery stores** Point of sale reaches chitterlings purchasers **Churches** Targets church goers Churches trusted source **Health Care providers** Doctors, hospitals, county clinics, WIC Waiting rooms **Media** *Targeted*: Gospel station talk show *Mass*: Reinforce focused message
Community leaders/ gatekeepers Heterogeneous group having authority to allow dissemination of information	Allow and encourage message dissemination to target group within their sphere of influence	**Perceived barriers** Extra work Potential political or economic repercussion **Perceived benefits** Image of promoting safety of children DHR did most of follow-up work	**Cover letters** For each sub-group **News release** **Medical fact sheets** **Samples of brochures & flyers** Can evaluate what they are being asked to distribute **Presentation** In person/phone to address questions	**Grocers' associations & large chains** Point of sale distribution **Church associations** Posting, bulletin insert, pulpit announcements **Media** Timely awareness of preventable health problem
Health Care providers Private doctors County clinic nurses & environmentalists WIC nutritionists Hospital infection control nurses & epidemiologists	To take exposure history and culture for *YE* in appropriate cases Disseminate prevention message	**Perceived barriers** Requires awareness & asking about chitterling exposure Extra cultures & cost **Perceived benefits** Correctly diagnosis *YE* Earlier treatment *YR* Simple prevention message	**Cover letter** **Medical fact sheets** **News release Samples of brochures & flyers** Distribution to their patient population **Presentations** In person/phone to address questions	**Work place/office** From supervisors State Epidemiologists Research investigator Emphasis on new, well documented medical information and timeliness of prevention issues

* Peterson & Koehler 1997, p. 6

A crucial area is that of counselling and particularly helpline counselling in sensitive areas such as child abuse, sexual assault, intimate partner violence, depression, and suicide. In these situations counsellors must be particularly skilled in obtaining the confidence of callers so as to keep them on the line long enough to defuse the crisis situation, then elicit their personal details so as to

refer them to appropriate counselling organisations. The *Freedom from Fear*
Men's Domestic Violence Helpline counsellors were crucial to the success of
that campaign (see chapter 14).

Concluding comment

The marketing mix provides the social marketer with a framework for planning
a comprehensive campaign. The elements of the marketing mix not only serve
to remind the campaign planner of all the elements that must be considered in
planning and implementing a campaign, but also provide a framework for generating ideas, an opportunity to be imaginative and innovative. The framework
also serves to remind the planner that all elements need to reinforce each other.
Even where one element may be given more emphasis in a particular combination the marketing mix should still be regarded as a single entity within which
each element supports and reinforces the others.

Chapter 11

Using Media in Social Marketing

Introduction

Consistent with Ric Young's (1989) statement that information is social marketing's primary product, Richard Manoff, one of the first social marketing practitioners, called mass media 'social marketing's primary tool' (Manoff 1985, p. 64). However, there continues to be some debate as to the power of the mass media, and not just among social marketers, public health professionals, and other social change professionals. Some argue that the mass media influence what topics we think about, but not how we think about those topics. Others claim an inordinate influence of the media—especially advertising and especially among children and young people with respect to promoting or exacerbating violence, sexual promiscuity, intolerance, and the negative stereotyping of women, the elderly, and people of colour (see Harris 1999; Strasburger 1993).

Of the different media, television has come in for most criticism, no doubt because of its capacity for dramatic, graphic images and its ability to evoke powerful emotions and to reach large segments of the population within a very short timeframe. So-called reality shows, magazine shows, and daytime shows such as the *Jerry Springer Show* all come in for criticism for promoting values antithetical to 'desirable' social norms.

Although the mass media are frequently criticised for their part in the development of antisocial attitudes and behaviours among children, *Sesame Street*, the prosocial children's television program that was established with the aim of providing children (particularly disadvantaged children) with skills to equip them for school, has been produced by the Children's Television Workshop

---

War of the Worlds: the power of the media?

In October 1938 tens of thousands of people panicked on hearing Orson Welles's radio production of H. G. Wells's *War of the Worlds*. Thinking they were listening to a real news report of an invasion from Mars they abandoned their homes in droves and attempted to flee to the countryside (Lowery & DeFleur 1995).

Television and the decline of social capital

Putnam (1995a) has claimed that the advent of television coincides with the observed decline in social capital over the past 50 years. He claims that time spent watching television led to reduced membership and participation in community activities and that the nature of television programming in terms of publicising and sensationalising crime and corruption led to declines in public trust. However, this simplistic analysis has been criticised by others (for example, Norris 1996). Donovan and Jones (1999) concluded that it is not how much television one watches, but rather the type of shows watched that best predicts civic engagement.

---

since 1969. As well as providing prereading skills and early numeracy skills, *Sesame Street* provides a positive social model for children, promoting sexual and racial equality. This latter objective has shown considerable benefits for both white and non-white children. It has been reported that minority children watching *Sesame Street* show increased cultural pride, confidence, and interpersonal cooperation, and that white children showed more positive attitudes toward children of other races (Harris 1999).

The potential power of the mass media has been recognised for many years, and long before television. The Nazis may not have been the first to realise the enormous potential of the modern mass media, but they appear to have been the first to systematically exploit it on a national scale. The Nazis were also aware that information (propaganda) could be transmitted via entertainment vehicles such as theatre and movies. Hence, the Nazis not only took control of news outlets, but cultural and arts organisations also. Goebbels's ministry was known as the Ministry for Popular Enlightenment and Propaganda (Rhodes 1975). Goebbels realised that the young were particularly vulnerable and easily reachable through schools. He supplied all German schools with radios so that children could be exposed to Nazi propaganda. Channel One in the USA (see box) operates in a way chillingly similar to that of the Nazis.

Effectiveness of the mass media to promote health and socially desirable causes

In the 1970s several large-scale community health promotion trials involving the mass media were carried out. Three of the best known were the Stanford

---

Targeting the young: Nazi Germany in the 1930s, the USA in the 1990s

Channel One in the USA places television and VCR equipment in schools. In return, the schools ensure that students watch Channel One programming, in which each telecast contains 2 minutes of ads for major youth marketers. As of 1998, 12 000 schools (8 million kids) had taken up Channel One's offer (Schwartz 1998).

three and five city studies in the USA (Maccoby, Farquhar, Wood & Alexander 1977), the North Karelia project in Finland (Puska, Toumilheto, Salonen et al. 1985), and the North Coast Health Lifestyle Program in Australia (Egger, Fitzgerald, Frape et al. 1983). These studies generally involved comparing control communities with mass media-only interventions and mass media plus community-based programs. The general conclusion from these studies was that maximum change is best achieved through the combination of mass media and community-based programs, but that mass media alone can have some impact, albeit limited. For example, road safety advertising and publicity alone can raise awareness of an issue and may even result in a minor short-term behaviour change. However, without concurrent visible enforcement activities, any behavioural effect will be short-lived. At the same time the impact of enforcement activities appears to be enhanced by accompanying advertising and publicity (Donovan, Henley, Jalleh & Slater 1995).

The effectiveness of the media, either alone or as a contributing element, in social marketing campaigns has been confirmed in a number of different areas including health and injury prevention, racism, domestic violence, recycling, and crime prevention (see, for example, Egger, Donovan & Spark 1993; Spark, Sinclair, Donovan et al. 1994; Middlestadt, Fishbein, Albarracin et al. 1995; Foerster, Kizer, DiSogra et al. 1995; Brannstrom & Lindblad 1994; France, Donovan, Watson et al. 1991; Donovan & Leivers 1993; Hindin, Kincaid, Kumah et al. 1994; Coleman & Meyer 1990; Donovan, Paterson & Francas 1999f; Donovan, Francas, Paterson & Zappelli 2000; Yzer, Siero & Buunk 2000). The effectiveness of the media in tobacco control via publicity and paid advertising is well established for well-designed and implemented campaigns (Elder, Edwards, Conway et al. 1996; Hafstad, Aaro & Langmark 1996; Hu, Sung & Keeler 1995; Pierce, Macaskill & Hill 1990; Popham, Potter, Bal et al. 1993; Reid 1996; Hassard 1999; 2000).

As with many areas, where the mass media have failed it is not so much that they are ineffective, but the message has been poor, the targeting ineffective, the objectives unrealistic, or the evaluation inappropriate (Egger et al. 1993). Where the campaigns have been based on sound social and cognitive models, where community activities are included, and where all the principles of social marketing are integrated the results have been positive (Marcus, Owen, Forsyth et al. 1998).

Too often unrealistic objectives are set for the media. It is unrealistic, for example, to expect that advertising alone will have a significant impact on a man's violent behaviour, but it can have a substantial influence on encouraging the violent man to seek help for his behaviour (Donovan et al. 1999f; see chapter 14). The media can certainly stimulate help seeking (for example, in calls to helplines) and screening behaviours, and can contribute to significant changes in beliefs and attitudes related to more complex behaviour changes (such as racism; Donovan & Leivers 1993). Figure 11.1 (below) shows a clear relationship between the amount of advertising and the number of calls to the Quitline for

Figure 11.1 National tobacco campaign: calls to the Quit line by media weight*

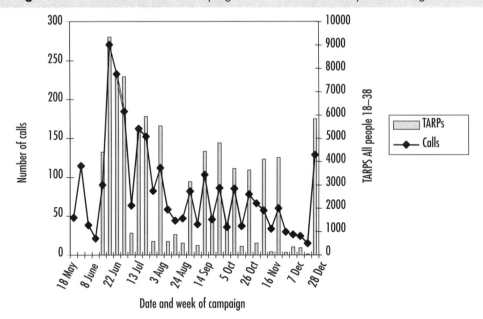

Date and week of campaign

* Donovan, Freeman, Borland & Boulter 1999b

Australia's national tobacco campaign (Donovan et al. 1999b; Donovan 2000a).

In short, it is crucial to determine just what are the objectives for media components of campaigns (dealt with later in this chapter).

Our experience suggests that media would have most behavioural effect where all or nearly all of the following apply:

- the desired behaviour change requires little time, effort, financial, or psychological cost

- where social norms are important and favour the desired change

- where there are clear and substantial benefits to the individual (that outweigh any costs)

Targeting fathers: Japanese style

Japan's Health Ministry has sponsored a $4 million media campaign aimed at encouraging fathers to become more involved in child rearing. The television advertisements and posters feature a famous Japanese dancer holding his infant son and bear the caption, 'A man who does not help in child rearing cannot be called a father'. The contentious campaign has created a public and media uproar as fathers take offence at the criticism of their lack of involvement (Jordan & Sullivan 1999). Japan's prime minister supports the campaign, saying that it increased his awareness of the importance of fathers' involvement in bringing up their children. It may be the case that focusing on the issue will encourage fathers to think about the amount of time they spend with their children.

Table 11.1 Summary of media methods*

TYPE	CHARACTERISTICS
Limited reach media	
PAMPHLETS	Information transmission. Best where cognition rather than emotion is desired outcome.
INFORMATION SHEETS	Quick convenient information. Use as series with storage folder. Not for complex behaviour change.
NEWSLETTERS	Continuity. Personalised. Labour intensive and requires detailed commitment and needs assessment before commencing.
POSTERS	Agenda setting function. Visual message. Creative input required. Possibility of graffiti might be considered.
T-SHIRTS	Emotive. Personal. Useful for cementing attitudes and commitment to program/idea.
STICKERS	Short messages to identify/motivate the user and cement commitment. Cheap, persuasive.
VIDEOS	Instructional. Motivational. Useful for personal viewing with adults as back-up to other programs.
Mass reach media	
TELEVISION	Awareness, arousal, modelling and image creation role. May be increasingly useful in information and skills training as awareness and interest in health increases.
RADIO	Informative, interactive (talkback). Cost effective and useful in creating awareness, providing information.
NEWSPAPERS	Long and short copy information. Material dependent on type of paper and day of week.
MAGAZINES	Wide readership and influence. Useful as in supportive role and to inform and provide social proof.

* Egger et al. 1999

- where there are no major environmental inhibitors
- where the individual's attitudes are neutral or already mildly positive towards the behaviour.

Hard-to-reach audiences

Egger et al. (1993) note that some criticism of the use of mass media has centred on the claim that mass media are ineffective in reaching important target groups. In some cases this is a valid criticism in that media campaigns have been directed toward various groups that would have been more effectively targeted via some other methods.

Hard-to-reach groups are usually defined in terms of their non-responsiveness to mainstream media campaigns. However, as Egger et al. (1993) point out, it is important to distinguish between those who are hard-to-reach because of low access to mainstream media and those who are hard to reach because of apparent imperviousness to media campaigns. The latter definition is the most used (for example, White & Maloney 1990), and accessibility is often included as a correlate of personality and lifestyle factors, such as a distrust of large government organisations, a sense of fatalism, and poor cognitive processing skills (Freimuth & Mettger 1990).

In keeping with Egger et al. (1993), we suggest that hard-to-REACH be used to refer to those simply not accessible via mainstream media, and hard-to-IMPACT be used to refer to those not responsive to media-delivered messages.

Groups most commonly thought of as not reachable include prostitutes, IV drug users, street kids and other homeless people, Aboriginal fringe dwellers, and non-English-speaking migrants. Yet there is now considerable evidence that such groups are accessible via mainstream media, including ethnic media, although care must be taken in scheduling and vehicle selection (Donovan, Jason, Gibbs & Kroger 1991; Bednall 1992; Research Triangle 1990). Furthermore, they are reachable by local media, including material distributed by hand and posters in local gathering spots.

As always with respect to both accessibility and responsiveness, the answer lies in carrying out adequate formative research to assess whether or not a potential target audience is firstly accessible and then, given accessibility, whether it is likely to be responsive to media messages. In some cases, the role of media may be limited to directing people to other campaign interventions such as telephone information services, interpreter services, and needle exchange locations, rather than to belief or attitude change.

A practical model for media use in social marketing programs

The framework presented here extends that presented elsewhere (Egger, Donovan & Spark 1993; Donovan & Owen 1994). We focus on five major media methods applied to health and social change promotion (advertising, publicity, edutainment, websites and interactive technology, and civic journalism) for three major objectives (education, motivation, and advocacy). This is shown in the table below where the number of asterisks indicates the relative use of the methods for the various objectives.

We first present the five major methods, then discuss the three major objectives.

Advertising

Advertising is generally defined as the paid placement of messages in media vehicles by an identified source, including the situation in which media organisations donate time or space for the placement of social change messages that

Table 11.2 A framework for using media in social marketing

	WAYS OF USING THE MEDIA				
	Advertising	Publicity	Edutainment	Websites	Civic journalism
OBJECTIVES					
Educate	**	**	****	*****	****
Motivate	****	**	****	**	***
Advocate	***	***	**	**	****

Donovan's (1991) guidelines for public health advertising

- Be credible, do not exaggerate claims.
- Arouse a strong relevant emotional response, whether this be positive or negative.
- For fear appeals show relevant, disabling harmful effects in otherwise healthy individuals rather than bedridden patients and ensure that anxiety results from a relevant self-assessment rather than just from the executional elements per se.
- Be sufficiently dramatic to generate word-of-mouth about the message (that is, not just the execution).
- Use simple concrete words and visual demonstrations of effects—both positive and negative.
- Show a means of attaining the desired behaviour and a source of assistance.
- Use modelling to enhance the trial and adoption of behavioural objectives.
- Use mnemonics for informational objectives.
- Where relevant, ensure that prescriptive norms and popular norms are congruent.

are clearly in the format of paid advertisements (community or public service announcements—CSAs or PSAs). There is a large number of advertising channels available, from direct mail to the rear of a toilet door, to shopping centre noticeboards, from packaging to sporting team jumpers, from local newspapers to nationwide (and international) television networks, and the worldwide web (see table 11.2). In fact, most media vehicles and features within media vehicles (sections in newspapers such as gardening, home improvements, etc.) exist simply to provide a channel for advertisers.

In commercial marketing advertising is the primary communication tool, although it is only one tool within the media mix. Other elements of the communication mix include tools such as publicity, sponsorship, trade shows, and instore and shopping centre demonstrations. For example, the launch of a new product may be accompanied by extensive mass media advertising to create awareness and a tentative positive attitude toward the product, press releases may be issued about the product's technological characteristics, its social benefits or its ecological soundness, special sales representatives may be on hand instore to describe and demonstrate the product, and entry to a sweepstake plus a substantial discount may be offered to the first 100 purchasers. Thus, in most commercial campaigns advertising, with a defined but limited set of objectives, is only one element of an integrated campaign. This is often forgotten by inexperienced social marketers who focus only on advertising.

Advertising is used to create awareness of and at least tentative positive attitudes towards brands and companies. This tentative positive attitude is assumed to lead to consideration of the brand at the point of sale (for example, in the supermarket or department store), or requesting more information (via coupon or telephone), or visiting an outlet to inspect the product. The actual sale then is determined by the product's packaging, price, perceived value relative to competitors' offerings, the salesperson's skill (where appropriate), the product's

> ### Advertising's communication objectives
>
> Following Rossiter and Percy's (1997) objectives for commercial advertising the communication objectives for the media components of social marketing campaigns can be listed as follows:
>
> * *awareness*: creating, maintaining or increasing awareness of an issue, product, service, or event
> * *attitudes*: creating, maintaining, or increasing positive attitudes towards an issue, product, service, or event
> * *behavioural intentions*: creating, maintaining, or increasing explicit or implicit intentions to behave in the recommended manner (including intermediate behaviours)
> * *behavioural facilitation*: facilitating acting on intentions by neutralising misperceptions and negatives and justifying costs and other factors that inhibit adoption of the recommended behaviour.

performance (where it can be observed), acceptance of the appropriate credit card, and so on—that is, all the elements of the marketing mix.

Similarly, in most social change areas, the major roles of advertising are first to create awareness of the issue and second, to create a tentative positive attitude toward the issue that predisposes the individual to other components of the campaign and to positive social pressures. The extent to which advertising can directly influence behaviour in health and social policy fields depends on the nature of the behaviour and the extent of prior public education. For example, non-threatening one-off behaviours such as cholesterol testing—even one-off behaviours with quite threatening consequences such as HIV testing—can be influenced directly by advertising campaigns (in conjunction with easily accessible test sites).

However, addictive and more complex behaviours requiring substantial lifestyle changes can rarely be influenced directly by advertising. Advertising's role in these instances is to maintain salience of the issue, to sensitise the target to intervention components that might otherwise have gone unnoticed, to provide directions to sources of assistance, to generate positive attitudes towards trying to adopt the desired behaviour change, and, where the behaviour has been adopted, to reinforce that behaviour.

Two other methods similar to advertising in that they involve payment for exposure of the marketer's products or messages to target audiences, are sponsorship and product placement.

Sponsorship

Sponsorship is generally defined as payment for the right to associate the sponsor's company name, products or services, with the sponsee (for example, Otker 1988; Sandler & Shani 1989). The subject of the sponsorship may vary from a one-off event (for example, a fun run), a season series (for example, the rugby league), a group of individuals (for example, the Sydney Swans football team), or an organisation (for example, an arts or crafts group) and its activities. Given that many high-profile commercial sponsorships are accompanied by promotional activities such as advertising, product samplings, trade promotions, or exclusive merchandising agreements, the more embracing term 'events marketing' is widely used in the USA, along with the term 'sports marketing' for sporting sponsorships. Sponsorship is covered in chapter 12.

Product placement

Product placement refers to the paid placement of brands and products in movies, books, and popular music. We have included this tactic under advertising, although others see it as a hybrid of advertising and publicity (Balasubramanian 1994). The tobacco companies, along with many others, appear to have used this tool quite extensively: Coca Cola, for example, features extensively in *Nutty Professor II*, Tom Cruise nearly collides with an Avis truck in *Mission Impossible II*, and in *What Women Want* part of the story involves making a television ad for Nike (Barber 2001).

Patricia Cornwell's book *Cause of Death* includes references to numerous brands across a broad range of product categories, including cigarettes (Marlboro, Camel, and Players). Furthermore—and perhaps true to its title—the book includes a sequence where the heroine smokes a Marlboro after 3 years of not smoking. She describes the feeling as follows

> The first hit cut my lungs like a blade, and I was instantly light-headed. I felt as I had when I smoked my first Camel at the age of sixteen. Then nicotine enveloped my brain, and the world spun more slowly and my thoughts coalesced. 'God, I have missed this,' I mourned as I tapped an ash.
>
> Cornwell 1996, pp. 211–12

Hmmmm.

Publicity

The high cost of advertising and an increasing understanding of media advocacy (see below) has led to social change practitioners paying more attention to unpaid methods to get their messages across. Publicity refers to the unpaid placement of messages in the media, usually in news or current affairs programs, but also in feature articles or documentaries. Unlike advertising, the source of the message is seen to be a presumably unbiased journalist rather than the organisation whose product or message is the subject of the news item or feature. Publicity involves attracting the media to run a particular story or cover a particular event in a way that creates, maintains, or increases the target audience's awareness of or favourable attitudes towards the organisation's products or message or towards the organisation itself.

Can advertising influence racist stereotype beliefs?*

A 2-week television, print, and radio advertising campaign was conducted in an Australian regional city. The aim was to assess the feasibility of using mass media to change discriminatory beliefs. Following formative research an advertising campaign was developed targeting the following beliefs about Aborigines and employment:
- very few Aborigines have a job
- very few Aborigines who have jobs hold them for a long time
- very few Aborigines have skilled jobs

These 'objective' beliefs were identified as the basis for subjective beliefs such as Aborigines are lazy, don't want to work, and can't handle responsibility. The results are shown below.

Figure 11.2a   Perceived proportion of Aborigines in paid employment

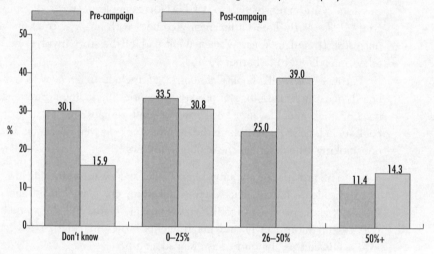

Figure 11.2b   Perceived proportion of employed Aborigines remaining in a job for more than a year

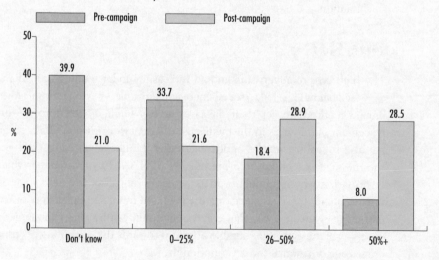

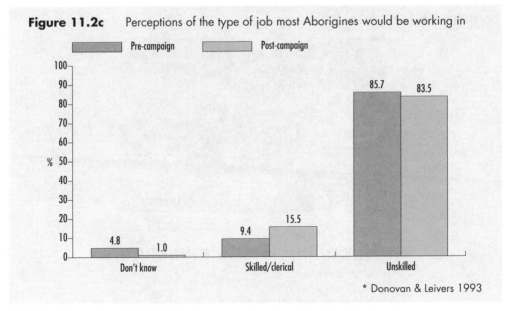

Figure 11.2c Perceptions of the type of job most Aborigines would be working in

* Donovan & Leivers 1993

Many social marketing campaigns now involve press conferences with celebrities and staged events that attract considerable photo coverage by the media (see figure 11.3). These events can be supported by activities such as providing the media with feature articles (for newspapers and magazines) and making experts available for interview on radio and television.

Publicity is part of the public relations mix, which refers to the activities an organisation undertakes to create and maintain positive relations with all of the organisation's publics, including customers, staff, suppliers, journalists, and politicians (Belch & Belch 1990). Public relations involves a number of activities other than seeking favourable publicity, such as employee magazines, loyalty magazines, educational materials, annual reports, research funding, and charitable donations.

Although a publicity strategy can be a long-term, planned strategy, in practice it tends to be more short term and focused on specific newsworthy events, such as a celebrity launching a campaign. Furthermore, even if the aim is longer-term, say, aiming for an article per month in a weekend newspaper, whether the article appears is up to the journalist or editor. A longer-term method that ensures continued coverage is where the news organisation itself takes responsibility for running a series of items with a socially desirable goal. This is known as civic (or public) journalism and is covered later in this chapter.

Edutainment

Edutainment (or enter–education) refers to the deliberate inclusion of socially desirable messages in entertainment vehicles such as television and radio soap operas, films, popular music, comics, novels, and short stories to achieve social

Figure 11.3 Spreading the waste message

Rotten job: Elephant Productions director-producer Chris Woodland starts to clean up rubbish dumped at his Leeming home. PICTURE: BILL HATTO

Spreading waste message

■ By Ruth Callaghan

THE graphic image of an average household's stinking, sweating waste on the front garden of a suburban Perth home will be used to encourage West Australians to recycle their waste.

A four-tonne pile of rubbish, dumped in front of a Leeming home on Friday, will star in a new recycling video to be distributed free to 138,000 WA homes.

Nine local government areas will receive the video which will give householders tips on environmentally friendly practices.

It is one of several new projects funded partly by the State's landfill levy program which diverts the cost of sending rubbish to the tip into recycling projects.

The $300,000 project, run by waste management company Cleanaway and production group Elephant Productions, received $70,000 from the levy fund.

Councils involved in the scheme also contributed to the project.

While the average WA household produces about 20kg of rubbish a week, West Australians recycle only 2.5kg — 40 per cent less than in New South Wales.

change objectives (Singhal & Rogers 1999). This may involve inserting prosocial messages in already existing or planned entertainment vehicles or actually developing the entertainment vehicles as part of a social change program. With the exception of the use of theatre in health education for schoolchildren (Ball 1994), the use of edutainment in the developed countries appears to consist primarily of the former, whereas in underdeveloped countries, it consists primarily of the latter. In fact, edutainment is a strategy used primarily in developing rather than in developed countries (Lettenmaier, Krenn, Morgan et al. 1993; Ranganath 1993; Helquist & Sealy 1992; Singhal & Rogers 1999).

Edutainment has clear advantages for presenting potentially threatening or sensitive topics in a non-threatening way and of reaching people who might otherwise not attend to the message when the source is clearly identified. That is, people might deliberately avoid a documentary or educational program deal-

CME points for watching television?

Some GPs claim that the information they get from shows such as *GP* and *A Country Practice* is so good that they should receive Continuing Medical Education (CME) points for watching. Another criterion to add to your selection of GP? (Maegraith 1994).

Edutainment: deceptive, or a valid social marketing tool?

A furore broke out in the USA in December 1999–January 2000 when it was disclosed that the Office of National Drug Control Policy (ONDCP) was negotiating with television stations to incorporate antidrug messages into program scripts in return for the stations not having to air a number of antidrug PSAs. (As part of the National Youth Anti-Drug Media Campaign, American networks were required to air one free slot for every paid slot.) Some critics lambasted both the stations and the ONDCP for allowing the stations to abrogate their civic responsibilities so easily. Others accused the ONDCP and the stations of deceptive conduct and social manipulation, and the ONDCP was accused of censoring television content because it allegedly wanted to approve the antidrug program scripts before they went to air. Only in America ... .

ing with race relations, but be quite happy to watch their favourite soap opera deal with the issue (Egger et al. 1993).

Edutainment appears to have been systematically adopted following a 1969 Peruvian soap opera (*Simplemente Maria*), which told the rags-to-riches story of Maria, who sewed her way to social and economic success with a Singer sewing machine. Wherever in South America the program was televised sales of Singer sewing machines were reported to have increased substantially (Singhal & Rogers 1989). A Mexican television producer and director, Miguel Sabido, is credited with being inspired by these results to develop a series of prosocial telenovellas in Mexico and hence, establishing the soap opera as a medium for social change. His methods have been studied and adapted to several countries, especially those where there is a strong cultural tradition of storytelling as a means of passing on knowledge. Most applications in underdeveloped countries have been directed primarily, but not exclusively, at social issues that influence economic development, particularly family planning, literacy, vocational training, agricultural methods, child rearing, female equality, and family harmony (Singhal & Rogers 1999; Coleman & Meyer 1990).

In Australia a recent series of three 1-hour programs on ABC-TV used a well-known comedy duo to present and discuss various health problems for men ('The trouble with men'). In the UK the BBC has produced television programs with the Health Education Authority (Reid 1996). Including ways of interaction with an audience can increase the effectiveness of the approach (Chapman, Smith, Mowbray et al. 1993).

Much of the rationale for edutainment is based on Bandura's social learning theory (Bandura 1977b). It is claimed that viewers will learn appropriate behaviours by observational learning (modelling). There is evidence that modelling of televised behaviours does occur (Winett, Leckliter, Chinn, Stahl & Love 1985; Wharton & Mandell 1985; Hawton, Simkin, Deeks et al. 1999). However, a comprehensive theory of how persuasion works via entertainment vehicles has yet to be developed. Advertising researchers have proposed that drama is processed differently to lecture or argument approaches to persuasion and that these differences might offer some advantages to persuasion by edutainment (Deighton, Romer & McQueen 1989).

Implementing edutainment

Achieving cooperation between social change professionals and entertainment industry professionals requires each to have a good understanding of the other's needs (Montgomery 1990). Social change professionals must accept and appreciate the commercial needs of the producers and the creative needs of the artists. They must accept that their messages must be subtle and secondary to the entertainment aspects. On the other hand, entertainment professionals must be convinced that prosocial messages can enhance audience appeal, and hence profitability of commercial productions (Coleman & Meyer 1990). In the ONDCP situation noted above the television stations were required—not without good reason—to submit the scripts to the ONDCP for approval, which instigated the accusation of government censorship. The ruckus may have been avoided had the antidrug people worked alongside the writers to jointly develop the antidrug related script components.

The potential application of edutainment to Aboriginal issues

Given the strong oral history tradition and use of storytelling to pass on cultural and religious beliefs among Indigenous Australians, an edutainment approach could be appropriate for this group. Ross Spark (Spark & Mills 1988; Spark, Donovan & Howat 1991; Spark, Binns, Laughlin, Spooner & Donovan 1992), in an innovative approach to Indigenous health promotion, used a community development model to elicit stories from Aboriginal communities that contained health messages about issues considered important to the community. Indigenous artists cooperated with community members to express the stories in pictures. These pictures then were developed into television advertisements shown through the Kimberley region of Western Australia. Evaluation of the project indicated a high level of awareness of these ads among Indigenous people and substantial satisfaction with the approach (Spark 1999).

Edutainment in action: *Soul City*

Soul City is a multimedia edutainment strategy that has been running in South Africa since 1992 and which 'aims to empower people and communities through the power of mass media' (CASE 1997, p. 1). *Soul City* utilises television, radio, print media, public relations and advertising, and education packages.

The television component, a half-hour drama that runs weekly for 13 weeks, has reportedly become one of the most popular programs on television and has won the Avanti award for excellence in broadcasting 2 years in succession (CASE 1997). The radio drama component consists of forty-five

Figure 11.4 *Soul City*

15-minute episodes (in eight different languages) and was developed to reach rural audiences.

Soul City's objectives (see CASE 1997) are to:

■ reach as many people as possible within a broad target market while specifically focusing on youth and women in marginalised and remote communities

■ generate discussion around health and lifestyle issues

■ encourage changing attitudes and behaviour in relation to certain diseases and health risks.

There have been four series of *Soul City* each of which has focused on specific issues, with ongoing underlying themes of the empowerment of women, prosocial issues, and community action for health and development. Series 1 (1994) focused largely on mother and child health. Series 2 (1996) focused on health issues, including smoking and communicable diseases such as tuberculosis and STDs, as well as land and housing issues. Series 3 (1996) included social issues such as violence, alcoholism, and household energy, and Series 4 (1999) with health issues such as HIV and hypertension as well as social issues including violence against women and teenage sexuality.

Key findings of the 1997 *Soul City* evaluation (as summarised in CASE 1997) included:

■ 61 per cent of all respondents were exposed to *Soul City* media

■ 95 per cent of people exposed to *Soul City* reported that they had learnt something from it

■ over half of those who accessed *Soul City* discussed it afterwards with friends, family, or at school

■ knowledge about the transmission of HIV increased significantly and there was a reported increase in condom use

■ there was a positive change in attitudes towards people with HIV/AIDS

■ there was an increase in awareness of tuberculosis and knowledge about its symptoms and treatment

■ there was an increase in awareness of land reform packages and processes for acquiring land.

Soul City has clearly had a considerable positive impact on the knowledge, attitudes, and beliefs of South African people across a range of social and health issues. In the words of one respondent, '*Soul City* taught me that if people unite around particular goals they ultimately succeed' (CASE 1997).

The Drum Beat

The Drum Beat (<http://www.comminit.com>), the email and web network from The Communication Initiative partnership—a joint venture between the Rockefeller Foundation, UNICEF, USAID, WHO, BBC World Service, CIDA, Johns Hopkins University Center for Communication Programs, *Soul City*, the Panos Institute, and UNFPA—provides details on its website of socially proactive media campaigns. For example, some of the programs featured include:

- News Agency for Child Rights (Brazil)—contributes to the development of a journalistic culture that supports the promotion of child rights, suggests guidelines for news on child and youth issues, and encourages the media to praise or denounce projects that relate to children and youth ('Communication and Change' 1998)
- Live Wise to Survive (Surinam)—Radio Muye, focusing on education and skill development for women, has been established with the support of UNESCO and reaches an audience of 5000 people in five villages ('Communication and Change' 1998)
- Call to Action (Brazil)—established to train radio producers and presenters to be effective advocates for the importance and value of education in their communities ('Communication and Change' 1998)
- *Children in Conflict* (global)—a ten-part radio series in nine languages produced by the BBC. The series will feature children from around the world telling their personal stories of the impact of war ('Media and Peace' 1999)
- *New Home, New Life* (Afghanistan)—this radio soap opera, also an initiative of the BBC, is broadcast three times a week. Initially focusing on the repatriation of refugees it now addresses social issues such as domestic and community disputes and health and financial issues ('Media and Peace' 1999)
- *Youth Television Network* (global)—this innovative program utilises video networking technology to bring together youth from around the world to talk about critical issues. The network's aim is to 'break through physical, cultural, and political barriers, helping shape a world where people better understand each other, and can work together creatively' ('Media and Peace' 1999).

Infonews (our term) is the news equivalent of edutainment: it refers to the placement of desired messages in news items. Journalists are provided with standard paragraphs that can accompany news about various topics. For example, in reporting any news about the tobacco industry or reports on tobacco-related illnesses, journalists can be encouraged to include closing statements such as 'Tobacco kills 18 000 people per annum in Australia'. Similarly, reports of road crashes can include closing statements that 'Crashes due to fatigue are estimated to constitute 30 per cent of crashes. Fatigue occurs not only on country roads, but in early morning traffic resulting from late nights or disturbed sleep'. For example, in cooperation with a local newspaper in the USA the reporting of road trauma was done in such a way as to include information from road trauma research and how injury can be avoided. Before and after surveys following an 8-week trial of the program revealed significant changes in people's perceptions of road trauma (Wilde & Ackersviller 1981). This method of media use, although not common, presents opportunities for the future.

Linking prosocial messages with entertainment vehicles

The Johns Hopkins Health Institutions have developed an innovative way of using people's interest in high-profile television soap operas *ER* and *Chicago Hope*: An informative 90-second health news segment dealing with the issue portrayed in that week's episode is produced to be aired immediately following the show. The segment also lists toll-free numbers and internet links to relevant information (Langlieb, Cooper & Gielen 1999).

Civic (public) journalism

As yet there is no specific agreed upon definition of civic journalism. Jay Rosen describes public journalism in the USA as

> an unfolding philosophy about the place of the journalist in public life [which] has emerged most clearly in recent initiatives in the newspaper world that show journalists trying to connect with their communities ... by encouraging civic participation or regrounding the coverage of politics in the imperatives of public discussion and debate (Rosen 1994).

This is not all altruistic. Media organisations hope to make themselves more valuable to their consumers by deepening their connections to the community. Nevertheless, while they may not have called it civic journalism or recognised the outcome as increasing social capital, journalists claim to have been using mass media to improve society for as long as they have been reporting news.

Civic journalism differs primarily from standard journalism in that standard journalism thrives on conflict and disagreement, whereas civic journalism attempts to build community consensus and cooperation. For example, whereas standard journalism seeks to emphasise differences and seek interviews with those known to have extremely opposing views on a topic, civic journalism emphasises similarities and seeks to emphasise more moderate views.

American examples of civic journalism appear to be based primarily on attempts to involve citizens more in political life. For example, in one of the first—and perhaps only—attempts to evaluate a civic journalism campaign, a field experiment supported by the Pew Center for Civic Journalism was designed to measure directly the impact of a multimedia civic journalism project in Madison, Wisconsin. The researchers wanted to find out whether a deliberate media campaign and related activities (for example, town hall meetings) could interest people in the elections, cause them to learn more about the candidates and the issues, and inspire them to get involved, particularly to vote. The attitudes and knowledge of the citizens were measured before, during, and after the campaign. The outcomes of the project (see Denton & Thorson 1995) included:

- a high level of awareness of the program
- an increased interest in public affairs
- people feeling more knowledgeable

- people aware of the program feeling more able to decide between the candidates
- people feeling encouraged to vote
- political cynicism did not increase (despite increased awareness of how campaign publicity can be used to distort issues)
- a substantial increase in positive feelings towards the media outlets involved in the campaign.

These results show a clear positive change in civic involvement and 'are very encouraging for those who want to improve the democratic process and to those who believe the news media can take a more active role in facilitating these processes' (Denton & Thorson 1995).

Civic journalism in action: the *Akron Beacon Journal*'s 'Coming Together' project

Following the riots that occurred in Los Angeles in 1992 after the Rodney King verdict a journalist with the *Akron Beacon Journal* decided to do something personally about race relations in the Akron–Canton area (and surrounding counties) of Ohio.

For the resulting series of articles aimed at improving race relations in Ohio, the *Akron Beacon Journal* won the 1994 Pulitzer Prize gold medal for public service journalism, the fourth Pulitzer for the newspaper.

The overall aims of the newspaper were initially very broad: to stimulate discussions of issues, to provide reasons behind the statistics (for example, that when controlling for race, neighbourhood crime rates were similar across white and black areas of similar socioeconomic status), to acquaint each group with the other's views, and to move people's beliefs and attitudes—and hence, behaviours—towards some common ground. In the spirit of civic journalism the idea was to present middle rather than extreme views and to promote agreement rather than division and conflict (the normal fodder for journalists).

It could be argued that one of the major points of this project was that it encouraged people to express views and fears that they would not normally have expressed for fear of being labelled 'racist' or 'alarmist', etc. If such views are continually internalised and repressed they become more difficult to challenge and change. Expressing such views in an atmosphere of cooperation rather than confrontation is the first stage to changing negative attitudes. By the reporting of views and the reasons behind these views the project also began to provide a greater understanding of each group's situation with respect to race. Apparently, one of the key outcomes of the project was that whites—some of whom rarely interacted with blacks and most of whom had never experienced discrimination of any sort and so had no appreciation of blacks' experiences—became far more aware that race was an issue for blacks, an issue they face every day in virtually all areas of their lives. Similar ignorances exist among most non-Indigenous Australians.

Civic journalism

The *Akron Beacon Journal*'s race relations project

The *Akron Beacon Journal* instituted a year-long series of articles entitled 'A Question of Colour', which dealt with five issues: racial attitudes, housing, education, economic status, and crime. Each topic was presented over 3 or 4 consecutive days, covering several pages each day, and including a number of graphics and people photos. The amount of space devoted to the series was a clear indicator to the reader of the importance placed on the issue by the newspaper.

The articles contained a mix of statistical information (percentage of home ownership by colour, percentage of occupational status by colour, etc.), traditional journalism reporting, and interpretation of past and current events, the identification of major changes and non-changes over the decades, reports on the results of focus groups among both blacks and whites that probed beliefs and attitudes held by the two groups towards each other (and postgroup interviews with participants), and reports on survey research of the extent to which people in the community held various beliefs and attitudes. The result was articles containing strong personal components expressing attitudes and beliefs that readers could identify with. For example, the issue on schooling commenced with a quote from a 16-year-old black student whose parents bus him to a nearby, predominantly white, school: 'I think the teachers put more effort into teaching because they have more white students in their classrooms. They probably feel more comfortable with white students than with a lot of black students in a class.' Next came a map of school attendance zones, statistics on race of students, race of teachers, and percentage of students in different grades passing proficiency tests. Next followed an article on the discrimination experienced by black children inside and outside of schools, with quotes from students, families, and school staff. Finally, an opinion piece titled 'Who's learning in integrated schools?' looked at the impact of colour on how students are treated, what is taught, what is learnt, and who benefits from the education process. The article was personalised by focusing on the prejudice experienced by two black students in a predominantly white school and included a large photograph of the two boys with their mother.

Right from the start, the *Journal*'s readers were invited to 'Tell us what you think' about race relations and 'how blacks and whites can better understand each other', by faxing, phoning, or writing to the newspaper. The newspaper periodically printed readers' contributions.

Following consultations with community groups the second in the series of articles was accompanied by a form inviting people and groups who wanted to become more involved in improving race relations to register with the *Journal*. This involvement of the community evolved into the Coming Together community project, which continued after the 'A Question of Colour' series finished in December 1993. The *Journal* continued to support the project by providing office space and salaries for two part-time community coordinators to the end of 1995, by which time it was hoped that other funding would be obtained to further continue the project. The role of the community coordinators (one black, one white) was to assist organisations to get together for various one-off or continuing events and to produce a monthly newsletter.

Research for the Council for Aboriginal Reconciliation (Donovan 1992a) predicted a potential backlash on Indigenous issues around some slogan such as 'Enough is enough' (which was, in fact, used by one Queensland One Nation candidate). A civic journalism approach was suggested to the council as a means of dealing with this anticipated backlash and for reconciliation issues generally (Donovan 1992a; 1996). One can only speculate as to whether the impact of Pauline Hanson's One Nation may have been defused somewhat had a civic journalism approach been adopted by the council.

Following interviews with many of those concerned with the Coming Together project, Donovan (1996) came to the following conclusions as to factors that facilitated this project:

- the personal commitment and enthusiasm of a number of individuals
- a supportive newspaper culture; the *Journal* has a history of involvement in community issues
- the newspaper ownership supported this community orientation with resources
- a commitment to a long-term project (initially, a year-long series of articles), not just a one-off, ad hoc approach
- the extensive use of focus group research that allowed 'ordinary' people and the so-called silent majority (of both races) to express their views and fears without being 'labelled' and the personalisation of stories
- the comprehensive background research for the articles and the presentation format of the articles (that is, use of graphics, photos)
- the timing was right; the Rodney King verdict and subsequent events resulted in an awareness throughout the USA that the racial question had to be confronted
- there was a recent release of extensive census data providing a rich source of material for the articles
- the *Journal* acted only as facilitator, requiring the community organisations themselves to develop and implement community interactions; the journalists also remained impartial in their articles and ensured that both sides' views were published—extreme views on either side were not included
- the project members and advisory council members deliberately kept the project from being taken over by any particular organisation wishing to promote a specific agenda by clearly positioning the project in a race relations context, not as a movement against institutional or other expressions of racism (though these are end goals); this facilitated the participation of people and groups who might otherwise have been deterred by the perceived dominance of some particular groups
- other media became involved as a result of community responses (for example, talkback radio)
- there were no unrealistic expectations, most of those interviewed referring to 'moving slowly', with the first goal relating to increasing familiarity between the two groups, then establishing trust before moving on to more

'No Viet Cong ever called me nigger'

Muhammed Ali

While the term 'civic journalism' may be new the roots of this growing ethos of prosocial news media in opposing racism stretch back many decades. Hudson (1999) cites four examples from the 1950s of the news media engendering support for civil rights and the eradication of racism in America's South. The coverage of these events—the murder of Emmett Till; the university suspension of Catherine Lucy, the first black student at the University of Alabama; the anti-apartheid bus boycott following the arrest in Alabama of Rosa Parkes, a black woman who refused to move to the back of a bus; and the integration of Central High School in Little Rock, Arkansas—'played an important part in galvanising support for the civil rights movement in the 1950s ... [awakening] America's conscience to flagrant abuses in the South' (Hudson 1999).

Hudson also points to press coverage of civil rights issues during the Second World War 'when some journalists questioned why black soldiers should have had to fight oppression overseas and then fight racism at home'. This issue was again canvassed by America's journalists after the Vietnam War following the oft-quoted words of Muhammad Ali—who threw away his Olympic gold medal following discrimination in his home town—as to why should he should go to Vietnam when 'No Viet Cong ever called me "nigger"'

concrete objectives, a principle that was stated as 'learning before doing'; it was stated that 'whites are task orientated and don't take time to develop relationships, whereas blacks required the building of trust before acting'; a similar cultural divide operates in Australia

- in keeping with others' recommendations for civic journalism, the articles were written in a down-to-earth style and dealt primarily with concrete issues rather than abstract concepts, which made the articles comprehensible
- perhaps most importantly, the project told people what they could personally do to have an impact and, furthermore, facilitated this involvement; this is crucial where people generally feel powerless or feel that their contribution would have no impact.

Websites—interactive information technology

The arrival of the internet has led to enormous advances in increasing people's access to information (provided they have a PC and an internet link), and for certain marketers has provided a sales channel without which they could only have reached markets in their small geographical catchment areas. However, it has not increased people's ability to interpret information, nor to judge the reliability and validity of the information provided. That is, the very accessibility of the internet not only provides an opportunity to provide prosocial messages, but also provides an avenue for the dissemination of racist, violent, and unhealthy psychological messages.

Figure 11.5 The runaway game promo

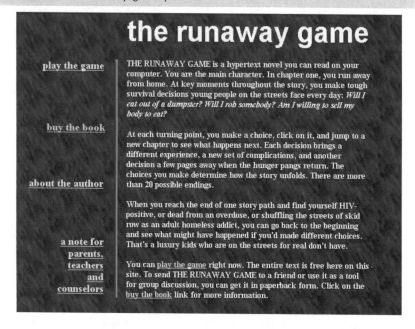

This unfettered access to the web (anyone can have a website; today's search engines are very efficient) increases the need for credible prosocial organisations not only to have a strong presence on the web, but also to continue to position themselves in the public eye as the credible, authoritative sources for information in their areas.

For social marketers the web provides a relatively efficient and inexpensive forum for the development and dissemination of social marketing projects and materials. For example, the website of The Communication Initiative partnership (<http://www.comminit.com>) lists numerous examples of prosocial websites, including:

- *Voices of Youth*—a UNICEF-supported site for young people for online discussion of issues such as child labour, girls' rights, urbanisation, and discrimination

- the *Creative Exchange*—a forum for the exchange of research and information for people working for change and development

- the *Sexuality Information and Education Council*—SIECUS' site assists them in the development, collection, and dissemination of information about sexuality and advocates for the rights of individuals

- *Asian Migrant Centre Online*—working to empower migrants to challenge unsustainable policies and to reintegrate into their home countries, helping to build local, regional, and international alternatives to migration.

Some new media developments with implications for social change marketers are as follows.

The new technology: Whatever happened to Springfield?

Springfield ('A new city. A new beginning'), on the outskirts of Brisbane, was reported in 1998 as Australia's first community where residents would have 24-hour online access to each other and to local services over an intranet. When contacted by the authors for an update, even the police seemed unsure as to just how far this online accessing had taken place.

Electronic communities

Electronic communities are where all households, retailers, businesses, schools, health, and welfare organisations, and so on, in a particular geographical (usually local government) area are given access to each other (and each other's products and services) via an intranet. The opportunities for direct emailing, marketing promotions, and information dissemination are clearly enormous. As the local copper in Springfield, Australia's first wired-up community said, 'The advantage is that you've got access to the whole community and they have access to you' (Murphy 1998, p. 5). Some might question whether this is in fact an advantage as the potential for information overload and hence people screening incoming information is also high.

One major concern with electronic communities is that, as for the web in general, interpersonal interactions will lessen as electronic interaction takes over, leading to a decline in social capital. Others argue that the web introduces a new kind of social capital, which is perhaps even more empowering because of greater access to a broader range of resources (Riedel, Dresel, Wagoner & Sullivan 1998).

Another concern is that, as in other areas, the more disadvantaged members of a community will either have less direct access to electronic devices or will have fewer skills to make the most of what is available.

Multimedia and interactive technology

It is these areas that hold most promise for the future, and not just for social marketers. Multimedia PCs are those with digital audio and a CD-ROM player. Unlike older PCs (remember the 486?) these can show pictures, sound, text, and graphics. Newer versions of the CD, such as the DVD (digital versatile disc or digital video disc), will not only store far more, but also have far greater capabilities (the film *Men In Black* runs for 114 minutes; the DVD version runs for 900 minutes). Hence, multimedia PC developments provide opportunities for elaborate message execution (combining messages from celebrities, film clips, computer-generated animations, demonstrations, etc.).

Sales of CD-ROMs (mainly for entertainment) are soaring in the USA (Postma 1999) and are being used frequently in direct mail campaigns. The Australian Taxation Office sent all owners of small businesses a CD-ROM that explained the new GST tax requirements and had inbuilt software to enable

The USA's national youth antidrug media campaign

This campaign is probably the world's most extensive interactive program, bringing together a number of interactive websites aimed at youth, parents, teachers, media personnel, and other stakeholders, placing messages on a variety of prosocial partners' websites, placing advertising on consumer websites and a major internet service provider (America On Line [AOL]), and developing messages and programs for leading child–parent news content sites. A key partnership includes a deal with Marvel Comic Books, which produces a special Spider Man comic book series (downloadable from the web) teaching kids antidrug messages and media literacy skills for deconstructing what they see and hear at the movies, on television, and in popular songs (Schwartz 2000).

them do their tax forms. Many social marketing campaigns use CD-ROMs as part of their communication mix.

Interactivity is concerned with mutual responsiveness (Postma 1999). At this stage the greatest opportunities for interactivity are via websites and CD-ROMs, although by the time this book is published interactive television may be far more commonplace than it is now (through cost reductions and technology advances). Comprehensive interactive television will add a whole new (visual) dimension to that currently offered by computers.

Many health organisations have developed interactive websites where visitors can, for example, answer a questionnaire with respect to their dietary habits and receive an immediate 'diagnosis' and 'prognosis' re dietary changes. Antitobacco campaigners are developing similar methods that classify smokers according to their stage of change and then present messages tailored to the smoker's stage of change and other characteristics (Borland, Balmford & Hunt, under review).

Regardless of these new media, social marketers should not be tempted to devote excess resources simply to follow what they see as exciting new trends. As Postma (1999) reminds us, people are still people and change at a far lesser rate than does technology. Furthermore, things actually change less than we often think: a recent survey of Australian children showed that the internet was not their most popular leisure activity outside school hours (47 per cent accessed in the past 12 months), nor were electronic games (69 per cent played in the past 2 weeks); the most popular was still 'watching television or videos': 97 per cent in past 2 weeks. Furthermore, 64 per cent rode bikes, 44 per cent spent time on art and craft activities, and 31 per cent skateboarded or rollerbladed (Australian Bureau of Statistics [ABS] 2000).

Choosing media and methods

The decision whether to use advertising, publicity, civic journalism, website technology edutainment, or some combination of these in any social marketing campaign is determined by the objectives of the campaign, the budget, the relative effectiveness of the different modes in reaching and impacting the target audiences, the complexity of the message, time constraints, relations with professionals in the various media, and the nature and types of media and media vehicles available (Egger et al. 1993).

The choice of print versus electronic media, television versus newspapers, radio versus magazines, and so on, also depends on budget, type of message required, target audience media habits, and so on. In general, television and outdoor media are intrusive and therefore have the capacity to reach those who might not normally attend to a message; newspapers and websites are passive in that only those interested in the topic will read further or deliberately access the site.

Egger et al. (1993) describe the following advantages and disadvantages of advertising, publicity, and edutainment. The primary advantages of paid advertising relate to control factors, that is, control over message content, message exposure—timing and location, and hence, target audience, and frequency of exposure. Advertising's major disadvantage is cost, both production costs (though creative advertising people can, and do, develop messages that do not require expensive production; see Donovan et al. 1999d) and media costs (by far the larger component). On the other hand, given the number of people exposed to, say, network television advertising, the cost per individual contact and impact is often quite low, especially relative to face-to-face methods.

Publicity in major media shares the ability of advertising to reach large numbers of people in a relatively short period of time, but has the disadvantage of less control over message content, message exposure, and message frequency (unless the issue is sufficiently newsworthy to attract continuing coverage for several days). A press release might be rewritten by a subeditor in a way that omits or distorts crucial information, be relegated to the later pages of a newspaper, only appear in a very late television or radio news spot, or even be totally ignored. On the other hand, publicity is generally perceived as more credible than paid advertising (because the source is presumably unbiased, or less biased) and is less costly.

Edutainment in major media has the ability to reach large numbers of people in a relatively short period of time (given a popular show), but, except where the show is produced by the social marketer, has the disadvantages of less control over message content and less control over message exposure and frequency—unless the theme continues for several episodes. On the other hand, a specifically produced show may not have the reach of an already popular show. The primary advantage of edutainment (which also, but to a lesser extent, applies to publicity) is the ability to attract the attention of people who might otherwise deliberately avoid messages that appear in an obvious educational form. Where the social marketer is not directly involved in producing the show edutainment can be quite inexpensive. However, where the social marketer is a joint or sole producer costs can be high. On the other hand, if a show is a commercial success the organisation might earn a profit (Coleman & Meyer 1990).

Websites are virtually *de rigueur* for any campaign, even if serving the same purpose as an entry in the *Yellow Pages*. However, useful websites allow target audience members to access information about the issue and allow stakeholders

Scenarios USA*

A variation on edutainment is where the target audience themselves become involved in making the production (as in Spark's approach). Scenarios USA brings together young people, film and television professionals, schools, and community organisations. The young people write the script on the topic (drugs, STDs, etc.), then act in and produce the film under the guidance of professionals. The short films are then distributed as widely as possible. A major benefit of this approach is that it engages many young at-risk teenagers who would reject a standard approach on these issues.

* Joiner, Minsky & Seals 2000

to access program information. Interactive elements can be built into the site as well as links established to other sites. Website design becomes expensive when interactive elements are included, but the major issues are maintaining and updating the site.

Civic journalism is most useful for complex issues requiring extensive information to be absorbed in a non-emotive atmosphere. The major difficulty in Australia is that there is no established tradition of civic journalism; newspapers appear focused on advertising revenue rather than quality journalism and hence, individual journalists have little support from their editors and publishers.

Roles of the media in social marketing campaigns

Egger et al. (1993) delineate three major roles for the media components of social marketing campaigns, two of which apply primarily to the targeting of individual behaviour change and the other to the achievement of sociopolitical objectives or structural change. All of these objectives involve the targeting of beliefs (knowledge and perceptions), attitudes (and opinions), and values. A fourth role is a directing or public announcement role. In this case the information is not about the issue in question, nor does it attempt to persuade; it simply directs people to further information about the issue (for example, promoting a telephone information service), to activities associated with the issue (for example, a cancer foundation Run for Life event), or to opportunities for community involvement in policy making (for example, announcing a public meeting to deal with local issues).

Targeting individual behaviour change

Most uses of the mass media in health promotion and social marketing have been directed towards individual behaviour change. This is particularly so in the USA where there is a strong cultural value on individual responsibility. The two primary communication objectives for campaigns that target individual behaviour change are (Donovan 1991):

TO EDUCATE (or INFORM)

and

TO MOTIVATE (or PERSUADE)

Education aims to create or maintain awareness, knowledge, and understanding of the health issue in question. Motivation aims to bring about attitude change, behavioural intentions, or explicit actions within the target group. Education is primarily a cognitive process; motivation involves cognition and emotional processes. Television advertising is most associated with and suited to persuasion, whereas most public health pamphlets, especially in years gone by, have focused on education.

The distinction between these two roles is blurred in that the provision of information is generally not intended for its own sake, but is usually meant to lead to desired behaviour changes. It was increasing evidence that knowledge alone was insufficient to achieve attitude and behaviour change among substantial proportions of the population that led public health officials to focus more attention on how to improve the motivational power of their health messages (Egger et al. 1993).

Targeting sociopolitical change: media advocacy

The ultimate goal of media advocacy is to create changes in policies that improve the health and wellbeing of communities (Wallack 1994). Those most associated with media advocacy to date—the quit smoking lobby—have used the media to define smoking as a public health issue of concern to all, and to attack the morals and motives of tobacco companies' marketing techniques (Chapman & Lupton 1994; Wallack, Dorfinan, Jernigan & Themba 1993). The subsequent arousal of public opinion has been used to support lobbying for legislative changes with respect to restrictions on tobacco advertising and sponsorship. This sort of media use is the third major role of media:

TO ADVOCATE

It can also be described as the use of media, usually via unpaid publicity, to place a particular point of view before the public with respect to some controversial issue with the aim of involving the public in the resolution of that issue. That is, a major aim of media advocacy is to empower the public to take part in policy making (see Rogers, Feighery, Tencati et al. 1995).

Some writers view media advocacy as an alternative, and hence separate from social marketing (for example, Wallack 1990b). However, we and others (for example, Slater, Kelly & Edwards 2000) view media advocacy as part of a comprehensive social marketing approach. Furthermore, advocacy per se involves far more than just media components and is a major tool for achieving change at the upstream, broader societal level.

Streetwize Communications in New South Wales is a non-profit organisation that develops materials appropriate for communicating social issues to young people and hard-to-reach groups. With the financial support of the New South Wales and Victorian Law Foundations Streetwize produces *Krunch*, a comic aimed at conveying socially positive messages in an entertaining format to young people. Stories address such topics as school bullying, the rights of kids when their parents separate, ways of dealing with domestic violence, drug and alcohol use, Indigenous issues, and the problem of coping with two cultures. All Streetwize material is produced in consultation with the community, especially young people and service providers, and involves the target audience in every stage of the development process. Streetwize can be found at <http://www.streetwize.com.au >.

Figure 11.6   Streetwize's Hep C comic

© Commonwealth of Australia, Communicable Diseases Branch 2000

The fight for public health: principles and practice of media advocacy

For those wanting to hone their media advocacy skills, read Chapman and Lupton's *The Fight for Public Health*. Simon Chapman is probably Australia's leading expert in media advocacy, best known for his media presence in tobacco control and gun control. One of the major early antitobacco campaigns involving Chapman was the attempt to remove Paul Hogan from Winfield advertising because of his appeal to children (Chapman 1980).

Both individual and structural change objectives should be part of any comprehensive social change campaign. In some cases it is likely that individual-targeted campaigns must have some impact first, not only on individual beliefs and attitudes towards the issue per se, but also on social norms towards the recommended behaviour, before advocacy objectives can be achieved. For example, it is unlikely that efforts to frame smoking as a public health issue would have been as successful without prior Quit campaigns that emphasised the ill-health effects of smoking. Similarly, graphic road safety ads served to create a positive social context within which harsher penalties and surveillance methods, such as speed cameras and random breath testing, could be introduced with minimal public opposition.

Specific objectives

There are a number of objectives that can be classified under the three overall roles of informing, persuading or advocating (see Donovan & Robinson 1992; Flora, Maibach & Maccoby 1989). However, it should be noted that the classification is not a mutually exclusive one. Egger et al. (1993) summarise these as follows.

Informational objectives

- *Informing* (or educating) people about the personal and community disbenefits of various undesirable behaviours, and the benefits of alternative behaviours.
- *Clarifying* misperceptions and/or confusions that people may have about various issues.
- *Reminding* people of the benefits and disbenefits of which they are already aware and maintaining the salience of this knowledge.

Motivational or persuasion objectives

- *Reinforcing* those already practising the desired behaviour (see figure 11.7).
- *Generating emotion arousal* to increase people's motivations to cease undesired behaviours and/or to adopt various desired behaviours.
- *Sensitising* or predisposing individuals to specific intervention components (arguably, the major role as a facilitator of behaviour change).
- *Increasing awareness* of prescriptive and, where appropriate, popular norms (Cialdini 1989), and hence, providing social support for those who wish to adopt the recommended behaviour.
- *Stimulating word-of-mouth* communications about the issue in question, and hence, encouraging peer (and other) group discussion and decision making—a very important role for the diffusion of social issues (Rogers 1995).

Figure 11.7 A National Environment Bureau recycling poster

Advocacy-related objectives

■ *Increasing community awareness* of the issue and placing the issue on the community's agenda (agenda setting; Ghorpade 1986).

■ *Creating or increasing community awareness* of a particular point of view with respect to the issue (*framing* the community agenda).

■ *Creating or maintaining a favourable attitude* towards this particular view.

■ *Creating a view* that the issue is a significantly serious one for community concern (*legitimising* the issue).

■ *Generating a positive community mood* within which regulatory and other policies can be introduced with minimal opposition and/or maximal support.

Concluding comment

The effective application of these media methods in social marketing requires close cooperation between media experts, marketing experts, content profes-

Figure 11.8 Friends of the Earth media release

Friends of the Earth Australia

Campaigns I Contacts I Home I Media Releases I Policy I Research Papers

Media Release

Wednesday, 28 March 2001

World faces Climate Disaster as Bush rats on Kyoto Treaty

The world is tottering on the brink of climate disaster today, as the White House confirmed that President Bush has decided to rat on the 1997 Kyoto Treaty. At Kyoto, the world's developed countries agreed for the first time to cut emissions of climate changing gases. White House officials have taken legal advice on how to pull out of the Treaty, which the US signed but which remains unratified by the Senate.

The United States, with 5% of the world's population, emits more than 20% of the world's carbon dioxide, the main climate changing gas. The US promised to cut emissions by 7% over 1990 levels by 2012 at the latest, but US emissions in fact rose by more than 10% between 1990 and 2000.

George Bush's campaign for the US presidency was backed by major US oil giants including Exxon, which also led the campaign in the US against the Kyoto Treaty. The Republican presidential campaign claimed that if Kyoto was ratified, US citizens might have to "walk to work".

Commenting, Charles Secrett, Director of Friends of the Earth England, Wales and Northern Ireland said: "George Bush's decision to rat on the Kyoto Treaty is grim news. When the Hague talks collapsed last year because of US intransigence, Friends of the Earth warned that the world would pay the price in tears. Millions of people - in the US as well as in other countries - face the loss of their homes, their jobs and even their lives because of climate change. But this ignorant, short-sighted and selfish politician, long since firmly jammed into the pockets of the oil lobby, clearly couldn't care less. The talks in Bonn in July must now concentrate on world action independent of the US."

For further information contact:

Ian Willmore	Media Co-ordinator	Mobile: 07887 641344 Work: 0207 566 1657 Home: 0208 885 3779

Direct access to FoE Melbourne Press Releases via `http://www.melbourne.foe.org.au/pr`
Direct access to FoE Australia Press Releases via `http://www.foe.org.au/pr`

sionals, and behavioural scientists with expertise in communication theory and attitude and behaviour change. A realisation of this has been a long time coming. Nevertheless, the Australian government's national tobacco campaign is directed by a special advisory group (headed by a behavioural scientist) and includes health promotion, social marketing, and consumer behaviour experts, all with considerable experience in tobacco control.

Chapter 12

Sponsorship[1]

Introduction

Sponsorship is generally defined as the payment for the right to associate the sponsor's company name, products, or services with the sponsee (Abratt, Clayton & Pitt 1987; Otker & Hayes 1987; Javalgi, Traylor, Gross & Lampman 1994; Cornwell & Maignan 1998). The sponsee could be an organisation (for example, the National Heart Foundation), a group of individuals or one individual (for example, Tiger Woods), an event (for example, the Olympic Games), or a season series (for example, Australian Football League).

In recent years the use of sponsorship as a promotional tool has increased dramatically in both commercial marketing and in health promotion. In 1966 the estimated worldwide sponsorship expenditure was US$13.4 billion (*International Events Group Sponsorship Report* 1996). In Australia in 1996–7, A$466.5 million was spent on sponsorship, of which A$281.9 million was channelled into sports, A$50.4 million to trade shows and conferences, A$37.3 million to education via grants and scholarships, and A$29.2 million to arts and culture (Australian Bureau of Statistics 1999). These figures indicate that sponsorship in Australia and elsewhere is substantial even though it is still small relative to total marketing expenditure.

The growth of sponsorship

The growth in sponsorship is attributable to the inherent benefits of sponsorship (for example, access to difficult-to-reach audiences) as well as to factors associated with advertising (for example, high costs and clutter in mass media advertising (Otker 1988; Wright 1988; Abratt & Grobler 1989; Crowley 1991), and to the phasing out of tobacco advertising. Sponsorship provides opportunities to access specific segments of an organisation's target audience (for exam-

---

1 This chapter is collated from extensive work by the Health Promotion Evaluation Unit (HPEU), Department of Public Health, University of Western Australia.

Figure 12.1 Water and Rivers Commission ad

WATER
AND RIVERS
COMMISSION

Expression of Interest
"Bringing Back the Swans"
Sponsorship opportunity

Your company could be involved in an exciting and important project to establish Black Swan habitat havens at prominent locations along the Swan River in Perth.

The Water and Rivers Commission has studied potential sites and how they could be modified to encourage more swans onto the river that is named after them.

But we need your help to build suitable habitat to bring this important environmental and cultural icon back to its rightful home.

The Water and Rivers Commission is offering a unique opportunity for organisations to be associated with a high profile environmental project by providing funds or in kind contributions of goods and services.

Closing: Friday, February 9th 2001 at 4.00pm WST.

Enquiries: Mr Peter Kent, Director, Business Development and Intergration Division. Tel: 9278 0314, Fax: 9278 0583, Email: peter.kent@wrc.wa.gov.au

Documents: Reception, Level 2 Hyatt Centre, 3 Plain St, East Perth WA 6004, or visit our website at: www.wrc.wa.gov.au/public/swans

Caring for WA's Most Vital Resource

ple, young people) and secondary audiences (for example, employees, shareholders, and clients) that are often difficult to reach through other media.

The growth in commercial sponsorship was led by the tobacco companies in an effort to continue to promote their brands following bans on television advertising and, later, other forms of promotion (Chapman & Lupton 1994; Meenaghan 1991). The apparent success of the tobacco companies' sponsorship in maintaining brand awareness and image encouraged other companies to embrace sponsorship, particularly the major brewery and soft drink marketers. Through a 'social proof' effect (Cialdini 1984), the highly visible sponsorship activities of these large companies may have been interpreted as proof that sponsorship is effective and therefore stimulated other companies to follow (Donovan, Corti, Holman, West & Pitter 1993).

The entry of large companies into sponsorship programs has also been stimulated by non-profit organisations actively promoting themselves as vehicles for sponsorship (for example, the Australian Institute of Sport and Kellogg's Sustain; the National Heart Foundation's 'tick' labelling).

In Australia (and elsewhere) in recent years, health promotion professionals have adopted many of the concepts and tools of commercial marketing (Egger, Donovan & Spark 1993), and now are enthusiastically embracing sponsorship as sponsors (mainly government agencies), and by actively promoting themselves to business as sponsees (non-government agencies). This has been facilitated by the fact that small-scale sponsorships at selected events are within the capacity of even small health agencies, and by a growing number of health and sporting organisations becoming more aware of the 'natural' link between both types of organisations' goals. While most applications of sponsorship in social marketing have been in health promotion, social marketers are becoming more aware of the potential of this marketing tool in other areas (Weinreich, Abbott & Olson 1999).

In Australia, the growth in health promotion sponsorship was initiated by the legislative phasing out of tobacco sponsorship and the creation in a number of Australian states of health promotion foundations that replaced tobacco sponsorship funds (Furlong 1994). Funded by a tobacco tax these foundations provide funds for health promotion research, intervention projects, and health sponsorship. Substantial funds are distributed to sports, arts, and racing organisations in return for these organisations' events being sponsored by health-promoting organisations. (For more information on the Australian health promotion foundations and the use of their funds, see Betts 1993; Carroll 1993; Court 1993; Galbally 1993; Frizzell 1993.) The replacement of tobacco sponsorship with health sponsorship occurs elsewhere; for example, in California (see Weinreich, Abbott & Olson 1999) and in New Zealand (via the Health Sponsorship Council).

Objectives of sponsorship

Most commercial sponsorships have trading and communication objectives, while most health sponsorships have structural and communication objectives.

Trading and structural objectives

The major objective of marketing activities is to influence or reinforce consumers' behaviour, including sales (Hoek, Gendall & Stockdale 1993). Trading objectives mainly refer to securing merchandising rights at events (Gross, Traylor & Shuman 1987). For example, Heineken sponsors a number of golf tournaments and, as part of their sponsorship arrangement, they seek to have exclusive merchandising rights so that only Heineken beer is available at these tournaments. It is hoped that (forced) trial of the product will lead to a more favourable attitude to the product and to repurchase in other situations.

Trading objectives for commercial sponsorships equate to structural change for health promotion sponsorships. For example, as a condition of the health sponsorship the sponsee may be required to establish smoke-free areas or to provide low-alcohol beer at their events. Such contractual requirements can reduce the degree of exposure to cigarette smoke (Giles-Corti, Clarkson, Donovan et al. 2001; Pikora, Corti, Clarkson, Jalleh & Donovan 1998), induce trial of low alcohol beers, and lead to the substitution of healthy foods for high-fat foods (Jalleh, Hamilton, Clarkson, Donovan & Corti 1998). Healthway's sponsorship program provides the opportunity for health agencies to work collaboratively with those in the health, recreational, and cultural sectors to introduce health-promotive policies in recreational settings (Giles-Corti et al. 2001).

Communication objectives

There are two main communication objectives of sponsorship:

■ to increase awareness of an organisation, brand name, or health issue among the general public or a specific target market (Otker & Hayes 1987; Wright 1988)

■ to increase or reinforce positive attitudes towards the organisation, brand name, or health issue through the association with the sponsee (Hansen & Scotwin 1995; Meenaghan 1994; 1996).

Also, while most commercial and health sponsorships are directed primarily at consumers they may have direct or indirect positive effects on other target groups such as potential employees, community leaders, politicians, and other relevant stakeholders. Sponsorship also can be used for client entertainment, special perks for key employees, and to provide incentives for the salesforce and distributors (Hastings 1984; Gross et al. 1987).

Differences between health and commercial sponsorship objectives

Health sponsorship attitude and belief objectives are more complex than those of commercial sponsors. Health sponsors promote a message, whereas commercial sponsors are primarily concerned with increasing awareness of brand names, trademarks, or logos. Health sponsorships have additional attitude and belief objectives that can be categorised as follows:

1 acceptance of the message as a legitimate health issue
2 acceptance of the personal relevance of the message
3 creation or reinforcement of a perception of the social norm with respect to acceptance of the message.

How sponsorship works

Sponsorship is similar to advertising as both are used to communicate an organisation's message and image for a product, brand, or service to the target market. Both advertising and sponsorship aim to increase the salience of the organisation or message. However, the process by which advertising and sponsorship achieve these communication objectives may be quite different. Advertising is a paid communication in which the medium and the message are controlled by the advertiser and can be explicitly linked to the relevant organisation or brand. Advertising is able to communicate complex messages both in terms of information and imagery (Hastings 1984). In contrast, sponsorship persuades indirectly by linking the sponsor's message to an event or organisation (Pham 1992) (although the sponsor's contract may include advertising at the event).

Commercial sponsors are concerned primarily with brand names or logos and associating these with the image attributes of the sponsee. Hence, most commercial sponsorship objectives require only limited cognitive processing, mainly via unconscious associative learning. Since social marketing sponsors promote a message, these sponsorship objectives require conscious processing, comprehension, and cognitive elaboration to achieve their objectives.

There are a number of ways in which attitude effects of sponsorship may occur.

1 Sheer exposure may lead to feelings of familiarity, and hence, positive feelings towards the message or organisation (Donovan et al. 1993). In this way sponsorship may reinforce a perception of the social norm or social acceptance of a message. Furthermore, awareness facilitates other promotional activities by sensitising the individual to such activities (Otker 1988).

2 Sponsorship results in positive affect transfer from the event to the sponsor (Keller 1993). Positive image or feelings (for example, fun, enjoyment, and excitement) associated with the event are transferred to the message or organisation via associative learning or cognitive inferencing.

3 As attitudes are based on a number of beliefs, an expressed attitude towards an organisation, brand name, or health message is dependent on what beliefs are most salient at the time (Klapper 1961). Hence, as sponsorship can increase the salience of a belief (Donovan et al. 1993), sponsorship can influence attitude.

Evaluation of sponsorship

The hierarchical communication model shown in figure 12.2 provides a basis for understanding how sponsorship can influence behaviour. However, it is not realistic to expect sponsorship or other promotional strategies in isolation to have a direct effect on behaviour. As with mass media promotions, sponsorship is likely to be more effective in the early stages of this hierarchy, whereas other elements of the marketing strategy and environmental factors are far more influential at the later behavioural stages. Therefore, it is important to measure sponsorship effects in terms of the earlier stages in the hierarchical communication model.

Until recently, the literature revealed little systematic evaluation of sponsorship. Academic papers have focused on topics such as questions of definitions, the role of sponsorship in the total marketing promotions mix, the setting of goals for sponsorship, and the criteria for the selection of events to sponsor (Otker 1988). Non-academic writings have focused on the benefits of sponsorship to sponsors and implementation factors (for example, Hobsons 1990; Dwyer 1997).

Figure 12.2 Steps in a hierarchical communication model

The lack of published commercial sponsorship evaluation research may be due in part to the proprietary nature of the data (Otker & Hayes 1987; Hansen & Scotwin 1995). It may also be due to the fact that advertising forms a major part of most marketing strategies, whereas sponsorship is usually one-off or event-based. Furthermore, it is difficult to separate the effects of sponsorship from advertising, sales promotion, and other promotional tools, especially for large organisations with multiple promotional activities (Rajaretnam 1994).

However, there have been a number of studies emanating from the Department of Public Health at the University of Western Australia (for example, Holman, Donovan, Corti, Jalleh, Frizzell & Carroll 1996; Donovan et al. 1993; Giles-Corti et al. 2001; Jalleh, Donovan, Giles-Corti & Holman 2002). We present the results of a number of these here.

Measures of effectiveness

Sponsorship has been evaluated in three main ways:

- measures of media exposure
- survey research on spectators' awareness and attitudes
- sales or behavioural data.

Media exposure

Sponsors often benefit from substantial publicity through media exposure associated with an event (for example, lineage in newspapers and magazines, television or radio mentions) (Scott & Suchard 1992). This means that sponsors

Figure 12.3 Michael Schumacher, a Marlboro winner

reach not only the audience at events, but also, those who watch, listen to, or read about the event via the various forms of media (Nicholls, Roslow & Laskey 1994). Given its objectivity and ready measurement (via commercial media watch organisations), media exposure is the most frequently nominated measure of sponsorship effectiveness by sponsors (Pope & Voges 1994). Backing a winner has big payoffs; pictures of a winning Michael Schumacher like the one shown in figure 12.3 appeared throughout the Formula 1 season in 2002. Levels of media exposure achieved via sponsorship can then be compared with levels reached by mainstream advertising or, more typically, can be calculated in terms of how much advertising would have been required to achieve the equiv-alent exposure (Hastings 1984; Nicholls et al. 1994). For example, the car man-ufacturer Volvo spent $5 million on sponsoring and promoting pro tennis. This was calculated to be equivalent to approximately $35 million in media exposure or a 7:1 ratio (Schlossberg 1996). Similarly, the value of 4 minutes of logo visi-bility during a game is estimated to be one-third to one-half the cost of buying 4 minutes of advertising on that game (Crimmins & Horn 1996).

Hence, sponsorship may be viewed as a cost-effective way of generating exposure. However, this comparison is only valid if sponsorship works in the same way as mainstream advertising. This is questionable as the message con-veyed through sponsorship is of a much simpler nature than that which can be transmitted through advertising (Abratt & Grobler 1989; Hansen & Scotwin 1995). Furthermore, the results of Pokrywczynski's (1994) experiments on arena displays versus advertising suggest that arena displays need 8–20 times more exposure than a commercial to achieve a similar impact (Crimmins & Horn 1996).

Nevertheless, despite its limitation, media exposure is a valuable process measure and a valuable comparative measure for assessing the audience reach of various sponsorships.

Sales and behavioural data

There are several methods to track sales data resulting from sponsorship. The appropriate method depends on the trading terms of the sponsorship. When sales are directly linked to a sponsored event (for example, coupons or label redemptions) it is relatively easy to measure the impact of the sponsorship on sales. Other possible methods include comparing sales for a period around the sponsorship with the same period in prior years, or in periods before and after the sponsored event, or in the event area against national sales (Kate 1995).

There are few published data on the impact of sponsorship on sales, which may again be due mainly to the proprietary nature of the data (Hansen & Scotwin 1995; Otker & Hayes 1987). Those that have been reported provide evidence that sponsorship can have a positive impact on sales. For example, the Los Angeles Cellular Telephone Company claimed that in 1994 every dollar spent on sponsorship of pro sports teams, ski areas, concerts, and festivals pro-duced almost $87 in incremental sales (Kate 1995). In 1992 Visa advertised that it would donate a small percentage of the value of each American transaction to the USA Olympic team. Visa's transaction volume increased by 17 per cent during the promotion. No other Visa advertising or promotion campaign had generated an increased volume of more than 3 per cent (Kate 1995).

A number of Health Promotion Development and Evaluation Program (HPDEP) (now known as the Health Promotion Evaluation Unit [HPEU]) studies (for example, Holman et al. 1996; Donovan, Jalleh, Clarkson & Corti 1999g), using self-reports, indicate that health sponsorships can lead to behav-ioural changes among those exposed to the messages. These will be noted below.

Survey research

Beside the opportunity for a sponsor to achieve sales at the event sponsorship aims to create a favourable image and hence increase the likelihood of later purchase of sponsored brands in the shopping situation (Nicholls et al. 1994). In recent years a number of studies have determined the effects of sponsorship in terms of awareness and attitudinal effects.

Awareness effects

There are two types of awareness that may result from sponsorship: awareness of the sponsor's sponsorship of an event and awareness of the sponsor's brand name or message regardless of any link with an event.

A number of publications on the impact of sponsorships are based on major international events such as the Olympic Games (for example, Abratt et al. 1987; Sandler & Shani 1989; 1993; Stotlar 1993; Hitchen 1995) and the Soccer World Cup (for example, Otker & Hayes 1987). The results of studies in terms of generating awareness of the sponsor's link to the event have been mixed. Since 1984 Sponsor Watch has tracked 102 official Olympic sponsors, of which only 51 per cent built a successful link between their brand and the Olympics (Crimmins & Horn 1996). Similarly, Sandler and Shani (1989) examined seven categories of official sponsors of the 1988 Winter Olympics and found that four of the seven official sponsors succeeded in building awareness of their sponsorship and three did not. Of the sponsors who ran advertising during the 1992 Olympic Games, 64 per cent succeeded in creating a link between the Olympics and their brand, whereas among official sponsors who did not run advertising during the Olympics, only one sponsor, *Sports Illustrated*, succeeded in creating a link between the Olympics and the brand (Crimmins & Horn 1996).

It is important to assess also the awareness of a sponsor's competitors to determine the strength of the link between the sponsor and the event or organisation (Crimmins & Horn 1996). For example, in 1993, Coca-Cola contracted to be the official soft drink of the American National Football League (NFL) for 5 years. In the 1994 NFL season, prompted recognition of Coke as a sponsor among NFL football fans who regularly consumed soft drinks was 35 per cent. However, 34 per cent of the sample mistakenly identified Pepsi as a sponsor of the NFL. That is, Coca-Cola's sponsorship failed to gain an advantage over its main competitor in terms of sponsor awareness. The larger the proportion of the target audience who recognise that the organisation or brand is a sponsor and its competitor is not, the stronger is the link (Crimmins & Horn 1996).

There is evidence that sponsorships can increase children's awareness of brand names. Ledwith (1984) showed that recognition levels of cigarette brands increased according to which brands had recently sponsored televised sporting events. Similarly, Aitken, Leathar, and Squair (1986) found that more than half of secondary school children in the UK were able to name cigarette brands of sponsored sports. In spite of cigarette advertising being banned on television for more than 25 years, 64 per cent of children aged between 9 and 15 claimed to have seen cigarette advertising on television. The reason is that there is an average of 1 hour of television coverage each day of sports directly associated with a major tobacco brand (Crompton 1993). This provides evidence that sponsorship acts much the same as advertising in increasing brand awareness.

Donovan et al. (1993) showed that 'lack of physical activity' as a factor contributing to heart disease increased from 20 per cent prior to a National Heart Foundation-sponsored event promoting physical activity to 49 per cent after the event.

Attitudinal effects

There are three attitudinal effects of interest:
- attitudes to sponsorship in general
- attitudes to the sponsor
- attitudes to the sponsor's products or services.

Studies have found positive attitudes towards sponsorship in general (for example, Sweeney 1992; Hitchen 1995). The Roper Organisation for the American Coalition for Entertainment and Sports Sponsorship study, as one example, found that: 93 per cent of adults believed that corporate sponsorships are a good thing, 76 per cent agreed that advertising and sponsorship are a fair price for the entertainment they provide, 82 per cent agreed that corporate sponsorships benefit local communities by presenting events that attract visitors and by helping to hold ticket prices down, and 76 per cent believed that corporate sponsorship is a fair price to pay to keep sports on free television (Saxton 1993). Many sponsors no doubt believe that goodwill towards sponsorship in general will, by association, flow on to their corporate reputation.

Attitudes to sponsors have been measured mainly by asking respondents to rate the sponsor on a number of statements related to corporate image (for example, Javalgi et al. 1994; Hitchen 1995; Jones & Dearsley 1995; Stipp & Schiavone 1996). It has been argued that sponsorship is better able to influence image than traditional advertising as advertising is too direct, whereas sponsorship is more subtle (Armstrong 1988; McDonald 1991). Hence, it has been suggested that sponsorship may be used to counter negative company images associated with unpleasant activities (for example, insurance companies) and environmental pollution (for example, oil companies) (Wolton 1988). Some studies have found positive effects of sponsorship on company image (for example, Rajaretnam 1994; Turco 1995), while others reported little or no effect (for example, Otker & Hayes 1987; Javalgi et al. 1994). No doubt Phillip Morris is hoping that its sponsorship of issues such as domestic violence will have a positive impact on its corporate image.

A number of studies have found that prompted awareness of a sponsor's link with an event can positively influence consumers' preference for the sponsor's products or services (for example, Sweeney 1992). Performance Research, for example, found that 48 per cent of NASCAR fans would 'almost always'

Figure 12.4 Healthway logo

Healthway. Healthy WA.

purchase a sponsor's product over that of a closely priced competitor and 42 per cent would switch to the sponsor's brands (Crimmins & Horn 1996). Crimmins and Horn (1996) found that about 60 per cent of the USA's adult population reported that they would buy a company's product if the company supported the Olympic Games and about 60 per cent felt they were contributing to the Olympics by purchasing the brands of Olympic sponsors.

A measure of attitude change less susceptible to demand effects than the above measure is simply to ask a sample of the target population to select which brand or company offers the best product or service in their category without *any* reference to sponsorship. In Crimmins and Horn's (1996) study, Visa's advantage over Mastercard in perceived superiority doubled during the Olympic Games from 15 per cent to 30 per cent and remained higher 1 month after the Olympics than it had been during the 3 months before the Olympics. Similarly, Seiko's average advantage over Timex in perceived superiority during the 3 months before the Olympics was 5 per cent, which increased to 20 per cent during the Olympics. However, only about half of the Olympic sponsors who built a link to the Olympic Games had an appreciable increase in their perceived superiority.

Crimmins and Horn (1996) compared the communications of the sponsors who succeeded and those who did not succeed in improving their perceived superiority and found that sponsors who were able to translate recognition of their sponsorship into improved brand perceptions were those who made the meaning of their sponsorship clear (that is, the message that the brand would like the sponsorship to communicate). As evident in the examples earlier, fans of an event or organisation are willing to change their perception of the brand, but they need to be informed how the perception should change. Crimmins and Horn (1996) concluded that even though the meaning of a link between a brand and an event or organisation seems direct, as in the link between athletics shoes and basketball, sponsors still need to reinforce the natural interpretation.

Overall then, there is substantial evidence that sponsorship can work for commercial organisations. Can it work for social marketing?

Figure 12.5 The Australian Health Promotion Foundations' sponsorship model*

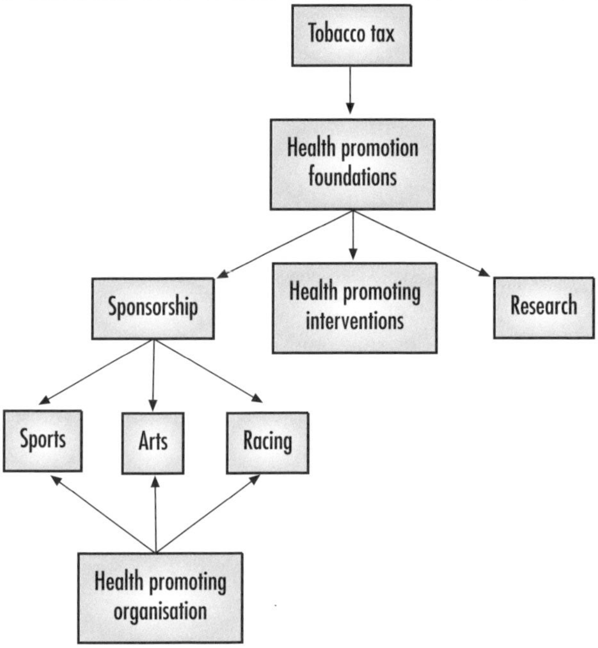

* Jalleh et al. 2002

Health promotion foundations: the case of Healthway

In Australia health promotion foundations now exist in four of the eight states and territories, the first being established in 1987 in Victoria (VicHealth). While no two of the Australian foundations are identical the following description of the Western Australia Health Promotion Foundation (known as Healthway) illustrates the principal concepts.

Healthway was established in 1991 under tobacco control legislation that outlawed the public promotion of tobacco products. Healthway is funded by a levy raised on the wholesale distribution price of tobacco products. It uses approximately 60 per cent of its funds to sponsor sport, arts, and racing groups (SARGs) (racing includes horse, greyhound, and motor car racing). SARGs may range from one-off small craft exhibitions to a series of State Theatre plays, or from coaching clinics for junior soccer players to professional league sports, such as AFL and NBA teams.

When Healthway provides sponsorship funds (a grant) to a SARG it simultaneously awards support funds to an independent health agency to promote a health message at the sponsored event. Health organisations (for example, the National Heart Foundation, the Cancer Foundation, Diabetes Australia, etc.)

and their messages (for example, 'Be Smoke-Free', 'Be Active Every Day', 'Eat More Fruit'n'Veg', 'Be Sun Wise', 'Drinksafe', etc.) for particular events are chosen primarily with respect to the nature of the event's audience or participants and the state's health priority areas. For very small grants, and especially for country SARGs, rather than allocating funds to a health agency, Healthway provides the SARG with a sponsorship support kit containing posters, decals, pamphlets, and ideas for activities with respect to a specific health message.

Healthway also attempts to create healthy environments by negotiating, where appropriate, the introduction of smoke-free areas, availability of low-alcohol and non-alcohol alternatives, safe alcohol-serving practices, provision of healthy food choices, and sun protection measures such as shaded spectator areas and protective clothing. The latter are the equivalent of merchandising and stocking agreements in commercial sponsorship. Healthway also negotiates, where appropriate, facilitation of access by people with disabilities or SES disadvantage.

Matching sports, arts, and racing events with health sponsors

In general, sponsors select organisations or events to sponsor for a combination of reasons, but the essential criteria are:

- the event's or organisation's spectators or members constitute the sponsor's target audience
- the event's or organisation's image attributes match—or at least are not inconsistent with—the sponsor's desired corporate or brand image
- the cost of the sponsorship in terms of target audience numbers delivered is competitive with other means of reaching the target audience.

In short, sponsors select events that attract their target market. In the commercial area Schick razors sponsors the National Basketball Association's championships in the USA as basketball followers match the company's target market of 18–34-year-old males (Schlossberg 1996). The Scottish F A Cup audience consisted mostly of working-class males, one of the Scottish Health Education Group's main target groups (Hastings et al. 1988).

Other reasons for selecting a particular sponsee may be to preempt a competitor sponsoring the event (for example, road safety authorities sponsoring a

Philanthropy or target marketing?*

The pharmaceutical company Novo Nordisk raised a few eyebrows with its sponsorship of the allegedly richest ever one-day swimming meet—the reason being that Novo Nordisk manufactures the performance enhancing growth hormone used by some swimming (and other) cheats. The meet was organised by US Olympic gold medallist Gary Hall Junior, a diabetic, and Novo Nordisk also manufactures diabetic medications. People were likening Novo Nordisk's sponsorship to that of tobacco or alcohol sponsorship—just not on!* Just as using celebrities has sometimes had embarrassing outcomes, sponsor partnerships should be approached with care.

* Jeffery 2001

Parenting sponsorship of the animal nursery*

Family and Children's Services of Western Australia sponsors the Animal Nursery pavilion at the Perth Royal Show. In 1997, it was estimated that 368 000 people visited the Animal Nursery, with 73 per cent being aware of parenting messages associated with the pavilion.

Sponsorship of the Animal Nursery offers Family and Children's Services an effective strategy for reaching young families, their primary target population, both metropolitan and rural. They estimate the marketing strategy is highly cost-effective at about 7c per person. The event is appropriate as it links to the theme of parenting, as well as being innovative. In return for the sponsorship, the Perth Royal Show offers exclusive naming rights (The Family and Children's Services Animal Nursery), signage, banners and other support.

* Family and Children's Services Annual Report 1997/8; 1998/9

local football team to preempt an alcohol sponsor), the event may deliver a specific subgroup that is difficult to reach any other way (for example, a surf carnival, a heavy metal concert), the event may provide a means of reaching important opinion leaders in the community (for example, a health authority taking a box at an international sporting event in order to meet local politicians who will receive tickets to the event), or the event is popular with staff and attendance and involvement will boost morale (applies to commercial rather than social sponsorships).

Through community surveys and surveys at events, Healthway has a good idea of the demographic and health profiles of audiences and spectators at various types of events. For example, racegoers have higher than average smoking prevalence and lower than average physical activity levels, youth concerts have higher than average alcohol levels, football spectators not only have higher than average levels of physical activity, but also higher levels of alcohol consumption, arts audiences have lower than average smoking prevalence, but lower levels of physical activity, most audiences have lower than average levels of fruit and vegetable consumption, and so on.

However, some matches of message and event have to be carefully considered. For example, the National Heart Foundation's 'Eat Less Fat' and 'Eat More Fruit'n'Veg' messages can yield the following sorts of problems at the races: the Eat Less Fat Stakes, the Fruit'n'Veg Handicap'. Similarly, the 'Diabetes Perth Cup' just does not seem to match the excitement of a big race and certainly does not have the glamour of even the 'Winfield Perth Cup'.

Engaging the sponsored organisation

An important aspect is getting the sponsored organisation's staff and participants involved in or adopting the message. This appears more difficult with arts organisations—who are sensitive to any sort of commercial intrusion on their artistic integrity, but appears to fit well with sporting organisations' members. For example, the Western Australian Football League (WAFL) is sponsored by the Office of Road Safety, primarily promoting the 'Belt Up' seatbelt message. The WAFL ensures that all the players are fully aware of the sponsorship and the implications of internalising the sponsorship message. Players are asked to sign a pledge to always wear their seat belt and each player is asked to sign up eighteen friends (the number of players in a team) to also make the pledge. On the other hand, things can go wrong as indicated in the following box.

'Drink drive, lose sponsor'*

The Victorian Traffic Accident Commission (TAC) sponsors the Richmond Tigers Aussie Rules team. This headline appeared in the *West Australian* following one of the team members being caught drink driving. The TAC, which runs the 'Drink Drive, Bloody Idiot' campaign was clearly not impressed and the Tigers ran the real risk of losing the sponsorship dollars. The TAC includes penalties in its sponsorships for players or officials who transgress road laws during the life of the sponsorship.

* Lyon 2002

In a new TAC sponsorship deal with the Collingwood AFL club players and officials will be given a personal breathalyser, a Cabcharge card for taxi use, and a hands-free mobile phone car kit in an effort to facilitate road safe behaviours. In addition, a code of conduct is being developed for players and officials.

Cooperation between the health organisation sponsor and sponsee

Most major Western Australian health organisations now employ sponsorship officers (often Healthway-funded); Healthway also employs several sponsorship officers. In many cases these health sponsorship officers have a more sophisticated understanding of sponsorship than do their commercial counterparts. Many of the larger arts, sporting, and racing organisations similarly employ sponsorship officers. Cooperation between the two is essential for effective implementation of the sponsorship. Whereas initially most sponsored arts, racing, and sports organisations were simply interested in the money and minimal compliance with Healthway's and the sponsor organisation's requirements, the situation has evolved to where many sponsored organisations have assumed partial responsibility for promotion of the health message and value its intrinsic

Keeping an eye on sponsees

In one incident, Healthway by chance discovered that a junior football club they sponsored was to hold a raffle in which first prize was a trailer of beer, second prize was a wheelbarrow of beer, and third prize was 'all you can carry'. This was hardly a message that Healthway wanted to be seen to be condoning in a junior football club.

benefits for its own members. Nevertheless, one must always be alert to potential problems (see box).

Evaluating health sponsorship: Does it work?

Sponsorship, like advertising, can be used to achieve individual changes in beliefs, attitudes, and behaviour. Sponsorship can also be used to negotiate structural change as a condition of the sponsorship. The Health Promotion Evaluation Unit (HPEU) at the University of Western Australia has undertaken a number of field studies as well as designing a systematic evaluation of all of Healthway's sponsorship activities. HPEU's research program includes sponsorship awareness measures as well as attempting to assess sponsorship's (actual and potential) behavioural effects and structural changes (see Donovan et al. 1999g; Corti, Holman, Donovan, Frizzell & Carroll 1997; Giles-Corti et al. 2001; Holman, Donovan & Corti 1993; 1994; Holman, Donovan, Corti et al. 1996; 1997b; Holman, Donovan, Corti & Jalleh 1997a for examples). The next sections show how Healthway has used sponsorship to achieve both individual and structural change.

Using sponsorship to achieve individual change

In 1992 the HPDEP (now HPEU) designed a system for the evaluation of health promotion and sponsorship projects sponsored by Healthway. The system, known as graduated project evaluation (GPE), attempts to systematically evaluate an organisation's sponsorship program. GPE aims to match an appropriate level of evaluation to each sponsorship project. The GPE structure originally consisted of four evaluation levels, with the main criterion for assignment of GPE levels being the dollar amount of sponsorship (that is, GPE level 1 for less than $10 000, level 2 for $10 001–25 000, level 3 for $25 001–100 000, and level 4 for greater than $100 000; for details of the GPE see Holman, Donovan & Corti 1993).

The evaluation required for GPE level 3 projects includes assessing the sponsored health message in terms of impact measures: health message awareness, comprehension, acceptance, intention, and action. These measures represent a hierarchy of cognitive and attitudinal effects (Donovan & Robinson 1992). The first three measures primarily refer to process evaluation as they relate specifically to the health message per se. The last two levels refer to impact and outcome evaluation as they relate to the effect of the message on behavioural intentions and actual behaviour.

In the section that follows, we first present results from Healthway's GPE analysis. We then present examples of field studies that more directly assess the effects of sponsorship on attitudes and on behaviour.

GPE results: 1996/7 compared with 1992/3

An earlier study examined all sponsorship projects funded by Healthway at the GPE level 3 from 1 July 1992 to 30 June 1993 (Holman, Donovan & Corti 1994). These results and those for 1996/7 are presented here.

Data were gathered at sponsored events by professional interviewers. A combination of self-administered and interviewer-administered questionnaires was used; there were also some variations by the life-stage of the respondents (that is, adult, teenager, or child). Children aged 10 years or above were eligible to participate in the surveys. The questionnaires contained a core set of items so as to allow the data—questionnaire type and respondent type—to be combined across projects. Interviews were conducted at the sponsored venues either during an interval or post event. Interviewers were assigned to specific locations at the venues and were given instructions on the selection of respondents so as to ensure, as far as possible, a random sample of patrons (Health Promotion Evaluation Unit 1998). Further details of the methodology can be found in Holman, Donovan & Corti (1993; 1994).

There were thirty-three projects included in the 1996/7 sample (n = 2579 respondents) and fifty-five in the 1992/3 sample (n = 5710 respondents). Approximately equal proportions of males and females were interviewed on each occasion. In 1992/3, 49 per cent of respondents were under 20 years of age, compared with 37 per cent of respondents in 1996/7. No attempt was made to attain similar sample demographics at each time point as the samples reflect the populations attending these Healthway sponsored events at that time.

There were sixteen different messages—across seven health areas—allocated to sponsorships in 1996/7 and twenty-one (nine areas) in 1992/3. In general, the distribution of message topics was similar for the most frequently allocated messages. The most frequent health areas (messages) in both periods were smoking (for example, Quit, Smoke Free), followed by nutrition (for example, Eat More Fruit'n'Veg), physical activity (for example, Be Active), and sun protection (for example, Sunsmart) (full details can be found in Donovan, Corti & Jalleh 1997a; Donovan, Jalleh, Clarkson, Corti & Pikora 1997b).

All respondents were first asked whether they could recall seeing or hearing any health messages at the event. Interviewer-administered questionnaires then measured prompted awareness by presenting respondents with a list of messages and asking which they recalled seeing or hearing at the event. Respondents who were aware of the message at the event were then asked what they understood the message to mean (comprehension) and, if correct, were asked their attitude toward the message (acceptance). All respondents accepting the message (other than the child self-administered questionnaire respondents) were asked what thoughts, if any, they had about the message. Further, if they had seen the mes-

Table 12.1 Cognitive impact measures as a proportion of each preceding level

Measure	1992/3 (n = 5684) Total sample (%)	1996/7 (n = 2579) Total sample (%)
Total awareness	67.2	75.8
Comprehension	82.2	90.0
Acceptance	88.2	88.2
Intention	8.6	12.2
Action	20.9	22.8

sage at a previous event, they were asked whether they had taken any action as a result. Respondents' stated thoughts were analysed and those who expressed an intention to take action as a result of exposure to the message were identified. Action (and intention) includes any actions (or intentions) related to the message, not just adoption and continuation of the recommended behaviour. It also includes not only personal actions, but also those related to encouraging others to adopt or continue a recommended behaviour. Table 12.1 shows the cognitive impact measures as a proportion of each preceding level in the hierarchy.

Total awareness of the sponsored health messages at events increased significantly from 67.2 per cent in 1992/3 to 75.8 per cent in 1996/7 (p <0.05). Respondents were asked what they thought the message meant. Message comprehension among respondents who were aware of the sponsored message increased slightly in 1996/7 from an already high level: 90.0 per cent (compared with 82.2 per cent in 1992/3). Acceptance of the message among those who were aware of and correctly understood the message remained high in 1996/7: 88.2 per cent (compared with 88.2 per cent in 1992/3).

Intention to act on the message increased, but not significantly: of respondents who agreed with the message 12.2 per cent (compared with 8.6 per cent in 1992/3) mentioned that they would or wanted to do the recommended behaviour. Respondents who were aware of the sponsored message at a previous event were asked what they did, if anything, as a result of being aware of the health message. In both 1992/3 and 1996/7 approximately one in five of these respondents took some relevant action (20.9 per cent and 22.8 per cent respectively).

Multiplying the preceding proportions down the hierarchy of measures provides an estimate of the percentage of the total sample who were sufficiently stimulated to take some relevant action as a result of exposure to a health message. For the total sample in 1996/7 this was 1.7 per cent (that is, 75.8 per cent × 68.2 per cent × 60.2 per cent × 12.2 per cent × 22.8 per cent = 1.7 per cent). This hierarchical multiplicative exercise shows the importance of achieving high levels of effects early in the hierarchy. Thus, the higher the level of awareness that can be achieved, the greater the likelihood of achieving behaviour change in the target group. These data show a substantial increase in action over

Figure 12.6 Results of the cognitive impact measures as a proportion of the total sample (%)

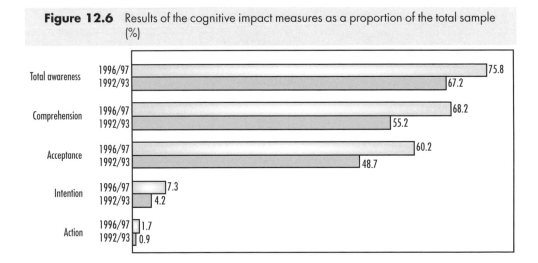

previous years (1.7 per cent compared with 0.9 per cent) and probably reflect the cumulative effect of many of these or related messages now having been seen for a number of years at the same types of events.

The results for the hierarchy of cognitive responses for both 1996/7 and 1992/3 are shown in figure 12.6 as a proportion of the total sample, that is, of all people attending Healthway sponsored events, 75.8 per cent were aware of a Healthway-sponsored message at the event, 68.2 per cent correctly understood the message, 60.2 per cent accepted or agreed with the message, 7.3 per cent formed some intention to act on the message, and 1.7 per cent claimed to have taken some action as a result of prior exposure.

With respect to process evaluation these data show that the sponsorship messages are receiving good exposure at events and that the health messages used are well understood and accepted by event patrons. These are clearly necessary prerequisites for persuasion and subsequent behaviour change. Intentions to act on the health messages and behavioural outcomes are also acceptable and show an increase from 1992/3 to 1996/7. While the absolute numbers are small commercial organisations would be quite happy to achieve behavioural effects in 1–2 per cent of the target audience (Rossiter & Percy 1997).

The marked increases of cognitive effects achieved for all stages in the hierarchy are likely to be related to increased exposure of audiences to health messages over time combined with more effective sponsorship strategies.

Field studies measuring awareness and attitudinal effects

Awareness (salience) effects

Donovan et al. (1993) showed that the first mentioned 'way of preventing heart disease' varied as to whether respondents had been exposed to a 'be active' versus a 'fruit'n'veg' sponsorship. The study was a quasi-experimental field design. The National Heart Foundation was the support sponsor to the State Theatre for a season of plays. The NHF chose two health messages to be featured during the season: 'Be active every day' and 'Eat more Fruit'n'Veg'. The nutrition slogan was allocated to one play and the exercise slogan to another (both slogans were promoted at a third play). Face-to-face interviews were conducted as people left the theatre. Prior to any questions about health or sponsorship respondents were asked, 'When you think of ways to prevent heart disease, what comes to mind?'. When 'be active' was the health message, exercise responses were first to mind for 49 per cent of the sample (15 per cent responded with nutrition responses); when fruit'n'veg was the health message, nutrition responses were first to mind for 50 per cent of the sample (26 per cent responded with exercise responses).

Attitudinal effects

Donovan et al. (1993) used a pre–post independent samples design to assess attitude effects of a health sponsor (Quit) and two commercial sponsors (a bank and a motor vehicle) at a major sporting event. Respondents in both pre and post interviews were presented, in turn, with a set of banks and a set of motor vehicles and asked, 'If you were going to [buy a new car; open a new bank account], which of these would you be most interested in receiving more information about? And next most? And next?' Respondents also were presented with a set of health behaviours and asked, 'If you were interested in becoming more healthy, which of these would you most like more information on? And next most? And next?' The behaviours included quitting smoking or assisting someone else to do so, diet, exercise, and relaxation.

The Quit sponsorship showed a near-significant pre–post increase in the proportion nominating smoking behaviour (first preference, 10.4–17.6 per cent), the car sponsor obtained a non-significant increase in pre–post preferences (first preference: 13.5–20.0 per cent), but there was no change in preferences for the bank sponsor. There was a positive relationship between sponsor recall and sponsorship impact: Quit was recalled as a sponsor by 40 per cent compared with 33 per cent for the car sponsor and 26 per cent for the bank sponsor. Donovan et al. (1993) concluded that sheer exposure to the Quit sponsorship appeared to result in a situational temporary increase in positive attitudes towards attempting to quit or encouraging someone else to do so.

Further field studies were conducted to extend the Donovan et al. (1993) study by measuring sponsorship effects on both awareness and attitudes and by investigating the cognitive processing that occurs as a result (Jalleh 1999). A pre–post independent samples design was used to assess sponsorship effectiveness in terms of awareness and attitude objectives at an Australian Rules football event. To allow assessment of both awareness and attitude effects without prior questions contaminating later measures, two pre and two post samples were taken at the event. One health and two commercial sponsors were assessed at the event: Respect Yourself (an alcohol moderation message) and two commercial sponsors, Holden and ANZ Bank. Only male drinkers aged 18–30 years were interviewed at the football as they are the major target group for the Respect Yourself message. Each of the evaluated sponsors had approximately the same area of perimeter and other signage at the event.

Face-to-face intercept interviewing of patrons was carried out by professional market research interviewers. Interviewers were assigned to specific locations at the venues and were given instructions on the selection of respondents so as to ensure, as far as possible, a random sample of patrons (HPEU 1998). Pre interviews were carried out prior to entry to the event. Post interviews were carried out in the venues from half time to the end of the event. Two sets of pre and post questionnaires were developed. One set of pre and post questionnaires focused on awareness, the other on attitude measures.

A recall (salience) measure was used to assess brand awareness: 'When you think of (cars, banks, alcohol) what (brands, banks, health messages or slogans) come to mind? Any others? Any others?' In both the pre and post awareness questionnaires these questions were asked immediately after the preliminary screening questions. Order of presentation of brand or health issue was rotated across respondents.

The brand attitude measure followed that of Donovan et al. (1993). Respondents in both pre and post conditions were presented, in turn, with a set of seven banks (including the ANZ) and a set of six motor vehicle manufacturers (including Holden) and asked, 'If you were going to [open a new bank account, buy a new car] which of these would you be most interested in receiving more information about? And next most? And next?' Respondents were also presented with a set of six health behaviours and asked, 'If you were interested in becoming more healthy, which of these would you most like more information on? And next most? And next?' The behaviours included quitting smoking, assisting someone to quit smoking, reducing alcohol consumption, nutrition, exercising, and relaxation methods. Order of presentation of brand or health issue was rotated across respondents. In both the pre and post attitude questionnaires these questions were asked immediately after the preliminary screening questions. A total of 400 football patrons was interviewed for the attitude study: pre, n = 204 and post, n = 196.

Awareness change

These was no impact on levels of awareness for the Holden and ANZ Bank football sponsorships, but a significant impact for the Respect Yourself sponsorship for both first mentions (pre, 28.4 per cent, post, 43.7 per cent; p = .002) and all mentions (pre, 42.7 per cent, post, 58.2 per cent; p = .003).

Pre-post awareness for sponsored brands and health message

Figure 12.7a Results

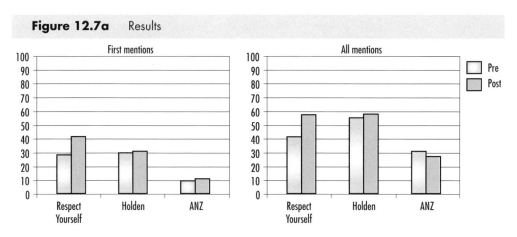

Attitude change

There was no impact on attitude for the Holden sponsorship, a significant impact for the ANZ bank sponsorship in terms of first preferences (pre: 9.8 per cent, post: 17.3 per cent; p=.027), and a significant impact for the Respect Yourself sponsorship for both first preferences (pre: 1.5 per cent, post: 8.2 per cent; p=.002) and top three preferences (pre: 17.6 per cent, post: 25.5 per cent; p=.056).

Pre-post preferences for sponsored brands and health message

Figure 12.7b Results

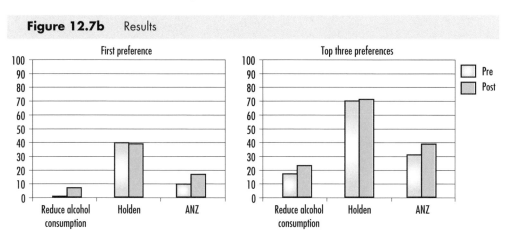

The apparently greater impact of the health message may be due, at least in part, to the scarcity of health messages at these events. Respect Yourself was the only health message promoted at the football. At both venues, while the commercial brand names were the only ones in their respective product categories, there were numerous other commercial sponsors. Furthermore, since health sponsorships began in the early 1990s they may still be a novelty and, as such, attract more attention relative to commercial sponsorships.

The superiority of the health sponsorships over the commercial sponsorships also may be due to the implementation of the sponsorships. The health sponsor was more enthusiastic and leveraged their sponsorship more through promotional strategies such as distributing merchandise. Furthermore, Healthway has negotiated the supply and prominent display of low-alcohol beer in bars at the football venue. In addition, Respect Yourself sponsors the Dockers football team in the Australian Football League. In contrast the commercial sponsors did not engage in any activities other than signage.

Hence, sponsorship can have a significant impact on awareness and attitude objectives; however, this impact appears dependent on how the sponsorship is implemented.

Field studies measuring behavioural effects

Quasi-experimental field studies are also used to assess behavioural effects. For example, as reported in chapter 6, observational data were collected at three junior sporting codes (rugby union, basketball, Australian Rules football) before and after a mouthguard sponsorship. The sponsorship was implemented in the rugby and basketball competitions, with the football serving as control. The sponsorship involved partnerships with dental organisations, which offered high-quality mouthguards at reduced prices. At both competition events and training sessions all players present on particular dates were inspected to see whether they were wearing a mouthguard. Face-to-face surveys of a sample of players and coaches were also undertaken to assess awareness of the sponsorship. Results showed a significant increase in mouthguard usage in competition events among both intervention codes (rugby, 77–84 per cent; basketball, 23–43 per cent) relative to the football controls (72–73 per cent) (Jalleh et al. 2001).

Using sponsorship to achieve structural change (Giles-Corti et al. 2001)

An important benefit for health sponsors is the implementation of policies that create healthier recreational and cultural environments. This is equivalent to a commercial sponsor's merchandising agreements. It involves, for example, depending on the nature of the venue and type of event, the introduction of smoke-free areas, sun protection, healthy food choices, and, where alcohol is served, policies favouring the sale of low- to mid-strength products, as well as the implementation of responsible serving practices.

Theoretical underpinnings

Working with other sectors to create health-enhancing environments in settings commonly used by people in the course of their daily lives is consistent with a social ecological approach to public health (McLeroy, Bibeau, Steckler & Glanz 1988; Stokols, Allen & Bellingham 1996). It acknowledges that individual behaviour change is more likely to be sustained if it takes place in supportive social and physical environments. This is because of a dynamic interplay between observable behaviour, an individual's cognitive response, and physical and social environments.

Why promote health in recreational settings?

Promoting health in recreational settings provides opportunities to reach hard-to-reach groups in the community (Olsen 1999). There is substantial evidence that large numbers of Australians regularly access these settings and many have elevated risk factors compared with the general population. This was particularly evident with those attending sports events, but also in those attending arts events for selected risk factor areas (for example, alcohol consumption) (for more details see Holman, Donovan, Corti & Jalleh 1997a). A review of national health policy reports found that many referred to the potential role that recreational or cultural settings could play in achieving national health goals, including injury, alcohol consumption, nutrition, sun protection, and passive smoking (NHMRC 1997a).

Healthway's main objective is related to tobacco control. To date Healthway has successfully negotiated for the main areas of the football, speedway, baseball, and soccer venues to be smoke-free—even substantial portions of outdoor seating areas.

Achieving healthy public policy reform involves a process of diffusion (Rogers 1983) which, in recreational settings in Western Australia, moved sport, arts, and racing groups along a continuum of change. At each stage of the diffusion process different strategies were required. Initially, as part of the sponsor benefit negotiations, Healthway requested the creation of smoke-free areas. However, these policies were expanded as sponsorship agreements were renegotiated to require organisations to become completely smoke-free. In 1996 Healthway's board voted in favour of making it a condition of sponsorship that all indoor areas under the control of the sponsored organisation must be smoke-free. This decision made way for Healthway to negotiate additional sponsor benefits, such as policies to serve low- or mid-strength beers in favour of full-strength beers.

Figure 12.8 Billboard at the baseball

A number of studies have shown that these policies have been effective. For example, following the introduction of a policy banning smoking in all indoor and outdoor seated areas at the home ground for two Western Australia-based national football teams sponsored by Healthway, spectator surveys were conducted to determine awareness of, agreement with, and support for the smoke-free venue policies (Jones, Corti & Donovan 1996). Approximately three-quarters of spectators were aware of the policy (74.1 per cent), and the vast majority of those aware of the policy were supportive (82.5 per cent). There were high levels of awareness or support of the policy in both smokers and non-smokers. In 1998 a similar survey was conducted. Awareness of the smoke-free policy increased to 81.4 per cent of respondents and the vast majority of those aware of the policy were supportive (almost 80 per cent).

To assess the extent to which smoke-free policies at sporting events were implemented and adhered to two observational studies were conducted (Pikora, Phang, Karro et al. 1999). One was conducted at Subiaco Oval, Perth's premier football oval, in 1997 and the other at the WACA, Perth's premier cricket ground, in 1998. These two major venues had introduced smoke-free policies in indoor and outdoor seated areas as a result of Healthway sponsorship. Some 4616 people were observed at Subiaco Oval and 3596 at the WACA. Using binoculars observers systematically scanned spectators seated in randomly selected smoke-free areas throughout the grounds to determine adherence to the policy. Table 12.2 shows the results of the observations. As can be seen there was a high level of compliance with the smoke-free policies at both events, suggesting that the policies were implemented and adhered to.

Mail surveys were conducted in mid 1992 (n = 269), 1994 (n = 511), and 1997 (n = 536) (Clarkson, Corti, Pikora, Jalleh & Donovan 1998) of all sport, arts, and racing organisations that had commenced Healthway-funded projects during the previous 12 months. Response rates of 91.3 per cent, 78.0 per cent, and 83.5 per cent respectively were achieved. Among other things organisations

Table 12.2 Results of observational studies, 1998

	Subiaco Oval	WACA
Estimated number of people in the study area	4616	3596
Estimated number of smokers in the study area*	969	539
Number observed smoking in study area	8	0
Number of butts found in the study area before the game	0	0
Number of butts found in the study area after the game	6	2

* Based on spectator surveys of those entering the venue

were asked whether they had introduced policies restricting smoking. As shown in table 12.3 the percentage of organisations reporting a smoke-free policy increased significantly between 1994 and 1997 (p <0.001).

Table 12.3 Smoke free policies in place in the majority of venues used by sport, arts, and racing organisations sponsored by Healthway, 1992–7

Year	n	%
1992[a]	118	77.1
1994	292	85.9
1997	434	95.6[b]

[a] Percentages for 1992 may overrepresent Healthway's influence because it includes policies within organisations and/or in the majority of venues they use.
[b] Compared with 1994: ***$p < 0.001$.

Community surveys were conducted in mid 1992 (n = 2629), 1994 (n = 2009), and 1998 (n = 1337) and involved randomly selected members of the general population aged 16–69 (Clarkson, Donovan, Giles-Corti, Bulsara & Jalleh 2000). Personal interviews were used in the metropolitan area and telephone interviews were used in country areas with the sample being based on randomly selected listed and unlisted private numbers. A quota was applied to ensure equal numbers of male and female respondents. One of the topics included access to smoke-free policies in the principal sport, racing, or arts clubs to which respondents belonged.

In 1992, 29 per cent of respondents reported that their club was entirely smoke-free and a further 11 per cent reported that the club was mostly smoke-free with special smoking areas (see table 12.4). In 1994 these proportions increased to 36 per cent and 16 per cent respectively; in 1998 they increased to 41 per cent and 25 per cent respectively. The trend towards entirely smoke-free sport, arts, and racing clubs was statistically significant (χ^2 test for trend =10.03, p = 0.001).

Comment on structural impact studies

These studies indicate that, with financial resources initially generated by a levy on tobacco products and an understanding of the process of bringing about

Table 12.4   Smoke-free area policies present in the main sport or racing club or arts organisation in which community members involved in 1992, 1994 and 1998

Smoke-free area policies	All Respondents					
	n			%		
	1992 1059	1994 755	1998 506	1992	1994	1998
No smoking allowed anywhere	302	265	205	29	36	41
No smoking, except for special smoking areas	119	122	126	11	16	25
Smoking allowed except for special non-smoking areas	98	60	41	9	8	8
Smoking allowed anywhere	528	295	126	50	40	25
Don't know	–	–	3	–	–	–
Not applicable/missing	–	–	5	–	–	–

change in organisations, health organisations can purchase healthy structural reform in sectors outside of health.

Consistent with international (Jeffery, Forster, Schmid et al. 1990) and national research (Jones, Wakefield & Turnbull 1999), the results indicate that the introduction of smoke-free policies may change community norms about smoking in public. Earlier surveys of smoking and non-smoking spectators at football events indicated that there was little support for the introduction of smoke-free policies in outdoor areas. However, following the introduction of these policies in Western Australia's premier football stadium, support among spectators for the smoke-free policies increased markedly, particularly among non-smokers who have most to gain from a reduction in exposure to passive smoking. The successful introduction of smoke-free policies may indeed normalise non-smoking within recreational and cultural settings.

The extent to which smoking restrictions in recreational settings contributes to a reduction in smoking is not clear. Studies conducted in the USA and Australia indicate that policies restricting smoking in the workplace (Farkas, Gilpin, Distenfan & Pierce 1999; Farrelly, Evans & Sfekas 1999; Owen & Borland 1997) and in households (Farkas et al. 1999) are associated with a reduction in smoking by smokers and lower rates of smoking by adolescents (Farkas, Gilpin, White & Pierce 2000). Although there is some evidence that the impact of smoking restrictions may diminish over time (Owen & Borland 1997), it appears that in the long term the net result is a reduction in cigarette consumption. While the direct influence on smokers of smoke-free policies in recreational settings remains unknown, it is likely these policies create supportive environments and positive social norms for non-smoking behaviours.

Giles-Corti et al. (2001) suggest that lessons from Healthway's experience have wider application, particularly in developing countries where the tobacco industry actively uses tobacco advertising and sponsorship to market tobacco products (Reynolds 1999; Hu 1997).

Healthway's approach to achieving reform in recreational and cultural settings is instructive and may be applied elsewhere. First, it involved working collaboratively with other agencies, including those in the health, recreational, and cultural sectors. Second, it involved a small wins incremental approach (Weick 1984) that increased the prevalence of smoke-free policies while at the same time gaining the support of various stakeholders, including the general public. Third, it involved comprehensive evaluation of its sponsorship activities, including community attitudes towards reform. Finally, it involved communicating evaluation results to all stakeholders.

Concluding comment

Since the use of health and commercial sponsorships will continue to grow, more research is required to build the knowledge base of how sponsorship works and sponsorship's impact on those exposed to it. Overall, a number of studies provide evidence that health sponsorships have an impact on awareness of health issues, attitudes towards various healthy behaviours, and on intentions and behaviour; however, this impact appears dependent on how the sponsorship is implemented.

You can't just buy a sponsorship and let it work by itself because all you've done is buy the potential ... it's like buying the air time and then not putting the ad on ... you have to go and make it work.

Graeme Hannan, New South Wales General Manager, International Management Group (Berich 1995, cited in Jalleh and Donovan 2000).

Chapter 13

Planning and Developing Social Marketing Campaigns

Introduction

This chapter attempts to bring together the various elements that have been discussed in the preceding chapters. It involves applying general principles of planning to the identification of needs and the development of strategies to meet these needs.

A number of planning models have been described or proposed in the social marketing and health promotion literature. Perhaps the simplest distillation is that below (after Green 1999).

According to Green (1999), phase 1 implies an epidemiological approach to identifying populations at risk and determining needs overall. In the health area this is reflected in Australia's defined health priorities. In phase 2 both behavioural (for example, alcohol, tobacco, physical inactivity, diet, unsafe driving behaviours) and structural (for example, poor housing, unemployment, unsafe work environments) risk factors are identified, along with Green's predisposing, enabling, and reinforcing factors (Green & Kreuter 1999). Phase 3 attempts to bring about changes in the determinants of the behaviours and conditions being

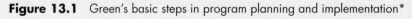

Figure 13.1   Green's basic steps in program planning and implementation*

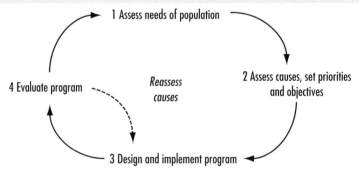

* **Green 1999,** with permission, from the Annual Review of Public Health, Volume 20, 1999 by Annual Reviews, <www.annualreviews.org>.

Figure 13.2 AED's basic steps in program planning and implementation*

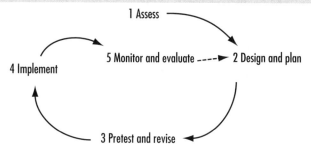

*Day & Monroe 2000

targeted, hence delivering the desired social outcomes. Evaluation of programs leads eventually to reassessments in phase 1 and, in the short term, to reassessment of program components and assessments in phase 2 (Green 1999).

Based apparently on a model from the Center for Communications Programs at Johns Hopkins University, the Academy for Educational Development (AED), Washington DC uses a similar framework to that in figure 13.1 (see figure 13.2) (Day & Monroe 2000; Graeff, Elder & Booth 1993).

Egger, Donovan & Spark (1993) elaborate these phases by delineating the general steps in planning:

1 collection and analysis of current and historical data
2 setting objectives
3 devising overall strategies
4 developing methods, materials, and intervention designs
5 reassessment of resources
6 finalising program procedures
7 implementation
8 monitoring the implementation process and revision where necessary
9 evaluation.

They then distil these nine stages into the five phases which take the acronym **SOPIE:**

■ situational analysis
■ objective setting
■ planning
■ implementation
■ evaluation

An important point is that all models stress that planning is an iterative process whereby objectives, strategies, and methods are continually revised in light of what is viable given such things as the nature and extent of the problem, the nature and accessibility of the target audience(s), and the limitations of financial and other resources.

Walsh, Rudd, Moeykens, and Moloney (1993) explored the social marketing literature, reviewed applications of social marketing in a number of areas, and conducted interviews with practitioners and scholars in the field. They identified the nine elements in table 13.1 as the bases for developing a comprehensive social marketing program over three phases: research and planning, strategy design, and implementation and evaluation. However, their process appears to start after the needs assessment has been done.

Table 13.1 sums up virtually all of the elements we would want to discuss, although some might argue about the sequencing of some of these elements. For example, we may want to form partnerships (that is, enlist collaborators, in phase III) much earlier, probably in phase I. In the *Freedom from Fear* campaign (chapter 15) it was in fact essential to ensure at least tentative collaboration from some key stakeholders before any planning went ahead.

One point we would add is the need to maintain political support for campaigns with long-term outcomes. This should be built in to the implementation phase. It is vital to brief and support incoming ministers and heads of department when changes occur in cabinet or in governing parties.

The PRECEDE-PROCEED model

No chapter on planning would be complete without including Lawrence Green's PRECEDE–PROCEED model, probably the most widely used planning model in the health promotion literature and in practice. A recent survey of members of the Australian Health Promotion Association found that PRECEDE–PROCEED was the model most frequently used for program planning and implementation (Jones & Donovan 2003).

The model is shown in figure 13.3. The value of Green's model (which has undergone a number of modifications since first presented as just PRECEDE) is that it makes explicit that the factors analysed in the planning and development phases (the PRECEDE phases) are the same factors to be considered in the implementation and evaluation phases (PROCEED).

PRECEDE is an acronym for predisposing, reinforcing, and enabling constructs in educational (and environmental) diagnosis and evaluation. Ross Spark, who applied the model to his PhD thesis on health promotion in Indigenous communities, provides the comments below on the model. According to Spark (1999) the PRECEDE framework was novel in that it focused on outcomes rather than inputs, forcing the health practitioner to begin the planning process from the outcome end. It was also comprehensive in that each of the five phases in PRECEDE allows a different layer of diagnosis: social, epidemiological, behavioural, educational, and administrative.

During the decade following the publication of PRECEDE there was an acknowledgment in the international public health community that health education, with its emphasis on behavioural or lifestyle-related choices and individually oriented programs, was neglecting the importance of social factors in the aetiology of many diseases. This was crystallised in the declaration of the *Ottawa Charter for Health Promotion* at a World Health Organization-sponsored

Table 13.1   Elements of the social marketing process*

Exhibit 1
Description of Social Marketing Process Elements

Social marketing process elements	Description of activities
Phase I: Research and planning	
Planning	Specifically realistic and measurable objectives Establish checkpoints for making go/no-go decisions Review existing research and map out a program prototype Select outcomes measures to judge progress and success
Consumer analysis	Conduct and analyze qualitative and/or quantitative consumer research Identify population segments of interest for whom the program may be most effective Study consumer motivational and resistance points
Market analysis	Designate the marketing mix (product, price, place, and promotion) Examine the fit between the chosen target group and the current product Analyze the market environment to identify competitors and allies
Channel analysis	Examine communication channels to determine which are best suited for reaching the target audience and achieving program goals Assess available vehicles to distribute the product Consider which organisations or institutions might collaborate
Phase II: Strategy design	
Development of marketing mix strategy	Translate the marketing mix into a program strategy by developing the product, generating methods of reducing the price (or increasing the benefits), selecting the place or system of distribution, and specifying the means of promotion Test the concepts and product prototypes with the target group Market test the strategy in a circumscribed area and refine as needed
Communication	Clarify ideas and information and develop pilot messages Test concepts and message strategies with the target group and refine Produce communication materials, testing and refining them as needed
Phase III: Implementation and evaluation	
Implementation	Enlist collaborators, clarifying the nature of their involvement and securing their commitment Train key players in executing the program and in product/service delivery Activate communication and distribution
Process evaluation	Assess quality of target group exposure to program communications Evaluate the delivery of the product or service Obtain data on use of the product (reasons for using/not using) Modify the product offerings or distribution and communication systems in response to consumer feedback
Outcome evaluation	Consider threats to the validity of research methodology and the degree to which the program assessment conforms to rigorous program evaluation design Assess program impact through statistical comparisons using preselected outcome measures Estimate cost-effectiveness of program

* Walsh et al 1993

Figure 13.3 The PRECEDE–PROCEED model for health promotion planning and evaluation (Green & Kreuter, 1991)*

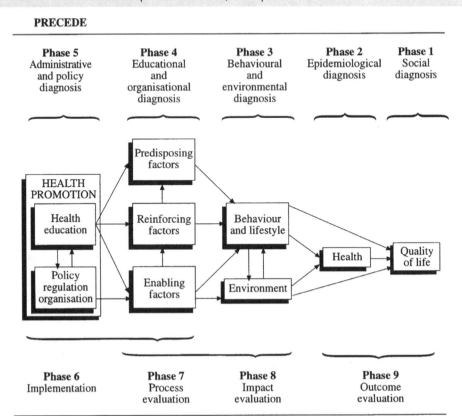

PRECEDE

Phase 5	Phase 4	Phase 3	Phase 2	Phase 1
Administrative and policy diagnosis	Educational and organisational diagnosis	Behavioural and environmental diagnosis	Epidemiological diagnosis	Social diagnosis

Phase 6	Phase 7	Phase 8	Phase 9
Implementation	Process evaluation	Impact evaluation	Outcome evaluation

PROCEED

* Reproduced with permission of the McGraw-Hill Companies.

conference in 1986 in Ottawa, Canada. The *Ottawa Charter* described five principles for health promotion action as the basis for a new public health: strengthening community action, developing personal skills, building healthy public policy, reorienting health services, and creating supportive environments (World Health Organization 1986).

Reflecting this broadened scope, Green amended the PRECEDE model to give greater emphasis to environmental factors and expanded it to include PROCEED, an acronym for **p**olicy, **r**egulatory and **o**rganisational constructs in educational and environmental development. PROCEED includes resource mobilisation and evaluation and is essentially an elaboration and extension of the administrative diagnosis phase of PRECEDE. Overall, the addition of PRO-CEED to the original model gave greater emphasis to the contribution of structural factors and community organisation processes to program implementation.

The social diagnosis involves assessing people's perceptions of their own needs and how the issue at hand impacts on their quality of life. For example, asthmatics and diabetics face certain restrictions on their lifestyle, have to comply with a medication schedule, and have to visit a medical practitioner more often than average. The epidemiological analysis identifies the relative importance of various health problems in various subgroups of the population, and the behavioural and environmental factors related to those health problems. For example, young males account for a higher proportion of road crashes than do other groups; alcohol, speed, and not wearing a seat belt are related to crashes, severity of injury, and mortality. Phases 1 and 2 correspond to the needs assessment phases in figures 13.1 and 13.2.

The behavioural and environmental analysis analyses in more depth the factors arising from epidemiological analyses as well as behaviours and environmental aspects that may arise from clinical or other evidence. In road safety, use of seat belts, driver education, driver skills, exceeding the speed limit, driving while tired, vehicular modifications, roadworthiness of vehicles, road conditions, and placement of warning signs, all require analysis in terms of such things as how important are they, how changeable are they, and what resources are required to change them.

The educational and organisational diagnosis is the heart of the model: it identifies the factors that must be changed to initiate or facilitate the desired behaviour and environmental changes. These factors then become the targets for the program. The model proposes three types of factors:

- *predisposing factors*—individuals' beliefs, attitudes, and perceptions that influence their decision to act (for example, a belief that alcohol increases feelings of wellbeing and reduces one's shyness predisposes one to consume alcohol; a belief that alcohol is a poison or may lead to loss of control predisposes one to not consume alcohol)
- *reinforcing factors*—environmental factors that serve to reward or punish expression of the behaviour (for example, friends' approval of one's speeding or drinking alcohol serves to reinforce the behaviour; a parent's clear disapproval of drug use serves to inhibit that behaviour)
- *enabling factors*—individual and environmental factors that make a behaviour possible (or not possible) to occur (for example, having time and money facilitates joining a health club, smoke-free policies facilitate smoking cessation) (that is, skills, resources, support policies and services).

Following research with respect to drink driving with male drivers in the Great Southern Region of Western Australia, NFO Donovan Research (Batini & Donovan 2001) proposed the following classification of factors as influencing drink driving in rural areas.

Predisposing factors

Convenience

Most believe that it is simply easier to drive than seek alternatives. They believe it is easier to drive home than collect their car the next day (includes fear of damage to or theft of car if left overnight).

Figure 13.4 Transperth's new timetables—enabling public transport use

Cultural acceptance

Rather than being morally unacceptable behaviour, drinking and driving is very much seen as being culturally acceptable—the actual social norm in their towns. However, they do distinguish between the terms 'drinking and driving' and 'drunk driving', the latter being generally considered far less acceptable.

Personal safety

In some towns many were fearful of being assaulted while walking home after having consumed alcohol.

Enabling factors

Lack of enforcement

Most participants knew that the police cannot be everywhere all the time. Many knew when the police knock off for the evening. High-profile blitzes (for example, booze bus, RBT stop) are highly visible and easily avoided (via the bush telegraph). There was a known lack of funding for regular patrols and a perception that if they have got away with it before they can get away with it again.

Lack of public transport

For many there are simply no (or very limited) public transport options, particularly within the smaller towns. In addition, those living out of town cite the distance as being too far to walk (30 kilometres, 50 kilometres, etc.).

Reinforcing factors

Expense of alternatives

Many are reluctant to pay the fare for a 30–50 kilometre taxi ride—often viewed as a 'waste of good drinking money'.

Confidence

While aware of the 0.05 limit many feel perfectly capable of driving above this limit, citing that they have 'driven from an early age on the farm' and have the 'ability to handle country roads'. Others try to drive more 'carefully' after drinking (for example, slower, concentrate more, etc.). There is a perception that if they have been able to successfully drive home after consuming alcohol before, they can do it again.

Administrative and policy diagnosis

The educational and organisational analysis identifies what needs to be done. The next phase looks at how it can be done.

Administrative and policy diagnosis involves assessing resources and looking at educational, motivational and regulatory alternatives for influencing the factors identified in phase 4. It involves establishing intersectoral collaboration where necessary and developing relationships with intermediaries.

Planning and designing the intervention are an outcome of phases 1–5, along with setting of process, impact, and outcome objectives. Implementation (phase 6) can include pretesting of methods and materials, perhaps even carrying out efficacy (or pilot) trials of the intervention. Process, impact, and outcome evaluation were covered in chapter 6. Process evaluation should be ongoing to ensure that timelines are met and to enable valid assessments of impact and outcomes (for example, failure to meet attitudinal and behavioural objectives might be due to non-delivery of communication materials, call analyses might reveal that only 20 per cent of calls to a helpline are being answered before the caller hangs up).

Applying PRECEDE–PROCEED to increasing fruit and vegetable consumption

In chapter 10 we referred to the Black Churches United for Better Health Project ('Praise the Lord and pass the fruit'n'veg'). Campbell et al (1999) used the PRECEDE–PROCEED model to develop a set of activities (their marketing mix) based on the predisposing, enabling, and reinforcing factors they identified as determinants of fruit and vegetable consumption and, ultimately, cancer incidence.

They report the following activities to address predisposing factors.
* *Tailored bulletins*—each individual received personalised, tailored messages and feedback based on questionnaire data with respect to their beliefs, attitudes and current behaviours, barriers, social support, and stage of change.
* *Printed materials*—monthly packages of brochures, posters, banners, idea sheets, and church bulletin inserts were provided to each church's Nutrition Action Team (church members recruited by the pastor to organise and implement activities).

The following activities addressed enabling factors.
* *Gardening*—churches were encouraged to plant fruit and vegetable gardens; training was available for master gardeners. (One program in Queensland encouraged schools to plant gardens as a way of creating and sustaining positive attitudes towards fruit and vegetables consumption; Viola 2002.)
* *Educational sessions*—Nutrition Action Team members attended educational sessions and were trained to conduct cooking sessions showing how to achieve five-a-day guidelines.
* *Cookbook and recipe tasting*—a trained cookbook person in each church showed members how to modify their favourite recipes to meet the five-a-day guidelines and conducted taste tests on the modified products. Recipes were included in a cookbook distributed to all participants.
* *Serving more fruit and vegetables at church functions*—a 'practice what you preach' orientation was encouraged to enable more trial of fruit and vegetable dishes

The following activities addressed reinforcing factors.
* *Lay health advisors*—natural helpers were identified and trained in topics such as social support and assisting others to advance through the stages of change.
* *Community coalitions*—each county formed a coalition of relevant stakeholders, such as local grocers, farmers, and church members, who received training in community action and organised community events.
* *Pastor support*—pastors were encouraged to promote the campaign in their sermons and church announcements, received a newsletter keeping them informed of all activities, reviewed educational materials, and were involved in generating tailored messages.
* Grocer–vendor involvement—promotional materials, such as recipe cards, coupons, and farmer's market posters, were distributed to church members and local stores.

Concluding comments

Planning and designing social marketing interventions follows a logical commonsense sequence. However, it is important to remember that subsequent stages can only be as good as the preceding stages. Hence, the needs assessment stage is the most important of all. Bearing this in mind, remember that stages are not reversible. The process is iterative and recursive, with later stages also informing earlier stages, especially evident when pretesting of methods and materials begins. Finally, no social marketing program, no matter how successful in achieving its objectives, is immune from political interference. Program planning should therefore include a political contingencies component.

Chapter 14

Two Case Studies: the Immunise Australia program[1] and TravelSmart®[2]

The Immunise Australia program

Introduction—The problem

The case study presented here represents the application of social marketing theory and practice to increase the levels of full age-appropriate childhood immunisation as part of the Immunise Australia program.

A significant proportion of Australian children were not being immunised in accordance with the schedule recommended by Australia's National Health and Medical Research Council. In 1995 an Australian Bureau of Statistics survey found that only 33 per cent of Australian children aged up to 6 years were fully immunised according to the schedule being recommended at the time and 52 per cent fully immunised according to the previous schedule (Australian Bureau Statistics 1996).

In response to this situation the Australian government formulated the Immunise Australia program. This program comprised a number of initiatives, including:

- improvements to immunisation practice and service delivery (product and place)
- establishment of a National Centre for Immunisation Research and Surveillance
- negotiation with state and territory governments to introduce requirements for immunisation prior to commencing school (regulatory factor)
- financial incentives for doctors, parents and guardians (price and intermediaries)

---

1 The Immunise Australia case is based on Carroll (1997) and other information provided by Tom E. Carroll, PhD, Social Marketing Consultant and Principal, Carroll Communications, New South Wales, Australia, and Laurie Van Veen, Director, Population Health Social Marketing Unit, Australian Department of Health and Ageing, Woden, ACT, Australia.
2 The TravelSmart® case is based on James (2002) and other information provided by Bruce James, Acting Executive Director, Metropolitan Department of Transport, Perth, Western Australia, <www.travelsmart.transport.wa.gov.au>.

- a national childhood immunisation education campaign (product information)
- a specific measles control campaign (product).

While recognising the key role played by structural and policy reform within the formulation and implementation of a social marketing strategy this chapter will primarily focus on the community education components of this program.

A social marketing approach

The contribution of a social marketing approach (Lefebvre & Flora 1988; Andreasen 1995) to designing strategies to increase population immunisation levels has been previously recognised in the Australian context (Nutbeam 1991; Donovan & Robinson 1992). Mass media campaigns supported by community level activities and longer-term reminder systems and incorporating service provider strategies appeared to offer good potential (Bazeley & Kemp 1994). The application of social marketing principles, and particularly the role of formative research, is illustrated through the development of the Immunise Australia Community Education Campaign and its comprehensive, integrated implementation.

Formative research

One of the key roles for formative research was to gain an understanding of the perceived costs and benefits associated with parents taking their children along to be immunised. In social marketing terms this relates to understanding the dynamics of the exchange that the social marketing program will be seeking to achieve. That is, what will parents and carers consider the range of costs— including psychological, emotional, time, and financial costs—involved in having their child immunised and what will they perceive as the benefits of paying these costs?

Because of the greater likelihood that mothers take primary responsibility for children's health care in Australian families, the primary target audience for the campaign, and hence for the formative research, were mothers of children up to the age of 5 years. Recognising a number of subsegments within this target audience, research samples included first-time mothers, mothers with additional children, and mothers from a range of socioeconomic backgrounds in metropolitan and regional areas throughout Australia. Qualitative research methodologies (primarily, focus groups and individual depth interviews) were employed because of their strength in allowing indepth exploration of attitudes and motivations.

Key findings from formative research (Carroll 1997)

It was evident that while most women expressed their support for childhood immunisation when asked, many did not perceive a high level of personal relevance or urgency in the issue. This was related to the fact that many had never seen children suffering the diseases that the vaccinations were designed to protect their children from.

Mothers were generally aware of the diseases against which children could be immunised, but had low levels of specific knowledge of these diseases and low perceptions of seriousness regarding getting these diseases. They also had low awareness of the particular details of the recommended immunisation schedule. Many mothers reportedly were not immunising against measles because it was often thought of as a fairly benign disease; the danger of pertussis (whooping cough) was typically underestimated in comparison to the perceptions of the risks of immunisation. Parents' perception of the seriousness of polio was partly due to memories of common permanent disabilities in the previous generation. Diphtheria was perceived as a frightening disease but knowledge of what the disease actually entailed was very low.

Furthermore, respondents' spontaneous associations with the act of immunisation were quite negative—needles, pain, screaming children, and possible side-effects. In addition there was a general concern over what was perceived to be an everincreasing number of immunisation injections for children and significant variation in advice and guidance on immunisation issues from doctors.

Motivations

On the other hand, immunising children was perceived to be the accepted norm. The key motivators toward immunisation were identified as emotional ones: fear of not being a good mother, potential guilt if their children did contract a disease and were not immunised, and fear of being socially ostracised.

Strategically important was the fact that, while the majority of mothers reported feeling that immunising their children was the right thing to do, they also claimed that they lacked the rational arguments to support this fundamental belief and reassurance that their actions were in fact the most responsible for their children.

Barriers

Three types of barriers to full immunisation were identified in this formative research:

- practical
- medical
- emotional.

Practical barriers

Practical barriers appeared to mainly affect mothers with lower socioeconomic backgrounds, and those with more than two children. These included:

- difficulty in remembering whether the children have been immunised or not
- difficulty in attending venues for immunisation at the appropriate times

- lack of belief in the importance of the precise timing and number of vaccinations
- lack of awareness of the exact details of immunisation schedules.

Medical factors
Medical factors affected some mothers. These included:
- postponing vaccinations because of a perception that their children are too sick to be immunised
- lack of belief in the seriousness of particular diseases
- disillusionment when a child still contracts a disease despite being immunised.

Emotional factors
Emotional factors operating as barriers to immunisation included:
- embarrassment of being reprimanded as a result of having missed vaccinations
- fear of possible side-effects.

The greatest concerns related to the perceived potential side effects of vaccination, which, for some mothers, included the frightening risk of long-term serious disability.

Target audience segmentation
Six segments were identified among these mothers, according to their attitudes toward immunisation. These were:
- *advocates*—actively, conspicuously pro immunisation, well informed about immunisation and most likely to be compliant
- *acceptors*—more passive in their attitudes toward immunisation, hold strong beliefs in social norms, and are firm in their acceptance of immunisation
- *defaulters*—basically pro immunisation, and fairly involved in the subject, whose failure to immunise usually related to not getting around to it, forgetting, or being unaware of timing and schedules
- *questioners*—interested in both sides of the immunisation debate, would most likely try to comply if possible, but are looking for proof to decide the argument one way or the other
- *lapsed immunisers*—have essentially stopped believing in immunisation, typically felt uncomfortable and vulnerable about deciding not to immunise, and many now believed that the risks of immunisation exceeded the risks of the diseases
- *rejectors*—were similar to the lapsed immunisers, but had found alternatives to immunisation such as homoeopathic or naturopathic alternatives, with some actively anti-immunisation.

Apart from rejectors who had found alternatives to immunisation support for the concept of immunisation was virtually universal across these groups. Campaign communications were therefore primarily directed towards the acceptors, defaulters, and questioners while providing information for the advocates to confirm their position and to challenge the position of lapsed immunisers.

Strategy—an integrated comprehensive approach

The community education campaign communication objectives were to:

- increase parents' awareness of the benefits of full childhood immunisation
- inform them that the risks associated with the diseases are much greater than risks associated with vaccinations
- reinforce existing positive attitudes toward immunisation
- reduce fears about possible side-effects.

Behavioural objectives were to:

- stimulate parents to check the immunisation status of their children
- seek further information if required
- undertake any necessary action to fully immunise their children.

The health belief model (Rosenstock 1974) provided a useful theoretical framework within which to conceptualise how the campaign could operate to achieve these objectives at an individual level. Initially, the campaign would need to generate in parents an awareness of their children's susceptibility to these childhood diseases and the severity of the consequences of their children experiencing them. This latter point was a central component of the campaign strategy given that formative research had indicated an alarming level of complacency about these diseases among some parents, driven primarily by the fact that most of this generation of parents had never seen children suffering from many of these diseases.

With respect to cues to action the campaign needed to increase knowledge levels about the particular ages at which immunisations fell due within the recommended schedule.

Implementation—the marketing mix

The primary target audience for the campaign was parents of children aged up to 5 years. Secondary target audiences included family and friends of parents, immunisation service providers, and immunisation information providers.

While immunisation service providers were a secondary target audience, the first phase of campaign activity was directed at this group to increase and reinforce their knowledge levels and support for immunisation, with the goal of increasing opportunistic recruitment by general practitioners. Further, as research indicated that parents would be likely to seek information from their general practitioner or immunisation service provider, it was important to inform these health professionals that a campaign targeting parents would soon be initiated and to assist them in being able to meet these requests.

The service provider component of the campaign commenced in February 1997 with the launch of the sixth edition *Australian Immunisation Handbook*

(NHMRC 1997b), which was distributed to over 60 000 immunisation providers. Other components of the strategy included a regular column in *Australian Doctor* (a peak provider publication), an interactive satellite program for rural and remote providers, development and distribution of a regular newsletter updating specialist media on the progress of the campaign or any emerging issues for providers, development of the Australian Childhood Immunisation Charter, which outlines key principles and practices of immunisation and includes signatories from professional and community organisations, a public relations strategy, and the development and distribution of a range of resource materials.

The community education advertising campaign, launched in August 1997 with 2 weeks exposure of the 60-second version of the 'Whooping Cough' television commercial, was designed to graphically show Australian parents exactly what it is like for a child to experience whooping cough. Television advertising continued over the next 17 weeks with a pattern of 1 week on air followed by 2 weeks off air. The initial period of the 'Whooping Cough' commercial was followed by introduction of the 'Amy/Hospital' commercial in week 8 of the campaign. This commercial was particularly targeted at parents with more than one child and added a focus on the potential seriousness of a disease that many parents had become quite complacent about—measles. The final 7 weeks of television advertising featured a rotation of the 30-seconds version of 'Whooping Cough' and 'Amy/Hospital'. Supporting communication was undertaken through advertising in women's magazines and through posters in health clinics, hospitals, and doctors' surgeries.

Other components of the integrated campaign strategy entailed three Immunisation Awareness Days conducted in August, October, and December at selected locations in each state and territory, a national telephone information line, and distribution of a booklet, *Understanding Childhood Immunisation*, developed for parents through the formative research process. Extensive public relations activities underpinned these campaign elements, including publicity strategies, media monitoring, issues management, stakeholder management, and an expert spokesperson program.

In addition a non-English-language component of the campaign was launched in August 1997. This strategy targeted parents from non-English-speaking backgrounds and included advertising, public relations, and education strategies in thirteen spoken languages.

Evaluation

Precampaign and postcampaign telephone surveys, conducted in July 1997 and November–December 1997 respectively, comprised nationally representative samples of approximately 800 parents and guardians in each survey (Cramer & Carroll 1998).

The campaign effectively reached and communicated with its target audience: recognition for 'Whooping Cough' was 80 per cent, with appropriate message recall among these respondents of 97 per cent; recognition for 'Amy/Hospital' was

49 per cent, possibly reflecting its lower media weight, but a similarly high level of appropriate message recall among these respondents of 93 per cent.

Consistent with the agenda-setting function of mass media campaigns there was an increase in reported discussion about immunisation in the home. Key findings from the study indicated that between the two surveys there was an increase in the proportion of respondents reporting correct ages for immunisation. In addition, there were increases in the proportion of respondents who believed it would be very serious to a child's health if the child caught whooping cough (from 49 per cent to 69 per cent) and measles (from 31 per cent to 43 per cent).

The proportion of parents who reported they had checked their child's immunisation status in the last 3 months also increased (from 36 per cent to 43 per cent) as did the number of parents who had reported they had taken their child to be immunised during this period (from 22 per cent to 33 per cent).

Data from the Australian Childhood Immunisation Register, which was established in January 1996 and provides a comprehensive database of children's immunisations in Australia, indicate that levels of full age-appropriate childhood immunisation have risen since the campaign and the implementation of the range of Immunise Australia program parent and service provider initiatives. At the end of June 1997, prior to the commencement of the 1997 campaign (but after a number of other initiatives), the proportion of children aged 12 months who were assessed as fully immunised for their age was 76 per cent (Department of Health and Family Services 1998). By the end of December 1998 the comparable figure had increased to 85 per cent (Department of Health and Aged Care 1999). April 1998 marked the commencement of the Immunise Australia program initiative of linking the eligibility for childcare rebate to the child's immunisation coverage rate. The combination of communication campaigns and such policy initiatives has resulted in a significant increase in the full immunisation coverage rates among this age cohort. By June 2000 the level of full immunisation for this group had reached 88 per cent (Department of Health and Aged Care 2000) and, by June 2001, 91 per cent (Department of Health and Aged Care 2001).

Service providers

Two national telephone surveys were conducted with immunisation providers. One survey was conducted at the beginning of the campaign, the other 1 year later. The research found that there was an increase in the number of service providers accessing the latest handbook and a high degree of satisfaction with it.

The 1998 measles-control campaign

Building on the achievements of the 1997 campaign and the favourable community environment for child immunisation that it had achieved, the Immunise Australia program then initiated the National Measles Control Campaign in 1998 as a first step towards eliminating measles in Australia. The objective was to increase the proportion of 5–12-year-old Australian children who have received their second measles, mumps and rubella vaccinations to 95 per cent.

The marketing mix for the campaign entailed national mass media and a direct marketing campaign to the parents of 1.75 million children to gain their consent for their children to be vaccinated at school by visiting teams of nurses (Promotion, Place, and People). In addition, an extensive range of information kits (Product and Promotion) was distributed to schools and local doctors (Place, Intermediaries), and a comprehensive public relations campaign was carried out promoting the purpose of the program and mobilising a firm issues management campaign answering concerns raised in the press by anti-immunisation groups (Promotion). Extensive consultation processes in the health and education sectors were initiated and maintained throughout the campaign (Partnerships).

In contrast to the 1997 campaign, in which formative research had clearly indicated the need to raise perceptions of the seriousness of the diseases children were being immunised against, the Measles Control Campaign's creative strategy reflected a positive, modelling approach. Developed and refined through further formative research this approach was premised upon, and reflected, the greater support for child immunisation achieved by the previous campaign; it adopted the voices of children themselves calling on parents, schools, and the community at large to 'Work Together To Beat Measles'.

Evaluation research for this campaign indicated that the target for the campaign was achieved, with 96 per cent (1.7 million) of the 1.78 million Australian school children aged 5–12 years receiving a dose of MMR vaccine during the campaign. A serosurvey conducted after the campaign showed that 94 per cent of children aged 6–12 years were immune to measles, an increase from 84 per cent before the campaign (Commonwealth Department of Health and Aged Care 2000). The campaign was assessed as averting an estimated 17 500 cases of measles (NCIRS 1999).

Comment

This case study illustrates the critical role played by formative research in the development of strategy and in the design and refinement of communication materials. By adopting a consumer orientation we gain an understanding through the eyes of our target audience of the perceived costs and benefits of the behaviour we are seeking to increase. It is this understanding that allows us to generate identification with and a sense of personal relevance in our communication. This case study illustrates that the application of social marketing can— and has—achieved significant positive gains in improving levels of childhood immunisation and consequently protection against preventable disease for Australian children. Critical to the sustainability of the social marketing intervention were the policy initiatives of providing ongoing incentives to doctors and parents, particularly the linking of eligibility for the childcare rebate to the child's immunisation coverage rate. This is a useful example of how a public education campaign can help create an environment that facilitates the implementation of policy initiatives, which, in turn, create structural support for the achievements of the campaign.

TravelSmart®: an individualised social marketing case study

Background

Traditionally, transport planning has been based on disciplines such as engineering, economics, and logistics planning. Using social marketing principles to deliver sustained behaviour change in the transport planning field is therefore an innovative approach—at least in Australia—but one being increasingly adopted in the transport area. The major advantage of adopting a social marketing approach from the government's point of view is that, if successful, it is likely to be much cheaper than building costly infrastructure.

TravelSmart® is the registered trade mark for voluntary behaviour change programs held by the Western Australian Department for Planning and Infrastructure. TravelSmart® was developed by the Western Australian Department for Planning and Infrastructure with the aim of reducing the number of car trips made in the Perth metropolitan area by replacing them with walking, cycling, and public transport trips. A key principle is that this project aims to change people's modes of transport without reducing the number of places (that is, shops, entertainment venues, recreational areas, etc.) people wish to access.

Individualised marketing was a proven intervention developed and implemented by Socialdata (a private transport consultancy) in several European countries to increase public transport patronage and cycling. The application of this intervention in the Western Australian context focused on changing car trips to walking, cycling, and public transport. This had not been attempted before in Australia. The approach is based on simplifying complex transport information, having a dialogue with the community, motivating people to choose alternative modes for trips that suit their circumstances, and offering incentives to trial alternative modes. The program is based on a personal selling strategy that involves bus drivers promoting the program direct to the target market by calling on people in their homes.

The benefits of reducing the number of car trips include:

- reducing the amount of traffic congestion and deferring the need to build expensive road infrastructure
- reducing air pollution, greenhouse gas emissions, and other negative environmental consequences of extensive car use

Figure 14.1 Travelsmart® logo

- increasing the level of physical activity within the community with associated improved health outcomes
- increasing the use of walking and cycling infrastructure, and patronage of public transport.

For example, the Sierra Club, an environmental activist club, reports that those US cities spending most on public transportation rather than on motor vehicle infrastructure have the least smog (*The Nation's Health* 2002). Smog contributes to diseases such as asthma, chronic lung disease and pneumonia.

The TravelSmart® intervention

The TravelSmart® intervention is shown in Figure 14.2. It involves a partnership between the Western Australia Department for Planning and Infrastructure (incorporating the previous Department for Transport) and local governments of areas in which the intervention is applied. The intervention is implemented by Socialdata Australia, a private company.

Residents are first contacted by phone or mail (see letters relating to the intervention sent to the first author's home). On completion of a simple questionnaire, respondents are classified into 'regular users of non-car modes of transport', 'interested in using non-car modes', and 'not interested' ('Who in the household would consider more frequent use of public transport, cycling as a form of transport, walking as a form of transport?'). Residents are also asked who in the household 'would be interested in FREE information about public transport and timetables, cycling, walking and other general information for your area (including maps)?'

Those identified as 'not interested' are left alone and not provided with any information. This minimises adverse reactions from people who have no interest in changing their behaviour. 'Regular users' of the alternative (that is, non-car) modes are given a reward (in this project it was a publication on the history of the city of South Perth) and the choice of receiving or not receiving information materials.

Pilot study

A pilot study was conducted from 1997 to 1999 with 800 randomly selected households within the City of South Perth. The pilot study showed that while the number of trips per person per day remained constant there were sustained increases in the number of walking and cycling trips together with reductions in the number of car as driver trips. There was also a small but sustained increase in the number of public transport trips. These changes were not observed in the control group. The pilot also provided evidence of negligible, if any, adverse community reaction to the intervention based on informal discussions with numerous stakeholders.

The main intervention

Given the success of the pilot study a full-scale intervention was applied in 2000 to all 15 300 households (35 000 people) in the City of South Perth (figure 14.2). Prior to contacting households, 180 bus stop-specific timetable modules were installed throughout the city. These serve not only to make it easier for people to use the public transport system, but also to increase awareness of the intervention among residents.

The project's main focus was on converting those who expressed an interest in using alternative modes into regular users of alternative modes of transport. This 'interested' group was offered information and home visits. The information focused on accessing the transport system rather than trying to persuade people to use their cars less. The home visits, by bus drivers from the local Transperth bus operator, were offered to those in the 'interested' group who expressed a strong interest but who did not have the confidence to catch the bus. Most households were offered a test ticket to encourage them to start their use of public transport. The evaluation travel surveys were undertaken after the tickets expired and the electronic public transport system excluded these tickets in the counts.

Results

The self-reported survey results are shown in table 14.1. While the control group showed no changes in behaviour, the intervention group showed substantial relative changes: car trips as a driver declined substantially, while walking, cycling, and public transport trips increased substantially.

The Transperth electronic ticketing system was also analysed to identify changes in public transport patronage for those routes operating within the City of South Perth. The monthly comparisons for 1999 (pre-intervention), 2000, and 2001 are shown in figure 14.3. The results show an average 24 per cent increase in patronage of public transport. (The drop in demand in April is due to a combination of factors in Perth at this time: Easter, Anzac Day, school holidays, and annual leave.)

Table 14.1 Self-reported behaviour change achieved by TravelSmart®

| Control group % | Base Sept 1997 (%) | Main mode | After TravelSmart | | Control |
			Oct 2000 (%)	Relative change (%)	After (%)
15	12	Walking	16	+35	13
4	2	Cycling	3	+61	4
56	60	Car as driver	52	-14	56
20	20	Car passenger	22	+9	22
5	6	Public transport	7	+17	5
	3.4	Trips per person per day	3.4		

Figure 14.2 TravelSmart® intervention process

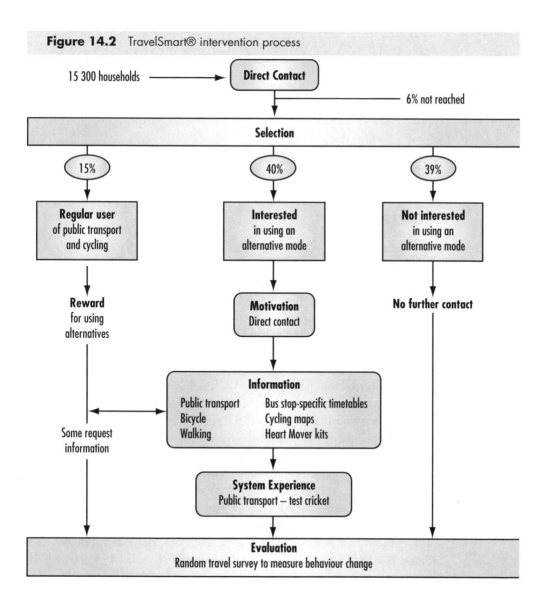

Figure 14.3 Public transport electronic ticketing patronage

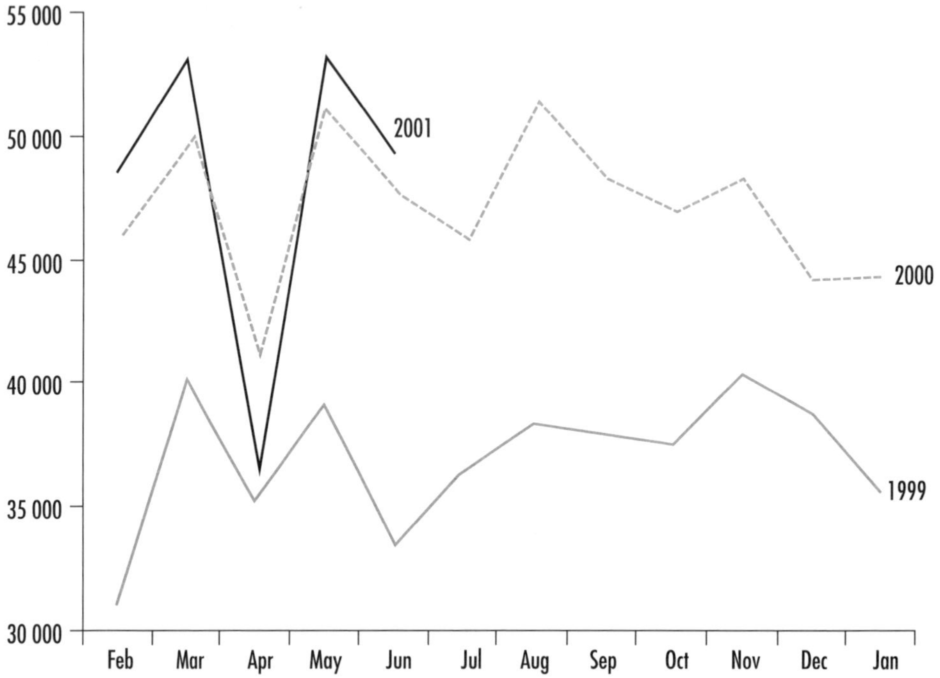

Comment

TravelSmart® attempts to achieve voluntary behaviour change by facilitating behaviour change among those already positive towards the desired behaviour (that is, those in the contemplation stage of change). Unlike many other social marketing campaigns, rather than rely on mass media only or community-led activities, the TravelSmart® intervention goes back to the marketing tool of personal selling and then individual tailoring of advice to the target household. The approach has clearly been successful and the South Perth results provided the evidence to argue for a major expansion of the intervention to other areas within the Perth metropolitan area. As a result, the Western Australian state government provided funding to expand the program in 2002, with the next stage targeting a further 30 000 potential public transport users. It is anticipated that TravelSmart® will eventually be applied throughout the Perth area.

TravelSmart® also shows the benefits of combining marketing principles with principles of applied behavioural analysis as suggested in chapter 5. Environmental reinforcers are introduced (for example, bus stop modules), incentives are offered, and there is a focus on facilitating the desired behaviours.

An alternative method that has been trialed in Australia is the so-called 'Travel Blending'® approach (Rose & Ampt 2001). However, while based on similar principles of individualised information and feedback, Travel Blend-

Figure 14.4 Letter from Department of Planning and Infrastructure to City of Subiaco residents

 Department for **Planning and Infrastructure**
Government of Western Australia

City of Subiaco

Dear City of Subiaco Resident,

Reducing traffic levels in your neighbourhood

Recent surveys of residents in Perth have shown that many people are concerned about increases in local traffic levels. High volumes of traffic create noise, congestion, air pollution and greenhouse gas emissions. These concerns are shared by the State Government and the City of Subiaco.

The Department for Planning and Infrastructure and the City of Subiaco have been working together on a solution - a project called *TravelSmart*.

This initiative helps to tackle local traffic issues by providing residents the opportunity to focus on healthy, environmentally positive alternatives to the motor car such as public transport, cycling and walking. It will help you to assess your individual daily travel needs and offer you information that will make taking the alternatives easier.

The benefits of *TravelSmart* would make a big difference to traffic levels and can be obtained by many people changing just a few trips per week.

Over the next few days our partner in this project, *Socialdata Australia*, (telephone number 9431 1864) will contact you with further information about this exciting *TravelSmart* Initiative. We ask that you consider the information carefully and discuss it with other members of your household.

This is a great opportunity to join a community effort that can make a big difference to the wellbeing of your neighbourhood. We hope you will be a part of it.

With kind regards, for and on behalf of the Department for Planning and Infrastructure and the City of Subiaco,

Alannah MacTiernan MLA
**MINISTER FOR PLANNING
AND INFRASTRUCTURE**

Tony Costa JP
MAYOR, CITY OF SUBIACO

August 2002

TRAVEL
SMART

It's how you get there that counts

Further information: *Socialdata Australia*, 45 Quarry Street, Fremantle WA 6160 - Telephone (08) 9431 1864

ing® is far more demanding on the respondent in terms of study participation (diaries and kits are completed and exchanged over a 9-week period) additional to any desired behaviour changes. The study of approximately 100 households in Adelaide showed a 10 per cent reduction in car driver kilometres. However, there was no control group and the participants were recruited from four related government departments (Department of Transport, Passenger Transport Board, Department of Environmental and Natural Resources, Department of Housing and Urban Development). Further trials of the program are underway in Australia and overseas.

Figure 14.5 Letter from Socialdata Australia to City of Subiaco residents

Socialdata Australia

45 Quarry Street
Fremantle WA 6160

PO Box 803
Fremantle WA 6959

Ph: +61 8 9431 1860
Fax: +61 8 9431 1865
Email:
socialdata@socialdata.com.au

August 2002

Dear City of Subiaco Resident,

We have been unable to contact your household by phone, but as we would like everyone to have the opportunity to take part in this exciting initiative, we are sending you this questionnaire.

The *TravelSmart* Initiative helps tackle local traffic issues by providing residents with the opportunity to seek advice and encouragement about environmentally positive and healthy ways of travelling. The Initiative provides information about public transport, cycling and walking in your local area, such as maps, timetables and other general information.

To participate in this *TravelSmart* Initiative, just fill in the questionnaire and return it in the envelope provided by Friday 6th September.

The information you provide will remain strictly confidential and will be used for statistical purposes only. There is a space on the back page of the questionnaire for you to make any comments you may have about transport related issues in your area. We welcome all comments, which will be forwarded anonymously to the Department for Planning and Infrastructure and the City of Subiaco.

Please do not hesitate to contact our office on 9431 1864, if you have any further questions about the initiative.

With kind regards,

HM Grey-Smith

Helen Grey-Smith
PROJECT CO-ORDINATOR

Chapter 15

Targeting Male Perpetrators of Intimate Partner Violence: Western Australia's *Freedom from Fear* campaign

Introduction

This chapter describes the development, implementation, and initial results of the Western Australian *Freedom from Fear* domestic violence prevention campaign targeting male perpetrators of intimate partner violence. Mass media advertising was used to create and maintain awareness of a men's domestic violence helpline and to encourage violent and potentially violent men to call that helpline. The primary aim of the helpline counsellors was to refer as many qualified callers as possible into no-fee, government-funded counselling programs provided primarily by private sector organisations. This chapter is based on Donovan, Paterson, and Francas (1999f)[1] and Donovan, Francas, Paterson, and Zappelli (2000[2]).

Costs of intimate partner violence

Violence against women by their partners is now recognised as a major international public health problem, in both developed and developing countries (Davidson 1996; Reppucci, Woolard & Fried 1999; WHO 1997). In a 1996 survey in Australia 2.6 per cent of women in a relationship reported a violent incident in the 12 months prior to the survey (ABS 1996b). It is estimated that each year in the USA 4 million women experience a serious assault by their partner (*APS Observer* 1997). In a 1993 Canadian survey, 3 per cent of women in a relationship reported a physical or sexual assault in the 12 months prior to interview, while in the UK it has been estimated that systematic violence occurs in 5 per cent of marriages. In the USA 12 per cent of husbands in a 1985 survey reported at least one physical assault on their wife and 3.4 per cent

---

1   Donovan, Paterson, and Francas's (1999f) paper won the Best Paper award—the Novelli Award for Excellence and Innovation in Social Marketing—at the Innovations in Social Marketing International Conference in Montreal, Canada, in 1999.

2   Mark Francas won the Best Paper Award at the Market Research Society of Australia National Conference in Sydney in 1999.

Figure 15.1 Freedom from Fear campaign logo

FReeDOM FROM FeaR
CAMPAIGN AGAINST DOMESTIC VIOLENCE

reported at least one act of severe violence (Tomison & Wolcott 1998). While intimate partner violence also involves female-to-male partner violence (and same sex partner violence as well), male-to-female partner violence occurs more frequently and with far more serious consequences in terms of injury and death (Sorenson, Upchurch & Shen 1996).

Intimate partner violence not only has major consequences for the physical and mental health of the women (Koss & Heslet 1992; Roberts, Lawrence, Williams & Raphael 1998), but there are also major consequences for children and other family members (Gomel 1997). Victim-related economic cost of partner violence in the USA has been estimated to be in the vicinity of $67 billion (*APS Observer* 1997). The costs of such violence cannot be calculated simply in terms of emergency ward treatments, hospital bed nights, refuge home placements, lives lost in homicides and suicides, and so on. There also are enormous costs in terms of children's lost happiness and subsequent dysfunctional behaviours. Incarceration costs for convicted perpetrators also must be taken into account.

While usually attracting little sympathy, violent men also suffer psychologically via guilt and remorse, feelings of helplessness, anxiety, and depression, often resulting in suicide (or murder–suicides). Furthermore, many violent men have themselves been the victims of violence when young, either directly or via exposure to parental violence (Hotaling & Sugarman 1986).

Traditional interventions

Most programs aimed at a reduction of abuse have been based around the criminal justice system, targeting both police and the judiciary. A feature of many current approaches is that women no longer have to lodge a complaint before police can charge the perpetrator with assault (thus removing one of the major barriers to women reporting incidents). A major target with the judiciary has been to obtain mandatory treatment programs for offenders (Healey & Smith 1998). Where public education components have accompanied such campaigns these have aimed at increasing the public's (and perpetrators') perception that domestic violence is a crime (Buchanan 1996). Such campaigns generally encourage women to report incidents and, where necessary, to leave the family home and to take out civil protection (or restraining) orders against violent partners.

While the incarceration of violent men and the issuing of protection orders are necessary components of domestic violence prevention interventions and do alleviate some violence (Keilitz, Davis, Efkeman et al. 1998), they do not—and cannot—remove the fear women experience in terms of the man reappearing some time, some place, often with tragic consequences (De Becker 1998). Furthermore, many women do not want to leave the relationship, nor do they want the man incarcerated; they simply want the violence to stop. The Western Australian *Freedom from Fear* campaign acknowledges these factors and aims to reduce women's and children's fear by encouraging perpetrators and potential perpetrators to voluntarily attend counselling (or batterer) programs.

The Western Australian *Freedom from Fear* campaign

The Western Australian *Freedom from Fear* campaign is a 10-year community education program complementing criminal justice and other community interventions. As far as we are aware this campaign is a unique initiative, being the first government-funded, mass media-based, non-punitive campaign focusing primarily on perpetrators of domestic violence and asking them to voluntarily seek help to change their violent ways.

Campaign goals and overall strategy

The overall goals of the campaign are the reduction of violence against women by male partners and, consequently, increased physical and mental health among victims. Consistent with Andreasen's (1995) inclusion of the concept of 'voluntary behaviour' in the definition of social marketing, the campaign aims to achieve the goal of reduced violence by voluntary behaviour change among male perpetrators, and the prevention of first and subsequent acts of violence among potential perpetrators. Figure 15.3 summarises the overall campaign strategy. In its first phase, given the nature of the primary target audience (men accepting of their need to change; see below), the campaign essentially used a 'pull' strategy (Kotler et al. 1998): mass media advertising (television advertising—especially in sporting programs, supported by radio advertising and posters) was used to create and maintain awareness among the primary target audience of a men's domestic violence helpline, and to encourage violent and potentially violent men to call the helpline.

The helpline was staffed by counsellors specifically trained to deal with violent men, who were able to assess callers, and to conduct lengthy telephone counselling with members of the primary target audience. The primary aim of the helpline counsellors was to refer as many as possible qualified callers into no-fee, government-funded counselling programs provided primarily by private sector organisations in twelve locations throughout the state. Although results vary counselling programs have been found to be effective in reducing violence (Davis & Taylor 1999; Healey, Smith & O'Sullivan 1998).

Figure 15.2 Campaign overview

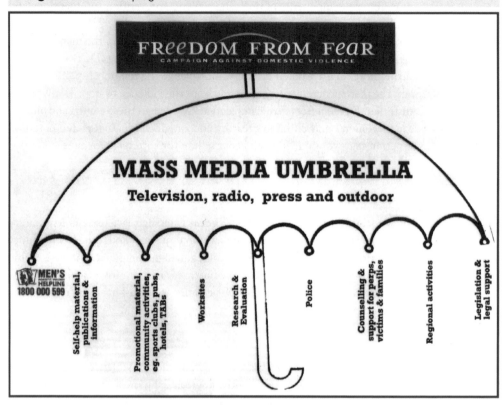

Anonymity was an important aspect of the strategy. There was no pressure on men to give their names when they called. If they wished to receive self-help materials they were able to nominate an address to which materials could be sent. This was considered appropriate because perpetrators may be aware their behaviour is wrong and that they should seek assistance but they are understandably resistant to seeking assistance that might result in legal sanctions.

Campaign target groups

The primary target audience was defined (and confirmed in formative research) as male perpetrators and potential perpetrators in Prochaska's contemplation, ready for action or action stages (Prochaska & DiClemente 1984) with respect to doing something about their violence or potential violence. While these men may still minimise and deny (at some level or on some occasions) full responsibility for their behaviour, they are reachable through mass media because they do accept some responsibility for their behaviour. Hardcore perpetrators still in a strong state of denial (Eisikovits & Buchbinder 1997) were not part of the primary target audience for this campaign. The stages of change concept has been recommended for social marketing programs (Andreasen 1995;

Figure 15.3 Program for target groups

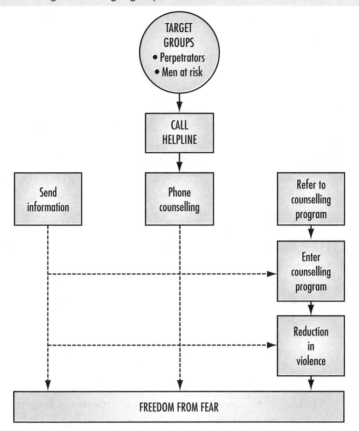

Donovan & Owen 1994) and is being used in an evaluation of the Milwaukee Women's Center's perpetrator interventions (National Center for Injury Prevention and Control 1999).

Potential perpetrators were defined as those subjecting their partner to non-physical forms of abuse (for example, emotional abuse, financial deprivation, social isolation). There is evidence that these non-physical forms of abuse are often precursors to physical abuse. Potential perpetrators also include men with undesirable attitudes towards partner abuse (for example, believed violence by the male partner was justified or often provoked in certain situations).

The secondary target audience consisted of 'all other 18–40 year old males'. A third target group consisted of those individuals who might encourage the primary target audience to seek assistance: victims, family members, friends, and professionals with whom they might come in contact (for example, lawyers, doctors, nurses, police officers, counsellors). Finally, the campaign targeted all members of the community in terms of maintaining the salience of domestic violence as a community concern and in terms of reinforcing men not engaged in violent behaviour.

The marketing mix

The following description is based on the four Ps of tangible product marketing, product, price, promotion, and place, and the fifth P (people) for services marketing (after Cowell 1984).

Product

The core product, that is, the end benefit being offered to violent men in relationships, was the opportunity to keep their relationship (family) intact by ending the violence towards their partner (and its impact on their children). Actual products and services were as follows.

- The primary end product consisted of counselling programs delivered by private service providers and subsidised by the government. Prior to the campaign launch there were few such programs available and most were attended by men under court orders. Six new perpetrator and five new victim and children's counselling programs were funded by the state government. These new services were mostly located in rural centres.

- Another major product was the Men's Domestic Violence Helpline staffed by trained counsellors who offered counselling over the phone (many calls were 45–60 minutes in duration) and attempted to get violent callers into counselling programs (referrals). Prior to this campaign there was no helpline specifically for perpetrators who voluntarily sought help; nor were counselling programs promoted. If the caller could not be encouraged to accept referral—which required the caller to provide contact details for forwarding to the service provider—the telephone counsellors delivered counselling over the phone. A further aim was to engage the callers sufficiently so as to obtain permission to send, at no cost, educational self-help materials to an address nominated by the caller and to encourage callers to call again when in need if they were reluctant or not able to enrol in a counselling program.

- Self-help booklets provided tips on how to control violence and how to contact service providers. These self-help booklets were also provided on audiocassettes for men with literacy difficulties.

People

The telephone counsellors were men who had considerable skills training and experience in dealing with violent men. These counsellors were able to gain the trust of men, listen to their stories, assess the level of denial and minimisation, yet confront men with these aspects of their behaviour and undertake counselling and encourage them into programs. The helpline advertising was not branded to the police department, as many campaigns are, and the content of the advertising was clearly non-punitive. The helpline advertising communicated the simple, clear message that help was available to violent (and potentially violent) men.

Figure 15.4 Self-help booklet cover

Promotion

The primary medium for reaching violent and potentially violent men was television advertising, especially in sporting programs; this was supported by radio advertising and posters. Extensive formative research was undertaken to ensure acceptance of the ad messages by the target group without negatively impacting victims and children and other relevant stakeholders. There was minor publicity of individual cases (willing to be photographed) who had undergone counselling.

Extensive public relations activities were undertaken with a number of relevant stakeholders, especially a range of women's groups, police, counselling professions, and other government departments. This involved repeated visits to these organisations and continually updating them on campaign developments. Further stakeholder issues are discussed below.

The main aim in phase 1 was to distribute posters advertising the helpline to worksites and to alert the appropriate worksite professionals (usually the occupational health and safety officer or human resources manager) about the campaign. The intention was to sensitise these persons to phase 2 initiatives of including the domestic violence counselling programs in the worksite offerings.

With the assistance of a number of trade unions, campaign information packs were distributed by mail to worksites.

Price

With respect to dollar costs, although domestic violence occurs across all income levels, preliminary investigations and service-provider experience suggested that fees for courses and materials could serve as a barrier (or be rationalised as such) for many members of the primary target audience. Hence, all materials and most counselling programs were to be provided at no cost to participants who were referred through the helpline. This pricing strategy was also considered more equitable to ensure that victims of low-income perpetrators would not be disadvantaged by their partner's limited income.

To minimise potential psychological and legal costs, the helpline assured anonymity and the counsellors were trained to deal with shame and embarrassment issues. It is the need for anonymity that required the strategy of the helpline as the first point of contact for these men, with mass media advertising creating awareness and motivating contact.

Place

Service providers were located throughout the metropolitan area and in six regional areas throughout the state. Programs were time scheduled to allow employed males access in non-working hours. It is acknowledged that access to programs (but not to telephone counselling) was geographically limited outside major population centres. Subsequent phases of the campaign will adopt distribution strategies designed to provide greater access to violence counselling service providers.

The telephone counselling and self-help booklets were especially useful for those not able to access a counselling program. The helpline was staffed by counsellors during the night to provide maximal access.

Communication and behavioural objectives

For all audiences the primary communication objectives of the promotional materials were that

- the perpetrator, not the victim, is responsible for the violence
- there are no circumstances in which violence is justified.

Among members of the primary and secondary target groups the main communication objectives were to increase awareness that non-punitive, anonymous help was available and to stimulate motivations and intentions to seek help. The intermediate behavioural objective was that they should call the helpline for assistance or seek assistance from some credible source. The final behavioural objectives, particularly following counselling, were a reduction in violent incidents—both physical and verbal—among perpetrators, and the prevention of violence among potentials.

Figure 15.5 Men's domestic violence helpline logo

Campaign development, execution and delivery considerations

Helpline staffing issues

Training of the helpline telephone counsellors and adequate staffing of service providers were crucial to the success of the campaign. Helpline staff faced a complex and delicate 'sales' interaction given the legal and social sanctions that accompany domestic violence. Skilful techniques were needed to engage the caller long enough for a meaningful counselling session, to obtain an address for materials, and to get to the referral stage.

The decision to make a call requires some courage on the part of the caller, with the act of calling often following a period of indecision. Hence, it was important that sufficient staff were always on hand to receive and act on calls. Putting callers on hold or asking them to call back can result in the caller losing motivation and cycling back one or more stages of change: for some perpetrators there is only a small window of opportunity when they actually make the call, usually in the remorse phase of what is known as the 'cycle of abuse' (Roberts 1984). Counsellors also encouraged repeat calls where the caller was not willing to accept a referral.

Where the caller accepted a referral the counsellor took details from the caller and completed a referral form, which was faxed to the appropriate service provider the same day. Service providers were required to contact callers within 2 days (most attempt to do so within 24 hours) to make an appointment for an assessment interview. Most callers were seen within 1 week. The referral process involved cooperation between two government departments and all (competing) service providers for the system to work. This cooperation was gained only after extensive consultation and interpersonal networking.

Partnerships and stakeholder issues

Directing resources towards male perpetrator programs is generally viewed rather negatively by female victim support organisations. Hence, it was crucial to gain women's organisations'—and female victims'—support for the program in principle, and then ensure their continued support for the various program materials as they were produced. This required an initial acceptance that prevention of violence via perpetrators' and potential perpetrators' voluntary entry into counselling was a legitimate and potentially effective violence prevention strategy, and then continued updating of developments and clearing of materials with these groups prior to final production. It was required that this sector be reassured that targeting perpetrators and funding perpetrator programs was consistent with the feminist philosophy with respect to domestic violence prevention; that is, that victim safety is paramount and that directing services towards men must ultimately be about victim safety and freedom from fear.

Police were encouraged to promote perpetrators' use of the telephone counselling service when called to 'domestics', particularly where no charges could or would be laid. It was also important to create and reinforce positive community attitudes to the counselling of violent men as a legitimate domestic violence prevention strategy (complementary to police arrest and sentencing and mandatory referral into counselling by courts), and hence worthy of government funding.

There were also important ramifications for developing the campaign's advertising component. It was necessary to avoid being judgmental so as to engage the attention and acceptance of members of the target audience. Simultaneously, it was essential—from victims' and other stakeholders' points of view—not to be seen to condone violence.

Formative research

Formative research was required to firstly 'get the right message' and then 'get the message right' (Egger, Donovan & Spark 1993). Getting the right message refers to establishing what message content would motivate violent men to seek help. Getting the message right refers to executing the message in a language and style that violent men would pay attention to, understand, and find believable, yet not be seen to either condemn or condone their violence. Furthermore, the ads could not make victims of domestic violence feel responsible, guilty, or more helpless.

Phase 1: getting the right message

The broad objectives of the first phase of research were to:

- examine the awareness, knowledge, attitudes, perceptions, and behaviours of men in general with respect to domestic violence

■ gain some understanding of perpetrators' beliefs and attitudes and hence assess whether reaching and impacting the primary target group was viable via mass media advertising

■ assess the effectiveness of five potential message themes for a community education campaign: Criminal Sanctions, Community Intervention, Social Disapproval, Consequences, and Help is Available (discussed below).

General population males

Fifteen focus groups were conducted with males aged 18–40 years, stratified by age and social economic status. Nine of the groups were conducted in Perth and six groups were held in four regional towns in Western Australia. The groups were recruited by a professional recruiting agency.

In order not to sensitise participants to the issue of domestic violence (which might have resulted in violent or potentially violent men or those with positive attitudes to partner violence excluding themselves), all potential group participants were told only that the groups would be discussing 'some important social issues'. Furthermore, the issue of violence in society was introduced as the initial topic of discussion. This allowed the issue of domestic violence to arise spontaneously in discussion (which it invariably did) and hence allow the moderator to focus on this area without being seen to impose the topic on the group.

The moderator probed men's general beliefs and attitudes about intimate partner violence (perceived causes, definitions, awareness of and reaction to previous campaigns, etc.) and attempted to elicit examples of physical or verbal or emotional abuse in participants' current or previous relationship(s) or in their friends' and relatives' relationships.

Perpetrators

Three group discussions, arranged through organisations providing counselling programs, were held with violent men. All participants were in treatment programs, some voluntarily and others court-mandated. Their participation in the group discussions was voluntary. Counsellors were on hand to debrief the men if issues were raised that needed attention; a criminologist assisted in the planning and moderating of the initial groups.

Because these men were in counselling programs for different lengths of time, the groups contained a mix of men in the various stages of change. The men's statements allowed identification of their stage status (statements with respect to responsibility and blame, whether the violence was 'deserved', empathy for the victim, attitude to the treatment program, etc.). Participants in the perpetrator groups were obviously not blind to the topic of discussion, hence, a warm-up discussion, common to most focus groups, was superfluous. Instead, the moderators got straight to the point of what sort of communication campaign could prevent men's violence against their partners.

Qualitative research results

Awareness, attitudes, and beliefs

Domestic violence was perceived by men in general as an important issue and men generally had an accurate understanding of what constitutes and what causes domestic violence—in all its forms. Hence, there was little need for a campaign to deal with these issues.

Three important points emerged from the research with perpetrators.

- The first time (that is, the first act of physical violence) is a critical event that facilitates subsequent violence. Hence, the campaign needed to attract potentially violent men to seek help before this first act of violence occurred.
- Many perpetrators expressed shame and guilt about their behaviour, yet were unaware of where or how to seek help without legal implications. Hence, the primary target audience and the underlying rationale of the campaign were confirmed.
- Many perpetrators exhibited a siege mentality and felt persecuted. They considered the allocation of 100 per cent blame for domestic violence to men as being grossly unfair. This highlighted that messages would need to avoid an accusatory or blaming tone to avoid being rejected by perpetrators.

Reaction to a priori message strategies

Criminal sanctions

This was not seen as a significant deterrent nor as entirely credible by males in general or perpetrators. Perpetrators with considerable experience with the criminal justice system commented that legal sanctions were often not particularly severe and therefore had little deterrent effect: 'The first couple of times you'd probably just get probation ... it wouldn't make you stop doing it.' Furthermore, many perpetrators had seen men getting away with domestic violence over the course of many years.

Community intervention

The theme of encouraging people to report or intervene in suspected cases of domestic violence was largely rejected by perpetrators (and males in general) as it was deemed inconsistent with social norms (that is, dobbing in was not acceptable in Australia). Furthermore, no doubt reinforced by their own experiences, the theme lacked credibility in that they felt other people would be reluctant to get involved.

Social disapproval

Non-perpetrators reacted favourably to the theme that violent behaviour towards a female is unacceptable for a man and that men who engage in such behaviour should be rejected by their peers. Perpetrators, however, doubted the credibility of such an approach and several of them reacted angrily to the peer rejection message; it seemed to exacerbate the siege mentality alluded to earlier.

Consequences

Two separate themes were tested: damage to partner and damage to children. Damage to partner was not an influencing factor among many perpetrators and lacked credibility among men in general who doubted, correctly, that perpetrators cared sufficiently about the damage to their partners. In contrast, damage to children was a powerful motivator among perpetrators. All expressed strong feelings for their children, recalling that their children's reactions to specific instances of domestic violence had a very vivid impact on them; many could relate to their own feelings towards violence committed against them when they were children. Thus, this theme had relevance whether or not they themselves had children. Furthermore, the damage to children theme was accepted by precontemplator perpetrators and hence had potential to move this group towards contemplation. This theme was also considered to be an effective theme by men in general and was selected as the key message strategy for the initial phase of the campaign.

Help is available

This theme was universally endorsed by perpetrators because it was seen as a positive message that addressed the siege mentality syndrome and because many were aware that they needed help but did not know how to go about getting it. The view of most perpetrators was that the focus should be on access to formal help (counselling programs, treatment programs) rather than informal help. This theme was also strongly endorsed by men in general. There was broad support for a media campaign to publicise this assistance.

Overall then, the phase 1 formative research confirmed a potentially substantial number of violent and potentially violent men who could be reached by, and would respond to, a mass media campaign that offered formal assistance. The key to reaching this audience was to avoid being judgmental and to focus on the effects on children of men's violence towards their partner as the motivator to take action.

Phase 2 pretesting of advertising executions: getting the message right

The pretesting was conducted in two stages: a qualitative concept screening stage and a quantitative animatic testing phase.

Concept screening

Six concepts based on the findings of the above qualitative research were tested in storyboard form against perpetrators and at risk males, general population males and females, victims, various stakeholder representatives, and children exposed to domestic violence.

Seventeen focus groups and eight individual interviews were conducted in Perth and country areas. Individual written reaction to the concepts was obtained prior to any group discussion using a modified ADTEST® questionnaire (see below), based on standard advertising pretest measures (Rossiter & Percy 1997). In the perpetrator groups, counsellors again were on hand to assist non-literate men complete the questionnaires and to deal with issues that required attention. The major focus of this stage was on the credibility of the concept message, the realism of the depicted situation, and the capacity of the message to stimulate violent men to think about seeking help to stop their violence.

As the key element of the message strategy was a focus on consequences for children, most of the concepts portrayed small children being exposed to domestic violence. However, it was crucial that the ads, although scheduled to be run only at adult times, did not trigger clinical stress symptoms in children, especially children of victims, and that children did not misunderstand the ads and think they were being asked to call the helpline or that they should ask their father to call the helpline. Groups of children at selected women's refuges were exposed to the advertising materials while a child psychologist observed and probed the children's reactions.

Quantitative ad testing

Three concepts considered potentially most effective were developed as animatics.

Nightmare

'Nightmare' depicts a child in bed, tossing and turning against a shadowy background and sound effects of a man abusing a woman; the ad ends with the caption 'This child is not having a nightmare, he is living one'.

Horror movie

Two children are watching television against a similar background as above; the caption states that the children are 'not watching a horror movie, they are living one'.

Back seat

A child's view, from the back seat of a car, of a male verbally abusing a woman in the front seat.

The ADTEST® procedure, based on published advertising pretest measures (Rossiter & Percy 1997), was used to test the animatics. This procedure has been used extensively in pretesting health and social issues advertising (for example, Donovan, Jalleh & Henley 1999d). Potential respondents were intercepted in the city centre, screened for age and SES, invited to the research agency's test centre, and randomly allocated to view one of the three animatics. The ad was exposed twice so that respondents had ample opportunity to understand what was going on in the ad and to make a judgment about its intended message (Rossiter & Percy 1997; Donovan et al. 1999d) Respondents were exposed to the animatic in groups of two to four; then completed a self-completion questionnaire (to facilitate frankness in responding), followed by a face-to-face, interviewer-administered questionnaire on the less sensitive aspects of their reactions (for example, likes and dislikes about the ad's execution). A total of 302 interviews was conducted with 18–40 year old males, of whom 24 per cent indicated they had come close to hitting their partner on at least one occasion.

All three animatics performed acceptably on all the crucial ADTEST measures, with the diagnostic data suggesting several ways to increase their effectiveness. Selected results (combined across all three ads) were as follows (Donovan Research 1998):

- all respondents correctly understood the ads' messages (that is, impact on children, help is available or call the helpline)
- cognitive response measures indicated high acceptance of the ads' messages and minimal counterarguing
- 90 per cent stated that the ads made them feel concerned for the children in the animatics
- approximately half thought 'a lot' or 'somewhat' that the ads suggested that men must take responsibility for their violent behaviour
- only 7 per cent thought the ads communicated that 'women who get beaten deserve it'
- 99 per cent found the ads believable (45 per cent 'very', 44 per cent 'fairly')
- approximately half thought 'a lot' or 'somewhat' that the ads would make violent men think they should do something about their behaviour
- there was overwhelming approval for an advertising campaign to encourage violent and potentially violent men to call a helpline.

Appropriate modifications were then made to the ads before final production. All finished ads were shown to stakeholders for final approval before going to air.

Evaluation research

Field surveys of changes in beliefs and attitudes

In the first 7 months of the campaign three statewide random telephone surveys were undertaken with approximately 400 males each wave, 18–40 years old, who were in a heterosexual relationship or intending to be in the future: one survey prior to the campaign (n = 359; designated 'pre' in the figures and tables), one 4 weeks into the campaign (wave 1) to assess initial impact, and the third 7 months into the campaign (wave 2). Respondents were selected at random from a selection of lower socioeconomic suburbs within the Perth metropolitan area and at random within the remainder of Western Australia. The sample was generated by a combination of computer-generated random digit telephone numbers for the country numbers and a random selection of metropolitan telephone numbers based on preselected postcode areas.

Questionnaire items measured the following:

- general awareness of, attitudes towards, and professed behaviours relating to domestic violence (that is, awareness of domestic violence as an important social issue, perceived acceptability of domestic violence under certain circumstances, propensity to commit various physical and emotional abuse behaviours)
- awareness of means for getting help (that is, knowledge about available support services, awareness of where to telephone for help, propensity to advise others to telephone the helpline)
- advertising reach and impact (that is, awareness of advertising (spontaneous and prompted), message take-out, attitudes towards the campaign).

To gain the men's confidence, the early part of the questionnaire asked about female to male intimate partner violence. This was done because of some men's negative reaction to surveys implying that only men commit violence against women (that is, ignore female to male partner violence), and to increase the likelihood of honest self-disclosure. Questions with respect to 'ever' and current abusive behaviours allowed the samples to be subclassified as never abused (23 per cent), ever or current emotional or verbal abusers (64 per cent), and ever or current physically violent (12 per cent). Hence, the samples were substantially consistent with the behavioural definitions of the primary and secondary target audiences.

Wave 1 was carried out primarily to assess advertising reach and impact so that any deficiencies could be detected and rectified as soon as practicable. Wave 2 was expected to show significant changes in awareness of sources of assistance, particularly the Men's Domestic Violence Helpline, and was to identify any early changes in beliefs and attitudes. However, it was felt premature at this stage to expect any substantial shifts in long-term beliefs and behaviours in relation to domestic violence. Selected results from the surveys are shown below.

Results

Program reach

Spontaneous awareness for any advertising about domestic violence increased substantially from benchmark (28 per cent), reaching 90 per cent in the Wave 2 survey. Prompted recognition of the specific television ads used showed 70 per cent recognition in Wave 1 and 79 per cent in Wave 2. Recognition of any campaign materials was 82 per cent in Wave 1 and 91 per cent in Wave 2.

Figure 15.6a Evaluation results—Overall campaign awareness

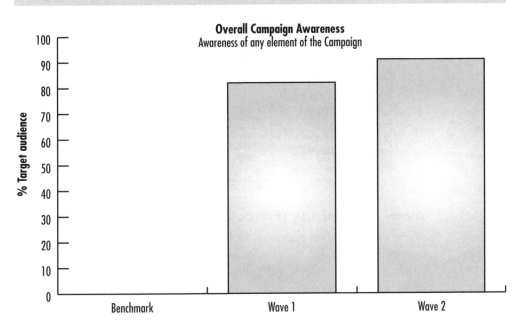

Figure 15.6b Evaluation results—Overall campaign awareness

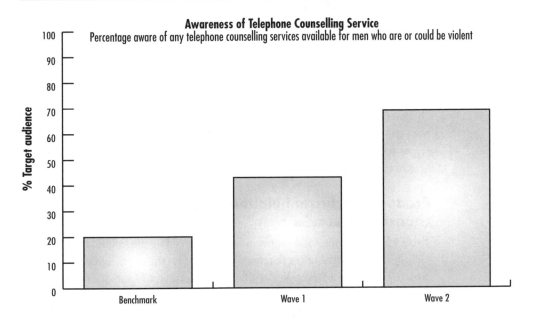

Figure 15.7 Campaign influence on beliefs

	Benchmark	Wave 1	Wave 2
Domestic violence affects the whole family	21%	34%	58%
Changed the way you think about domestic violence	9%	14%	21%
Occasional slapping is *never* justified	38%	47%	52%

Awareness of the (men's domestic violence) helpline

When asked the open-ended question 'Where can violent and potentially violent men go for help?' the proportion of respondents nominating a telephone helpline increased from a nil response prior to the campaign to 23 per cent in Wave 1, which further increased to 53 per cent in Wave 2. When prompted, the percentages went from 20 per cent at baseline, 43 per cent at Wave 1, and 69 per cent at Wave 2. The Wave 1 results indicated that the 'help is available' message was not coming through strongly. For this reason, in future ads the tagline was held on screen longer and a 15-second ad was made showing a man holding a telephone. Substantial increases in calls in the next 2 months reflected modifications to the ads as a result of Wave 1 findings.

Attitudinal effects

A number of positive belief and attitude effects began to emerge. In Wave 2, 21 per cent of respondents exposed to the campaign stated that the campaign had 'changed the way they thought about domestic violence'. When asked who suffered most from domestic violence, 58 per cent of all respondents in Wave 2 agreed that 'domestic violence affects the whole family' rather than just the children or the woman victim (versus 21 per cent prior to the campaign and 34 per cent in Wave 1). The proportion of the total sample agreeing that 'occasional slapping of their partner' is never justified increased from 38 per cent at benchmark to 47 per cent in Wave 1 and 52 per cent in Wave 2.

Product purchase: helpline calls and referrals to counselling services

Table 15.1 shows the total number of calls received by the helpline, the number identified as perpetrators or potential perpetrators (the campaign primary target group), the number who self-identified as perpetrators (a subset of the previous category), and the number of victim callers. The number of self-identified perpetrators who were referred to counselling is also shown. (Only self-identifying perpetrators were referred to counselling programs.)

Table 15.1 Number and breakdown of calls received by the helpline

%	TOTAL
All calls	3610 (100%)
Calls from Campaign Target Group	2250 (63% of all calls)
Self-identifing Perpetrators/Men at Risk	1487 (41% of all calls)
Referrals to Counselling	758 (20% of all calls, 50% of self-identifying perpetrators)
Victim Callers	394 (10% of all calls)

By late 1999 the Men's Domestic Violence Helpline had received 3610 calls, 2250 from members of the primary target group, including 1487 men who reported physically abusing their female partner. Of these self-identified perpetrators just over half (n = 758) agreed to a referral to a service provider.

Discussion and implications of early results

This innovative campaign has clearly demonstrated the feasibility of using social marketing principles to achieve voluntary behaviour change in an area where the emphasis has traditionally been—and continues to be—on criminal justice threats. This has been a significant breakthrough in the domestic violence area where support for funds directed at perpetrators has not been readily forthcoming. These positive outcomes reflect that the investment in money, time, and effort to ensure that the message strategy was right and that the ads were executed appropriately was a sound investment. This was particularly important for a campaign that would be subject to intense scrutiny because of its departure from traditional approaches and the scarcity of funds in this area.

The success of the campaign has been facilitated by:

■ the integration of all aspects of the campaign (price, promotion, people, place, and product)
■ the extensive and sensitive use of research
■ the use of conceptual frameworks (stages of change, communication principles in message design)
■ the formation of partnerships with all relevant stakeholders across the public and private sectors in a highly political and socially sensitive area.

The absolute numbers calling the helpline and being referred to counselling programs are considered sufficient from both a financial and social cost point of view to justify continuing and extending the campaign. Initial estimates put the cost per referral to completion of the counselling program at approximately A$2500—3000. In Western Australia in 1989 it was estimated that it cost more than A$50 000 to treat one victim of domestic violence (including cost of policing, hospital and medical, court services, social security payments, housing, and potential income loss) (Department of Community Development 1989). From the view of domestic violence prevention stakeholders the campaign strategy of targeting perpetrators to voluntarily seek assistance is confirmed as an effective strategy. It is now hoped that the counselling programs—including maintenance products—will deliver the overall goal of a sustained change in the abusive behaviour of those who complete the courses.

Future campaign directions

The next phase of the campaign is focusing on establishing distribution channels for counselling services. There are two major areas of focus: worksites and rural and remote areas. One primary distribution channel being targeted is a network of employers who offer employees counselling services for a variety of individual needs, not just work-related issues (Employee Assistance Program [EAP]). The human resources managers in companies in the EAP refer their workers to a number of linked service organisations. The *Freedom from Fear* campaign will form partnerships with these employers to increase employer awareness of their role in domestic violence, to include domestic violence counsellors among the list of service providers employees may be directed to, and to increase employee opportunity to disclose and seek help. Another specific channel consists of a similar apparatus within the defence forces. The overall aim is to widen the number of referral intermediaries who have direct face-to-face contact with members of the primary target audience, and hence more direct promotion of counselling services to these men. This next phase involves substantial targeting of a wide variety of intermediaries, all with specific needs and requirements that must be satisfied before agreeing to adopt and disseminate the *Freedom from Fear* product.

Postscript

The large number of men entering counselling programs as a result of the *Freedom from Fear* campaign has had the effect of increasing the focus on outcomes of these programs. Preliminary research for the Domestic Violence Prevention Unit shows that very little evaluation is done by service providers. It is hoped that effective evaluation processes can be built in to future programs.

For more information see <www.freedomfromfear.wa.gov.au>.

References

Aaker, J.L. (1997). Dimensions of brand personality. *Journal of Marketing Research*, 34, 347–356.

Abratt, R., Clayton, B. & Pitt, L. (1987). Corporate objectives in sports sponsorship. *International Journal of Advertising*, 6, 299–311.

Abratt, R. & Grobler, P. (1989). The evaluation of sports sponsorship. *International Journal of Advertising*, 8, 351–362.

Action on Smoking and Health (ASH) (2000). *PR in the playground: Tobacco industry initiatives on youth smoking.* Available online at <http://www.ash.org.uk>.

Advertising Standards Board website: <advertising standardsboard.com.au>.

Aidman, A. (1995). *Advertising in schools. ERIC Digest.* ERIC Identifier ED389473. Retrieved October 27, 2001 from <http://www.ed.gov/databases/ERIC_Digests/ed 389473.html>.

AIDS Action Committee (1989). SafetyNet© program: Small group parties for safer sex education. *Australian Journal of Public Health*, 79(9), 1305–1306.

Aitken, P.P., Leathar, D.S. & Squair, S.I. (1986). Children's awareness of cigarette brand sponsorship of sports and games in the UK. *Health Education Research*, 1(3), 203–211.

Ajzen, I. (1988). *Attitudes, Personality, and Behavior.* Chicago: The Dorsey Press.

Alderson, W. (1957). *Marketing behavior and executive action.* Homewood: Irwin.

Allen, J., Fuller, D.A. & Glaser, M. (1994). Understanding recycling behaviour: A public policy perspective. In D.J Ringold (Ed.), *Marketing and public policy conference proceedings*, vol. 4. Washington D.C.: American Marketing Association.

Amba-Rao, S.C. (1993). Multinational corporate social responsibility, ethics, interactions and Third World governments: An agenda for the 1990s. *Journal of Business Ethics*, 12(7), 553–573.

American Dietetic Association (1999). Position of the American Dietetic Association: Functional Foods. *Journal of the American Dietetic Association*, 99(10), 1278–86.

American Marketing Association Committee on Definitions (1960). *Marketing definitions: A glossary of marketing terms.* Chicago: American Marketing Association.

Amonini, C. (2001). The relative influence of morality, legitimacy, and other determinants on your alcohol, tobacco and marijuana use. Unpublished doctoral dissertation, Graduate School of Management, University of Western Australia, Perth, Western Australia.

Amonini, C. & Donovan, R.J. (2001, June). The relationship between morality and adolescents' tobacco use: An exploratory study. Paper presented at National Tobacco Conference, Adelaide.

Anderson, D.M., Duffy K. & Hallett, C. (1992). Cancer prevention counseling on telephone helplines. *Public Health Reports, 107*, 278–283

Andreasen, A. (1995). *Marketing social change: Changing behavior to promote health, social development, and the environment.* San Francisco: Jossey-Bass.

Andreasen, A. (1997). Prescriptions for theory-driven social marketing research: A response to Goldberg's alarms. *Journal of Consumer Psychology, 6*(2), 189–196.

Andreasen, A. (2000). '60 Minutes'. Message posted to social marketing listserver 14 January; archived at <soc-mktg@listproc.georgetown.edu>.

Andreasen, A. (Ed.) (2001). *Ethics in social marketing.* Washington, D.C.: Georgetown University Press.

Andreasen, A. (2002). Marketing social marketing in the social change marketplace. *Journal of Public Policy and Marketing, 21*(1), 3–14.

Andreasen, A. and Drumwright, M. (2001). Alliances and ethics in social marketing. In A. Andreasen (Ed.), *Ethics in social marketing.* Washington, D.C.: Georgetown University Press, 95–124.

American Psychological Society (1997, October). Human capital initiative—Reducing Violence: A behavioral science research plan for violence. *APS Observer.* Washington, D.C.

Armstrong, C. (1988, May). Sports sponsorship: A case-study approach to measuring its effectiveness. *European Research*, 97–102.

Associated Press (1998, April 27). Barbie needs limit ... *Marketing News, 32*(9)

Australian Bureau of Statistics (ABS) (1996a). *Children's immunisation Australia.* Canberra: Australian Government Publishing Servuce (AGPS), catalogue no. 4352.0.

Australian Bureau of Statistics (ABS) (1996b). *Women's safety Australia.* Canberra: AGPS, catalogue no. 4128.0.

Australian Bureau of Statistics (ABS) (1999). *Business sponsorship, Australia, 1996–97.* Canberra: AGPS, catalogue no. 4144.0.

Australian Bureau of Statistics (ABS) (2000). *Children's participation in cultural and leisure activities, Australia.* Canberra: AGPS, catalogue no. 4901.0.

Backer, T.E., Rogers, E.M. & Sopory, P. (1992). *Designing health communication campaigns: What works?* Newbury Park: Sage.

Bagozzi, R.P. & Moore, D.J. (1994). Public service advertisements: Emotions and empathy guide prosocial behaviour. *Journal of Marketing, 58*, 56–70.

Bagozzi, R.P. & Warshaw, P.R. (1990). Trying to consume. *Journal of Consumer Research, 17*, 127–140.

Baker, M.J. (1996). *Marketing: An introductory text* (6th ed.). London: Macmillan.

Balasubramanian, S.K. (1994). Beyond advertising and publicity: Hybrid messages and public policy issues. *Journal of Advertising, 23*, 29–46.

Ball, S. (1994). Theatre and health education: Meeting of minds or marriage of convenience? *Health Education Journal, 53*, 222–225.

Bandura, A. (1977a). Self-efficacy: Toward a unifying theory of behaviour change. *Psychological Review, 84*, 191–215.

Bandura, A. (1977b). *Social learning theory.* Englewood Cliffs: Prentice Hall.

Bandura, A. (1986). Social foundations of thought and action: A social cognitive theory. Englewood Cliffs: Prentice-Hall.

Banks, S.M., Salovey, P., Greener, S., Rothman, A.J., Moyer, A., Beauvais, J. & Epel, E. (1995). The effects of message framing on mammography utilization. *Health Psychology, 14*, 178–184.

Barber, L. (2001, January 20–1). Product misplacement. *The Weekend Australian Review*, 23.

Batini, C. & Donovan, R.J. (2001). *Stage One Qualitative Research Report to Great Southern Public Health Services.* Perth: NFO Donovan Research.

Batini, C. & Farley, R. (2001). *Road Safety Council community education campaigns on speeding February 1998–March 2001*. Paper presented at the National Conference of Road Safety: Gearing up for the Future, Perth, Western Australia.

Bayer, R. (1992). Review of *Free to be foolish: Politics and health promotion in the United States and Great Britain. Science*, 255(5043), 480–482.

Bayly, L. & Bull, F. (2001). *How to build social capital: A case study of an enduring community walking group*. Perth: Eastern Perth Public and Community Health Unit, University of Western Australia.

Bazeley, P. & Kemp, L. (1994). *Childhood immunisation: The role of parents and service providers. A review of the literature*. Canberra: Commonwealth Department of Human Services and Health.

BBC News online (2002, January 24). *Scientists Cross Pigs With Spinach*. Retrieved January 30, 2002 from <http://news.bbc.co.uk/hi/english/world/asiapacific/newsid_1780000/1780541.stm>.

Becker, M.H. (1974). The health belief model and personal health behaviour. *Health Education Monographs*, 2, 324–473.

Bednall, D. (1992). *Media and Immigrant Settlement*. Canberra: AGPS.

Beenstock, S. (1999, March 26). Meg@hurts. *Times Educational Supplement*, B8–9.

Belch, G.E. & Belch, M.A. (1990). *Introduction to Advertising and Promotion Management*. Homewood: Irwin.

Bender, K.L. & Westgren, R.E. (2001). Social construction of the market(s) for genetically modified and nonmodified crops. *American Behavioral Scientist*, 44(8), 1350–1370.

Benn, S.I. (1988). *The theory of freedom*. New York: Cambridge University Press.

Bennett, R. (1998). Shame, guilt and responses to nonprofit and public sector ads. *International Journal of Advertising*, 17(4), 483–499.

Bernhardt, J.M. (2001). Tailoring messages and design in a web-based skin cancer prevention intervention. *International Electronic Journal of Health Education*, 4, 290–297. Retreieved from <http://www.iejhe.org>.

Betts, L. (1993). Sponsorship and the VicHealth Model. *Health Promotion Journal of Australia*, 3(1), 13–15.

Bevins, J. (1988, September 22). Reducing communication abuse. *Workshop Proceedings Vol. 1*, Third National Drug Educators Workshop. Fremantle.

Biener, L. & Siegel, M. (2000. Tobacco marketing and adolescent smoking: More support for a causal influence. *American Journal of Public Health*, 90(3), 407–411.

Black, G. (2000, January 10). *60 Minutes*. Message posted to social marketing listserver. Archived at <soc-mktg@listproc.georgetown.edu>.

Blasi, A. (1980). Bridging moral cognition and moral action: A critical review of the literature. *Psychological Bulletin*, 88, 593–637.

Bloom, P.N. & Novelli, W.D. (1981). Problems and challenges in social marketing. *Journal of Marketing*, 45 (Spring), 79–88.

Blue, C.L. (1995). The predictive capacity of the theory of reasoned action and the theory of planned behavior in exercise research: An integrated literature review. *Research in Nursing & Health*, 18, 105–121.

Boer, H. & Seydel, E.R. (1996). Protection motivation theory. In M. Conner & P. Norman (Eds.), *Predicting health behaviour*. Buckingham: Open University Press, 95–120.

Bonniface, L. (2002). *Correlations of collective efficacy with environmental behaviour: Implications for social marketing*. Unpublished Master of Business (Marketing) thesis proposal, Edith Cowan University, Perth, Western Australia.

Booth, M.L., Macaskill, P., Owen, N., Oldenburg, B., Marcus, B.H. & Bauman, A. (1993). Population prevalence and correlates of stages of change in physical activity. *Health Education Quarterly*, 20, 431–440.

BoozeNews (2001, May 9). Statement of George A. Hacker on the marketing of 'alcopops' to teens. Retrieved April 20, 2003 from <http://www.cspinet.org>.

Borland, R., Balmford, J. & Hunt, D. (under review). The effectiveness of personally tailored computer generated advice letters for smoking cessation. *Addiction*.

Boster, F.J. & Mongeau, P. (1984). Fear-arousing persuasive messages. *Communication Yearbook*, 8, 330–375.

Botvin, G.J., Goldberg, C.J., Botvin, E.M. & Dusenbury, L. (1993). Smoking behavior of adolescents exposed to cigarette advertising. *Public Health Reports*, 108(2), 217–224.

Brandt, A.M. & Rozin, P. (1997). *Morality and health*. New York: Routledge.

Brannstrom, I. & Lindblad, I. (1994). Mass communication and health promotion: The power of the media and public opinion. *Health Communication*, 6(1), 21–36.

Brehony, K.A., Frederiksen, L.W. & Solomon, L.J. (1984). Marketing principles and behavorial medicine: An overview. In L.W. Frederiksen, L.J. Solomon & K.A. Brehony (Eds.), *Marketing health behavior. Principles, techniques, and applications.* New York: Plenum Press, 5–22.

Brenkert, G.G. (2001). The ethics of international social marketing. In A. Andreasen (Ed.), *Ethics in Social Marketing*. Washington, D.C.: Georgetown University Press, 39–69.

Brown, D. (2001). *Depressed men: Angry women: Non-stereotypical gender responses to anti-smoking messages in older smokers.* Unpublished masters dissertation, Edith Cowan University, Perth, Western Australia.

Brown, G. (1985). Tracking studies and sales effects: A UK perspective. *Journal of Advertising Research*, 25(1), 52–64.

Brown, L. (2002, May 31). In for the showbag. *The Australian*, 17.

Brown, W.J., Mummery, K., Eakin, E., Trost, S., Schofield, G. & Abernethy, P. (2002). 10 000 steps Rockhampton: Top down and bottom up approaches to increasing levels of physical activity. In S. Miilunpalo & R. Tulimaki (Eds.). *Health enhancing physical activity (HEPA): Evidence-based promotion of physical activity.* Book of Abstracts. Tampere: UKK Institute.

Brown, W.J. & Singhal, A. (1993). Ethical considerations of promoting prosocial messages through the popular media. *Journal of Popular Film and Television*, 21(3), 92–100.

Brownlee, S. (2001, December). The big fat question. *Self*, 124–127, 162–163.

Bryant, C., Lindenberger, J., Brown, C., Kent, E., Mogg Schreiber, J., Bustillo, M. & Walker, M. (2001). A social marketing approach to increasing enrollment in a public health program: A case study of the Texas WIC Program. *Human Organization*, 60(3), 234–246.

Bryant, J. & Zillmann, D. (Eds.) (2002). *Media effects: Advances in theory and research.* Mahwah: Lawrence Erlbaum.

Buchanan, F. (1996). Zero tolerance in South Australia: A statewide community initiative. *Australian Journal of Primary Health-Interchange*, 2(1), 107–112.

Buchanan, D. R., Reddy, S. & Hossain, Z. (1994). Social marketing: a critical appraisal. Social marketing and communication in health promotion. *Health Promotion International*, 9(1), 49–57.

Bull, F.C., Schipper, E.C., Jamrozik, K. & Blanksby, B.A. (1995). Beliefs and behaviour of general practitioners regarding promotion of physical activity. *Australian Journal of Public Health*, 19(3), 300–304.

Bull, F.C. & Jamrozik, K. (1998). Advice on exercise from a family physician can help sedentary patients to become active. *American Journal of Preventative Medicine*, *15*(2), 85–94.

Bullock, K.A. (2002, February 25). Family physicians to Governors: Help us discourage smoking. *American Academy of Family Physicians Statement*. Retrieved July 30, 2002 from <http://www.aafp.org/news/20020225stmt.html>.

Burbury, R. (1999, March 15). The 'third wave' of branding. *The Australian Financial Review*, 15.

Callaghan, R. (2001, October 6). No business like kid business. *The West Australian, Big Weekend* , 1–2.

Campbell, M.K., Demark-Wahnefried, W., Symons, M., Kalzbeek, W.D., Dodds, J., Cowan, A., Jackson, B., Motsinger, B., Hoben, K., Lashley, J., Demissie, S. & McClelland, J.W. (1999). Fruit and vegetable consumption and prevention of cancer: The Black Churches United for Better Health Project. *American Journal of Public Health*, *89*(9), 1390–1396.

Campbell, M.K., Symons, M., Demark–Wahnefried, W., Polhamus, B., Bernhardt, J.M., McClelland, J.W. & Washington, C. (1998). Stages of change and psychological correlates of fruit and vegetable consumption among rural African-American church members. *American Journal of Health Promotion*, *12*(3), 185–191.

Caragay, A.B. (1992). Cancer-preventive foods and ingredients. *Food Technology*, *46*(4), 65–68.

Carroll, A. (1993). Western Australian Health Promotion Foundation—Healthway. *Health Promotion Journal of Australia*, *3*, 42–43.

Carroll, T. (1997). The 1995 mass communication campaign for the national childhood immunisation program: An overview of the research conducted for the development, implementation and evaluation of the campaign. Sydney: Commonwealth Department of Human Services and Health.

Carroll, T. (2001). The role of social marketing in preventing harm associated with teenage drinking. Paper presented at the 2nd International Conference on Drugs and Young People. Melbourne. Retrieved April 21, 2003 from <http://www.adf.org.au/cyds/2dyp/carroll.pdf>.

Carroll, T. & Donovan, R.J. (2002). Alcohol marketing on the internet: New challenges for harm reduction. *Drug and Alcohol Review*, *21*, 83–91.

Carroll, T., Taylor, J. & Lum, M. (1996). *Evaluation of the Drug Offensive "Speed Catches up with you" amphetamines campaign—1993–1995*. Sydney: Commonwealth Department of Health and Family Services. Retrieved April 21, 2003 from <http://www.health.gov.au/pubhlth/publicat/document/reports/speedtr.pdf>.

Carter, S., Borland, R. & Chapman, S. (2001). *Finding the strength to kill your best friend: Smokers talk about smoking and quitting*. Sydney: Australian Smoking Cessation Consortium and GlaxoSmithKline Consumer Healthcare.

Casey, K.M. (n.d.). *The runaway game*. Retrieved April 22, 2003 from <http://www.therunawaygame.com>.

Centers for Disease Control and Prevention (1996). *The prevention marketing initiative: Applying prevention marketing*. Washington, D.C.: U.S. Department of Health and Human Services. Public Health Service.

Center for Media Education (CME) (1998). *Alcohol advertising targeted at youth on the internet: An update*. Washington, D.C.: Center for Media Education.

Center for a New American Dream (CNAD) (1997). *Poverty, race and consumerism*. Available online at <http://www.newdream.org>.

Centre for Behavioural Research in Cancer (1992). *Health warnings on cigarette packs*. Unpublished report, Victorian Anti-Cancer Council, Melbourne.

Chaika, G. (1998). The selling of our schools: Advertising in the classroom. *Education World*. Retrieved October 29, 2001 from <http://www.education-world.com/a_admin/admin083.shtml>

Chaiken, S. (1987). Heuristic versus systematic information processing and the use of source versus message cues in persuasion. *Journal of Personality and Social Psychology, 45*, 805–818.

Chaloupka, F.J. (1995). Public policies and private anti-health behavior. *The Economics of Health and Health Care, 85*(2), 45–49.

Chambers, J., Killoran, A., McNeill, A. & Reid, D. (1991). Smoking. *British Medical Journal* (editorial), *303*(6808), 973–977.

Chang, Y. (2002, June 10). 93-year-old man quits smoking habit. *Taipei Times*. Retrieved October 7, 2002 from <http://taipeitimes.com/news/2002/06/10/story/0000139712>.

Chapman, S. (1980). A David and Goliath story: Tobacco advertising in Australia. *British Medical Journal, 281*, 1187–1190.

Chapman, S. & Lupton, D. (1994). *The fight for public health: Principles and practice of media advocacy*. London: BMJ Publishing Group.

Chapman, S., Marks, R. & King, M. (1992). Trends in tans and skin protection in Australian fashion magazines, 1982 through 1991. *American Journal of Public Health, 82*, 1677–1680.

Chapman, S. and Reynolds, C. (1987). Regulating tobacco—The South Australian Tobacco Products Control Act 1986. *Community Health Studies, 11*(1), 9–15.

Chapman, S., Smith, W., Mowbray, G., Hugo, C. & Egger, G. (1993). Quit and win cessation contests: How should they be evaluated? *Preventative Medicine, 22*, 423–432.

Chapman, S. & Wakefield, M. (2001). Tobacco control advocacy in Australia: Reflections on 30 years of progress. *Health Education & Behaviour, 28*(3), 274–289

Checkup at the checkout counter (1999). *New World*, II. Retrieved July 31, 2002 from <http://w3.siemens.de/newworld/PND/PNDG/PNDGB/PNDGBB/pndgbb2_e.htm>.

Chen, P. (1996). Social marketing: Principles and practices for planned social change. *Media Asia, 23*(2), 79–85.

Chu, G.C. (1966). Fear arousal, efficacy, and imminency. *Journal of Personality and Social Psychology, 4*, 517–524.

Cialdini, R.B. (1984). *Influence: The new psychology of modern persuasion*. New York: Quill.

Cialdini, R.B. (1989). Littering: When every litter bit hurts. In R.E. Rice & C.K. Atkin (Eds.), *Public communication campaigns*. Newbury Park: Sage.

Cialdini, R.B. (1994). Interpersonal influence. In S. Shavitt & T.C. Brock (Eds.). *Persuasion: Psychological insights and perspectives*. Boston: Allyn and Bacon, 195–218.

Clarkson, J., Corti, B., Pikora, T., Jalleh, G. & Donovan, R.J. (1998). *Organisational survey 1992–1997. Healthy environment policies in sponsored organisations*. Perth: Health Promotion Evaluation Unit, University of Western Australia.

Clarkson, J., Donovan, R.J., Giles-Corti, B., Bulsara, M. & Jalleh, G. (2000). *Survey on recreation and health 1992–1998: Volume 5: Health environments in recreation venues*. Perth: Health Promotion Evaluation Unit, University of Western Australia.

Clarkson, J., Donovan, R.J., Giles-Corti, B. & Watson, N. (2002). *A study of smoking promotion in the mass media*. Report to Healthway by Health Promotion Unit. Perth: Department of Public Health, University of Western Australia.

Close, H. & Donovan, R.J. (1998). *Who's my market? Researching audience for the arts*. Sydney: Australian Council.

Coleman, P.L. & Meyer, R.C. (Eds.) (1990). *Proceedings from the enter-educate confer-ence: Entertainment for social change.* Baltimore: Johns Hopkins University Center for Comunication Programs.

Collins, M. (1993). Global corporate philanthropy—Marketing beyond the call of duty? *European Journal of Marketing, 27*(2), 46–59.

Commonwealth of Australia (1999, April 15). *Communicable Disease Intelligence, 23*(4). Canberra: Commonwealth of Australia, Department of Health and Aged Care.

Commonwealth of Australia (1998, March 19). *Communicable Disease Intelligence, 22*(3). Canberra: Commonwealth of Australia, Department of Health and Family Serv-ices.

Commonwealth of Australia (2000). *Let's work together to beat measles: A report on Aus-tralia's measles control campaign.* Canberra: Commonwealth of Australia. Canberra: Commonwealth of Australia, Department of Health and Aged Care.

Commonwealth of Australia (2000, July). *Communicable Disease Intelligence, 24*(7). Can-berra: Commonwealth of Australia, Department of Health and Aged Care.

Commonwealth of Australia (2001, September). Australian Childhood Immunisation Register. Coverage report. Canberra: Commonwealth of Australia, Department of Health and Aged Care.

Communication and change. News and Issues (1998, November 23). *Drum Beat, 7.* Retrieved April 21, 2003 from <http://www.comminit.com/drum_beat_7.html>.

Communities that care … A complete prevention planning system for a healthy commu-nity. Retrieved January 29, 2002 from <http://www.drp.org/ctc/CTC.html >.

Community Agency for Social Enquiry (CASE) (1997). *Let the sky be the limit: Soul City evaluation report.* Braamfontein: Community Agency for Social Enquiry.

Conner, M. & Norman, P. (Eds.) (1996). *Predicting health behaviour: Research and practice with social cognition models.* Buckingham: Open University Press.

Conner, M. & Sparks, P. (1996). The theory of planned behaviour and health behav-iours. In M. Conner & P. Norman (Eds.). *Predicting health behaviour.* Buckingham: Open University Press, 121–163.

Consumers Union (1998). *Captive kids: A report on commercial pressures on kids at schools.* Retrieved October 27, 2001 from <http://www.igc.org/consunion/other/cap-tivekids/summary.htm>.

Cooke, C. (2001, March 27). Hard to reach audiences. Message posted to social market-ing listserver. Archived at <mailto:soc-mktg@listproc.georgetown.edu>.

Cooper-Martin, E. & Smith, N.C. (1994). *Target marketing: Good marketing or bad ethics.* Washington, D.C.: Georgetown University, School of Business Administration, Working Paper Series, MKTG–1777–15–1294.

Cornwell, P. (1996). *Cause of death.* London: Little, Brown.

Cornwell, T.B. & Maignan, I. (1998). An international review of sponsorship research. *Journal of Advertising, 27*(1), 1–21.

Corti, B. (1998). *The relative influence of, and interaction between, environmental and indi-vidual determinants of recreational physical activity in sedentary workers and home mak-ers.* Unpublished doctoral dissertation, Department of Public Health, University of Western Australia, Perth.

Corti, B., Donovan, R.J. & Holman, C.D.J. (1996). Using sponsorship to promote health messages to children. *Health Education Quarterly, 24*(3), 276–286.

Corti, B., Holman, C.D.J., Donovan, R.J., Frizzell, S.K. & Carroll, A.M. (1997). Warn-ing: Attending a sport, racing or arts venue may be beneficial to your health. *Aus-tralian and New Zealand Journal of Public Health, 21*(4), 371–376.

Corti, B., Holman, C.D.J., Donovan, R.J., Frizzell, S.K. & Carroll, A.M. (1995). Using sponsorship to create health environments in sport, racing and arts venues. *Health Promotion International, 10*(3), 185–197.

Cosmetics on 1, lingerie on 2, mammograms on 3? (1997, June). *Self*.

Court, M. (1993). The South Australian Health Promotion Foundation—Foundation S.A. *Health Promotion Journal of Australia, 3,* 25–26.

Cowell, D. (1984). *The marketing of services*. Oxford: Heinemann.

Coyle, S.L., Boruch, R.F. & Turner, C.F. (Eds.) (1989). *Evaluating AIDS prevention programs*. Washington D.C.: National Academy Press.

Craig-Lees, M., Joy, S. & Browne, B. (1995). *Consumer Behaviour*. Brisbane: John Wiley & Sons.

Cramer, P. & Carroll, T. (1998). *Immunise Australia: Community education campaign. Benchmark and tracking research*. Sydney: Department of Health and Family Services.

Crimmins, J. & Horn, M. (1996). Sponsorship: from management ego trip to marketing success. *Journal of Advertising Research, 35*(4), 11–21.

Crompton, J. (1993). Sponsorship of sport by tobacco and alcohol companies: A review of the issues. *Journal of Sport and Social Issues, 17,* 148–167.

Crompton, J.L. (1981). The role of pricing in the delivery of community services. *Community Development Journal, 16*(1), 44–54.

Crowley M.G. (1991). Prioritising the sponsorship audience. *European Journal of Marketing, 25*(11), 11–22.

Curry, S.J., Kristal, A.R. & Bowen, D.J. (1992). An application of the stage model of behaviour change to dietary fat reduction. *Health Education Research, 7,* 97–105.

Cushman, P. (1990). Why the self is empty: Toward a historically situated psychology. *American Psychologist, 45*(5), 599–611.

Daniels, L. (1977). *Fear: A history of horror in the mass media*. London: Granada Publishing.

Dann, S. (1998). More ethics issues: Different cultures and different beliefs. Message posted to social marketing listserver July 28, archived at <soc-mktg@listproc.georgetown.edu>.

Davidson, L.L. (1996). Editorial: Preventing injuries from violence towards women. *American Journal of Public Health, 86*(1), 13–14.

Davis, R.C. & Taylor, B.G. (1999). Does batterer treatment reduce violence? A synthesis of the literature. In L. Feder (Ed.), *Women and domestic violence: An interdisciplinary approach*. New York: Haworth.

Day, B.A. & Monroe, M.C. (Eds.) (2000). *Environmental education and communication for a sustainable world: Handbook for international practitioners*. Washington D.C.: Academy for Educational Development and GreenCom.

De Becker, G. (1998). *A gift of fear: Survival signals that protect us from violence*. New York: Dell.

Deighton, J., Romer, D. & McQueen, J. (1989). Using drama to persuade. *Journal of Consumer Research, 16,* 335–343.

Della-Giacoma, J. (1993, April 24). User-pays system to cut cost, water use. *Weekend Australian*.

De Musis, E.A. & Miaoulis, G. (1988). Channels of distribution and exchange concepts in health promotion. *Journal of Health Care Marketing, 8,* 60–68.

Denton, F. & Thorson, E. (1995). *Civic journalism: Does it work?* Washington, D.C.: Pew Center for Civic Journalism.

Department of Community Development (1989). *Domestic violence information kit*. Perth: Government of Western Australia.

DeYoung, K. (2001, May 17). Organisations find big changes in Bush's A-list. *Washington Post*, 21. Retrieved May 28, 2001 from.<http://www.washingtonpost.com/wp-dyn/articles/A36643-2001May16.html>.

DiClemente, C.C., Prochaska, J.A., Fairhurst, S.K., Velicer, W.F., Velasquez, M.M. & Rossi, J.F. (1991). The process of smoking cessation: An analysis of precontemplation, contemplation and preparation stages of change. *Journal of Consulting and Clinical Psychology*, 59(2), 295–304.

Dillard, J.P., Plotnick, C.A., Godbold, L.C., Friemuth, V.S. & Edgar, T. (1996). The multiple affective outcome of AIDS PSAs: Fear appeals do more than scare people. *Communication Research*, *23*, 44–72.

Dishman, R.K. (1988). Exercise adherence research: Future directions. *American Journal of Health promotion*, *3*(1), 52–56.

Dishman, R.K. (1990). Determinants of participation in physical activity. In C. Bouchard (Ed.). *Exercise, fitness, and health*. Champaign: Human Kinetics Publishers.

Donovan, R.J. (1991). Public health advertising: Execution guidelines for health promotion professionals. *Health Promotion Journal of Australia*, *1*, 40–5.

Donovan, R.J. (1992a). *Aboriginal reconciliation research*. Report to Aboriginal Reconciliation Unit, Department of Prime Minister and Cabinet, Canberra.

Donovan, R.J. (1992b). *Using media for road safety public education campaigns*. Report to Traffic Board of Western Australia.

Donovan, R.J. (1995a). *Guidelines for creating effective road safety advertising.* Report to Federal Office of Road safety. Perth: Donovan Research.

Donovan, R.J. (1995b). *Unsafe alcohol consumption amongst young men in remote areas of Western Australia*. Report to Health Department of Western Australia. Perth: Donovan Research.

Donovan, R.J. (1996). *Using newspapers and community action to further the Aboriginal Reconciliation Process: A submission to the Council for Aboriginal Reconciliation.* Perth: University of Western Australia.

Donovan, R.J. (1997). *A Model of Alcohol Consumption to Assist in Developing Communication Strategies for Reducing Excessive Alcohol Consumption By Young People.* Report to Health Department of Western Australia. Perth: Donovan Research.

Donovan, R.J. (2000a). Tracking phase two of the national tobacco campaign. In K. Hassard (Ed.), *Australia's national tobacco campaign: evaluation report volume two*, 115–54. Canberra: Comonwealth Department of Health and Aged Care.

Donovan, R.J. (2000b). Understanding the social determinants of health. *Social Marketing Quarterly*, 6(3), 55–57.

Donovan, R.J. (2001). The effect of tobacco warnings: Expert statement. Submitted by Canadian Cancer Society, in the case of JTI-MacDonald Corp., Imperial Tobacco Canada Ltd and Rothman, Benson & Hedges Inc., vs the Attorney-General of Canada, Montreal.

Donovan, R.J. & Batini, C. (1997). *Strategy development and concept testing research for road safety campaign*. Summary report to Marketforce. Perth: Donovan Research.

Donovan, R.J., Close, H.K., Woodhouse, M. & Hogben, J. (1979). *The resident and urban renewal*. Melbourne: Australian Housing Research Council.

Donovan, R.J., Corti, B., Holman, C.D.J., West, D. & Pitter, D. (1993). Evaluating sponsorship effectiveness. *Health Promotion Journal of Australia*, 3(1), 63–67.

Donovan, R.J., Corti, B. & Jalleh, G. (1997a). Evaluating sponsorship effectiveness: An epidemiological approach to analysing survey data. *Australian Journal of Market Research*, 5(2), 9–23.

Donovan, R.J. & Egger, G. (1997). *A conceptual framework for achieving drug compliance in sport*. Report to Australian Sports Drug Agency. Perth: Donovan Research.

Donovan, R.J. & Egger, G.J. (2000). *Men's health beliefs: A qualitative research report to the "Healthy Blokes" project*. Centre for Behavioural Research in Cancer Control. Perth: Donovan Research.

Donovan, R.J., Egger, G.J. & Francas, M. (1999a). TARPARE: A method for selecting target audiences for public health interventions. *Australian and New Zealand Journal of Public Health, 23*(3), 280–4.

Donovan, R.J., Egger, G., Kapernick, V. & Mendoza, J. A. (2002). A conceptual framework for achieving drug compliance in sport. *Sports Medicine, 32*(4), 269–284.

Donovan, R.J. & Francas, M. (1985). *Cigarette pack health messages research*. Report to Department of Health. Perth: Donovan Research.

Donovan, R.J. & Francas, M. (1987). *Child value*. Report to Department for Community Services. Perth: Donovan Research.

Donovan, R.J. & Francas, M. (1990). Understanding Motivation and Communication Strategies. *Australian Health Review, 13*, 103–114.

Donovan, R.J., Francas, M., Paterson, D. & Zappelli, R. (2000). Formative research for mass media-based campaigns: Western Australia's 'Freedom from Fear' campaign targeting male perpetrators of intimate partner violence. *Health Promotion Journal of Australia, 10*(2), 78–83.

Donovan, R.J., Freeman, J., Borland, R. & Boulter, J. (1999b). Tracking the national tobacco campaign. In K. Hassard (Ed.), *Australia's national tobacco campaign: Evaluation report volume one,* 127–187. Canberra: Commonwealth Department of Health and Aged Care.

Donovan, R.J. & Henley, N. (1997). Negative outcomes, threats and threat appeals: Towards a conceptual famework for the study of fear and other emotions in social marketing communications. *Social Marketing Quarterly, 4*(1), 56–67.

Donovan, R.J. & Henley, N. (2000). A conceptual framework for fear arousal and threat appeals in health promotion communications. *Health Promotion Journal of Australia, 10*(2), 84–88.

Donovan, R.J., Henley, N., Jalleh, G. & Slater, C. (1995). *Road safety advertising: An empirical study and literature review*. Report to Federal Office of Road Safety. Perth: Donovan Research.

Donovan, R.J. & Holden, S.J.S. (1985). Projective techniques in attitude research. *Australian Marketing Researcher, 9*, 55–62.

Donovan, R.J. & Jalleh, G. (1999a). *Risk behaviours by stages of change*. Unpublished research report to the Western Australian Health Promotion Foundation. Department of Public Health and Graduate School of Management, University of Western Australia, Perth, Western Autsralia.

Donovan, R.J. & Jalleh, G. (1999b). Positive versus negatively framed product attributes: The influence of involvement. *Psychology & Marketing, 28*(4), 215–234.

Donovan, R.J. & Jalleh, G. (2000). Positive versus negative framing of a hypothetical infant immunisation: The influence of involvement. *Health Education and Behaviour, 27*(1), 82–95

Donovan, R.J., Jalleh, G., Clarkson, J., Corti, B. & Pikora, T. (1997b). *Sponsorship monitor evaluation results 1996/97*. Health Promotion Evaluation Unit, Department of Public Health and Graduate School of Management, University of Western Australia, Perth, Western Australia.

Donovan, R.J., Jalleh, G., Clarkson, J., Corti, B. & Pikora, T. (1998b). *Sponsorship monitor evaluation results 1997/98*. Health Promotion Evaluation Unit, Department of Public Health and Graduate School of Management, University of Western Australia, Perth, Western Australia.

Donovan, R.J., Jalleh, G., Clarkson, J., Corti, B. (1999g). Evidence for the effectiveness of sponsorship as a health promotion tool. *Australian Journal of Primary Health— Interchange, 5*(4), 81–91.

Donovan, R.J., Jalleh, G., Corti, B. & Clarkson, J. (1999c). *Multiple Messages Study Results*. Health Promotion Evaluation Unit, Department of Public Health and

Graduate School of Management, University of Western Australia, Perth, Western Australia.

Donovan, R.J., Jalleh, G. & Henley, N. (1999d). Effective road safety advertising: Are big production budgets necessary? *Accident Analysis and Prevention, 31*, 243–252.

Donovan, R.J., Jason, J., Gibbs, D.A. & Kroger, F. (1991). Paid advertising for AIDS prevention: Would the end justify the means? *Public Health Reports, 106*, 645–651.

Donovan, R.J. & Jones, S. (1999). *Social capital and the media.* Keynote address, Australian Health Promotion Professionals National Conference, Perth.

Donovan, R.J. & Leivers, S. (1988). *Young women and smoking.* Report to Department of Human Services and Health. Canberra: Donovan Research.

Donovan, R.J. & Leivers, S. (1993). Using paid advertising to modify racial stereotype beliefs. *Public Opinion Quarterly, 57*, 205–218.

Donovan, R.J., Leivers, S. & Hannaby, L. (1999e). Smokers' responses to anti-smoking advertisements by stage of change. *Social Marketing Quarterly, 5*(2), 56–63.

Donovan, R.J., Mick, L., Holden, S.J.S. & Noel, J. (1997c). *Underage drinking amongst Aboriginal and Islander Youth in the Northern Territory.* Report to Northern Territory Department of Health. Perth: Donovan Research.

Donovan, R.J. & Owen, N. (1994). Social marketing and population interventions. In R.K. Dishman (Ed.), *Advances in Exercise Adherence* (2nd ed.). Illinois: Human Kinetics, 249–290.

Donovan, R.J., Paterson, D. & Francas, M. (1999f). Targeting male perpetrators of intimate partner violence: Western Australia's *Freedom from Fear* campaign. *Social Marketing Quarterly, 5*(3), 127–143.

Donovan, R.J. & Robinson, L. (1992). Using mass media in health promotion: The Western Australia immunisation campaign. In R. Hall & J. Richter (Eds.), *Immunisation: The old and the new.* Canberra: Public Health Association.

Donovan, R.J. & Spark, R. (1997). Towards guidelines for researching remote Aboriginal communities. *Australian and New Zealand Journal of Public Health, 21*(1), 89–95.

Donovan, R.J., Weller, N. & Clarkson, J. (2003). *Incidental smoking in the media study.* Report to the Commonwealth Department of Health and Aged Care. Centre for Behavioural Research in Cancer Control, Curtin University, Perth, Western Australia.

Donovan Research 1998. *Concept Screening and ADTEST®.* Reports to Domestic Violence Prevention Unit. Perth: Donovan Research.

Dorfman, L. & Wallack, L. (1996). *The news on alcohol—Media advocacy strategies to promote prevention policy.* Toronto: Paper presented at the Tenth International Alcohol Conference.

Downie, R.S. & Calman, K.C. (1994). *Healthy respect. Ethics in health care* (2nd ed.). Oxford: Oxford University Press.

Drumwright, M.E. (1996, October). Company advertising with a social dimension: The role of noneconomic criteria. *Journal of Marketing, 60*, 71–88.

Durgee, J. (1986). How consumer sub-cultures code reality: A look at some code types. In R. Lutz (Ed.), *Advances in Consumer Research, 13*, 332–337. Association of Consumer Research.

Dworkin, G. (1988). *The theory and practice of autonomy.* Cambridge: Cambridge University Press.

Dwyer, C. (1997, November). Sponsorship. *The Australian Financial Review Magazine*, 20–22.

Eaton, L. (2001, June 9). Tobacco companies exploit women, says WHO. *British Medical Journal, 322*, 1384.

Egan, C. (2002, January 14). Depressing truth about child offenders. *The Australian*, 6.

Egger, G., Bolton, A., O'Neill, M. & Freeman, D. (1996). Effectiveness of an abdominal obesity reduction programme in men: The GutBuster "weight loss" programme. *International Journal of Obesity*, 20, 227–231.

Egger, G., Donovan, R.J. & Corti, B. (1998). *Development of national physical activity guidelines*. Report to Commonwealth Department of Health and Aged Care. Perth: Health Promotion Evaluation Unit, University of Western Australia.

Egger, G., Donovan, R.J., Giles-Corti, B., Bull, F. & Swinburn, B. (2001). Developing national physical activity guidelines for Australians. *Australian and New Zealand Journal of Public Health*, 25(6), 561–563.

Egger, G., Donovan, R.J. & Spark, R.A. (1990a). A component circuit approach to needs assessment and strategy selection in health promotion. *International Journal of Health Promotion*, 5(4), 299–302.

Egger, G., Donovan, R.J. & Spark, R.A. (1993). *Health and the media: Principles and practises for health promotion*. Sydney: McGraw-Hill.

Egger, G., Fitzgerald, W., Frape, G., Monaem, A., Rubinstein, P., Tyler, C. & Mackay, B. (1983). Results of a large scale media anti-smoking campaign in Australia: The North Coast Healthy Lifestyle Programme. *British Medical Journal*, 287, 1125–1287.

Egger, G. & Mowbray, G. (1993). A qualitative assessment of obesity and overweight in working men. *Australian Journal of Nutrition and Diet*, 50(1), 10–14.

Egger, G., Spark, R. & Lawson, J. (1990b). *Health promotion strategies and methods*. Sydney: McGraw-Hill.

Egger, G., Spark, R. & Lawson, J. & Donovan, R.J. (1999). *Health promotion strategies and methods* (2nd ed.). Sydney: McGraw-Hill.

Egger, G., Wolfenden, K., Pares, J. & Mowbray, G. (1991). Bread. It's a great way to go. *Medical Journal of Australia*, 155(11–12), 820–821.

Eisikovits, Z. & Buchbinder, E. (1997). Talking violent: A phenomenological study of metaphors battering men use. *Violence Against Women*, 3(5), 482–498.

Elder, J.P., Edwards, C.C., Conway, T.L., Kenney, E., Johnson, C.A. & Bennett, E.D. (1996). Independent evaluation of the California tobacco education program. *Public Health Reports*, 111, 353–358.

Elder, J.P., Geller, E.S., Hovell, M.F. & Mayer, J.A. (1994). *Motivating heath behaviour*. New York: Delmar.

Elliott, B. (1995, May). The inapplicability of the exchange concept to social marketing. *Marketing and Public Policy Conference*, Atlanta.

Family and Children's Services (1997/8). *Family and Children's Services Annual Report*. Perth: Family and Children's Services.

Family and Children's Services (1998/9). *Family and Children's Services Annual Report*. Perth: Family and Children's Services.

Farkas, A.J., Gilpin, E.A., Distenfan, J.M. & Pierce, J.P. (1999). The effects of household and workplace smoking restrictions on quitting behaviours. *Tobacco Control*, 8, 261–265.

Farkas, A.J., Gilpin, E.A., White, M.M. & Pierce, R.P. (2000). Association between household and workplace smoking restrictions and adolescent smoking. *Journal of the American Medical Association*, 284(6), 717–722.

Farrelly, M.C., Evans, W.N. & Sfekas, A.E.S. (1999). The impact of workplace smoking bans: Results from a national survey. *Tobacco Control*, 8, 272–277.

Faulkener, R.A. & Slattery, C.M. (1990). The relationship of physical activity to alcohol consumption in youth, 15–16 years of age. *Canadian Journal of Public Health*, 81, 168–169.

Fawcett, G.M., Heise, L.L., Isita-Espejel, L. & Pick, S. (1999). Changing community responses to wife abuse: A research and demonstration project in Iztacalco, Mexico. *American Psychologist*, 54(1), 41–49.

Feder, L.K. (1998). Branding culture: Nonprofits turn to marketing to improve image and bring in the bucks. *Marketing News, 32*(1), 1.

Fennell, G. (1978). Consumers' perceptions of the product-use situation. *Journal of Marketing, 42*(2), 38–47.

Ferriman, A. (2001, May 19). Editor resigns from post after tobacco gift. *British Medical Journal, 322,* 1200. Available online at <http://bmj.com.cgi/content/full/322/7296/1200/e>.

Festinger, L. (1957). *A theory of cognitive dissonance.* Stanford: Stanford University Press.

Field, A., Cheung, L., Wolf, A.M., Herzog, D.B., Gortmaker, S.L. & Colditz, G.A. (1999). Exposure to the mass media and weight concerns among girls. *Pediatrics, 103*(3). Retrieved April 20, 2003 from <http://www.pediatrics.org/cgi/content/full/103/3/e36>.

Fighting the good fight (2001). Message posted to culture jammers listserver, October 17. Archived at <jammers@lists.adbusters.org>.

Fine, S.H. (1990). *The marketing of ideas and social issues* (2nd ed.). New York: Praeger.

Fishbein, M. (1967). *Readings in attitude theory and measurement.* New York: Wiley.

Fishbein, M. & Ajzen, I. (1975). *Belief, attitude, intention and behaviour: An introduction to theory and research.* Reading: Addison-Wesley.

Fishbein, M., Middlestadt, S. & Hitchcock, P.J. (1991). Using information to change sexually transmitted disease-related behaviours: An analysis based on the theory of reasoned action. In J.N. Wasserheit, S.O. Aral & K.K. Holmes (Eds.), *Research issues in human behvior and sexually transmitted diseases in the AIDS era.* Washington, D.C.: American Society for Micro-Biology.

Flora, J.A., Maibach, E.W. & Maccoby, N. (1989). The role of media across four levels of health promotion intervention. *Annual Review of Public Health, 10,* 181–201.

Foerster, S.B., Kizer, K.W., DiSogra, L.K., Bal, D.G., Krieg, B.F. & Bunch, K.L. (1995). California's '5 a Day—For Better Health!' Campaign: An innovative population-based effort to effect large-scale dietary change. *American Journal of Preventive Medicine, 11*(2), 124–131.

Forbes, A. (2000). *Differences in social marketing–commercial marketing.* Message posted to social marketing listserver (April 3). Archived at <soc-mktg@listproc.georgetown.edu>.

Fox, K.F.A. & Kotler, P. (1980, Fall). The marketing of social causes: The first 10 years. *Journal of Marketing, 44,* 24–33.

Francas, M. & Donovan, R.J. (2001). *Perpetrator research.* Report to Domestic Violence Prevention Unit. Perth: NFO Donovan Research.

France, A., Donovan, R.J., Watson, C. & Leivers, S. (1991). A chlamydia awareness campaign aimed at reducing HIV risks in young adults. *Australian Health Promotion Journal, 1*(1), 19–28.

Frankenberger, K.D. & Convisser, J. (1995). Evaluating the distribution component of an HIV/AIDS social marketing program aimed at urban youth. In P. Scholder Ellen & P.J. Kaufman (Eds.). *Marketing and public policy conference proceedings,* Atlanta, 5, 276–286.

Freedman, J.L. & Fraser, S.C. (1966). Compliance without pressure: The foot-in-the-door technique. *Journal of Personality and Social Psychology, 4,* 195–202.

Freimuth, V.S. & Mettger, W. (1990). Is there a hard-to-reach audience? *Public Health Reports, 105,* 232–238.

French, S.A., Jeffrey, R.W., Story, M., Breitlow, K.K., Baxter, J.S, Hannan, P. & Snyder, M.P. (2001). Pricing and promotion effects on low-fat vending snack purchases: The CHIPS study. *American Journal of Public Health, 91*(1), 112–117.

French, S.A., Jeffrey, R.W., Story, M., Hannan, P. & Snyder, M.P. (1997). A pricing strategy to promote low-fat snack choices through vending machines. *American Journal of Public Health, 87*(5), 849–851.

Frizzell, S. (1993). Healthway—A catalyst in the community. *Health Promotion Journal of Australia, 3,* 68–69.

Frizzell, S. (2001). Healthy communities report card. *Healthway News, 31,* 12.

FTC News Summary (1981, September 11). Tobacco industry spent more than $1 billion in 1979 to promote cigarette sales. 1.

Functional food fights (1999). *Environmental Health Perspectives, 107*(9), 446–447.

Furnham, A., Ingle, H., Gunter, B. & McClelland, A. (1997). A content analysis of alcohol portrayal and drinking in British television soap operas. *Health Education Research, 12*(4), 519–529.

Furlong, R. (1994). Tobacco advertising legislation and the sponsorship of sport. *Australian Business Law Review, 22*(3), 159–189.

Galbally, R. (1993). The Victorian Health Promotion Foundation—Vic Health. *Health Promotion Journal of Australia, 3,* 4–5.

Geller, E.S. (1989). Applied behavior analysis and social marketing: An integration for environmental preservation. *Journal of Social Issues, 45,* 17–36.

Ghorpade, S. (1986). Agenda setting: A test of advertising's neglected function. *Journal of Advertising, 26,* 23–27.

Giles-Corti, B. & Donovan, R.J. (2002). The relative influence of individual, social and physical environment determinants of physical activity. *Social Science and Medicine, 54,* 1793–1812.

Giles-Corti, B., Clarkson, J., Donovan, R.J., Frizzell, S.K., Carroll, A.M., Pikora, T. & Jalleh, G. (2001). Creating smoke-free environments in recreational settings. *Health Education & Behavior, 28*(3), 341–351.

Gillespie, M.A. & Ellis, L.B.M. (1993). Computer-based education revisited. *Journal of Medical Systems, 17*(3/4), 119–125.

Gintner, G.G., Rectanus, E.F., Achord, K. & Parker, B. (1987). *Parental history of hypertension and screening attendance: Effects of wellness appeal versus threat appeal.* Mahwah: Lawrence Erlbaum.

Glantz, S. (2002). Rate movies with smoking 'R'. <../pdf/ECPglantz.pdfL, 5, 31–34.

Godfrey C. & Maynard A. (1988). Economic aspects of tobacco use and taxation policy. *British Medical Journal, 297,* 339–343.

Godin, G. (1993). The theory of reasoned action and planned behaviour: Overview of findings, emerging research problems and usefulness for exercise promotion. *Journal of Applied Sport Psychology, 5,* 141–157.

Godin, G. (1994). Social cognitive models. In R.K. Dishman (Ed.), *Advances in Exercise Adherence* (2nd ed.). Illinois: Human Kinetics.

Godin, G. & Kok, G. (1996). The theory of planned behavior: A review of its applications to health-related behaviors. *American Journal of Health Promotion, 11*(2), 87–98.

Goldberg, M.E. (1995). Social marketing: Are we fiddling while Rome burns? *Journal of Consumer Psychology, 4*(4), 347–370.

Goldberg, M.E. & Bechtel, L.J. (n.d.) (circa 1996). ADSMARTS: An intervention invoking reactance to combat alcohol usage by youths. Unpublished manuscript. University Park, PA: Penn State University.

Goldstein, A.O., Sobel R.A. & Newman, G.R. (1999, March 24). Tobacco and alcohol use in G-rated children's animated films. *Journal of the American Medical Association, 281,* 1131–1136

Gomel, M. (1997). *A focus on women. Nations for Mental Health.* Geneva: World Health Organization.

Government of Western Australia (1999). Information about sponsorship and advertising. In *School Education Act 1999* (WA). Retrieved October 4, 2001 from <http://www.edreview.wa.gov.au/bill/topics/sponship.htm>.

Graeff, J.A., Elder, J.P. & Booth, E.M. (1993). *Communication for health and behaviour change: A developing country perspective.* San Francisco: Jossey-Bass.

Green, L.W. (1999). Health education's contributions to public health in the twentieth century: A glimpse through health promotion's rear-view mirror. *Annual Review of Public Health, 20,* 67–88.

Green, L.W. & Kreuter, M.W. (1991). *Health promotion planning: An educational and ecological approach.* Mountain View: Mayfield Publishing.

Green, L.W. & Kreuter, M.W. (1999). *Health promotion planning: An educational and ecological approach* (3rd ed.). Mountain View: Mayfield Publishing.

Grey Advertising (1990). Road safety: The Transport Accident Commission Campaign. In Advertising Federation of Australia, *Effective Advertising: Casebook of the AFA Advertising Effectiveness Awards 1990.* Sydney: Advertising Federation of Australia.

Grimley, D.M., Prochaska, G.E. & Prochaska, J.O. (1997). Condom use adoption and continuation: A transtheoretical approach. *Health Education Research, 12*(1), 61–75.

Gross, A., Traylor, M. & Shuman, P. (1987). Corporate sponsorship of art and sports events in North America. *European Research, 15,* 9–13.

Grube, J. & Wallack, L. (1994). Television beer advertising and drinking knowledge, beliefs, and intentions among schoolchildren. *American Journal of Public Health, 84*(2), 254–259.

Gruskin, S., Plafker, K. & Smith-Estelle, A. (2001). Understanding and responding to youth substance use: The contribution of a health and human rights framework. *American Journal of Public Health, 91*(12), 1954–1963.

Hafstad, A., Aaro, L.E. & Langmark, F. (1996). Evaluation of an anti-smoking mass media campaign targeting adolescents: The role of affective response and interpersonal communication. *Health Education Research, 11*(1), 29–38.

Hahn, A. & Craythorn, E. (1994). Inactivity and physical environment in two regional centres. *Health Promotion Journal of Australia, 4*(2), 43–45.

Haire, M. (1950). Projective techniques in marketing research. *Journal of Marketing, 14,* 649–656.

Hansen, W.G. (1959). How accessibility shapes land use. *Journal of the American Institute of Planners, 15,* 73–76.

Hansen, F. & Scotwin, L. (1995). An experimental inquiry into sponsoring: What effects can be measured? *Marketing and Research Today, 23*(3), 173–181.

Harachi, T. W., Ayres, C. D., Hawkins, D., Catalano, R. & Cushing, J. (1996). Empowering communities to prevent substance abuse: Process evaluation results from a risk- and protection-focused community mobilization effort. *Journal of Primary Prevention, 16,* 233–254.

Hardy, F. (1950, 1972). *Power Without Glory.* Melbourne: Lloyd O'Neill.

Harris, E., Wise, M., Hawe, P., et al. (1995). *Working Together: intersectoral action for health.* Canberra: AGPS.

Harris, R.J. (1999). *A cognitive psychology of mass communication* (3rd ed.). Mahhaw, N.J.New Jersey: Lawrence Erlbaum.

Harrison, J.A., Mullen, P.D. & Green, L.W. (1992). A meta-analysis of studies of the health belief model with adults. *Health Education Research: Theory & Practice, 7*(1), 107–116.

Harvey, B. (2001, January 18). Firms fight for police job. *The West Australian,* 4.

Hassard, K. (Ed.) (1999). *Australia's national tobacco campaign: Evaluation report,* vol. 1. Canberra: Commonwealth of Australia.

Hassard, K. (Ed.) (2000). *Australia's national tobacco campaign: Evaluation report,* vol. 2. Canberra: Commonwealth of Australia.

Hastings, G. (1984). Sponsorship works differently from advertising. *International Journal of Advertising, 3*, 171–176.

Hastings, G. & Donovan, R.J. (2002). International initiatives: introduction and overview. *Social Marketing Quarterly, 8*(1), 3–5.

Hastings, G. & Haywood, A. (1991). Social marketing and communication in health promotion. *Health Promotion International, 6*, 135–145.

Hastings, G. & Haywood, A. (1994). Social marketing: A critical response. *Health Promotion International, 9*(1), 59–63.

Hastings, G., MacAskill, S., McNeill, R. & Leathar, D. (1988). Sports sponsorship in health education. *Health Promotion, 3*, 161–169.

Hastings, G. & MacFadyen, L. (2000). *Keep smiling: No one's going to die.* London: British Medical Association.

Hastings, G., MacFadyen, L. & Anderson, S. (2000). Whose behavior is it anyway? The broader potential of social marketing. *Social Marketing Quarterly, 6*(2), 46–58.

Hastings, G., MacKintosh, A. & Aitken, P. (1992). Is alcohol advertising reaching the people it shouldn't reach? *Health Education Journal, 51*(1), 38–42.

Hawkins, D.I., Best, R.J. & Coney, K.A. (1995). *Consumer behavior: Implications for marketing strategy.* Chicago: Irwin.

Hawkins, J.D., Catalano, R.F. & Associates (1992). *Communities that care: Action for drug abuse prevention.* San Francisco: Jossey-Bass.

Hawkins, J.D., Catalano, R.F. & Miller, J.Y. (1992). Risk and protective factors for alcohol and other drug problems in adolescence and early adulthood: Implications for substance abuse prevention. *Psychological Bulletin, 112*, 64–105.

Hawkins, J.D., Catalano, R.F., Kosterman, R., Abbott, R. & Hill, K.G. (1999). Preventing adolescent health-risk behaviors by strengthening protection during childhood. *Archives of Pediatrics & Adolescent Medicine, 153*(3), 226–247.

Hawkins, J.W. & Aber, C.S. (1988). The content of advertisements in medical journals: Distorting the image of women. *Women & Health, 14*(2), 43–59.

Hawton, K., Simkin, S., Deeks, J.J., O'Connor, S., Keen, A., Altman, D.G., Philo, G. & Bulstrode, C. (1999). Effects of a drug overdose in a television drama on presentations to hospital for self poisoning: Time series and questionnaire study. *British Medical Journal, 318*, 972–977.

Hawton, K., Townsend, E., Deeks, J., et al. (2001). Effects of legislation restricting pack sizes of paracetamol and salicylate on self poisoning in the United Kingdom: Before and after study. *British Medical Journal, 322*, 1–7.

Hay, P.J. (1998). Eating disorders: anorexia nervosa, bulimia nervosa and related syndromes—an overview of assessment and management. *Australian Prescriber, 21*, 100–103. Retrieved April 20, 2003 from <http://www.australianprescriber.com/magazines/vol21no4/eating_disorders.htm>.

Health Promotion Evaluation Unit (1998). *Guidelines for Evaluating Healthways sponsorships.* Perth: Department of Public Health and Graduate School of Management, University of Western Australia.

Healey, K.M. & Smith, C. (1998). Batterer programs: What criminal justice agencies need to know. *National Institute of Justice,* Research in Action. Available online at <www.ojp.usdoj.gov/nij/pubs-sum/171683.htm>.

Healey, K.M., Smith, C. & O'Sullivan, C. (1998). Batterer intervention: Program approaches and criminal justice strategies. *Issues and Practices in Criminal Justice, National Institute of Justice,* NCJ 168638. Available online at <www.ncjrs.org.pdf-files/168638.pdf>.

Helquist, M. & Sealy, G. (1992). *Using theater for AIDs education.* Washington, D.C. AIDSCOM, Academy for Educational Development.

Henderson, G. (2000, September 5). Globalised protest won't stop globalisation. *The Age*. Retrieved January 31, 2002 from <http://www/theage.com.au/news/2000905/A45936-2000Sep4.html>.

Henley, N. (1995). Fear literature review. In R.J. Donovan, N. Henley, G. Jalleh & C. Slater (Eds.), *Road safety advertising. Report to federal Office of Road Safety*. Perth: Donovan Research, 92–120.

Henley, N. (1999). Using threat appeals in social marketing. In M. Harker, D. Harker, P. Graham & M.J. Baker (Eds.). *Marketing trends in Australasia: Essays and case studies.*: Macmillan, 230–242.

Henley, N. (2002). You will die! Mass media invocations of existential dread. *M/C: A journal of media and culture*, 5(1). Available online at <http://www.media-culture.org.au/0203/youwilldie.html>.

Henley, N. & Donovan, R.J. (1999a). Threat appeals in social marketing: Death as a special case. *International Journal of Nonprofit and Voluntary Sector Marketing*, 4(4), 300–319.

Henley, N. & Donovan, R.J. (1999b). *Unintended consequences of arousing fear in social marketing*. Paper presented at Australia and New Zealand Marketing Academy Conference, Sydney, N.S.W.

Henley, N. & Donovan, R.J. (2002). Identifying appropriate motivations to encourage people to adopt healthy nutrition and physical activity behaviours. *Journal of Research for Consumers*, 4. Available online at <http://www.jrconsumers.com/>.

Henley, N. & Donovan, R.J. (2003). Young people's response to death threat appeals: Do they really feel immortal? *Health Education Research*, 18(1), 1–14.

Henley, N., Donovan, R.J. & Moorhead, H. (1998). Appealing to positive motivations and emotions in social marketing: Example of a positive parenting campaign. *Social Marketing Quarterly*, 4(4), 48–53.

Henry, P. (2001). An examination of the pathways through which social class impacts health outcomes. *Academy of Marketing Science Review*. Retrieved April 26, 2001 from <http://www.amsreview.org/amsrev/theory/henry03-01.html>.

Higbee, K.L. (1969). Fifteen years of fear arousal. Research on threat appeals: 1953–1968. *Psychological Bulletin*, 72, 426–439.

Hindin, M.J., Kincaid, D.L., Kumah, O.M., Morgan, W., Kim, Y.M. & Ofori, J.K. (1994). Gender differences in media exposure and action during a family planning campaign in Ghana. *Health Communication*, 6(2), 117–135.

Hitchen, A.L. (1995). Sponsorship gold at the '92 Olympics. In T. Meenaghan (Ed.), *Researching commercial sponsorship*. Amsterdam: ESOMAR, 120–138.

Hobsons, . (1990). *Hobsons sponsorship yearbook 1991*. Cambridge: Hobsons Publishing.

Hoek, J.A., Gendall, P. & Stockdale, M. (1993). Some effects of tobacco sponsorship advertisements on young males. *International Journal of Advertising*, 12, 25–35.

Hofstetter, C.R., Hovell, M.F. & Sallis, J.F. (1990). Social learning correlates of exercise self-efficacy: Early experiences with physical activity. *Social Science Medicine*, 31(10), 1169–1176.

Hollingsworth, P. (1997). Beverages: Redefining New Age. *Food Technology*, 51(8), 44–50.

Hollingsworth, P. (1999). Graying boomers are still a hot market. *Food Technology*, 53(5), 24.

Hollingsworth, P. (2000). The European food blender. *Food Technology*, 54(1), 38–42.

Hollingsworth, P. (2001a). Margarine: The over-the-top functional food. *Food Technology*, 55(1), 59–63.

Hollingsworth, P. (2001b). Yoghurt reinvents itself. *Food Technology*, 55(3), 43–46.

Hollingsworth, P. (2001c). Convenience is key to adding value. *Food Technology*, 55(5), 20.

Holman, C.D.J., Donovan, R.J. & Corti, B. (1993). Evaluating projects funded by the Western Australian Health Promotion Foundation: A systematic approach. *Health Promotion International*, 8(3), 199–208.

Holman, C.D.J., Donovan, R.J. & Corti, B. (1994). *Report of the evaluation of the Western Australian Health Promotion Foundation*. Perth: Health Promotion Development and Evaluation Program, Department of Public Health and Graduate School of Management, University of Western Australia.

Holman, C.D.J., Donovan, R.J., Corti, B. & Jalleh G. (1997a). The myth of 'healthism' in organised sport: Implications for health promotion sponsorship of sport and the arts. *American Journal of Health Promotion*, 11(3), 169–175.

Holman, C.D.J., Donovan, R.J., Corti, B., Jalleh, G., Frizzell, S.K. & Carroll, A.M. (1996). Evaluating projects funded by the Western Australian Health Promotion Foundation: First results. *Health Promotion International*, 11, 75–88.

Holman, C.D.J., Donovan, R.J., Corti, B., Jalleh G., Frizzell S.K. & Carroll A.M. (1997b). Banning tobacco sponsorship: Replacing tobacco with health messages and creating health-promoting environments. *Tobacco Control*, 6(2), 115–121.

Holt, T. (1995). *The rise of the nanny state: How consumer advocates try to run our lives*. U.S.: Capital Research Center.

Homel, R., Carseldine, D. & Kearns, I. (1988). Drink-driving countermeasures in Australia. *Alcohol, Drugs and Driving*, 4(2), 113–144.

Hornery, A. (2000, December 7). In some quarters ethics get a run. Some agencies are proving there is room for social principles in advertising. *The Pitch*. Retrieved April 18, 2001 from <www.smh.com.au/news/0012/07/text/business8.html>.

Hotaling, G.T. & Sugarman, D.B. (1986). An analysis of risk markers in husband to wife violence: The current state of knowledge. *Violence and Victims*, 1(2), 101–124.

Hovland, R. & Wilcox, G.B. (1987). The future of alcoholic beverage advertising, *Communications and the Law*, 9(2), 5–14.

Hu, T. (1997). Cigarette taxation in China: lessons from international experience. *Tobacco Control*, 6, 136–140.

Hu, T., Sung, H. & Keeler, T.E. (1995). Reducing cigarette consumption in California: Tobacco taxes vs an anti-smoking media campaign. *American Journal of Public Health*, 85, 1218–1222.

Hudson, D. (1999). Panel discusses crucial role of media in civil rights movement. First Amendment Center. Available online at <http://www.firstamendmentcenter.org/>.

International Events Group Sponsorship Report (1996). 1996 Annual sponsorship survey. Cited in T.B. Cornwell & I. Maignan (1998). An international review of sponsorship research. *Journal of Advertising*, 27(1), 1.

Intl-tobacco mailing list (2002). Archived at <http://lists.essential.org/mailman/listinfo/intl-tobacco>.

Isaacs, S.L. & Schroeder, S.A. (2001). Where the public good prevailed. *The American Prospect*, 12(10). Available online at <http://www.prospect.org>.

Jalleh, G. (1999). *Evaluating sponsorship effectiveness: Health vs commercial sponsorship*. Unpublished Master of Public Health thesis, University of Western Australia, Perth, Western Australia.

Jalleh, G. & Donovan, R.J. (2000). *Evaluation of Westar Rules and the West Australian Country Football League "Belt up" Sponsorship*. Perth: Centre for Behavioural Research in Cancer Control, Curtin University.

Jalleh, G. & Donovan, R.J. (2001). Beware of product labels! *Journal of Research for Consumers*, 2. Retrieved January 20, 2003 from <http://www.jrconsumers.com/>.

Jalleh, G., Donovan, R.J., Clarkson, J., March, K., Foster, M. & Giles-Corti, B. (2001). Increasing mouthguards usage among junior rugby and basketball players. *Australian and New Zealand Journal of Public Health*, 25(3), 250–252.

Jalleh, G., Donovan, R.J., Giles-Corti, B., Holman, C.D.J. (2002). Sponsorship: Impact on brand awareness and brand attitudes. *Social Marketing Quarterly*, 8(1), 35–45.

Jalleh, G., Hamilton, A., Clarkson, J., Donovan, R.J. & Corti, B. (1998). *Healthy food choices at Healthway sponsored Events*. Perth: Health Promotion Evaluation Unit, Department of Public Health and Graduate School of Management, University of Western Australia.

James, B. (2002). TravelSmart: An individualised social marketing case study. *Social Marketing Quarterly*, 8(1), 46–51.

Janz, N. & Becker, M. (1984). The health belief model: A decade later. *Health Education Quarterly*, 11, 1–47.

Javalgi, R., Traylor, M., Gross, A. & Lampman, E. (1994). Awareness of sponsorship and corporate image: An empirical investigation. *Journal of Advertising*, 23(4), 47–58.

Jazzybooks Media Pack (n.d.). Available from APN Educational Media, Sydney.

Jeffery, N. (2001, October 11). Sponsor quizzed over unsporting conduct. *The Australian*, 20.

Jeffery, R.W., Forster, J.L., Schmid, T.L., McBride, C.M., Rooney, B.L. & Pirie, P.L. (1990). Community attitudes toward public policies to control alcohol, tobacco, and high-fat food consumption. *American Journal of Preventive Medicine*, 6(1) 12–19.

Job, R.F.S. (1988). Effective and ineffective use of fear in health promotion campaigns. *American Journal of Public Health*, 78(2), 163–167.

Joiner, K., Minsky, M. & Seals, B.F. (2000). By and for youth: Lessons from the Sahel and Paris come to the USA. *Social Marketing Quarterly*, 6(3), 138–151.

Jones, K., Wakefield, M. & Turnbull, D. (1999). Attitudes and experiences of restaurateurs regarding smoking bans in Adelaide, South Australia. *Tobacco Control*, 8, 62–66.

Jones, M. & Dearsley, T. (1995). Understanding sponsorship. In T. Meenaghan (Ed.), *Researching commercial sponsorship*. Amsterdam: ESOMAR, 41–54.

Jones, S., Corti, B. & Donovan, R.J. (1996). Public response to a smoke-free policy at a major sporting venue (letter). *Medical Journal of Australia*, 164, 759.

Jones, S. & Donovan, R.J. (2001). Messages in alcohol advertising targeted to youth. *Australian and New Zealand Journal of Public Health*, 25(2), 126–131.

Jones, S.C. & Donovan, R.J. (2002). Self-regulation of alcohol advertising: Is it working for Australia? *Journal of Public Affairs*, 2/3, 153–165.

Jones, S.C. & Donovan, R.J. (2003), in press. Does theory inform practice in health promotion in Australia? *Health Education Research*.

Jordan, M. & Sullivan, K. (1999, May 13). Japan urges dads to spend more time with kids- ad campaign sparks renewed debate. *Seattle Times*, A20.

Kahneman, D. & Tversky, A. (1979). Prospect theory: An analysis of decision making under risk. *Econometrica*, 6, 621–630.

Kahneman, D. & Tversky, A. (1982). The psychology of preferences. *Scientific American*, 46, 160–173.

Karmanos Cancer Institute Somerset and Berkley Prevention Centers (2000, October 25). New motivation to get a mammogram. Retrieved July 31, 2002 from <http://www.karmanos.org/news/newmotivation2k.html>.

Kate, N.T. (1995, June). And now, a word from our sponsor. *American Demographics*, 46–52.

Katris, P., Donovan, R.J. & Gray, B.N. (1996). The use of targeted and non-targeted advertising to enrich skin cancer screening samples. *British Journal of Dermatology*, 135, 268–274.

Kawachi, I., Kennedy, B.P., Lochner, K. & Prothrow-Smith, D. (1997). Social capital, income inequality, and mortality. *American Journal of Public Health, 87*(9), 1491–1498.

Keilitz, S.L., Davis, C., Efkeman, H.S., Flango, C. & Hannaford, P.L. (1998). Civil protection orders: Victims' views on effectiveness. *National Institute of Justice*, Research preview. Available online at <www.ojp.usdoj.gov/nij/pubs-sum/171683.htm>.

Keller, K.L. (1993). Conceptualizing, measuring and managing customer-based equity. *Journal of Marketing, 57*, 1–22.

Kellogg's Kids Helpline Australia. Available online at <http://www.kellogg.com.au/06/03/0603.asp>. Accessed September 18, 2001.

King, D. (2001, November 1). Promoting sexual health through high street shops. HEDIR listserver.

King, A.C., Jeffery, R.W., Fridinger, F., Dusenbury, L., Provence, S., Hedlund, S.A. & Spangler, K. (1995). Environmental and policy approaches to cardiovascular disease prevention through physical activity: Issues and opportunities. *Health Education Quarterly, 22*(4), 499–511.

King, K.W. & Reid, L.N. (1990). Fear arousing anti-drinking and driving PSAs: Do physical injury threats influence young adults? *Current Issues in Research in Advertising, 13*, 155–175.

Kirby, S. (2000). Brand identity in public health: A CD.C. case study. *Social Marketing Quarterly, 6*(30), 117–118.

Kirby, S. & Andreasen, A. (2001). Marketing ethics to social marketers. A segmented approach. In A. Andreasen (Ed.), *Ethics in social marketing* Washington, D.C.: Georgetown University Press.

Klapper, J.T. (1961). *The effects of mass communication*. Glencoe: The Free Press.

Klein, N. (2000). *No Logo*. London: Flamingo.

Knag, S. (1997). The almighty, impotent state: or, the crisis of authority. *Independent Review, 1*(3), 397–413.

Koss, M.P. & Heslet, L. (1992). Somatic consequences of violence against women. *Archives of Family Medicine, 1*, 53–59.

Kotler, P. (1988). *Marketing management: Analysis, planning, implementation and control*. Englewood Cliffs: Prentice-Hall.

Kotler, P. (1989). *Principles of marketing*. Englewood Cliffs: Prentice-Hall.

Kotler, P. (2001). *A framework for marketing management*. Upper Saddle River: Prentice-Hall.

Kotler, P. & Andreasen, A.R. (1987). *Strategic marketing for nonprofit organizations*. Englewood Cliffs: Prentice-Hall.

Kotler, P., Armstrong, G., Brown, L. & Adam, S. (1998). *Marketing* (4th ed.). Sydney, : Prentice-Hall.

Kotler, P., Chandler, P.G., Brown, L. & Adam, S. (1994). *Marketing Australia and New Zealand* (3rd ed.). Sydney, : Prentice-Hall.

Kotler, P. & Roberto, E.L. (1989). *Social marketing: Strategies for changing public behaviour*. New York: The Free Press.

Kotler, P., Roberto, N. & Lee, N. (2002). *Social marketing: Improving the quality of life*, Thousand Oaks: Sage.

Kotler, P. & Zaltman, G. (1971). Social marketing: An approach to planned social change. *Journal of Marketing, 35*, 3–12.

Kreuter, M., Farrell, D., Olevitch, L., Brennan, L. & Rimer, B.K. (2000). *Tailoring health messages: Customising communication with computer technology*. Mahwah: Lawrence Erlbaum.

Kulik, J.A. & Carlino, P. (1987). The effect of verbal commitment and treatment choice on medication compliance in a pediatric setting. *Journal of Behavioural Medicine,* *10*(4), 367–376.

Kurzer, M.S. (1993). Planning and interpreting 'Designer Food' feeding studies. *Food Technology,* *47*(4), 80–85.

Kwok, Y. (2000, April 12). Charity defends using tobacco industry cash. *South China Morning Post.* Message posted on international tobacco admin listserver. Archived at <intl-tobacco@lists.essential.org>.

Laczniak, G.R., Lusch, R.F. & Murphy, P. (1979, Spring). Social marketing: Its ethical dimensions. *Journal of Marketing,* *43*, 29–36.

Laczniak, G.R. & Murphy, P. (1993). *Ethical marketing decisions: The higher road.* Needham Heights: Allyn and Bacon.

Lamont, L. (1996). Fears over McDonald's school sponsorship deal. *Sydney Morning Herald* (13 December). Retrieved October 26, 2001 from <http://www.mcspotlight.org/media/press/smherald_13dec96.html>.

Lancaster, K.J. (1966). A new approach to consumer theory. *Journal of Political Economy,* *14*, 132–157.

Lancaster, W., McIlwain, T. & Lancaster, J. (1983). Health marketing: Implications for health promotion. *Family and Community Health,* *5*, 41–51.

Langlieb, A.M., Cooper, C.P. & Gielen, A. (1999). Linking health promotion with entertainment television. *American Journal of Public Health,* *89*, 1116–1117.

Lasker, A.D. (1963, 1987). *The Lasker story: As he told it.* Lincolnwood.: NTC Business Books

LaTour, M.S., Snipes, R.L. & Bliss, S.J. (1996). Don't be afraid to use fear appeals: An experimental study. *Journal of Advertising Research,* *36*(2), 59–67.

Ledford, J. (1999, April 7). Alternative transportation catching on. *Atlanta-Journal-Constitution.*

Ledwith, F. (1984). Does tobacco sports sponsorship on television act as advertising to children? *Health Education Journal,* *43*, 85–88.

Lee, M.Y., Campbell, A.R. & Mulford, C.L. (1999). Victim-blaming tendency toward people with AIDS among college students. *Journal of Social Psychology,* *139*(3), 300–339.

Lefebvre, R.C. & Flora, J.A. (1988). Social marketing and public health intervention. *Health Education Quarterly,* *15*, 299–315.

Lehman, D., Hawkins, J.D. & Catalano, R.F. (1994). Reducing risks and protecting our youths: A community mission. *Corrections Today,* *56*(5), 92–100.

Lehrman, S. (1999, September 9). GM backlash leaves U.S. farmers wondering how to sell their crops. *Nature,* 107.

Lettenmaier, C., Krenn, S., Morgan, W., Kols, A. & Piotrow, P. (1993). Africa: Using radio soap operas to promote family planning. *Hygie,* *12*, 5–10.

Leventhal, H. & Cameron, L. (1994). Persuasion and health attitudes. In S. Shavitt & T.C. Brock (Eds.), *Persuasion: Psychological insights and perspectives.* Boston, MT: Allyn and Bacon, 219–249.

Leventhal, H. & Trembly, G. (1968). Negative emotions and persuasion. *Journal of Personality,* *36*, 154–168.

Levin, I.P. & Gaeth, G.J. (1988). How consumers are affected by the framing of attribute information before and after consuming the product. *Journal of Consumer Research,* *15*, 374–378.

Levitt, T. (1969). *The marketing mode.* New York: McGraw-Hill.

Lewis, G., Morkel, A. & Hubbard, G. (1993). *Australian strategic management: Concepts, context and cases* (Case 21, Smoking and health: An industry under siege). Sydney, : Prentice-Hall.

Lex, L. (1997, September 15). School's back, and so are the marketers. *The Wall Street Journal*, B1.

Ligerakis, M. (2001, February 23). Never underestimate the power of kids. *B&T Weekly*, 8.

Lilienfeld, A.M. & Lilienfeld, D.E. (1980). *Foundations of epidemiology*. New York: Oxford University Press.

Link, B.G. & Phelan, J.C. (1995). Social conditions as fundamental causes of disease. *Journal of Health and Social Behavior*, extra issue, 80–95.

Link, B.G. & Phelan, J.C. (1996). Why are some people healthy and others not? The determinants of health of populations. *American Journal of Public Health*, 86(4), 598–599.

Liu, C. (1999, March 30). Online hate sites target children, report warns. *The West Australian*, 30.

Locke, J. (1690, 1961). *An essay concerning human understanding* (ed. J.W. Yolton). London: J.M. Dent & Sons.

Lomas, J. (1998). Social capital and health: Implications for public health and epidemiology. *Social Science and Medicine*, 47(9), 1181–1188.

Lord, C.G., Ross, L. & Lepper, M.R. (1979). Biased assimilation and attitude polarisation: The effects of prior theories on subsequently altered evidence. *Journal of Personality and Social Psychology*, 37, 2098–2109.

Lowery, S.A. & DeFleur, M.L. (1988). The invasion from Mars. *Milestones in Mass Communication Research* (2nd ed.). New York: Longman.

Lowery, S.A. & DeFleur, M.L. (1995). *Milestones in mass communication research* (3rd ed.). White Plains: Longman.

Lunn, T. (1986). Segmenting and constructing markets. In R.M. Worcester & J. Downham (Eds.), *Consumer market research handbook*. Amsterdam: North Holland, 287–424.

Lusch, R.F., Laczniak, G.R. & Murphy, P. (1980). The 'ethics of social ideas' vs the 'ethics of marketing social ideas'. *Journal of Consumer Affairs*, 14(1), 156–164.

Lyderson, K. (1998). Did somebody say shut down McDonald's? *Chicago Ink*, 55–78.

Lyderson, K. (2002, July 3). In Iowa, there's not always room for Jello. *Washington Post*, A2.

Lyon, K. (2002, February 5). Drink drive, lose sponsor. *The West Australian*, 105 (reproduced from *The Age*).

Maccoby, N., Farquhar, J., Wood, P.D. & Alexander, J. (1977). Reducing the risk of cardiovascular disease: Effects of a community-based campaign on knowledge and behavior. *Journal of Community Health*, 3(2), 100–114.

MacCoun, R.J. (1998). Toward a psychology of harm reduction. *American Psychologist*, 53(11), 1199–1208.

MacIntyre, A. (1999). Social structures and their threat to moral agency. *Philosophy*, 74, 311–329. Retrieved October 4, 2001 from <http://www.royalinstitutephilosophy.org/articles /macintyre_lecture.htm>.

Maegraith, D. (1994, August 26). GP soaps not always just froth and bubble. *Australian Doctor*, 30.

Maheswaran, D. & Meyers-Levy, J. (1990). The influence of message framing and issue involvement. *Journal of Marketing Research*, 27, 361–367.

Maibach, E. (1993). Social marketing for the environment. Using information campaigns to promote environmental awareness and behavior change. *Health Promotion International*, 8(3), 209–224.

Maibach, E.W. & Cotton, D. (1995). Moving people to behavior change: A staged social cognitive approach to message design. In E. Maibach & R.L. Parrott (Eds.), *Designing Health Messages*. London: Sage.

Maiman, L.A. & Becker, M.H. (1974). The health belief model: Origins and correlates in psychological theory. *Health Education Monographs*, *2*(4), 336–353.

Mankell, H. (2000). *Sidetracked*. London: The Harvill Press.

Manoff, R.K. (1985). *Social marketing*. New York: Praeger.

Marcus, B.H. & Owen, N. (1992). Motivational readiness, self-efficacy and decision-making for exercise. *Journal of Applied Social Psychology*, *22*, 3–16.

Marcus, B.H., Owen, N., Forsyth, L.H., Cavill, N.A. & Fridinger, F. (1998). Interventions to promote physical activity using mass media, print media and information technology. *American Journal of Preventive Medicine*, *15*(4), 362–378.

Marcus, B.H., Rakowski, W. & Rossi, J.S. (1992). Assessing motivational readiness and decision making for exercise. *Health Psychology*, *11*, 257–261.

Marcus, B.H., Selby, V., Niaura, R.S. & Rossi, J.S. (1992). Self-efficacy and the stages of exercise behaviour change. *Research Quarterly for Exercise and Sport*, *63*, 60–66.

Marks, A. (1997). *Private sector collaboration in social marketing health research: examples from South Africa*. Paper presented to the Innovations in Social Marketing Conference, Boston.

Marmot, M.G. (2000). Social determinants of health: From observation to policy. *Medical Journal of Australia*, *172*, 379–383.

Marmot, M.G., Rose, H., Shipley, M. & Hamilton, P.J.S. (1978). Employment grade and coronary heart disease in British civil servants. *Journal of Epidemiology and Community Health*, *32*(4), 244–249.

Marmot, M.G., Smith, G.D., Stansfield, S., Patel, C., North, F., Head, J., White, I., Brunner, E. & Feeney, A. (1991). Health inequalities among British civil servants: The Whitehall II study. *Lancet*, *338*(8758), 58–59.

Marmot, M.G. & Wilkinson, R.G. (1999). *Social Determinants of Health*. Oxford: Oxford University Press.

Mayer, S.E. (1997). *What Money Can't Buy. Family income and children's life chances*. Cambridge: Harvard University Press.

McAuley, E. & Jacobson, L. (1991). Self-efficacy and exercise participation in sedentary adult females. *American Journal of Health Promotion*, *5*(3), 185–192.

McAvoy, B.R., Donovan, R.J., Jalleh, G., Saunders, J.B., Wutzke, S.E., et al. (2001). General practitioners, prevention and alcohol—a powerful cocktail? Facilitators and inhibitors of practising preventive medicine in general and early intervention for alcohol in particular: A 12-nation key informant and general practitioner study. *Drugs: Education, Prevention and Policy*, *8*(2), 103–117.

McCarthy, E.J. (1960). *Basic Marketing: A managerial approach*. Illinois: Richard Irwin.

McCoy, M. (2000). Good business for good citizens. *The Qantas Club*, Winter, 6–11.

McDermott, L. (2001). *An investigation of socio-cultural factors which promote the desirability of a suntan among adolescents*. Unpublished Masters thesis, University of Queensland, St Lucia, Queensland.

McDonald, C. (1991). Sponsorship and the image of the sponsor. *European Journal of Marketing*, *25*(11), 31–38.

McEwen, B.S. (1998). Protective and damaging effects of stress mediators. *New England Journal of Medicine*, *338*, 171–179.

MacFadyen, L., Hastings, G. & MacKintosh, A.M. (2001). Cross sectional study of young people's awareness of and involvement with tobacco marketing. *British Medical Journal*, *322*, 513–517.

McGuire, W.J. (1985). Attitudes and attitude change. In G. Lindsey & E. Aronsen (Eds.). *The handbook of social psychology, Volume II* (3rd ed.). New York: Random House.

McKee, N. (1992). *Social mobilisation and social marketing*. Penang: Southbound.

McLeroy, K.R., Bibeau, D., Steckler, A. & Glanz, K. (1988). An ecological perspective on health promotion programs. *Health Education Quarterly*, 15(4), 351–377.

McNeal, J.U. (1992). *Kids as customers: A handbook of marketing to children*. New York: Lexington.

Mead, L. (1998). Telling the poor what to do. *Public Interest*. Available online at <www.britannica.com/bcom>.

Mechanic, D. (1999). Issues in promoting health. *Social Science and Medicine*, 48, 711–718.

Media and peace (1999). *Drum Beat*, 16. Retrieved April 21, 2003 from <http://www.comminit.com/drum_beat_16.html>.

Mediascope (2000a). Body image and advertising. *Issue Briefs*. Studio City: Mediascope Press. Retrieved April 20, 2003 from <http://www.mediascope.org/pubs/ibriefs/bia.htm>.

Mediascope (2000b). Muscle madness: The ugly connection between body image and anabolic steroid use. *Issue Briefs*. Studio City: Mediascope Press.

Meenaghan, T. (1991). The role of sponsorship in the marketing communications mix. *International Journal of Advertising*, 10(1), 35–47.

Meenaghan, T. (1994, September). Point of view: Ambush marketing: Immoral or imaginative practice? *Journal of Advertising Research*, 77–88.

Meenaghan, T. (1996). Ambush marketing: A threat to corporate sponsorship. *Sloan Management Review*, 38(1), 103–113.

Meyerowitz, B.E. & Chaiken, S. (1987). The effect of message framing on breast self-examination attitudes, intentions, and behavior. *Journal of Personality and Social Psychology*, 52, 500–510.

Middlestadt, S.E., Fishbein, M., Albarracin, D., Francis, C., Eustace, M.A., Helquist, M. & Schneider, A. (1995). Evaluating the impact of a national aids prevention radio campaign in St. Vincent and the Grenadines. *Journal of Applied Social Psychology*, 25(1), 21–34.

Mill, J.S. (1859, 1991). *On Liberty and Other Essays*. (Ed. J. Gray). Oxford: Oxford University Press.

Molnar, A. & Reaves, J.A. (2001). *Buy me! Buy me! The fourth annual report on trends in schoolhouse commercialism*. Year 2000–2001. Commercialism in Education Research Unit, EPSL-0109-101-CERU. Tempe: Arizona State University.

Montgomery, K.C. (1990. Promoting health through entertainment television. In C. Atkin & L. Wallack (Eds.), *Mass communication and public health: complexities and conflicts*. Newbury Park: Sage.

Moor, K. & Rice, E. (2000, November 12). Tobacco giant targets women through fashion. *Adelaide Advertiser*.

Morley-John, J., Swinburn, B.A., Metcalf, P.A. & Raza, F. (2002). Fat content of chips, quality of frying fat and deep-frying practices in New Zealand fast food outlets. *Australian and New Zealand Journal of Public Health*, 26, 101–107.

Mugford, S., Mugford, J. & Donnelly, D. (1999). *Social research project: Athletes' motivations for using or not using performance enhancing drugs*. Canberra: Australian Sports Drug Agency.

Mulilis, J.-P. & Lippa, R. (1990). Behavioral changes in earthquake preparedness due to negative threat appeals: A test of protection motivation theory. *Journal of Applied Social Psychology*, 20(8), 619–638

Mummery, K. & Schofield, G. (2002, September 20). 10 000 Steps Rockhampton. *Health Promotion Queensland, Inaugural Seminar*, 20, Brisbane.

Murphy, K. (1998, April 25–26). Welcome to cyberbia. *The Weekend Australian*.

Murphy, M. and Mee, V. (1999). The impact of the National Tobacco Campaign on Aboriginal communities: A study in Victoria. *Australia's National Tobacco Campaign: Evaluation Report, Vol. 1.* Canberra: Commonwealth of Australia.

Murphy, P.E. & Bloom, P.N. (1990). Ethical issues in social marketing. In S. Fine (Ed.), *Social marketing. Promoting the causes of public and nonprofit agencies.* Boston: Allyn and Bacon.

Murphy, T. (1994, July 15). Patients encouraged to reveal abuse. *Australian Doctor,* 50.

Murray, I. (1997, April 23). "Chocolate" carrots a stick to beat cancer, *The Australian,* 8.

National Academy of Sciences, Institute of Health (2000). Promoting health: Intervention strategies from social and behavioral research. National Academies Press. Available online at <http://books.nap.edu/books/0309071755/html/6.html#pagetop>. Retrieved April 18, 2003.

National Cancer Institute (1982). *Pretesting in health communications.* NIH Publication No. 83–1493. Washington, D.C.: U.S. Government Printing Office.

National Center for Injury Prevention and Control (1999). Family and intimate violence prevention program: Multifaceted community-based projects. at <http://www.cdc.gov/ncipc/dvp>.

National Centre for Immunisation Research and Surveillance of Vaccine Preventable Diseases (NCIRS) 1999. *The Australian measles control campaign 1998 outcomes evaluation.* Unpublished report to the Commonwealth Department of Health and Aged Care.

National Health and Medical Research Council (NHMRC) (1997a). *Health-promoting sport, racing and arts settings. New challenges for the health sector.* Canberra: AGPS.

National Health and Medical Research Council (NHMRC) (1997b). *The Australian immunisation handbook* (6th ed.). Canberra: AGPS.

Neill, R. (2001, August 31). Incredible shrinking fashion victims waste away to nothing. *The Australian.*

New South Wales Government Health (2002, May 9). Media release: Retail therapy has a new meaning at David Jones. Retrieved July 20, 2002 from <http://www.health.nsw.gov.au/health-public-affairs/mediareleases/2002/May/09-05-02.htm>.

NFO Donovan Research (2000). *Qualitative research for the "Smarter Than Smoking" project.* Report to Smarter Than Smoking Management Group. Perth.

Nicholas, D., Huntington, P. & Williams, P. (2002). The impact of location on the use of digital information systems: Case study health information kiosks. *Journal of Documentation, 58*(3), 284–301.

Nicholls, J.A., Roslow, S. & Laskey, H.A. (1994). Sports event sponsorship for brand promotion. *Journal of Applied Business Research, 10*(4), 35–41.

Noble, G., Martin, D., Ford, J., Harbilas, R., Hornsey, A., Noble, E. & Nolan, J. (1990). *Portrayals of driving and alcohol in popular television programmes screened in Australia.* CR 90. Canberra: Federal Office of Road Safety.

Norman, P., Bennett, P. & Lewis, H. (1998). Understanding binge drinking among young people: An application of the theory of planned behaviour. *Health Education Research: Theory and Practice, 13*(2), 163–169.

Norman, P. & Connor, M. (1996). The role of social cognition models in predicting health behaviours: Future directions. In M. Conner & P. Norman (Eds.), *Predicting health behaviour.* Buckingham: Open University Press, 197–225.

Norris, P. (1996). Does television erode social capital? A reply to Putnam. *PS: Political Science and Politics,* September, 474–480.

Novelli, W.D. (1984). Developing marketing programs. In L.W. Frederickson, L.J. Solomon & K.A. Brehony (Eds.), *Marketing health behavior: Principles, techniques and applications.* New York: Plennum.

Novelli, W.D. (1990). Applying social marketing to health promotion and disease prevention. In K. Glantz, F.M. Lewis & B.K. Rimer (Eds.), *Health behavior and health education: Theory, research and practice*. San Francisco: Jossey- Bass, 342–369.

Nozick, R. (1974). *Anarchy, state and utopia*. New York: Basic Books.

Nutbeam, D. (1991). Consumers not patients: the application of social marketing principles to the improvement of immunisation uptake. In *Immunisation: the old and the new*. Public Health Association of Australia, 12–16.

O'Connell, J.K. & Price, J.H. (1983). Ethical theories for promoting health through behavioral change. *Journal of School Health*, 53(8), 476–479.

Office of National Drug Control Policy (ONDCP) (1997). *National Youth Anti-Drug Media Campaign*. Washington, D.C.: ONDCP.

Ohigashi, H., Murakami, A. & Koshimizu, K. (1996). An approach to functional food: Cancer preventive potential of vegetables and fruits and their active constituents. *Nutrition Reviews*, 54(11), S24–30.

O'Keefe, D.J. (1990). *Persuasion: Theory and research*. San Francisco: Sage.

Olsen, C.K. (1999). Countering pro-tobacco influences at the racetrack. *American Journal of Public Health*, 89(9), 1431–1432.

Oman, R.F. & King, A.C. (1998). Predicting the adoption and maintenance of exercise participation using self-efficacy and previous exercise participation rates. *American Journal of Health Promotion*, 12(3), 154–161.

Ontario School Bus Association (1999). *Policy statement #1000. External advertising on school buses*. Retrieved October 29, 2001 from <http://www.shantz-coach.com/external.html>.

Orleans, C.T., Gruman, J., Ulmer, C., Emont, S.L. & Hollendonner, J.K. (1999). Rating our progress in population health promotion: Report card on six behaviors. *American Journal of Health Promotion*, 14(2), 75–82.

Ornstein, R.E. (1986). *Multi mind*. London: Macmillan.

Orwall, B. (1997, November 24). Why are school kids eating Dimitri's fudge? *The Wall Street Journal*, B1.

Osterhus, L.T. (1997). Pro-social consumer influence strategies: When and how do they work? *Journal of Marketing*, 61, 16–29.

Otker, T. (1988). Exploitation: the key to sponsorship success. *European Research*, 16(2), 77–86.

Otker, T. & Hayes, P. (1987). Judging the efficiency of sponsorship: Experience from the 1986 soccer World Cup. *ESOMAR Congress*, 3–13.

Ottman, J.A. (1993). *Green marketing—challenges and opportunities for the new marketing age*. NTC Business Books.

Owen, J. (2002). Unpublished PhD progess report. University of Western Australia, Perth, Western Australia.

Owen, N. & R. Borland. (1997). Delayed compensatory cigarette consumption after a workplace smoking ban. *Tobacco Control*, 6, 131–135.

Pallonen, U.E., Velicer, W.F., Prochaska, J.O., et al. (1998). Computer-based smoking cessation interventions in adolescents: Description, feasibility, and six-month follow-up findings. *Substance Use and Misuse*, 33(4), 935–965.

Palmgreen, P., Donohew, L., Lorch, E.P., Hoyle, R.H. & Stephenson, M.T. (2001). Television campaigns and adolescent marijuana use: Tests of sensation seeking targeting. *American Journal of Public Health*, 91(2), 292.

Parker, B. (1995). *Snakebites, hammers and hand grenades*. Working paper. Peoria: Bradley University.

Parker, D., Manstead, A.S.R. & Stradling, S.G. (1995). Extending the theory of planned behaviour: The role of personal norm. *British Journal of Social Psychology*, 34, 127–137.

Parsons, S., Rissel, C. & Douglas, W. (1999). Alcohol portrayal in Australian prime time television in 1990 and 1997. *Australian and New Zealand Journal of Public Health, 23*(1), 67–71.

Pasick, R.J., D'Onofrio, C.N. & Otero-Sabogal, R. (1996). Similarities and differences across cultures: Questions to inform a third generation for health promotion research. *Health Education Quarterly, 23* (Supplement), SS142–161.

Patterson, P. & Wilkins, L. (1991). *Media ethics, issues and cases.* Dubuque: Wm. C. Brown Publishers.

Pechmann, C. & Shih, C.F. (1999). Smoking scenes in movies and antismoking advertisements before movies: Effects on youth. *Journal of Marketing, 63*, 1–13.

Pelto, G.H. (1981). Anthropological contributions to nutrition education research. *Journal of Nutrition Education, 13*, S2.

Perman, F. & Henley, N. (2001). Marketing the anti-drug message: Source credibility varies by use/non-use of marijuana. *Australia and New Zealand Marketing Academy Conference 2001 Proceedings*, New Zealand: Massey University.

Perry, C.L. (1999). The tobacco industry and underage youth smoking: Tobacco industry documents from the Minnesota litigation. *Archives of Pediatric and Adolescent Medicine, 153*, 935–941.

Persaud, R. (2000). Suicide rate rises after funeral of Princess of Wales. *British Medical Journal, 321*, 1246.

Peters, C. (1999). Teacher, there's a brand name in my math problem!! ZNET Daily Commentaries. Available online at <http://www.zmag.org>.

Peterson, E.A. & Koehler, J.E. (1997, May). *Changing traditions: Preventing illness associated with chitterlings.* Paper presented to the Innovations in Social Marketing Conference, Boston.

Pettigrew, S.F. (2000). *Culture and consumption : A study of beer consumption in Australia.* Unpublished doctoral dissertation, University of Western Australia, Perth Western Australia.

Petty, R.E. & Cacioppo, J.T. (1983). Central and peripheral routes to persuasion: Application to advertising. In L. Percy & A. Woodside (Eds.). *Advertising and consumer psychology.* Lexington: Lexington Books.

Petty, R.E. & Cacioppo, J.T. (1986). Elaboration Likelihood Model of persuasion. *Advances in Experimental Social Psychology, 19*, 123–193.

Pham, M.T. (1992). Effects of involvement, arousal, and pleasure on the recognition of sponsorship stimuli. In J.F. Sherry Jr. & B. Sternthal (Eds.), *Advances in consumer research*, 19. Provo: Association for Consumer Research, 85–96.

Pierce, J.P., Choi, W.S., Gilpin, E.A., Farkas, A.J. & Berry, C.C. (1998). Tobacco industry promotion of cigarettes and adolescent smoking. *Journal of the American Medical Association, 279*(7), 511–515.

Pierce, J.P., Macaskill, P. & Hill, D. (1990). Long-term effectiveness of mass-media-led antismoking campaigns in Australia. *American Journal of Public Health, 80*(5), 565–569.

Piercy, N. (1991. *Market-led strategic change: Making marketing happen in your organisation.* Oxford: Butterworth-Heinemann.

Pikora, T., Corti, B., Clarkson, J., Jalleh, G. & Donovan, R.J. (1998) *Evaluation of the smoke-free policy at the WACA ground.* Perth: Health Promotion Evaluation Unit, Department of Public Health and Graduate School of Management, University of Western Australia.

Pikora, T., Phang, J.W., Karro, J., Corti, B., Clarkson, J., Donovan, R.J., Frizzell, S. & Wilkinson, A. (1999). Are smoke-free policies implemented and adhered to at sporting venues? *Australia and New Zealand Journal of Public Health, 23*(4), 407–409.

Pokrywczynski, J. (1994). An examination of the exposure potential of in-stadium advertising in displays during televised sports coverage. In L.N. Reid (Ed.), *Proceedings of the 1992 conference of the American Academy of Advertising.* Athens, GA: , 150–155.

Pollay, R. (1986). The distorted mirror: Reflections on the unintended consequences of advertising. *Journal of Marketing, 50,* 18–36.

Pomazal, R.J. & Jaccard, J.J. (1976). An informational approach to altruistic behavior. *Journal of Personality and Social Psychology, 33,* 317–326.

Pope, N.K. & Voges, K.E. (1994). Sponsorship evaluation: Does it match the motive and the mechanism? *Sport Marketing Quarterly, 3*(4), 37–45.

Popham, W.J., Potter, L.D., Bal, D.G., Johnson, M.D., Duerr, J,M. & Quinn, V. (1993). Do anti-smoking media campaigns help smokers quit? *Public Health Reports, 108*(4), 510–513.

Post, J.E. (1985). Assessing the Nestle boycott: Corporate accountability and human rights. *California Management Review, 27*(2), 113– 142.

Postma, P. (1999). *The new marketing era.* New York: McGraw-Hill.

Pozzi, R., James, R., Kirby, G. & Cassells, J. (1996). Using media to increase community discussion: The rural alcohol campaign in Western Australia. *Health Promotion Journal of Australia, 6*(3), 50–52.

Prentice-Dunn, S. & Rogers, R.W. (1986). Protection motivation theory and preventive health: Beyond the health belief model. *Health Education Research: Theory & Practice, 1*(3), 153–161.

Prochaska, J.O. (1997). Interactive communication technologies and risk reduction. Keynote address at Innovations in Social Marketing Conference, Boston.

Prochaska, J.O. & DiClemente, C.C. (1984). *The transtheoretical approach: Crossing the traditional boundaries of therapy.* Illinios: Dow-Jones/Irwin.

Prochaska, J.O. & DiClemente, C.C. (1986). Toward a comprehensive model of change. In W.R. Miller & N. Heather (Eds.), *Treating addictive behaviours: Processes of change.* New York: Plenum Press.

Prochaska, J.O. & Marcus, B.H. (1994). The transtheoretical model: Applications to exercise. In R.K. Dishman (Ed.), *Advances in Exercise Adherence.* Champaign: Human Kinetics.

Prochaska, J.O., Norcross, J.C. & DiClemente, C.C. (1994a). *Changing for good.* New York: Avon Books.

Prochaska, J.O., Velicer, W.F., DiClemente, C.C. & Fava, J. (1988). Measuring processes of change: Applications to the cessation of smoking. *Journal of Consulting and Clinical Psychology, 56,* 520–528.

Prochaska, J.O., Velicer, W.F., Rossi, J.S., Goldstein, M.G., Marcus, B.H., Rakowski, W., Fiore, C., Harlow, L.L., Redding, C.A., Rosenbloom, D. & Rossi, S.R. (1994b). Stages of change and decisional balance for 12 problem behaviours. *Health Psychology, 13,* 39–46.

Puska, P., Toumilehto, J., Salonen, J., Neittaanmaki, L., Maki, J. & Virtamo, J. (1985). The community based strategy to prevent heart disease: Conclusions of the ten years of the North Karelia Project. *Annual Review of Public Health, 6,* 147–193.

Putnam, R.D. (1995a). Tuning in, tuning out: The strange disappearance of social capital in America. *PS: Political Science and Politics,* December, 664–683.

Putnam, R.D. (1995b). Bowling alone. America's declining social capital. *Journal of Democracy, 6,* 65–78.

Putnam, R.D. (2000). *Bowling alone: The Collapse and Revival of American Community.* New York: Simon and Schuster.

Raats, M.M. (1992). *The role of beliefs and sensory responses to milk in determining the selection of milks of different fat content.* Unpublished doctoral thesis, University of Reading, Reading, Hertfordshire.

Rajaretnam, J. (1994). The long-term effects of sponsorship on corporate and product image: Findings of a unique experiment. *Marketing & Research Today, 21*(1), 62–73.

Rangan, V. K., Karim, S. & Sandberg, S.K. (1996). Do better at doing good. *Harvard Business Review, 7*(3), 42–54.

Ranganath, H.K. (1993. Indian culture—symbols as communication tools. *Hygie, 12,* 19–22.

Rawls, J. (1971). *A theory of justice.* Cambridge: Harvard University Press.

Reid, D. (1996). Tobacco control: overview. *British Medical Bulletin, 52*(1), 108–120.

Reppucci, N.D., Woolard, J.L. & Fried, C.S. (1999. Social, community, and preventive interventions. *Annual Review of Psychology, 50,* 387–418.

Research Triangle Institute 1990. *Feasibility study regarding paid advertising: Evaluation design studies.* Report to Centers for Disease Control, contract no. 200 88 0643.

Reynolds, C. (1999). Tobacco advertising in Indonesia: 'The defining characteristics for success'. *Tobacco Control, 8,* 85–88.

Rhodes, A. (1975). *Propaganda: The art of persuasion: World War II.* London: Angus & Robertson.

Rice, R.E. & Atkin, K.J. (1989). *Public communication campaigns.* Newbury Park: Sage.

Riedel, E., Dresel, L., Wagoner, M.J., Sullivan, J.L. & Borgida, E. (1998). Electronic communities: Assessing equality of access in a rural Minnesota community. *Social Science Computer Review, 16*(4), 370–390.

Rippetoe, P.A. & Rogers, R.W. (1987). Effects of components of protection-motivation theory on adaptive and maladaptive coping with a health threat. *Journal of Personality and Social Psychology, 52*(3), 596–604.

Robberson, M.R. & Rogers, R.W. (1988). Beyond fear appeals: Negative and positive appeals to health and self-esteem. *Journal of Applied Social Psychology, 18,* 277–287.

Roberts, A.R. (Ed.) 1984. *Battered women and their families: Intervention strategies and treatment programs.* New York: Springer.

Roberts, D., Henriksen, L., Christenson, P.G. & Kelly, M. (1999, April). *Substance use in popular movies and music.* Washington, D.C.: Office of National Drug Control Policy.

Roberts, D., Christenson, P.G., Henriksen, L. & Bandy, E. (2002). *Substance use in popular movies and videos.* Washington, D.C.: Office of National Drug Control Policy.

Roberts, G. (2002). *Alcohol portrayal in* The Secret Life of Us *(Series 1): A preliminary analysis.* Melbourne: Centre for Youth Drug Studies, University of Melbourne.

Roberts, G.L., Lawrence, J.M., Williams, G.M. & Raphael, B. (1998). The impact of domestic violence on women's mental health. *Australian and New Zealand Journal of Public Health, 22*(7), 796–801.

Roberts, I. & Coggan, C. (1994). Blaming children for child pedestrian injuries. *Social Science and Medicine, 38*(5), 749–754.

Robertson, R. (1999, March 15). Body Shop bares itself to scrutiny. *Australian Financial Review,* 15.

Roche, A.M. & Ober, C. (1997). Rethinking smoking among Aboriginal Australians: The harm minimisation abstinence conundrum. *Health Promotion Journal of Australia, 7*(2), 128–133.

Rogers, E.M. (1983). *Diffusion of innovations* (3rd ed.). New York: The Free Press.

Rogers, E.M. (1995). *Diffusion of Innovations* (4th ed.). New York: The Free Press.

Rogers, R.W. (1975). A protection motivation theory of fear appeals and attitude change. *Journal of Psychology, 91,* 93–114.

Rogers, R.W. (1983). Cognitive and physiological process in fear appeals and attitude change: A revised theory of protection motivation. In J. Cacioppo & R. Petty (Eds.), *Social Psychophysiology.* New York: Guilford Press.

Rogers, T., Feighery, E.C., Tencati, E.M., Butler, J.L. & Weiner, L. (1995). Community mobilization to reduce point-of-purchase advertising of tobacco products. *Health Education Quarterly, 22*(4), 427–442.

Rose, G. (1985). Sick individuals and sick populations. *International Journal of Epidemiology, 14*(1), 32–38.

Rose, G. (1992). *The strategy of preventive medicine.* Oxford: Oxford University Press.

Rose, G. & Ampt, E. (2001). 'travel Blending': An Australian travel awareness initiative. *Transportation Research, 6*(2), 95–110.

Rosen, J. (1994). Public journalism: First principles. In J. Rosen & D. Merritt Jr. (Eds.), *Public journalism: Theory and practice.* Dayton: Kettering Foundation.

Rosenstock, I.M. (1974a). Historical models of the health belief model. In M.H. Becker & N.J. Thorofare (Eds.), *The health belief model and personal health behavior.* New Jersey: Charles B. Slack.

Rosenstock, I.M. (1974b). The health belief model and preventive health behaviour. *Health Education Monograph, 2*(4), 354–386.

Rosenstock, I.M., Strecher, V. & Becker, M. (1988). Social learning theory and the health belief model. *Health Education Quarterly, 15,* 175–183.

Ross, H. S. & Mico, P. R. (1980). *Theory and practice in health education.* Palo Alto: Mayfield.

Ross, W.D. (1930, 1963). *The Right and the Good.* Oxford: Clarendon Press.

Rossiter, J.R. (1987). Market segmentation: A review and proposed resolution. *Australian Marketing Researcher, 11*(1), 36–58.

Rossiter, J.R. & Donovan, R.J. (1983). Why you shouldn't test ads in focus groups. *Australian Marketing Researcher, 7,* 43–48.

Rossiter, J.R. & Percy, L. (1987). *Advertising and promotion management.* New York: McGraw-Hill.

Rossiter, J.R. & Percy, L. (1997). *Advertising communications and promotion management* (2nd ed.). New York: McGraw-Hill.

Rossiter, J.R., Percy, L. & Donovan, R.J. (1984). The advertising plan and advertising communication models. *Australian Marketing Researcher, 8,* 7–44.

Rossiter, J.R., Percy, L. & Donovan, R.J. (1991). A better advertising grid. *Journal of Advertising Research, 31,* 11–22.

Rothman, A.J. & Salovey, P. (1997). Shaping perceptions to motivate healthy behavior: The role of message framing. *Psychological Bulletin, 121*(1), 3–19.

Rothman, A.J. & Salovey, P., Antone, C., Keough, K. & Martin, C.D. (1993). The influence of message framing on intentions to perform health behaviors. *Journal of Experimental Social Psychology, 29,* 408–433.

Rothschild, M.L. (1979). Marketing communications in nonbusiness situations or why it's so hard to sell brotherhood like soap, *Journal of Marketing, 43,* 11–20.

Rothschild, M.L. (1997). A marketing view of behavior management in the social and public domains. Innovations in Social Marketing Conference, May, Boston.

Rothschild, M.L. (2001. Ethical considerations in the use of marketing for the management of public health and social issues. In A. Andreasen (Ed.), *Ethics in Social Marketing.* Washington, D.C.: Georgetown University Press, 17–38.

Rudd, C. (2003). *Merging General Practice-driven reforms and public sector strategies in the 1990s: A framework for health policy.* Unpublished doctoral dissertation. University of Western Australia, Perth, Western Australia.

Rudd, R.E., Moeykens, B.A. & Colton, T.C. Health and literacy 1999. A review of medical and public health literature. In *The annual review of adult learning and literacy, Vol. 1.* National Center for the Study of Adult Learning and Literacy. Retrieved April 28, 2003 from <http://ncsall.gse.harvard.edu/ann_rev/vol1_5.html>.

Ruggiero, L., Redding, C.A., Rossi, J.S. & Prochaska, J.O. (1997. A stage-matched smoking cessation program for pregnant smokers. *American Journal of Health Promotion, 12*(1), 31–3.

Rust, R. & Cooil, B. (1994. Reliability measures for qualitative data: Theory and implications. *Journal of Marketing Research, 31*, 1–14.

Salkowski, J. (1997, April 8). We'll return to history class after these messages. Schools learn how to ad; multiply their revenues. *StarNet Dispatches*. Retrieved October 29, 2001 from <http://dispatches.azstarnet.com/features/ad.htm>.

Sallis, R., Hovell, M.F., Hofstetter, C.R., et al. (1990). Distance between homes and exercise facilities related to frequency of exercise among San Diego residents. *Public Health Reports, 105*(2), 179–185.

Salmon, C.T. (Ed.) (1989). *Information campaigns: Balancing social values and social change*. Newbury Park: Sage.

Sanders, M.R. (2001). Helping families change: From clinical interventions to population-based strategies. In A. Booth, A.C. Crouter et al (Eds.), *Couples in conflict*. Mahwah: Lawrence Erlbaum, 185–219.

Sanders, M.R., Markie-Dadds, C. & Tully, L.A. (2001). Behavioural family therapy reduced disruptive behaviour in children at risk for developing conduct problems. *Evidence-Based Mental Health, 4*(1), 20–22.

Sanders, M.R., Markie-Dadds, C., Tully, L.A. & Bor, W. (2000). The Triple P-Positive Parenting Program: A comparison of enhanced, standard, and self-directed behavioral family intervention for parents of children with early onset conduct problems. *Journal of Consulting and Clinical Psychology, 68*(4), 624–640.

Sandler, D.M. & Shani, D. (1989). Olympic sponsorship vs 'ambush' marketing: Who gets the gold? *Journal of Advertising Research, 29*(4), 9–14.

Sandler, D.M. & Shani, D. (1993). Sponsorship and the Olympic Games: The consumer perspective. *Sport Marketing Quarterly, 2*(3), 38–43.

Sargeant, A. (1999). *Marketing management for nonprofit organizations*. Oxford: Oxford University Press.

Saxelby, C. (1997). More (chocolate-coated) carrots, please! *Nutrition News, 21*, 1.

Saxton, E. (1993, December). Motorsports. *Marketing News*, 5.

Schlossberg, H. (1996). *Sports marketing*. Cambridge: Blackwell Business.

Schlosser, E. (2001). Fast food nation: What the all-American meal is doing to the world. London: Allen Lane, The Penguin Press.

Schmidt, C.W. (2000). Frankenstein foods. *Chemical Innovation, 30*(1), 42–49.

Schwartz, B. (2000). *Fact sheet: Interactive program*. Washington, D.C.: Fleishman Hillard. Posted on Social Marketing listserver January 9.

Schwartz, J. (1998). Schools for sale? *Marketing News, 32*(17), 12.

Schwartz, S.H. & Tessler, R.C. (1972). A test of a model for reducing measured attitude-behavior discrepancies. *Journal of Personality and Social Psychology, 24*(2), 225–223.

Schwarzer, R. & Fuchs, R. (1996). Self-efficacy and health behaviours. In M. Conner & P. Norman (Eds.), *Predicting Health Behaviour*. Buckingham: Open University Press, 163–196.

Scott, D. & Suchard, H. (1992). Motivations for Australian expenditure on sponsorship: An analysis. *International Journal of Advertising, 11*, 325–332.

Shapiro, S.J. (1990). Canada seeks support for a case. In S.H. Fine (Ed.), *Social marketing. Promoting the causes of public and nonprofit agencies*. Boston: Allyn and Bacon, 275–288.

Sheeran, P. & Abraham, C. (1996). The health belief model. In M. Conner & P. Norman (Eds.), *Predicting health behaviour: Research and practice with social cognition models*. Buckingham: Open University Press, 23–61.

Sheppard, B.H., Hartwick, J. & Warshaw, P.R. (1988). The theory of reasoned action: A meta-analysis of past research with recommendations for modification and future research. *Journal of Consumer Research, 15*, 325–343.

Sherif, C. W., Sherif, M. & Nebergall, R. E. (1965). *Attitude and attitude change: The social judgment-involvement approach.* Philadelphia: W.B. Saunders.

Sheth, J.N. & Frazier, G.L. (1982). A model of strategy mix choice for planned social change. *Journal of Marketing, 46*, 15–26.

Sibbald, B. (2000). U of A refuses tobacco-sponsored scholarship donation. *Canadian Medical Association Journal, 164*(1), 81.

Siegel, M. & Doner, L. (1998). *Marketing public health: Strategies to promote social change.* Gaithersburg: Aspen Publishers.

Silburn, S.R., Zubrick, S.R., Garton, A., Gurren, L., Burton, P., Dalby, R., Carlton, J., Shepherd, C. & Laurence, D. (1996). *Western Australian child health survey: Family and community health.* Perth: Australian Bureau of Statistics and the Institute for Child Health Research.

Singhal, A. & Rogers, E.M. (1989). Prosocial television for development in India. In R.E. Rice & C.K. Atkin (Eds.), *Public Communication Campaigns.* Newbury Park: Sage.

Singhal, A. & Rogers, E.M. (1999). *Entertainment-education: A communication strategy for social change.* Mahwah: Lawrence Erlbaum.

Siska, M., Jason, J., Murdoch, P., Yang, W.S. & Donovan, R.J. (1992). Recall of AIDS public service announcements and their impact on the ranking of AIDS as a national problem. *American Journal of Public Health, 82*, 1029–1032.

Skoglund, K. (2001). The Dongara Project. *Healthway News, 31*, 13.

Slater, M.D., Kelly, K. & Edwards, R. (2000). Integrating social marketing, community readiness and media advocacy in community-based prevention efforts. *Social Marketing Quarterly, 6*(3), 125–137.

Sloan, A.E. (1998). Food industry forecast: Consumer trends to 2020 and beyond. *Food Technology, 52*(1), 37–43.

Sloan, A.E. (2000a). The top ten functional foods. *Food Technology, 54*(4), 33–51.

Sloan, A.E. (2000b). Adding value in 2000+. *Food Technology, 54*(1), 22.

Sloan, A.E. (2001). Clean foods. *Food Technology, 55*(2), 18.

Smith, A. (1992). Setting a strategy for health. *British Medical Journal, 304*(6823), 376–379.

Smith, B. (1998). Forget messages … Think about structural change first. *Social Marketing Quarterly, 4*(3), 13–19.

Smith, B. (1999). Ethics and the social marketer: Is the glass half-full, half-empty, or hemorrhaging? *Social Marketing Quarterly, 5*(3), 74–75.

Smith, B., Bauman, A.E., Bull, F., Booth, M.L. & Harris, M.F. (2000). Promoting physical activity in general practice: A controlled trial of written advice and information materials. *British Journal of Sports Medicine, 34*, 262–267.

Smith, C., Roberts, J.L. & Pendleton, L.L. (1988). Booze on the box: The portrayal of alcohol on British television: A content analysis. *Health Education Research, 3*(3), 267–272.

Smith, G., Goldman, M., Greenbaum, P. & Christiansen, B. (1995). Expectancy for social facilitation from drinking: The divergent paths of high-expectancy and low-expectancy adolescents. *Journal of Abnormal Psychology, 104*, 32–40.

Smith, M. (2000, June 30). Germany opposes cigarette curbs. *Financial Times.* Message posted to intl-tobacco mailing list. Archived at inti-tobacco@lists.essential.org; <http://lists.essential.org/mailman/listinfo/inti-tobacco>.

Smith, W.A. (2001). Ethics and the social marketer: A framework for practitioners. In A. Andreasen (Ed.), *Ethics in social marketing*. Washington, D.C.: Georgetown University Press, 1–16.

Snipes, R.L., LaTour, M.S. & Bliss, S.J. (1999). A model of the effects of self-efficacy on the perceived ethicality and performance of fear appeals in advertising. *Journal of Business Ethics, 19*(3), 273–285.

Solomon, D. (1984). Social marketing and community health promotion. In L.W. Frederiksen, L.J. Solomon & K.A. Brehony (Eds.), *Marketing health behavior. Principles, techniques, and applications*. New York: Plenum Press, 115–136.

Solomon, D.S. (1989). A social marketing perspective on communication campaigns. In R.E. Rice & C.K. Atkin (Eds.), *Public communication campaigns*. Newbury Park: Sage.

Sorenson, S.B., Upchurch, D.M. & Shen, H. (1996). Violence and injury in marital arguments: Risk patterns and gender differences. *American Journal of Public Health, 86*(1), 35–40.

Soutar, G.N., Ramaseshan, B. & Molster, C.M. (1994). Determinants of pro-environmental consumer purchase behaviour: Some Australian evidence. *Asia Pacific Advances in Consumer Research, 1*, 1–8.

Spark, R. (1999). *Developing Health Promotion Methods in Remote Aboriginal Communities*. Unpublished doctoral dissertation, Curtin University, Perth, Western Australia.

Spark, R., Binns, C., Laughlin, D., Spooner, C. & Donovan, R.J. (1992). Aboriginal people's perceptions of their own and their community's health: Results of a pilot study. *Health Promotion Journal of Australia, 2*(2), 60–64.

Spark, R., Donovan, R.J. & Howat, P. (1991). Promoting health and preventing injury in remote Aboriginal communities: A case study. *Health Promotion Journal of Australia, 1*(2), 10–16.

Spark, R. & Mills, P. (1988). Promoting Aboriginal health on television in the Northern Territory: A bicultural approach. *Drug Education Journal of Australia, 2*(3), 191–198.

Spark, R., Sinclair, D., Donovan, R.J., Hanna, J. & Whitehead, K. (1994). Campaigns that bite: The Dengue Fever prevention campaign in far North Queensland. *Health Promotion Journal of Australia, 4*(2), 28–32.

Sparks, P., Shepherd, R. & Frewer, L.J. (1995). Assessing and structuring attitudes toward the use of gene technology in food production: the role of perceived ethical obligation. *Basic and Applied Social Psychology, 16*, 267–285.

Stipp, H. & Schiavone, N. (1996). Modeling the impact of Olympic sponsorship on corporate image. *Journal of Advertising Research*, July/August, 22–28.

Stokols, D. (1992). Establishing and maintaining healthy environments: Towards a social ecology of health promotion. *American Psychologist, 47*, 6–22.

Stokols, D. (1996). Translating social ecological theory into guidelines for community health promotion. *American Journal of Health Promotion, 10*(4), 282–298.

Stokols, D., Allen, J. & Bellingham, R.L. (1996). The social ecology of health promotion: Implications for research and practice. *American Journal of Health Promotion, 10*(4), 247–251.

Stotlar, D. (1993). Sponsorship and the Olympic Winter Games. *Sport Marketing Quarterly, 2*(1), 35–43.

Stout, P.A. (1989). *Fear arousal and emotional response to AIDS messages*. Paper presented at the Annual Convention of the Association for Consumer Research, New Orleans.

Stout, P.A. & Sego, T. (1994). *Emotions elicited by threat appeals*. Unpublished paper. University of Texas.

Strasburger, V.C. (1993). Children, adolescents, and the media: Five crucial issues. *Adolescent Medicine: State of the Art Reviews, 4*(3). Retrieved June 15, 2003 from Children Youth and Family Consortium Electronic Clearinghouse at <www.cyfc.umn.edu/adolescents/research/crissues.html>.

Streetwize Comics 2000. *The Streetwize Hep C Comic*. Sydney: Streetwize.

Strong, J.T., Anderson, R.E. & Dubas, K.M. (1993). Marketing threat appeals: A conceptual framework and implications for practitioners. *Journal of Managerial Issues, 5*, 532–546.

Stuart, P. (2001). The Narrogin Project. *Healthway News, 31*, 14–15.

Sutherland, M. (1993). *Advertising and the mind of the consumer: What works, what doesn't, and why*. Sydney: Allen & Unwin.

Sutton, S.R. (1982). Fear-arousing communications: A critical examination of theory and research. In J.R. Eiser (Ed.), *Social Psychology and Behavioural Medicine*. New York: John Wiley.

Sutton, S.R. (1992. Shock tactics and the myth of the inverted U. *British Journal of Addiction, 87*, 517–19.

Sweeney, B.L. (1992). *Australians and sport*. Melbourne: Brian Sweeney and Associates.

Swinburn, B. (1999). Dissecting obesogenic environments, *Preventive Medicine, 29*, 563–570. Available online at <../person/eggerga.htm> and <../person/razaxfe.htm>.

Tanner, J.F., Day, E. & Crask, M.R. (1989). Protection motivation theory: An extension of fear appeals theory. *Journal of Business Research, 19*, 267–276.

Task Force of the National Advisory Council on Alcohol Abuse and Alcoholism (2002, April). How to reduce high-risk college drinking: Use proven strategies, fill research gaps. Final report of the Panel on Prevention and Treatment. US Department of Health and Human Services. Retrieved April 19, 2003 from <http://www.college-drinkingprevention.gov/images/Panel02/FINALPanel2.pdf>.

Teo, J. (1992). Evaluation of a social marketing program to encourage graduate mothers in Singapore to have more children. Unpublished paper. Edith Cowan University, Perth, Western Australia.

The Nation's Healt (2002, February). Transit spending linked to less smog in U.S. cities, 14.

Think global, act prejudiced? (1996, February 24), *The Economist*, 77.

Thomas, K. (1997). Health and morality in early modern England. In A.M. Brandt & P. Rozin (Eds.), *Morality and health*. New York: Routledge, 15–34.

Thompson, C.J. (1995). A contextualist proposal for the conceptualization and study of marketing ethics. *Journal of Public Policy and Marketing, 14*(20), 177–202.

Tomison, A. & Wolcott, I. (1997). Family violence. In D. DeVaus & I. Wolcott (Eds.), *Australian family profiles: Social and demographic perspectives*. Melbourne: Australian Institute of Family Studies, 119–127.

Too wacky veg (1997). General International Highlights INPR/22/1997 Retrieved July 15, 2002 from <http://www.mintel-iis.com/inprdemo/INPR/HL/0/INPR_22_1997/6.html>.

Triandis, H.C. (1977). *Interpersonal behavior*. Monterey: Brooks/Cole Publishing.

Tsahuridu, E. & McKenna, R.J. (2000). Moral autonomy in organisational decisions. *Current Topics in Management, 5*, 167–185.

Turco, D.M. (1995). The influence of sponsorship on product recall and image among sport spectators. In K. Grant & I. Walker (Eds.), *World marketing congress proceedings*. Melbourne: Academy of Marketing Science, 7(3), 11.6–11.10.

Twitchell, J.B. (1996). *ADCULTUSA: Triumph of advertising in American culture*. New York: Columbia University Press.

Tyler, T.R. (1997). Misconceptions about why people obey laws and accept judicial decisions. *American Psychological Society Observer*, September, 12–46.

Tyler, T.R. (1990). *Why people obey the law*. New Haven: Yale University Press.

United Nations, Office of the High Commissioner of Human Rights (1948). *Universal declaration of human rights*. Retrieved September 18, 2001 from <http://www.unhchr.ch/udhr/lang/eng.htm>.

Urban, G.L., Hauser, J.R. & Dholakia, N. (1987). *Essentials of new product management*. Englewood Cliffs: Prentice Hall.

Van Elswyk, M.E. (1993). Designer foods: Manipulating the fatty acid composition of meat and eggs for the health conscious consumer. *Nutrition Today, 28*(2), 21–30.

Varadarajan, P.R. & Menon, A. (1988). Cause-related marketing: A coalignment of marketing strategy and corporate philanthropy. *Journal of Marketing, 52,* 58–74.

Vaughn, R. (1980). How advertising works: A planning model. *Journal of Advertising Research, 20*(5), 27–33.

Vaughn, R. (1986). How advertising works: A planning model revisited. *Journal of Advertising Research, 26*(1), 57–66.

VicHealth Centre for Tobacco Control (2001). *Tobacco control: A blue chip investment in public health*. Melbourne: Cancer Council of Victoria.

Vidmar, N. & Rokeach, M. (1974). Archie Bunker's bigotry: A study in selective perception and exposure. *Journal of Communication, 24,* 36–47.

Vining, J. & Ebreo, A. (1992). Predicting recycling behavior from global and specific environmental attitudes and changes in recycling opportunities. *Journal of Applied Social Psychology, 22*(20), 1580–1607.

Viola, A. (2002). Building Healthy Queensland Communities Inaugural Seminar. Brisbane: Health Promotion Queensland.

Wallack, L. (1990a). Media advocacy: promoting health through mass communications. In K. Glanz, F.M. Lewis & B.K. Rimer (Eds.), *Health behaviour and health education*. San Fancisco: Jossey Bass.

Wallack, L. (1990b). Improving health promotion: Media advocacy and social marketing approaches. In C. Atkin & L. Wallach (Eds.), *Mass communication and public health: Complexities and conflicts*. Newbury Park: Sage.

Wallack, L. (1994). Media advocacy: A strategy for empowering people and communities. *Journal of Public Health Policy, 155*(4), 420–436.

Wallack, L., Dorfman, L., Jernigan, D. & Themba, M. (1993). *Media advocacy and public health: Power for prevention*. Newbury Park: Sage.

Wallack, L., Grube, J., Madden, P. & Breed, W. (1990). Portrayals of alcohol on prime-time television. *Journal of Studies on Alcohol, 51,* 428–437.

Walsh, D. (1995). *Selling out America's children: How America puts profits before values and what parents can do*. Minneapolis: Fairview Press.

Walsh, D.C., Rudd, R.E., Moeykens, B.A. & Moloney, T.W. (1993). Social marketing for public health. *Health Affairs, 12*(2), 104–119.

Wansink, B. & Kim, J. (2001). The marketing battle over genetically modified foods. *American Behavioral Scientist, 44*(8), 1405.

Wardlaw, M.J. (2000). Three lessons for a better cycling future. *British Medical Journal, 321,* 1582–1585.

Webb, D.J. and Mohr, L.A. (1998). A typology of consumer responses to cause-related marketing: From skeptics to socially concerned. *Journal of Public Policy & Marketing, 17*(2), 226–238.

Weick, K. (1984). Small wins: Revising the scale of social problems. *American Psychologist, 39,* 40–49.

Weimann, G. (1991). The influentials: Back to the concept of opinion leaders? *Public Opinion Quarterly, 55,* 267–279.

Weinreich, N.K., Abbott, J. & Olson, C.K. (1999). Social marketers in the driver's seat: Motorsport sponsorship as a vehicle for tobacco prevention. *Social Marketing Quarterly, 5*(3), 108–112.

Weinstein, N.D. (1988). The precaution adoption process. *Health Psychology, 7,* 355–386.

Weitzman, E. & Kawachi, I. (2000). Giving means receiving: The protective effect of social capital on binge drinking on college campuses. *American Journal of Public Health, 90*(12), 1936–1939.

Wharton, R. (2001). "That thing in the paper": The prostate cancer phone-in. Paper presented at Western Australian 2nd State Cancer Conference, Perth.

Wharton, R. & Mandell, F. (1985). Violence on television and imitative behavior: Impact on parenting practices. *Pediatrics, 75*(6), 1120–1122.

White, C. (1998). Food is a public health issue. *British Medical Journal, 316*(7), 416.

White, S.L. & Maloney, S.K. (1990). Promoting healthy diets and active lives to hard-to-reach groups: Market research study. *Public Health Reports, 105,* 224–231.

Whitelaw, S., MacHardy, L., Reid, W. & Duffy, M. (1999). *The stages of change model and its use in health promotion: A critical review.* Health Education Board of Scotland Research Centre.

Wiebe, G. (1952). Merchandising commodities and citizenship on television. *Public Opinion Quarterly, 15,* 679–691.

Wiegman, O., Taal, E., Van Den Bogaard, J. & Gutteling, J. M. (1992). Protection Motivation Theory variables as predictors of behavioural intentions in three domains of risk management. In J.A.M. Winnubst & S.Maes (Eds.). *Lifestyles, stress and health: New developments in health psychology.* Leiden: DSWO Press, 55–70.

Wikler, D. (1978). Persuasion and coercion for health. Ethical issues in government efforts to change life-styles. *Millbank Memorial Fund Quarterly, Health and Society, 56*(3), 303–338.

Wilde, G.J.S. & Ackersviller, M.J. (1981). Accident journalism and traffic safety education, Report No. TP 3659 E/CR 8202. Ottawa: Transport Canada, Traffic Safety.

Wilkinson, R. & Marmot, M. (1998). *Social determinants of health. The solid facts.* Copenhagen: World Health Organization Europe. Available online at <http://www.who.dk/document/E59555.pdf>.

Williams, A., Zubrick, S. & Silburn, S. (2001). *Foundations of social and emotional development: A continuum.* Report for Students at Educational Risk Project. Perth: Education Department of Western Australia.

Williams, C. (2001, June 15). Doll that gets a tan. *Daily Mail,* 27.

Williford, H.N., Barfield, B.R., Lazenby, R.B. & Olson, M.S. (1992). A survey of physicians' attitudes and practices related to exercise promotion. *Preventative Medicine, 21*(5), 630–636.

Wilson, D.H., Wakefield, M.A., Esterman, A. & Baker, C.C. (1987). 15's: They fit in everywhere, especially the schoolbag. *Community Health Studies, 11*(1), 16–20.

Wilson, D.K., Kaplan, R.M. & Schneiderman, L.J. (1987). Framing of decisions and selections of alternatives in health care. *Social Behavior, 2,* 51–59.

Wilson, D.K., Wallston, K.A. & King, J.E. (1987, August). *The effects of message framing and self-efficacy on smoking cessation.* Paper presented at the Annual Southeastern Psychological Association Convention, Atlanta.

Wilson, M.G. & Olds, R.S. (1991). Application of the marketing mix to health promotion marketing. *Journal of Health Education, 22*(4), 254–259.

Winett, R.A., Leckliter, I.N., Chinn, D.E., Stahl, B. & Love, S.Q. (1985). Effects of television modeling on residential energy conservation. *Journal of Applied Behaviour Analysis, 18*(1), 33–44.

Winzelberg, A.J., Taylor, C.B., Sharpe, T., Eldredge, K.L., Dev, P. & Constantinou, P.S. (1998). Evaluation of a computer-mediated eating disorder intervention program. *International Journal of Eating Disorders, 24*(4), 339–349.

Witte, K. (1993). Message and conceptual confounds in fear appeals: The role of threat, fear and efficacy. *Southern Communication Journal, 58*(2), 147–155.

Witte, K. (1998). Fear as motivator, fear as inhibitor. Using the Extended Parallel Process Model to explain fear appeal successes and failures. In P.A. Andersen & L.K. Guerrero (Eds.), *The handbook of communication and emotion: Research, theory, applications, and contexts.* San Diego: Academic Press, 423–450.

Witte, K. & Allen, M. (2000). A meta-analysis of fear appeals: Implications for effective public health campaigns. *Health Education and Behavior, 27*(5), 591–615.

Wolf, S., Gregory, W.L. & Stephan, W.G. (1986). Protection motivation theory: Prediction of intentions to engage in anti-nuclear war behaviors. *Journal of Applied Social Psychology, 16*(4), 310–321.

Wolff, C.G., Schroeder, D.G. & Young, M.W. (2001). Effect of improved housing on illness in children under 5 years old in northern Malawi: cross sectional study. *British Medical Journal, 322,* 1212–1213.

Wolton, C. (1988, May). Arts sponsorship: harmony or discord? *European Research,* 87–94.

Womersley, T. (2000, April 20). Magazines ban anorexic models. *Electronic Telegraph.* Retrieved April 20, 2003 from<http://www.telegraph.co.uk/news/main.jhtml?xml= %2Fnews%2F2000%2F06%2F22%2Fbody22.xml>.

Woodruff, K. (1996). Alcohol advertising and violence against women: A media advocacy case study. *Health Education Quarterly, 23*(3), 330–345.

World Health Organization (WHO) (1986). The Ottawa Charter for health promotion. *Health Promotion International, 1,* 3–5.

World Health Organization (WHO) (1997). *Violence against women: A priority health issue.* Geneva: Women's Health and Development.

World Health Organization (WHO) (2000). *100% condom use programme in entertainment establishments.* Manila: Regional Office for the Western Pacific. Retrieved April 21, 2003 from <http://www.google.com.au/search?q=cache:8VJehkmprWMC:www.wpro. who.int/pdf/condom.pdf+%22teahouses%22+%22health+education%22&hl=en&ie =UTF-8>.

World Health Organization (WHO) (2001). Women and the tobacco epidemic: Challenges for the 21st century. Retrieved from <http://tobacco.who.int/page.cfm? pid=49>.

Wrick, K.L., Friedman, L.J., Bewda, J.K. & Carroll. J.J. (1993). Consumer viewpoints on 'designer foods'. *Food Technology, 47*(3), 94–100.

Wright, R. (1988). Measuring awareness of British football sponsorship. *European Research,* May, 104–108.

Wurtele, S.K. & Maddux, J.E. (1987). Relative contributions of protection motivation theory components in predicting exercise intentions and behavior. *Health Psychology, 6*(5), 453–466.

Wutzke, S., Gomel, M.K. & Donovan, R.J. (1998). Enhancing the delivery of brief interventions for hazardous alcohol use in the general practice setting: A role for both general practitioners and medical receptionists. *Health Promotion Journal of Australia, 8*(2), 105–108.

Wyllie, A., Zhang, J. & Casswell, S. (1998). Responses to televised alcohol advertisements associated with drinking behaviour of 10–17 year olds. *Addiction, 93*(3), 361–371.

Yen, I.H. & Syme, S.L. (1999). The social environment and health: A discussion of the epidemiologic literature. *Annual Review of Public Health, 20,* 287–308.

Young, E. (1989). Social marketing in the information era. Paper presented at the American Marketing Association Conference, Social Marketing for the 1990s, Ottawa.

Yzer, M.C., Siero, F.W., Buunk, B.P. (2000). Can public campaigns effectively change psychological determinants of safer sex? An evaluation of three Dutch campaigns. *Health Education Research, 15*(3), 339–352.

Zaltman, G. & Coulter, R.H. (1995). Seeing the voice of the customer: Metaphor-based advertising research. *Journal of Advertising Research, 35*, 35–51.

Zeithaml, C.P. & Zeithaml, V.A. (1984). Environmental management: Revising the marketing perspective. *Journal of Marketing, 48*, 46–53.

Zubrick, S.R., Northey, K., Silburn, S.R., Williams, A.A., Blair, E., Robertson, D. & Sanders, M. (under review). Prevention of child behaviour problems via universal implementation of a group behavioural family intervention. *Prevention Science*.

Zuckerman, M. & Reis, H.T. (1978). Comparison of three models for predicting altruistic behavior. *Journal of Personality and Social Psychology, 36*(5), 498–510.

Index